GREEN LANTERN CORPS

EMERALD ECLIPSE

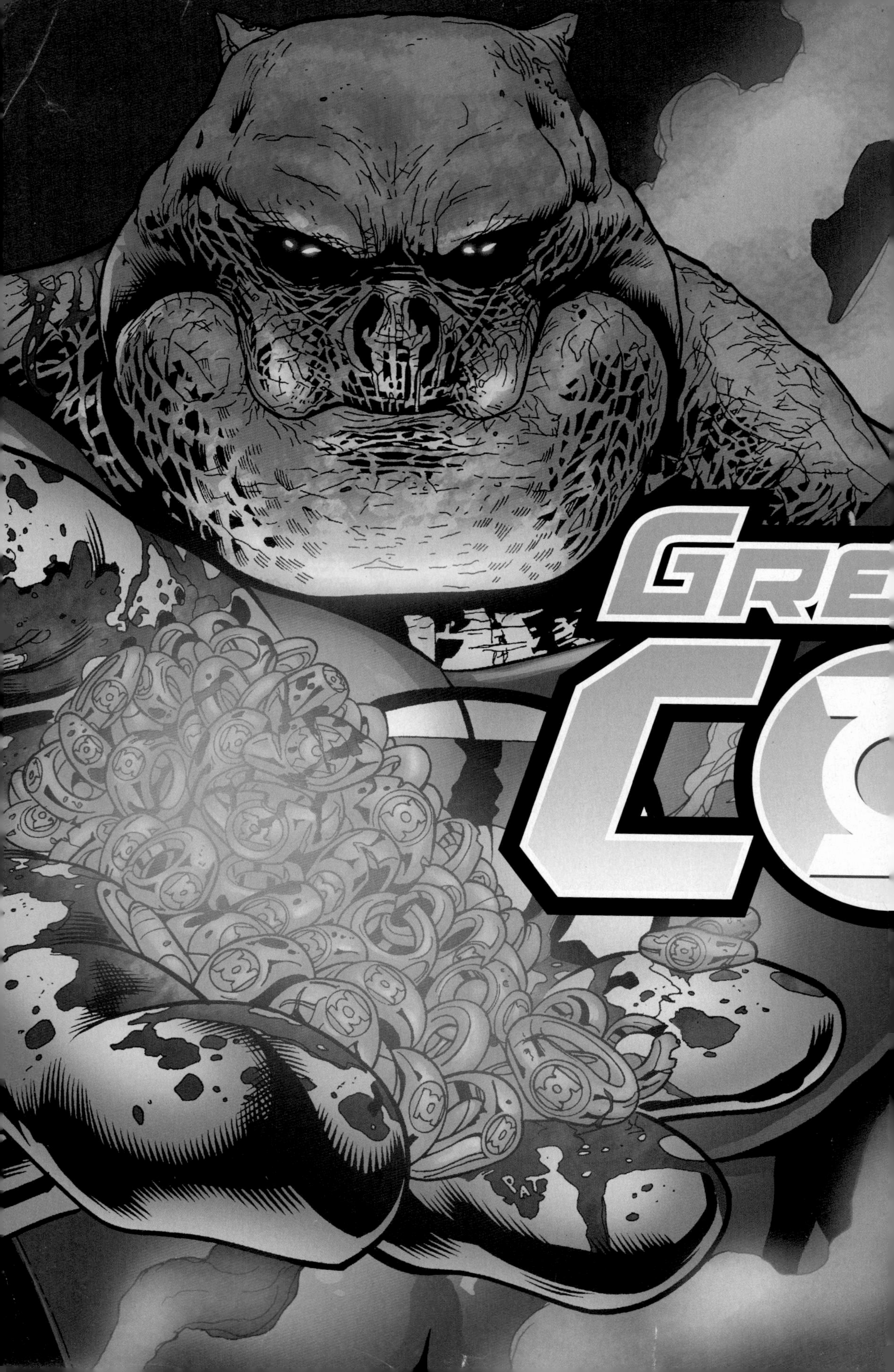

EN LANTERN ORPS

EMERALD ECLIPSE

PETER J. TOMASI Writer **PATRICK GLEASON** Penciller **REBECCA BUCHMAN** Inker

CHRISTIAN ALAMY (Part Two) **PRENTIS ROLLINS** (Part Four) **TOM NGUYEN** (Parts Five & Six)
Additional Inks

RANDY MAYOR **GABE ELTAEB**
Colorists

STEVE WANDS
Letterer

Adam Schlagman Editor - original series
Bob Harras Group Editor - Collected Editions
Bob Joy Editor
Robbin Brosterman Design Director - Books

DC COMICS
Diane Nelson President
Dan DiDio and Jim Lee Co-Publishers
Geoff Johns Chief Creative Officer
Patrick Caldon EVP - Finance and Administration
John Rood EVP - Sales, Marketing and Business Development
Amy Genkins SVP - Business & Legal Affairs
Steve Rotterdam SVP - Sales & Marketing
John Cunningham VP - Marketing
Terri Cunningham VP - Managing Editor
Alison Gill VP - Manufacturing
David Hyde VP - Publicity
Sue Pohja VP - Book Trade Sales
Alysse Soll VP - Advertising and Custom Publishing
Bob Wayne VP - Sales
Mark Chiarello Art Director

Cover by Patrick Gleason, Rebecca Buchman & Randy Mayor

GREEN LANTERN CORPS: EMERALD ECLIPSE
Published by DC Comics.

DC Comics, 1700 Broadway, New York, NY 10019
A Warner Bros. Entertainment Company
Printed by RR Donnelley, Salem, VA, USA 10/13/10.
First Printing.

SC ISBN: 978-1-4012-2529-2

SUSTAINABLE FORESTRY INITIATIVE
Certified Chain of Custody
Promoting Sustainable Forest Management

Fiber used in this product line meets the sourcing requirements of the SFI program.
www.sfiprogram.org NFS-SPICOC-C0001801

GREEN LANTERN CORPS #33
Cover by Patrick Gleason, Rebecca Buchman & Nei Ruffino

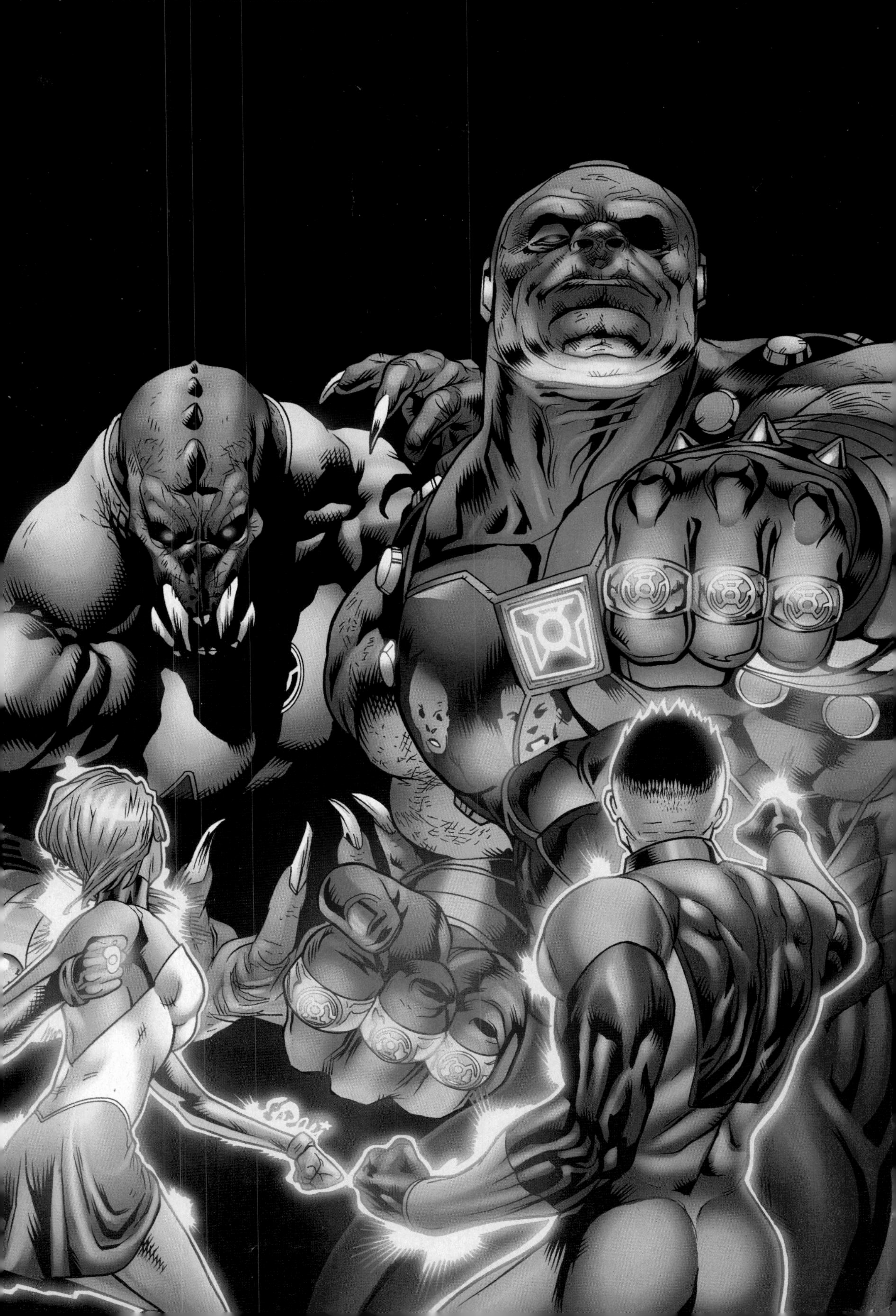

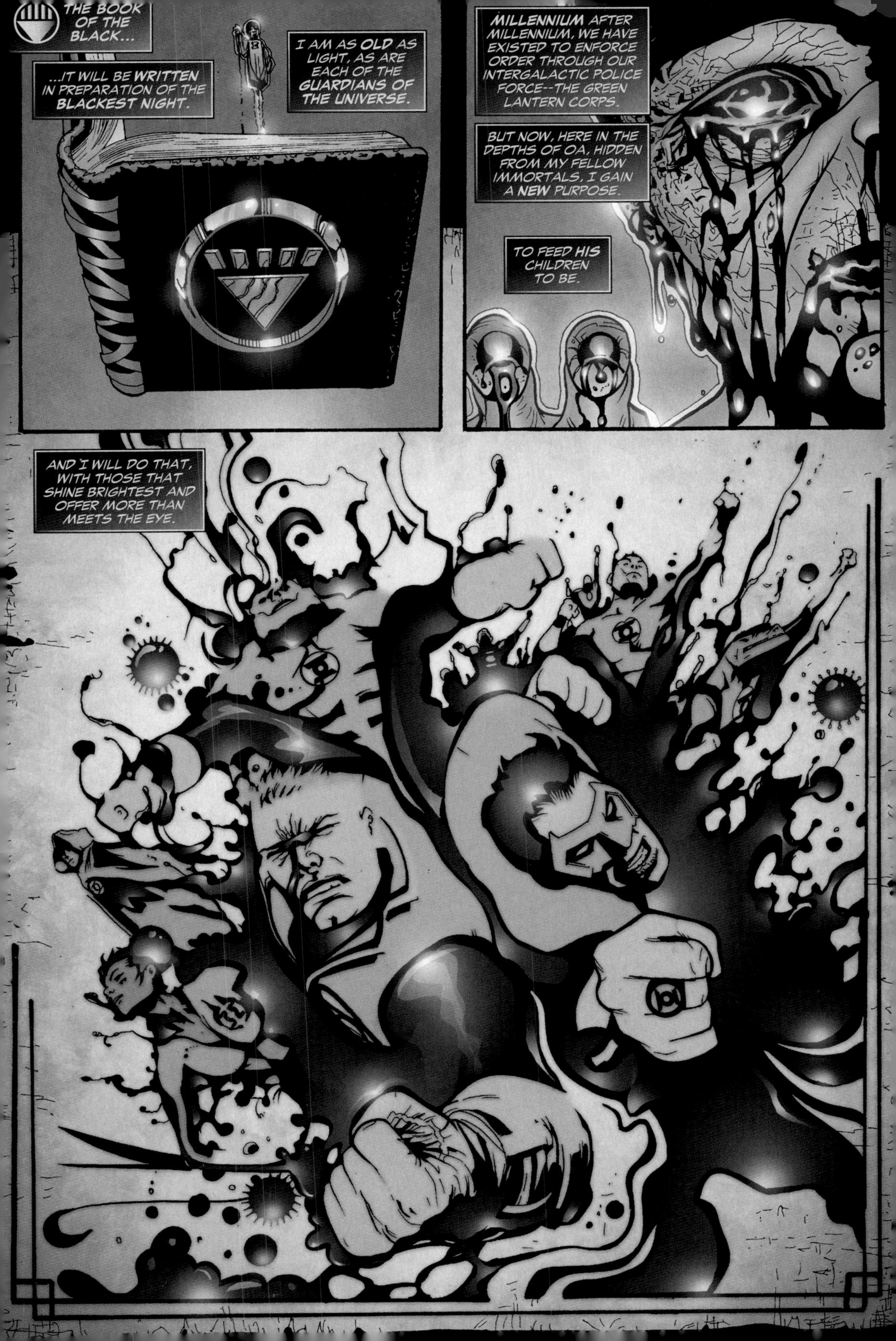
THE BOOK OF THE BLACK...
...IT WILL BE WRITTEN IN PREPARATION OF THE BLACKEST NIGHT.
I AM AS OLD AS LIGHT, AS ARE EACH OF THE GUARDIANS OF THE UNIVERSE.
MILLENNIUM AFTER MILLENNIUM, WE HAVE EXISTED TO ENFORCE ORDER THROUGH OUR INTERGALACTIC POLICE FORCE--THE GREEN LANTERN CORPS.
BUT NOW, HERE IN THE DEPTHS OF OA, HIDDEN FROM MY FELLOW IMMORTALS, I GAIN A NEW PURPOSE.
TO FEED HIS CHILDREN TO BE.
AND I WILL DO THAT, WITH THOSE THAT SHINE BRIGHTEST AND OFFER MORE THAN MEETS THE EYE.

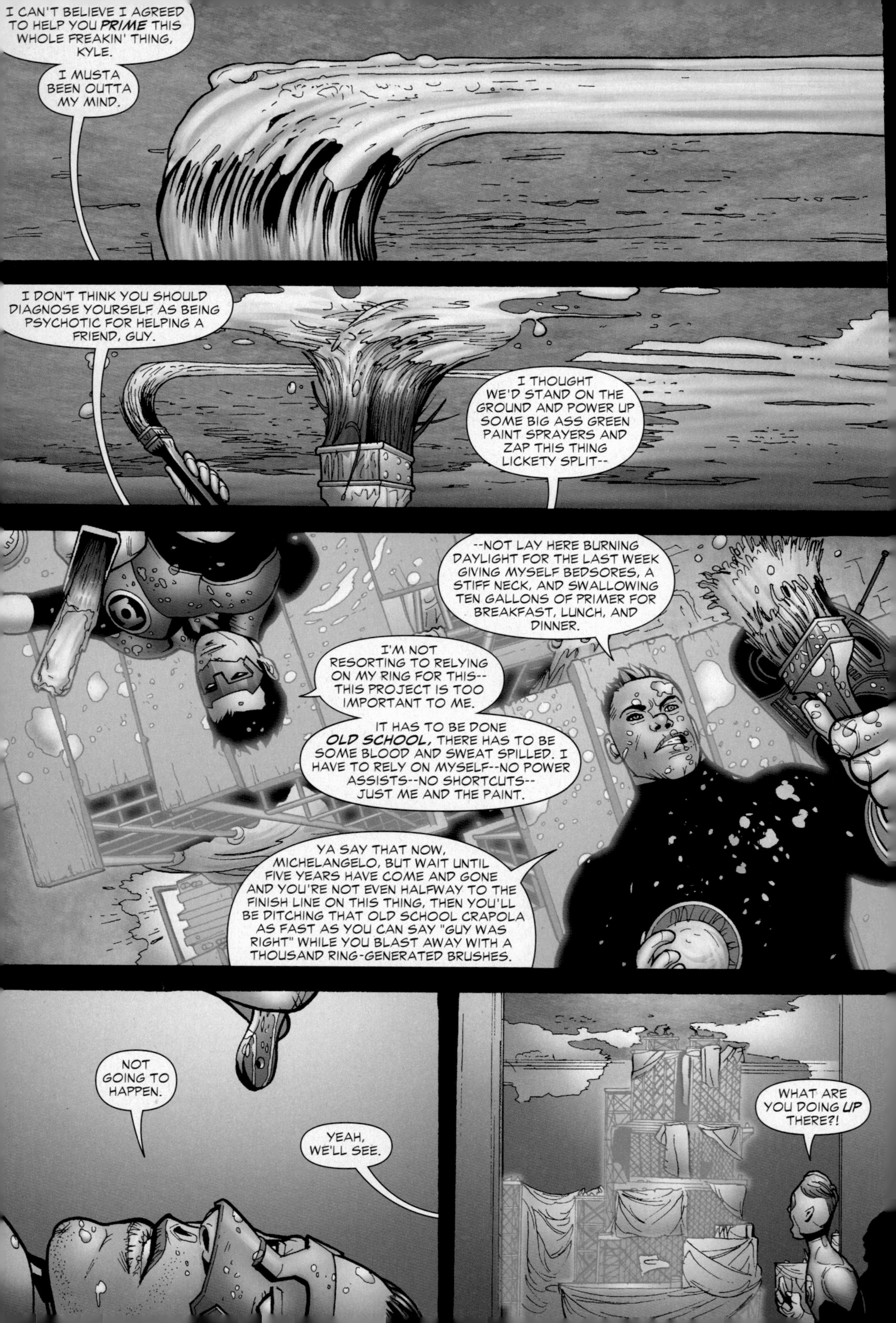
I CAN'T BELIEVE I AGREED TO HELP YOU *PRIME* THIS WHOLE FREAKIN' THING, KYLE.
I MUSTA BEEN OUTTA MY MIND.
I DON'T THINK YOU SHOULD DIAGNOSE YOURSELF AS BEING PSYCHOTIC FOR HELPING A FRIEND, GUY.
I THOUGHT WE'D STAND ON THE GROUND AND POWER UP SOME BIG ASS GREEN PAINT SPRAYERS AND ZAP THIS THING LICKETY SPLIT--
--NOT LAY HERE BURNING DAYLIGHT FOR THE LAST WEEK GIVING MYSELF BEDSORES, A STIFF NECK, AND SWALLOWING TEN GALLONS OF PRIMER FOR BREAKFAST, LUNCH, AND DINNER.
I'M NOT RESORTING TO RELYING ON MY RING FOR THIS-- THIS PROJECT IS TOO IMPORTANT TO ME.
IT HAS TO BE DONE ***OLD SCHOOL,*** THERE HAS TO BE SOME BLOOD AND SWEAT SPILLED. I HAVE TO RELY ON MYSELF--NO POWER ASSISTS--NO SHORTCUTS-- JUST ME AND THE PAINT.
YA SAY THAT NOW, MICHELANGELO, BUT WAIT UNTIL FIVE YEARS HAVE COME AND GONE AND YOU'RE NOT EVEN HALFWAY TO THE FINISH LINE ON THIS THING, THEN YOU'LL BE DITCHING THAT OLD SCHOOL CRAPOLA AS FAST AS YOU CAN SAY "GUY WAS RIGHT" WHILE YOU BLAST AWAY WITH A THOUSAND RING-GENERATED BRUSHES.
NOT GOING TO HAPPEN.
YEAH, WE'LL SEE.
WHAT ARE YOU DOING *UP* THERE?!

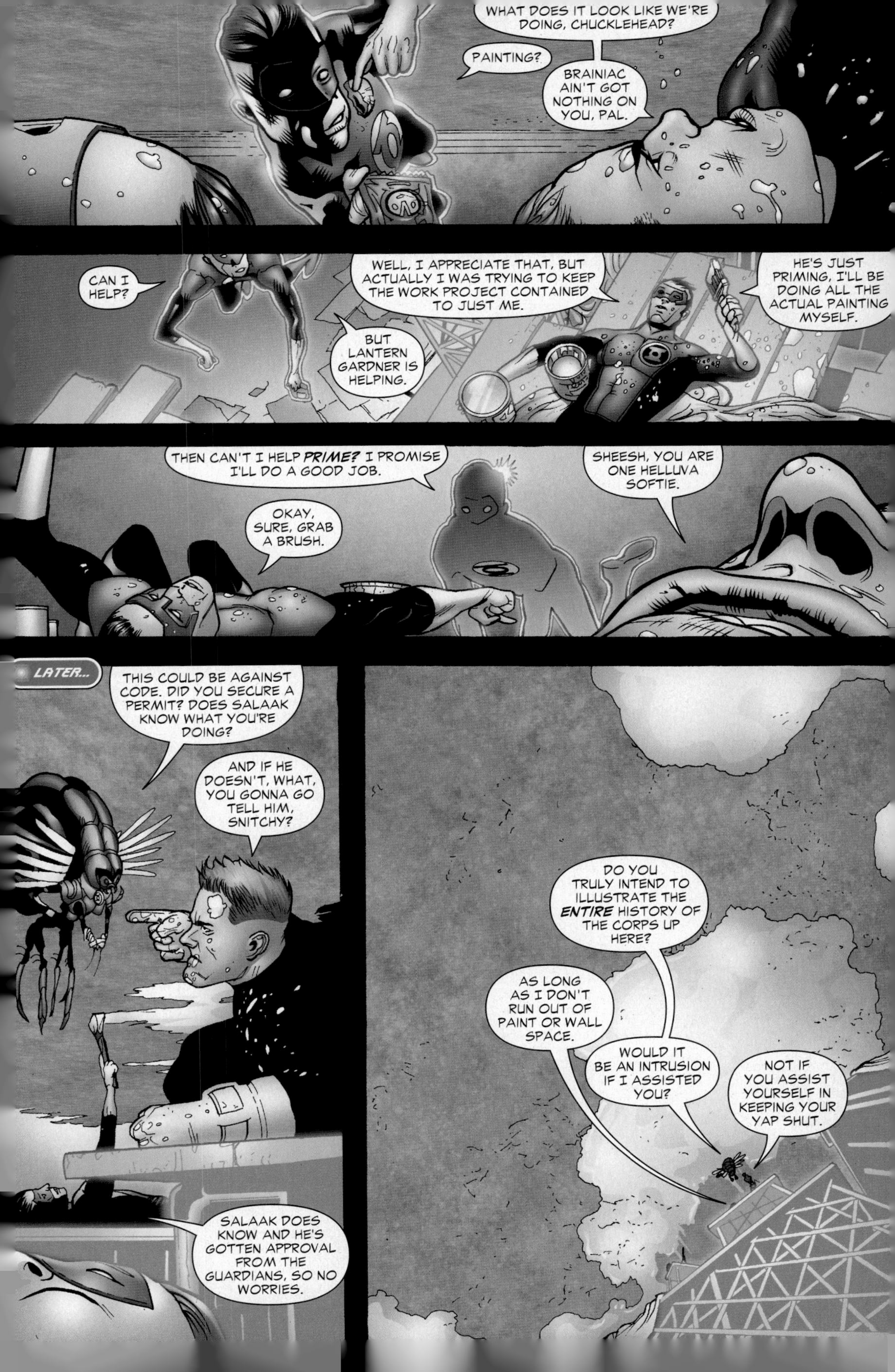
WHAT DOES IT LOOK LIKE WE'RE DOING, CHUCKLEHEAD?
PAINTING?
BRAINIAC AIN'T GOT NOTHING ON YOU, PAL.
CAN I HELP?
WELL, I APPRECIATE THAT, BUT ACTUALLY I WAS TRYING TO KEEP THE WORK PROJECT CONTAINED TO JUST ME.
BUT LANTERN GARDNER IS HELPING.
HE'S JUST PRIMING, I'LL BE DOING ALL THE ACTUAL PAINTING MYSELF.
THEN CAN'T I HELP *PRIME?* I PROMISE I'LL DO A GOOD JOB.
OKAY, SURE, GRAB A BRUSH.
SHEESH, YOU ARE ONE HELLUVA SOFTIE.
LATER...
THIS COULD BE AGAINST CODE. DID YOU SECURE A PERMIT? DOES SALAAK KNOW WHAT YOU'RE DOING?
AND IF HE DOESN'T, WHAT, YOU GONNA GO TELL HIM, SNITCHY?
SALAAK DOES KNOW AND HE'S GOTTEN APPROVAL FROM THE GUARDIANS, SO NO WORRIES.
DO YOU TRULY INTEND TO ILLUSTRATE THE *ENTIRE* HISTORY OF THE CORPS UP HERE?
AS LONG AS I DON'T RUN OUT OF PAINT OR WALL SPACE.
WOULD IT BE AN INTRUSION IF I ASSISTED YOU?
NOT IF YOU ASSIST YOURSELF IN KEEPING YOUR YAP SHUT.

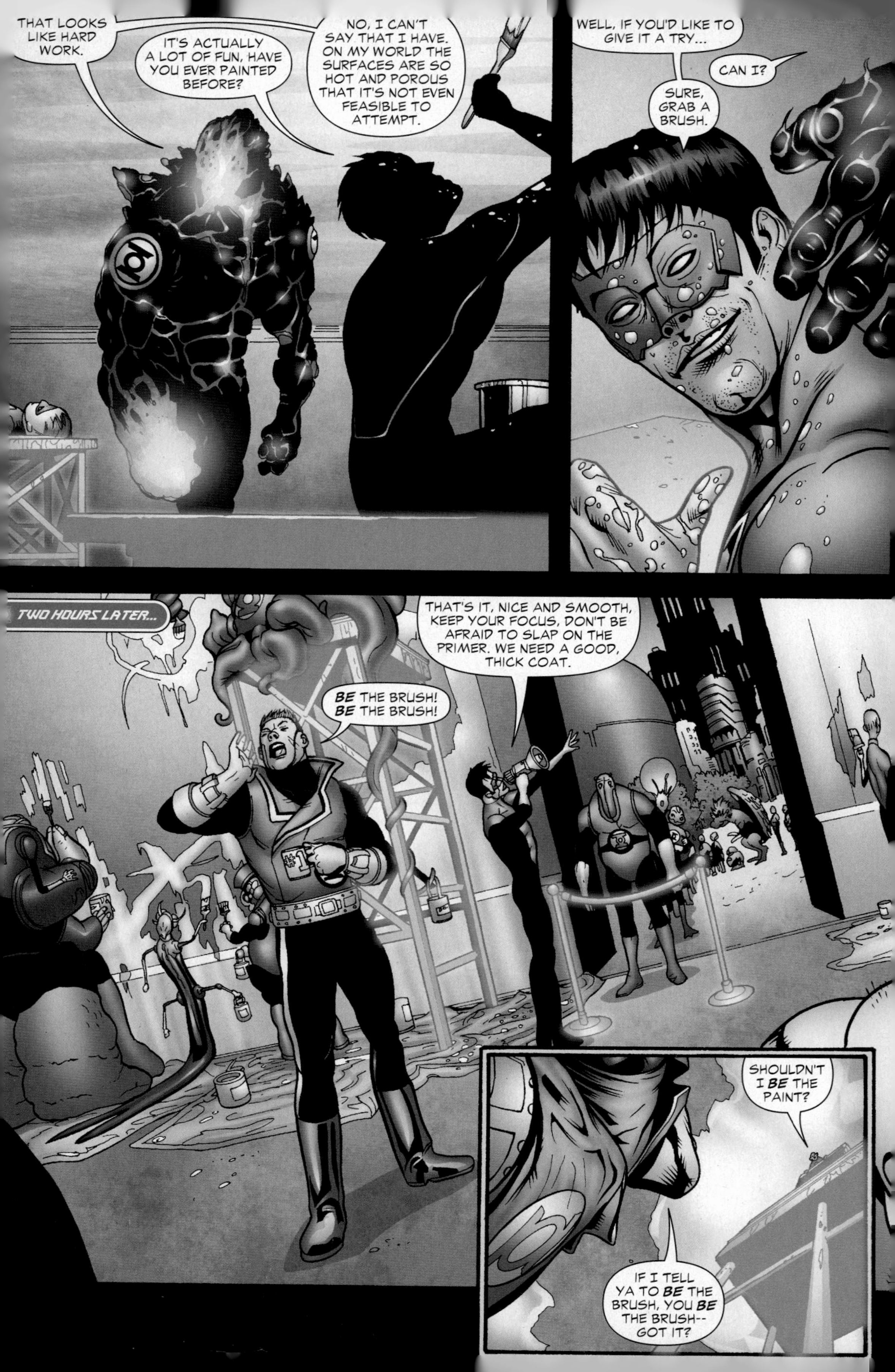
THAT LOOKS LIKE HARD WORK.
IT'S ACTUALLY A LOT OF FUN, HAVE YOU EVER PAINTED BEFORE?
NO, I CAN'T SAY THAT I HAVE. ON MY WORLD THE SURFACES ARE SO HOT AND POROUS THAT IT'S NOT EVEN FEASIBLE TO ATTEMPT.
WELL, IF YOU'D LIKE TO GIVE IT A TRY...
CAN I?
SURE, GRAB A BRUSH.
TWO HOURS LATER...
THAT'S IT, NICE AND SMOOTH, KEEP YOUR FOCUS, DON'T BE AFRAID TO SLAP ON THE PRIMER. WE NEED A GOOD, THICK COAT.
BE THE BRUSH! *BE* THE BRUSH!
SHOULDN'T I *BE* THE PAINT?
IF I TELL YA TO *BE* THE BRUSH, YOU *BE* THE BRUSH--GOT IT?

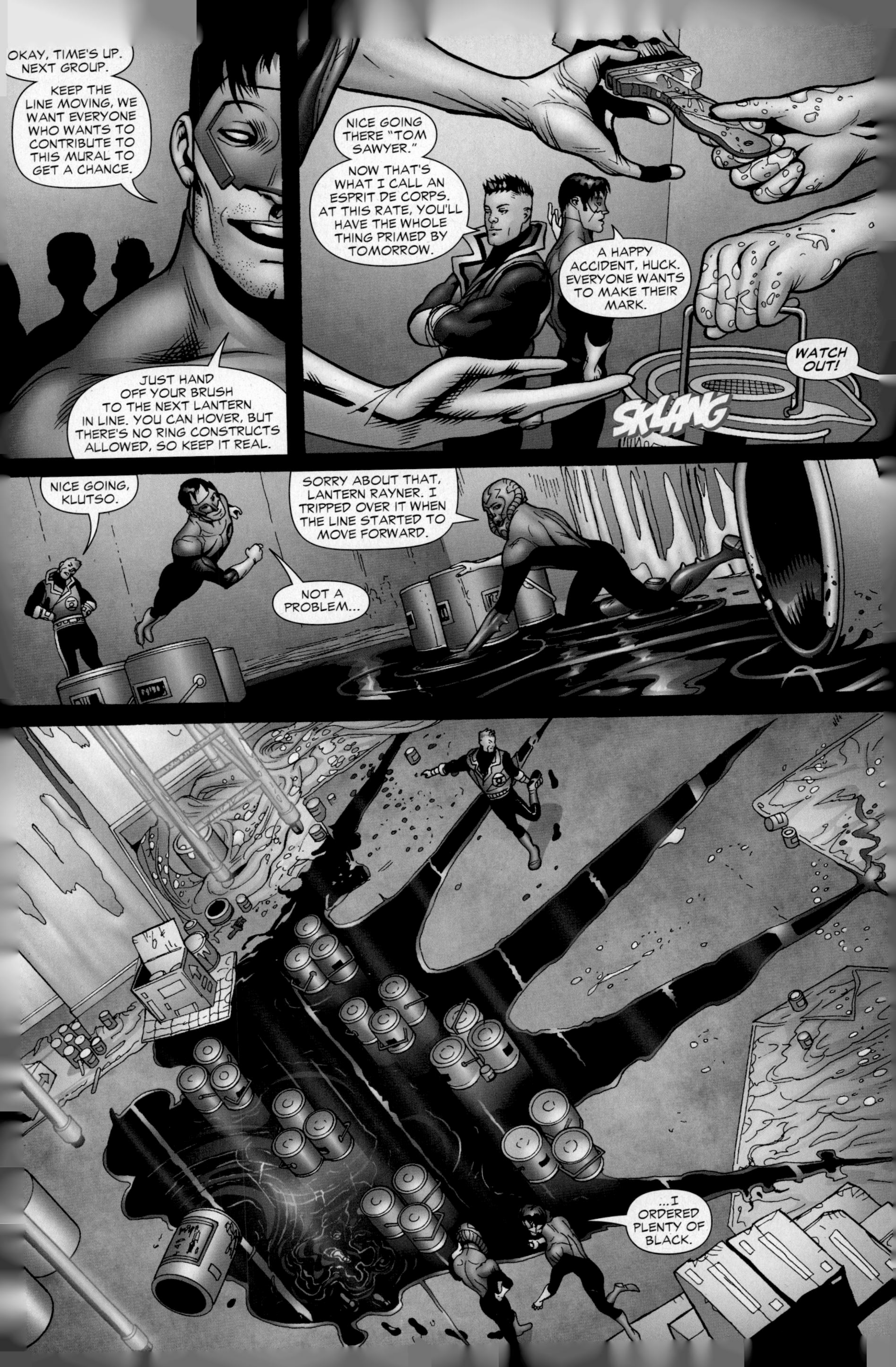
OKAY, TIME'S UP. NEXT GROUP.
KEEP THE LINE MOVING, WE WANT EVERYONE WHO WANTS TO CONTRIBUTE TO THIS MURAL TO GET A CHANCE.
JUST HAND OFF YOUR BRUSH TO THE NEXT LANTERN IN LINE. YOU CAN HOVER, BUT THERE'S NO RING CONSTRUCTS ALLOWED, SO KEEP IT REAL.
NICE GOING THERE "TOM SAWYER."
NOW THAT'S WHAT I CALL AN ESPRIT DE CORPS. AT THIS RATE, YOU'LL HAVE THE WHOLE THING PRIMED BY TOMORROW.
A HAPPY ACCIDENT, HUCK. EVERYONE WANTS TO MAKE THEIR MARK.
WATCH OUT!
SKLANG
NICE GOING, KLUTSO.
SORRY ABOUT THAT, LANTERN RAYNER. I TRIPPED OVER IT WHEN THE LINE STARTED TO MOVE FORWARD.
NOT A PROBLEM...
...I ORDERED PLENTY OF BLACK.

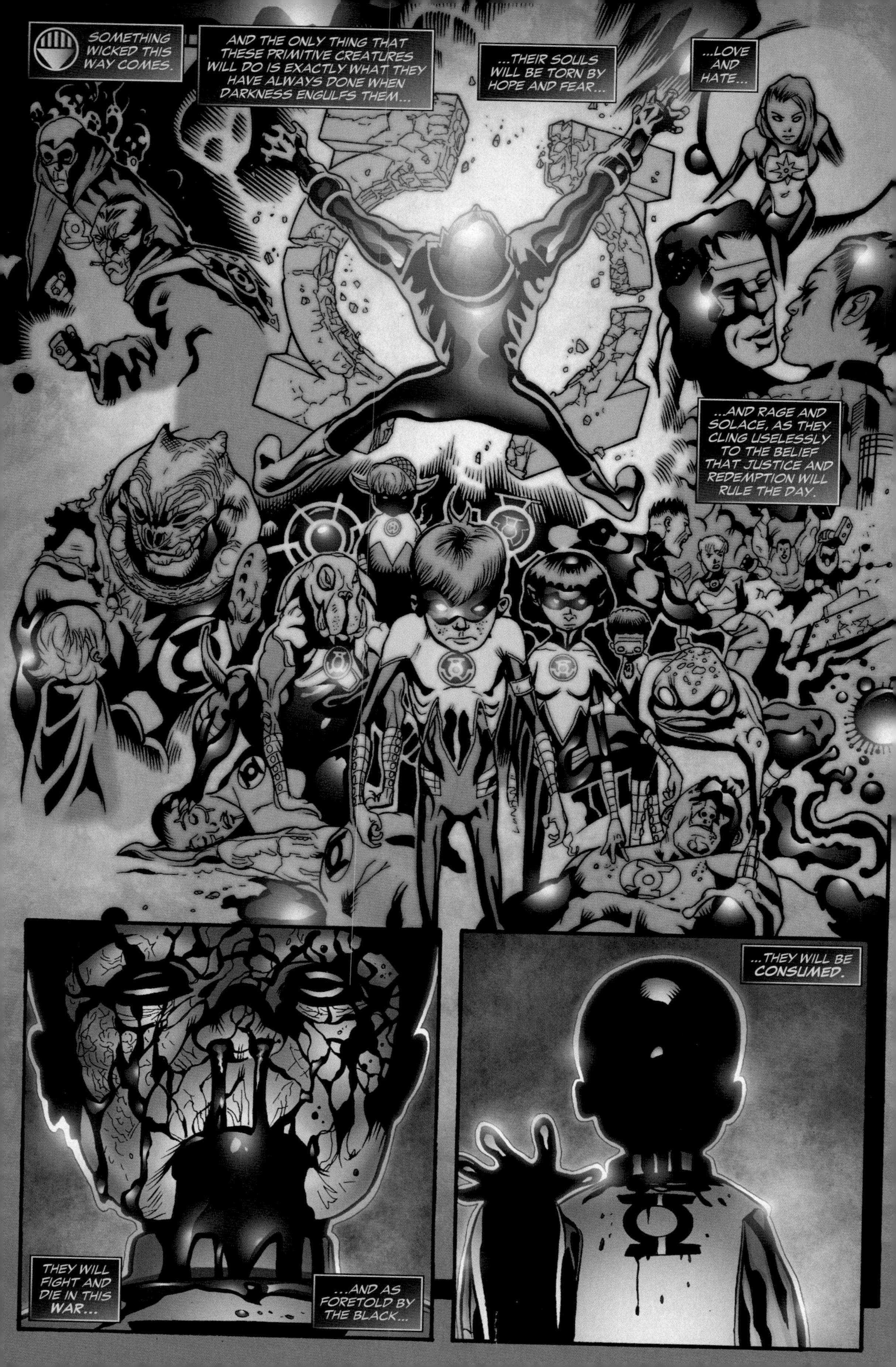
SOMETHING WICKED THIS WAY COMES.
AND THE ONLY THING THAT THESE PRIMITIVE CREATURES WILL DO IS EXACTLY WHAT THEY HAVE ALWAYS DONE WHEN DARKNESS ENGULFS THEM...
...THEIR SOULS WILL BE TORN BY HOPE AND FEAR...
...LOVE AND HATE...
...AND RAGE AND SOLACE, AS THEY CLING USELESSLY TO THE BELIEF THAT JUSTICE AND REDEMPTION WILL RULE THE DAY.
THEY WILL FIGHT AND DIE IN THIS WAR...
...AND AS FORETOLD BY THE BLACK...
...THEY WILL BE CONSUMED.

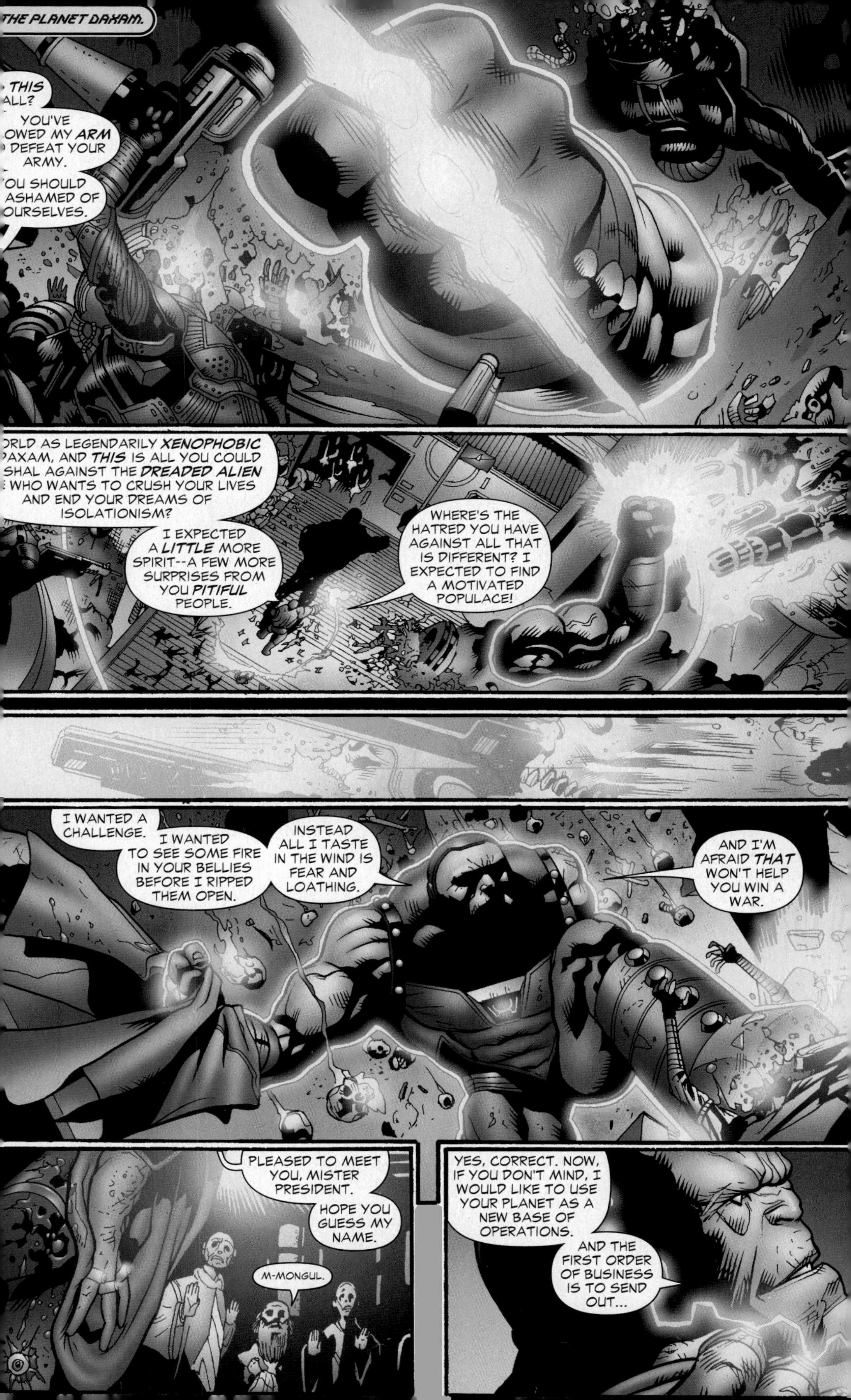

THE PLANET DAXAM.
THIS
ALL?
YOU'VE
OWED MY ARM
DEFEAT YOUR
ARMY.
OU SHOULD
ASHAMED OF
OURSELVES.
ORLD AS LEGENDARILY XENOPHOBIC
AXAM, AND THIS IS ALL YOU COULD
SHAL AGAINST THE DREADED ALIEN
WHO WANTS TO CRUSH YOUR LIVES
AND END YOUR DREAMS OF
ISOLATIONISM?
I EXPECTED A LITTLE MORE SPIRIT--A FEW MORE SURPRISES FROM YOU PITIFUL PEOPLE.
WHERE'S THE HATRED YOU HAVE AGAINST ALL THAT IS DIFFERENT? I EXPECTED TO FIND A MOTIVATED POPULACE!
I WANTED A CHALLENGE.
I WANTED TO SEE SOME FIRE IN YOUR BELLIES BEFORE I RIPPED THEM OPEN.
INSTEAD ALL I TASTE IN THE WIND IS FEAR AND LOATHING.
AND I'M AFRAID THAT WON'T HELP YOU WIN A WAR.
PLEASED TO MEET YOU, MISTER PRESIDENT.
HOPE YOU GUESS MY NAME.
M-MONGUL.
YES, CORRECT. NOW, IF YOU DON'T MIND, I WOULD LIKE TO USE YOUR PLANET AS A NEW BASE OF OPERATIONS.
AND THE FIRST ORDER OF BUSINESS IS TO SEND OUT...

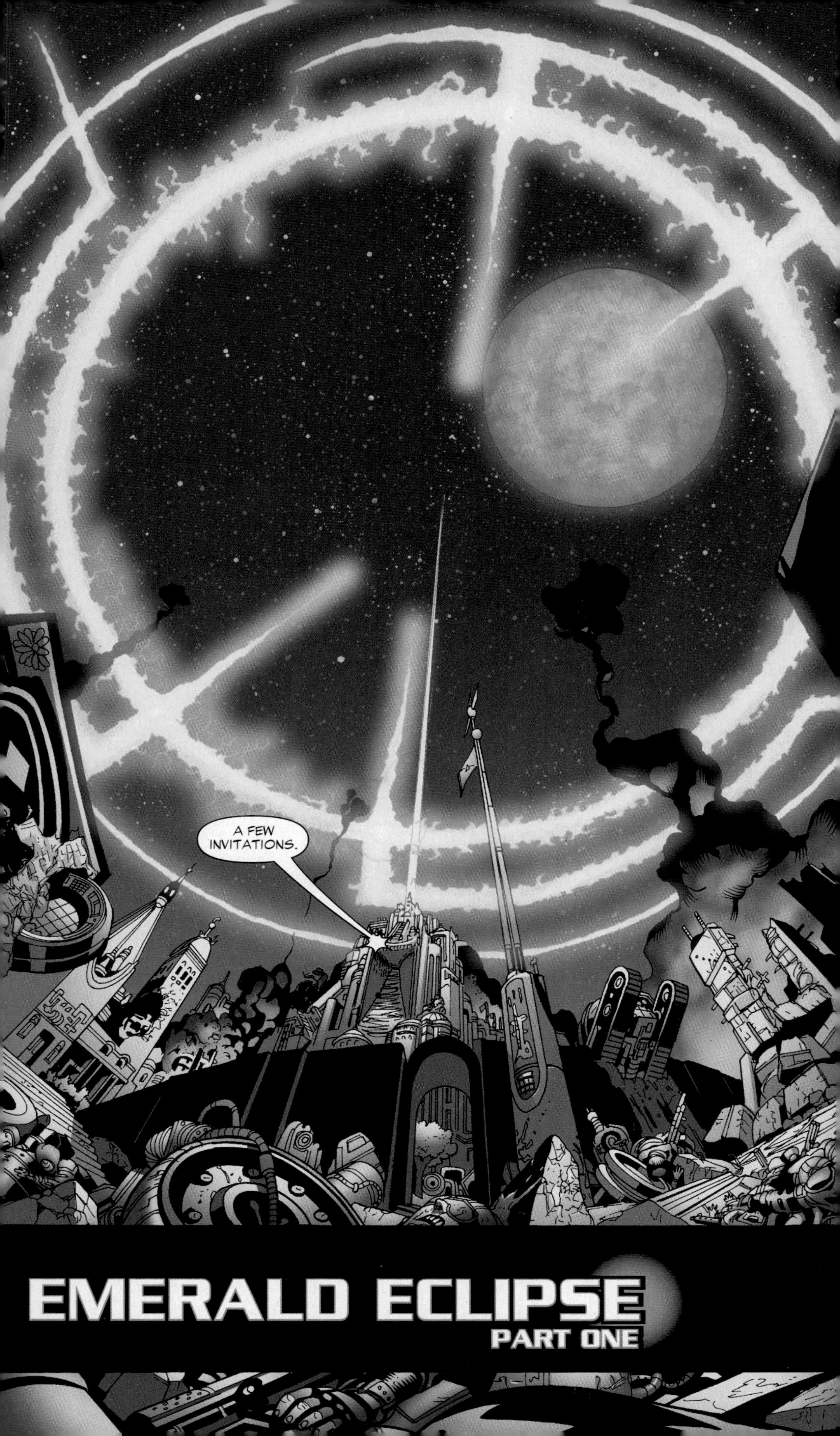
A FEW INVITATIONS.
EMERALD ECLIPSE
PART ONE

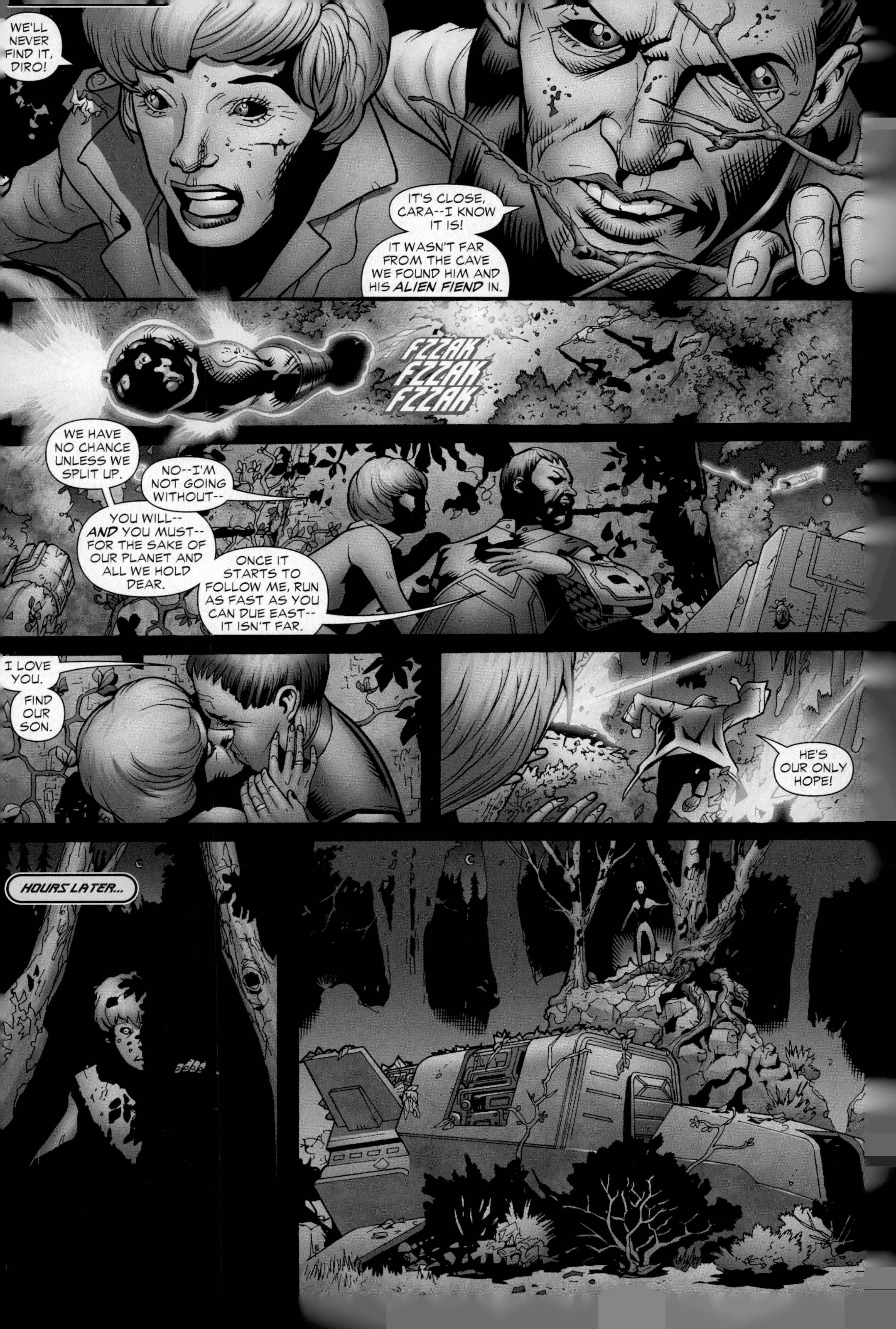
WE'LL NEVER FIND IT, DIRO!
IT'S CLOSE, CARA--I KNOW IT IS!
IT WASN'T FAR FROM THE CAVE WE FOUND HIM AND HIS ALIEN FIEND IN.
FZZAK FZZAK FZZAK
WE HAVE NO CHANCE UNLESS WE SPLIT UP.
NO--I'M NOT GOING WITHOUT--
YOU WILL-- AND YOU MUST-- FOR THE SAKE OF OUR PLANET AND ALL WE HOLD DEAR.
ONCE IT STARTS TO FOLLOW ME, RUN AS FAST AS YOU CAN DUE EAST-- IT ISN'T FAR.
I LOVE YOU.
FIND OUR SON.
HE'S OUR ONLY HOPE!
HOURS LATER...

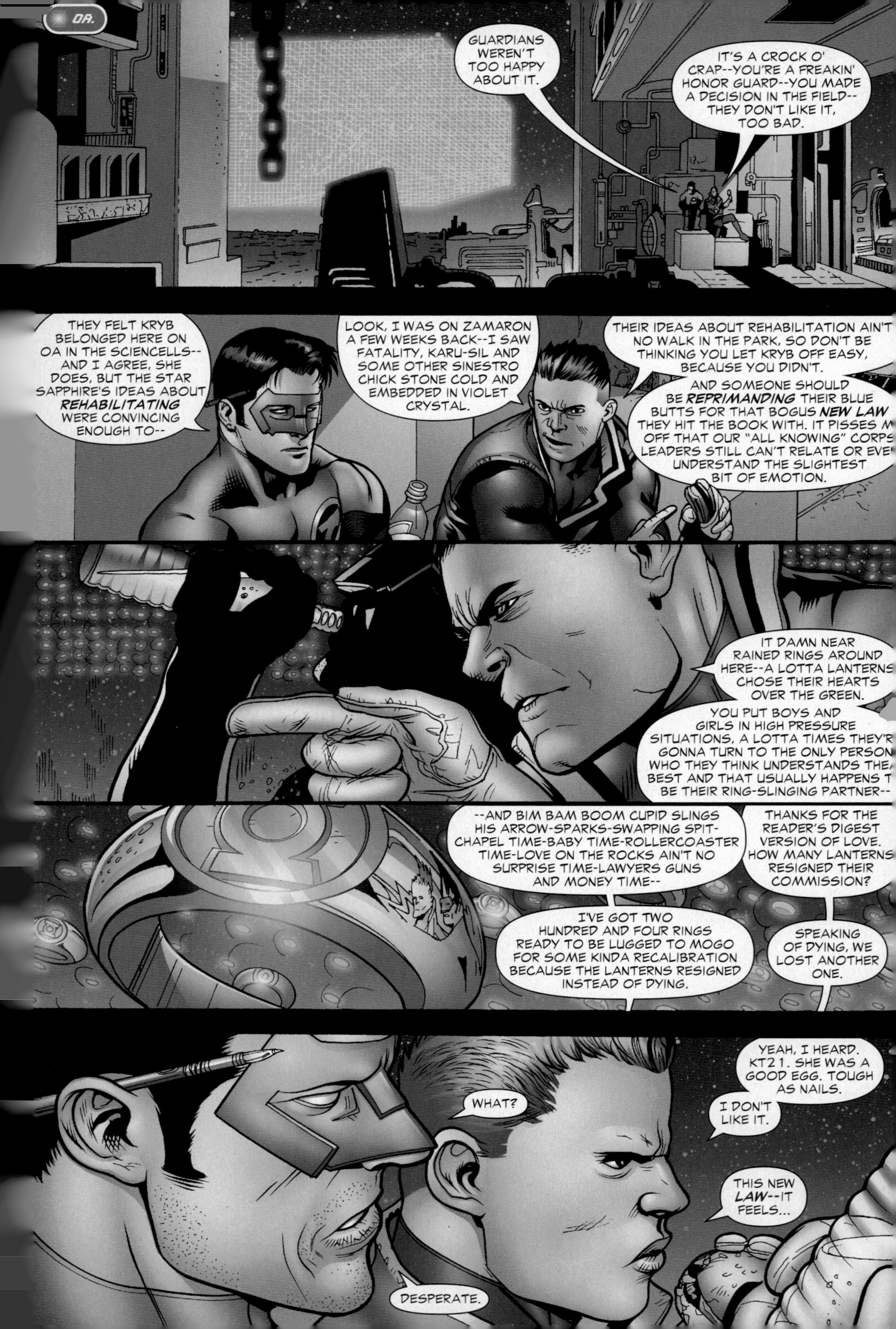
OA.
GUARDIANS WEREN'T TOO HAPPY ABOUT IT.
IT'S A CROCK O' CRAP--YOU'RE A FREAKIN' HONOR GUARD--YOU MADE A DECISION IN THE FIELD--THEY DON'T LIKE IT, TOO BAD.
THEY FELT KRYB BELONGED HERE ON OA IN THE SCIENCELLS--AND I AGREE, SHE DOES, BUT THE STAR SAPPHIRE'S IDEAS ABOUT REHABILITATING WERE CONVINCING ENOUGH TO--
LOOK, I WAS ON ZAMARON A FEW WEEKS BACK--I SAW FATALITY, KARU-SIL AND SOME OTHER SINESTRO CHICK STONE COLD AND EMBEDDED IN VIOLET CRYSTAL.
THEIR IDEAS ABOUT REHABILITATION AIN'T NO WALK IN THE PARK, SO DON'T BE THINKING YOU LET KRYB OFF EASY, BECAUSE YOU DIDN'T.
AND SOMEONE SHOULD BE REPRIMANDING THEIR BLUE BUTTS FOR THAT BOGUS NEW LAW THEY HIT THE BOOK WITH. IT PISSES M OFF THAT OUR "ALL KNOWING" CORPS LEADERS STILL CAN'T RELATE OR EVE UNDERSTAND THE SLIGHTEST BIT OF EMOTION.
IT DAMN NEAR RAINED RINGS AROUND HERE--A LOTTA LANTERNS CHOSE THEIR HEARTS OVER THE GREEN.
YOU PUT BOYS AND GIRLS IN HIGH PRESSURE SITUATIONS, A LOTTA TIMES THEY'R GONNA TURN TO THE ONLY PERSON WHO THEY THINK UNDERSTANDS THE BEST AND THAT USUALLY HAPPENS T BE THEIR RING-SLINGING PARTNER--
--AND BIM BAM BOOM CUPID SLINGS HIS ARROW-SPARKS-SWAPPING SPIT-CHAPEL TIME-BABY TIME-ROLLERCOASTER TIME-LOVE ON THE ROCKS AIN'T NO SURPRISE TIME-LAWYERS GUNS AND MONEY TIME--
THANKS FOR THE READER'S DIGEST VERSION OF LOVE. HOW MANY LANTERNS RESIGNED THEIR COMMISSION?
I'VE GOT TWO HUNDRED AND FOUR RINGS READY TO BE LUGGED TO MOGO FOR SOME KINDA RECALIBRATION BECAUSE THE LANTERNS RESIGNED INSTEAD OF DYING.
SPEAKING OF DYING, WE LOST ANOTHER ONE.
YEAH, I HEARD. KT21. SHE WAS A GOOD EGG. TOUGH AS NAILS.
I DON'T LIKE IT.
WHAT?
THIS NEW LAW--IT FEELS...
DESPERATE.

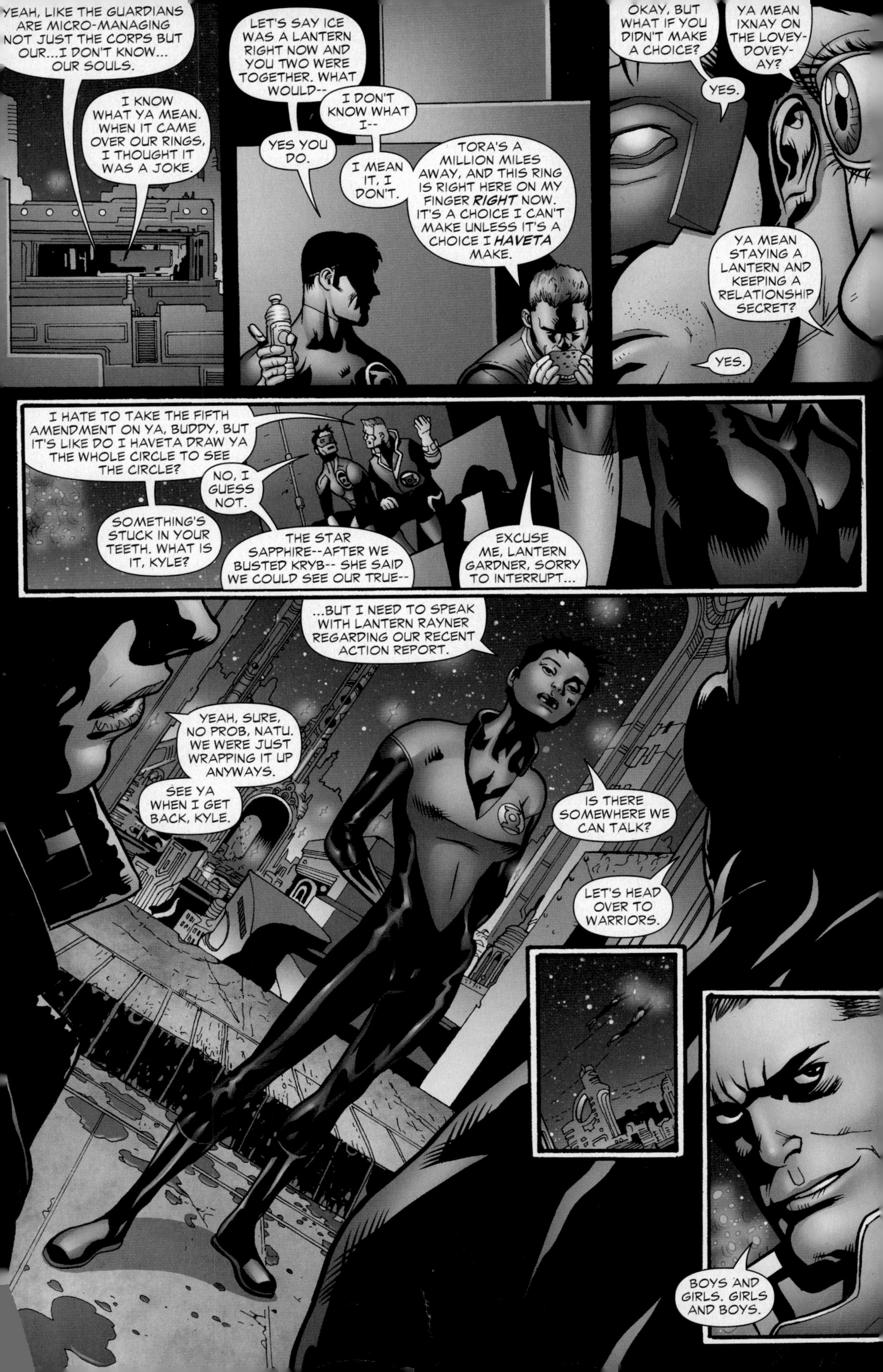
YEAH, LIKE THE GUARDIANS ARE MICRO-MANAGING NOT JUST THE CORPS BUT OUR...I DON'T KNOW... OUR SOULS.
I KNOW WHAT YA MEAN. WHEN IT CAME OVER OUR RINGS, I THOUGHT IT WAS A JOKE.
LET'S SAY ICE WAS A LANTERN RIGHT NOW AND YOU TWO WERE TOGETHER. WHAT WOULD--
I DON'T KNOW WHAT I--
YES YOU DO.
I MEAN IT, I DON'T.
TORA'S A MILLION MILES AWAY, AND THIS RING IS RIGHT HERE ON MY FINGER RIGHT NOW. IT'S A CHOICE I CAN'T MAKE UNLESS IT'S A CHOICE I HAVETA MAKE.
OKAY, BUT WHAT IF YOU DIDN'T MAKE A CHOICE?
YA MEAN IXNAY ON THE LOVEY-DOVEY-AY?
YES.
YA MEAN STAYING A LANTERN AND KEEPING A RELATIONSHIP SECRET?
YES.
I HATE TO TAKE THE FIFTH AMENDMENT ON YA, BUDDY, BUT IT'S LIKE DO I HAVETA DRAW YA THE WHOLE CIRCLE TO SEE THE CIRCLE?
NO, I GUESS NOT.
SOMETHING'S STUCK IN YOUR TEETH. WHAT IS IT, KYLE?
THE STAR SAPPHIRE--AFTER WE BUSTED KRYB-- SHE SAID WE COULD SEE OUR TRUE--
EXCUSE ME, LANTERN GARDNER, SORRY TO INTERRUPT...
...BUT I NEED TO SPEAK WITH LANTERN RAYNER REGARDING OUR RECENT ACTION REPORT.
YEAH, SURE, NO PROB, NATU. WE WERE JUST WRAPPING IT UP ANYWAYS.
SEE YA WHEN I GET BACK, KYLE.
IS THERE SOMEWHERE WE CAN TALK?
LET'S HEAD OVER TO WARRIORS.
BOYS AND GIRLS. GIRLS AND BOYS.

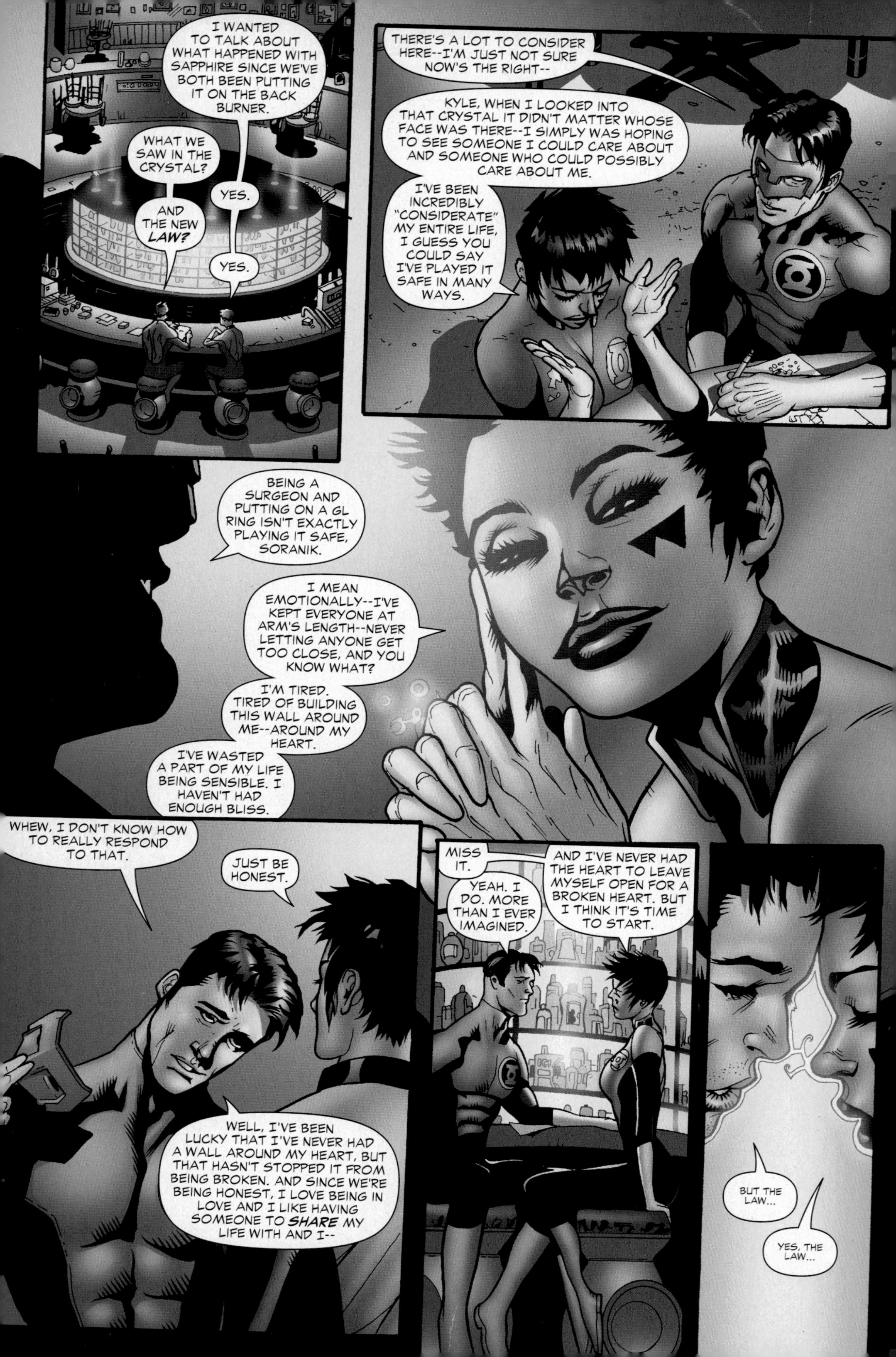
I WANTED TO TALK ABOUT WHAT HAPPENED WITH SAPPHIRE SINCE WE'VE BOTH BEEN PUTTING IT ON THE BACK BURNER.
WHAT WE SAW IN THE CRYSTAL?
YES.
AND THE NEW *LAW?*
YES.
THERE'S A LOT TO CONSIDER HERE--I'M JUST NOT SURE NOW'S THE RIGHT--
KYLE, WHEN I LOOKED INTO THAT CRYSTAL IT DIDN'T MATTER WHOSE FACE WAS THERE--I SIMPLY WAS HOPING TO SEE SOMEONE I COULD CARE ABOUT AND SOMEONE WHO COULD POSSIBLY CARE ABOUT ME.
I'VE BEEN INCREDIBLY "CONSIDERATE" MY ENTIRE LIFE, I GUESS YOU COULD SAY I'VE PLAYED IT SAFE IN MANY WAYS.
BEING A SURGEON AND PUTTING ON A GL RING ISN'T EXACTLY PLAYING IT SAFE, SORANIK.
I MEAN EMOTIONALLY--I'VE KEPT EVERYONE AT ARM'S LENGTH--NEVER LETTING ANYONE GET TOO CLOSE, AND YOU KNOW WHAT?
I'M TIRED. TIRED OF BUILDING THIS WALL AROUND ME--AROUND MY HEART.
I'VE WASTED A PART OF MY LIFE BEING SENSIBLE. I HAVEN'T HAD ENOUGH BLISS.
WHEW, I DON'T KNOW HOW TO REALLY RESPOND TO THAT.
JUST BE HONEST.
WELL, I'VE BEEN LUCKY THAT I'VE NEVER HAD A WALL AROUND MY HEART, BUT THAT HASN'T STOPPED IT FROM BEING BROKEN. AND SINCE WE'RE BEING HONEST, I LOVE BEING IN LOVE AND I LIKE HAVING SOMEONE TO *SHARE* MY LIFE WITH AND I--
MISS IT.
YEAH. I DO. MORE THAN I EVER IMAGINED.
AND I'VE NEVER HAD THE HEART TO LEAVE MYSELF OPEN FOR A BROKEN HEART. BUT I THINK IT'S TIME TO START.
BUT THE LAW...
YES, THE LAW...

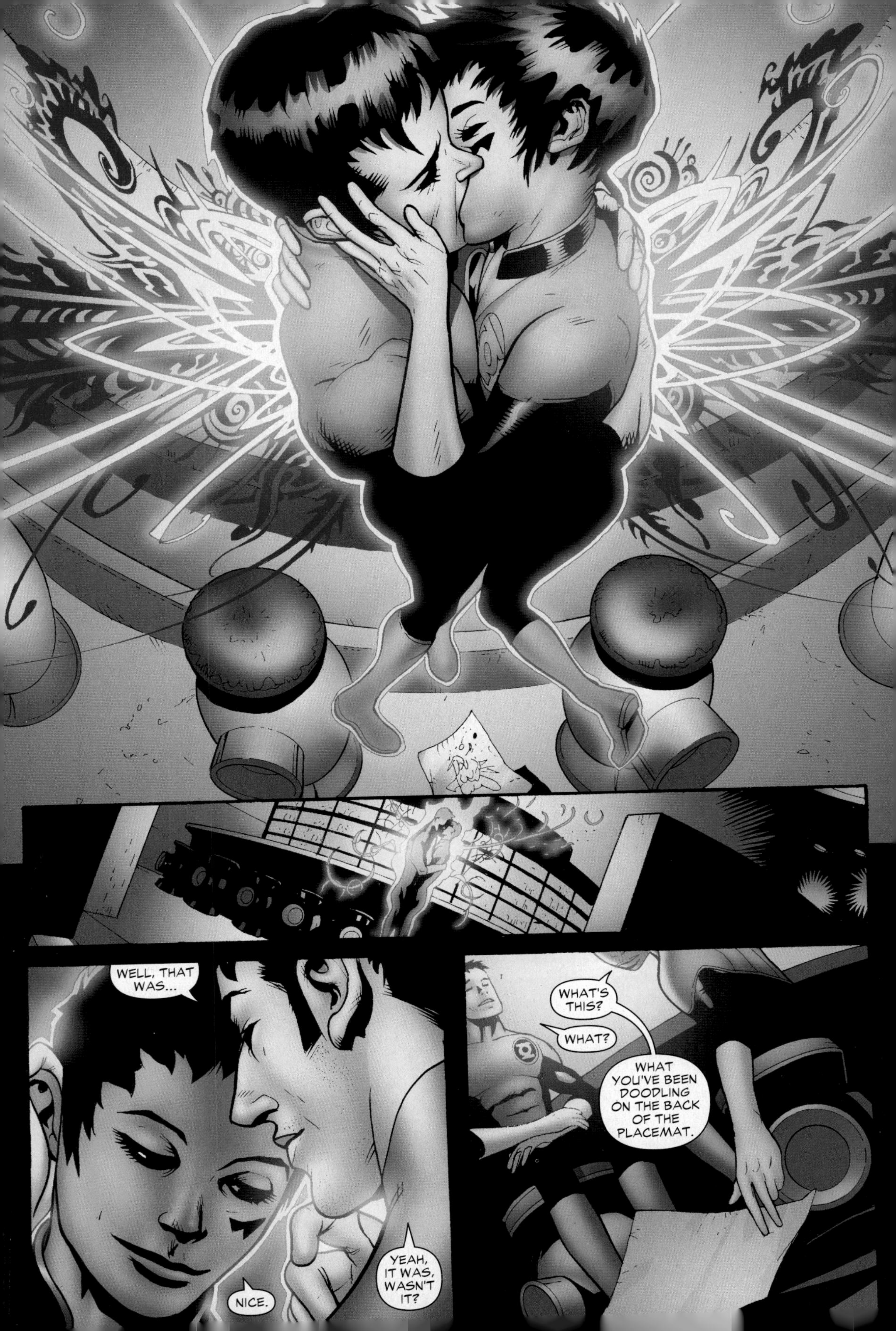
WELL, THAT WAS...
NICE.
YEAH, IT WAS, WASN'T IT?
WHAT'S THIS?
WHAT?
WHAT YOU'VE BEEN DOODLING ON THE BACK OF THE PLACEMAT.

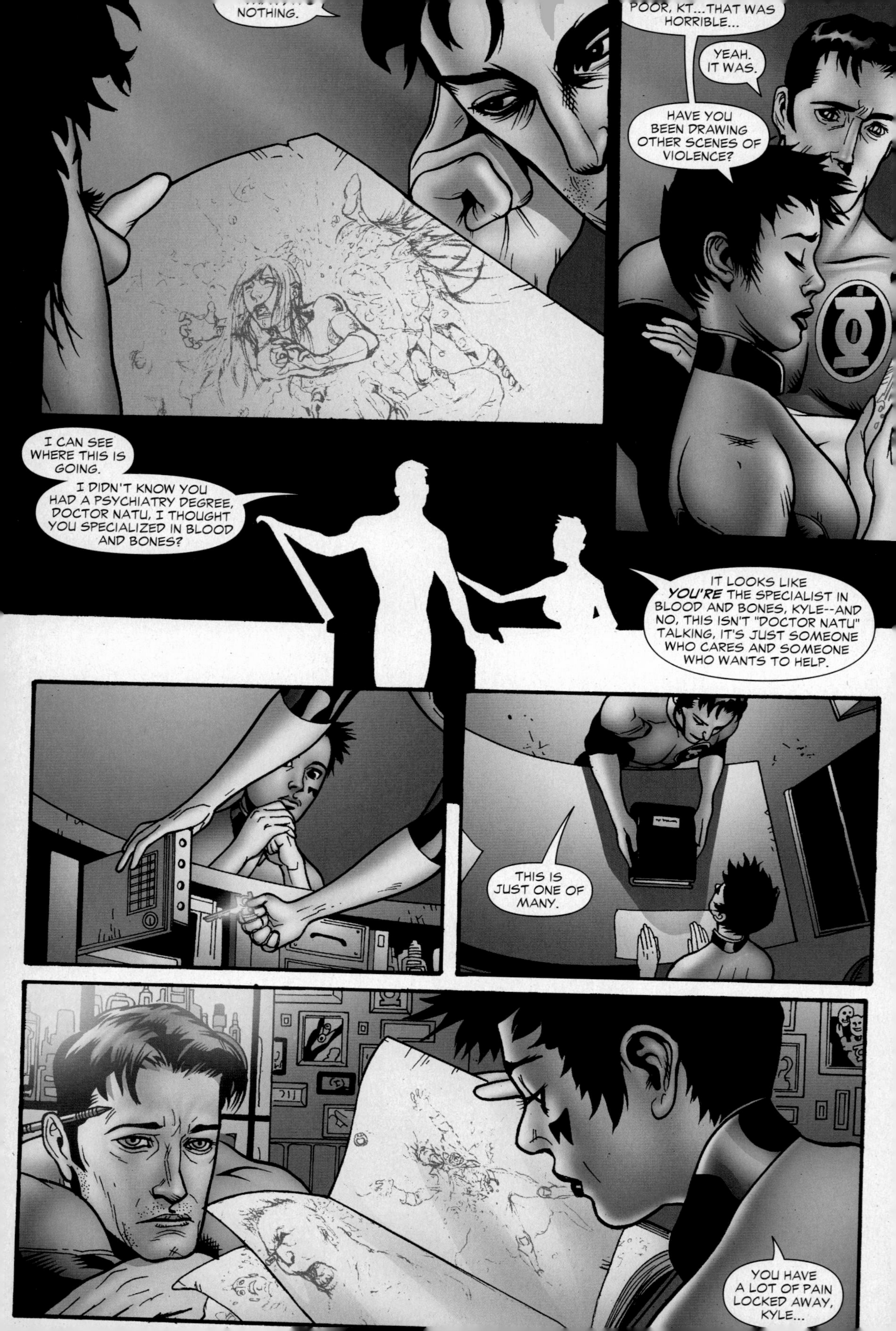
NOTHING.
POOR, KT...THAT WAS HORRIBLE...
YEAH. IT WAS.
HAVE YOU BEEN DRAWING OTHER SCENES OF VIOLENCE?
I CAN SEE WHERE THIS IS GOING.
I DIDN'T KNOW YOU HAD A PSYCHIATRY DEGREE, DOCTOR NATU. I THOUGHT YOU SPECIALIZED IN BLOOD AND BONES?
IT LOOKS LIKE *YOU'RE* THE SPECIALIST IN BLOOD AND BONES, KYLE--AND NO, THIS ISN'T "DOCTOR NATU" TALKING, IT'S JUST SOMEONE WHO CARES AND SOMEONE WHO WANTS TO HELP.
THIS IS JUST ONE OF MANY.
YOU HAVE A LOT OF PAIN LOCKED AWAY, KYLE...

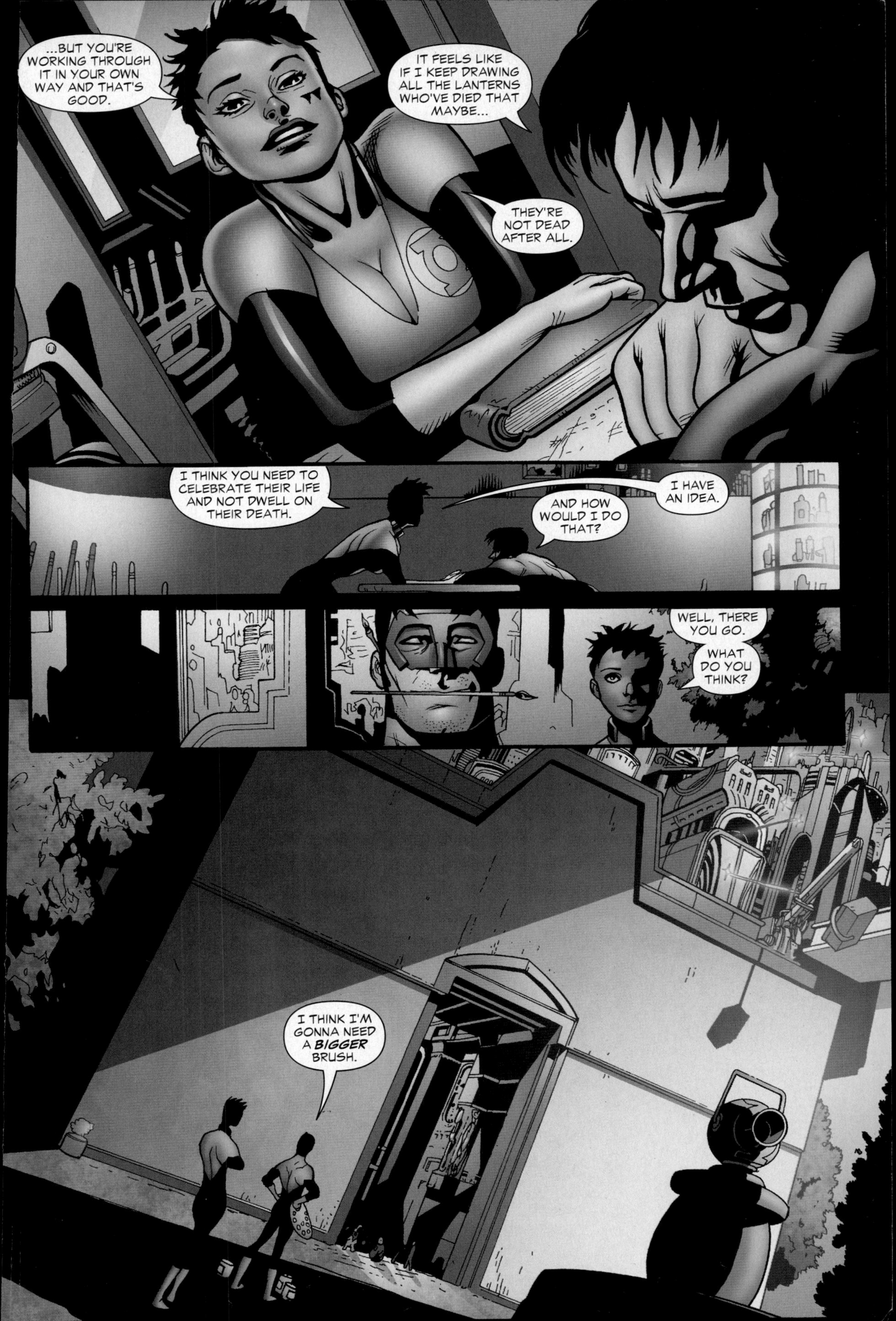
...BUT YOU'RE WORKING THROUGH IT IN YOUR OWN WAY AND THAT'S GOOD.
IT FEELS LIKE IF I KEEP DRAWING ALL THE LANTERNS WHO'VE DIED THAT MAYBE...
THEY'RE NOT DEAD AFTER ALL.
I THINK YOU NEED TO CELEBRATE THEIR LIFE AND NOT DWELL ON THEIR DEATH.
AND HOW WOULD I DO THAT?
I HAVE AN IDEA.
WELL, THERE YOU GO.
WHAT DO YOU THINK?
I THINK I'M GONNA NEED A BIGGER BRUSH.

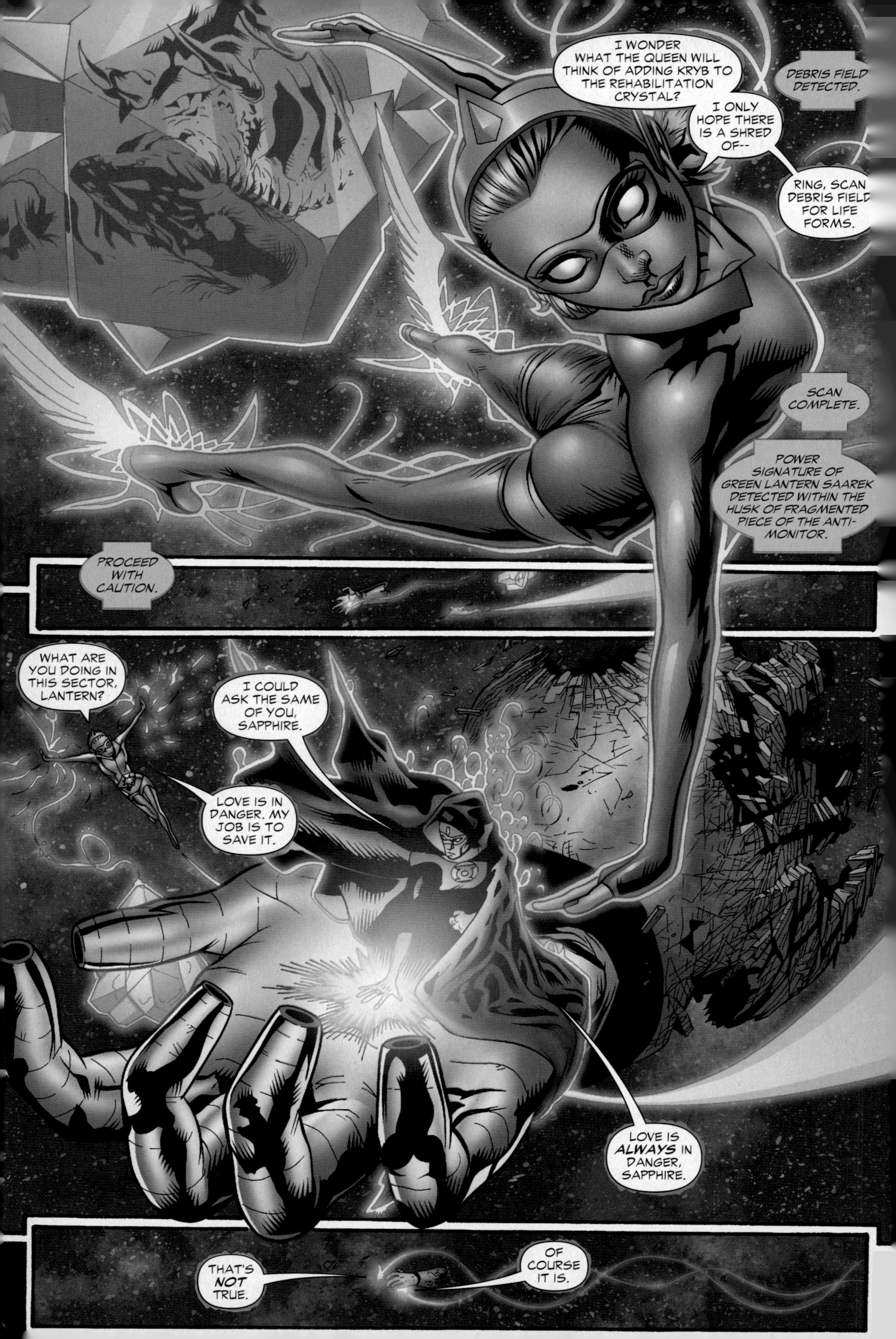
I WONDER WHAT THE QUEEN WILL THINK OF ADDING KRYB TO THE REHABILITATION CRYSTAL?
DEBRIS FIELD DETECTED.
I ONLY HOPE THERE IS A SHRED OF--
RING, SCAN DEBRIS FIELD FOR LIFE FORMS.
SCAN COMPLETE.
POWER SIGNATURE OF GREEN LANTERN SAAREK DETECTED WITHIN THE HUSK OF FRAGMENTED PIECE OF THE ANTI-MONITOR.
PROCEED WITH CAUTION.
WHAT ARE YOU DOING IN THIS SECTOR, LANTERN?
I COULD ASK THE SAME OF YOU, SAPPHIRE.
LOVE IS IN DANGER. MY JOB IS TO SAVE IT.
LOVE IS ALWAYS IN DANGER, SAPPHIRE.
THAT'S NOT TRUE.
OF COURSE IT IS.

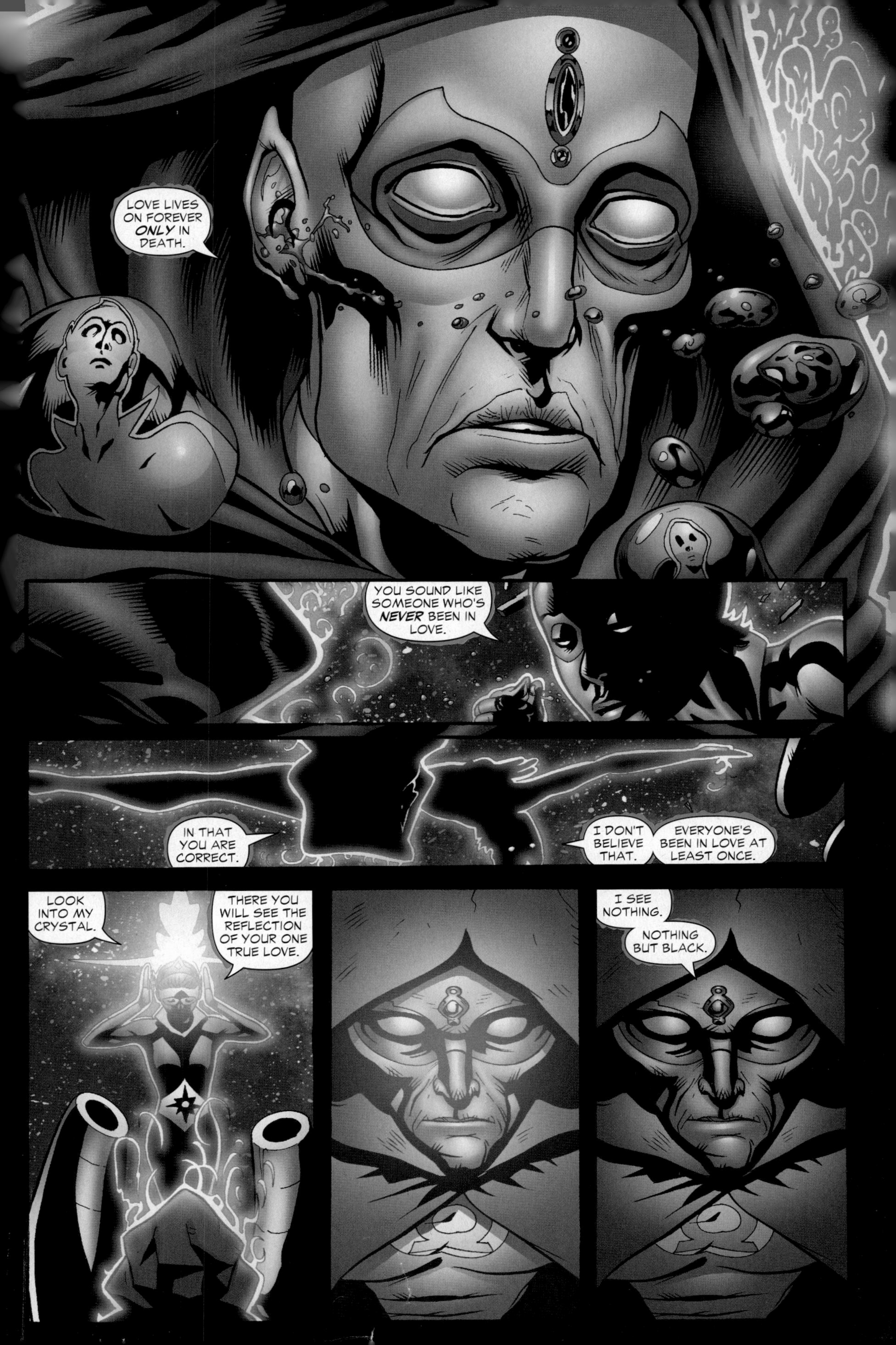
LOVE LIVES ON FOREVER *ONLY* IN DEATH.
YOU SOUND LIKE SOMEONE WHO'S *NEVER* BEEN IN LOVE.
IN THAT YOU ARE CORRECT.
I DON'T BELIEVE THAT.
EVERYONE'S BEEN IN LOVE AT LEAST ONCE.
LOOK INTO MY CRYSTAL.
THERE YOU WILL SEE THE REFLECTION OF YOUR ONE TRUE LOVE.
I SEE NOTHING.
NOTHING BUT BLACK.

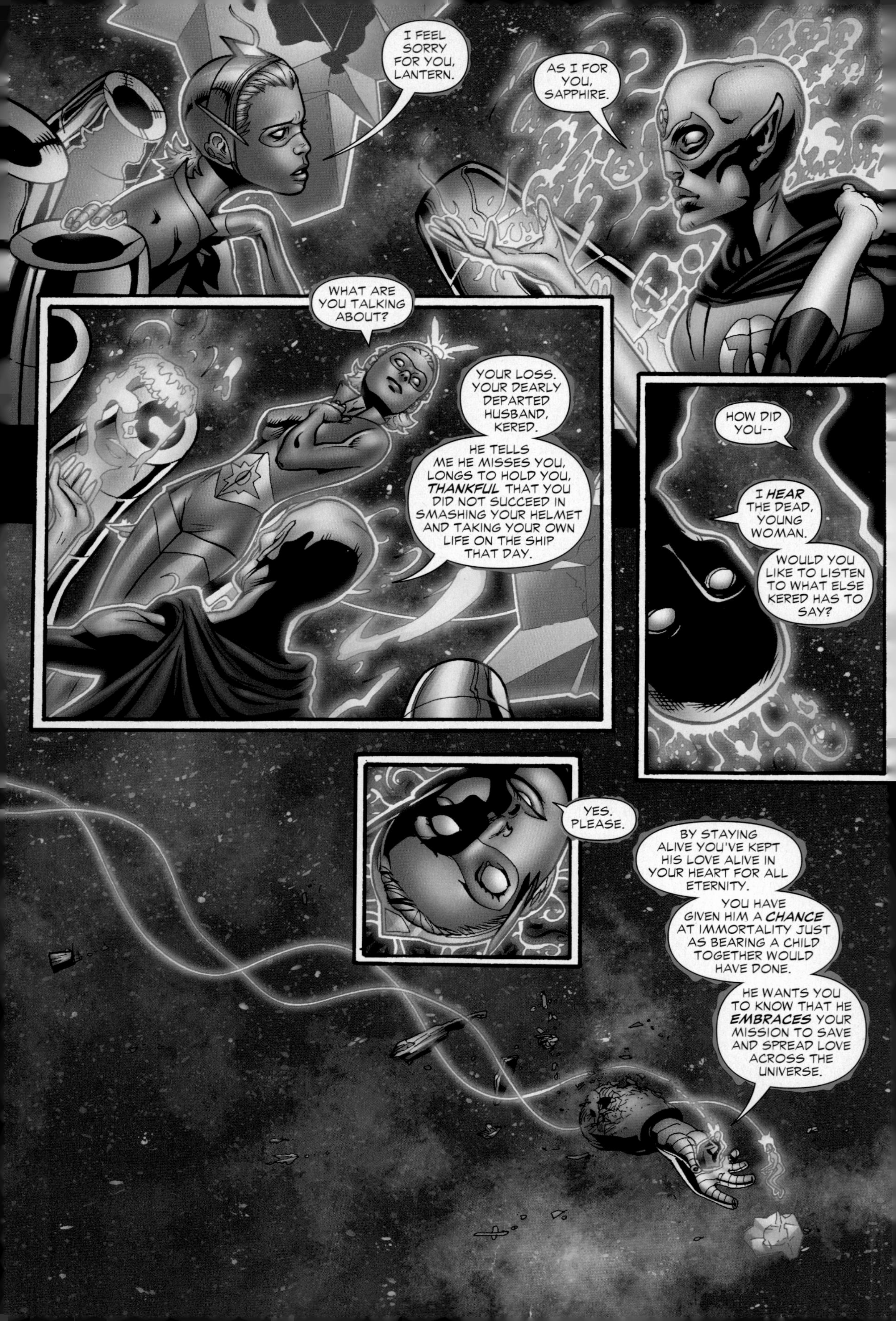
I FEEL SORRY FOR YOU, LANTERN.
AS I FOR YOU, SAPPHIRE.
WHAT ARE YOU TALKING ABOUT?
YOUR LOSS. YOUR DEARLY DEPARTED HUSBAND, KERED.
HE TELLS ME HE MISSES YOU, LONGS TO HOLD YOU, *THANKFUL* THAT YOU DID NOT SUCCEED IN SMASHING YOUR HELMET AND TAKING YOUR OWN LIFE ON THE SHIP THAT DAY.
HOW DID YOU--
I *HEAR* THE DEAD, YOUNG WOMAN.
WOULD YOU LIKE TO LISTEN TO WHAT ELSE KERED HAS TO SAY?
YES. PLEASE.
BY STAYING ALIVE YOU'VE KEPT HIS LOVE ALIVE IN YOUR HEART FOR ALL ETERNITY.
YOU HAVE GIVEN HIM A *CHANCE* AT IMMORTALITY JUST AS BEARING A CHILD TOGETHER WOULD HAVE DONE.
HE WANTS YOU TO KNOW THAT HE *EMBRACES* YOUR MISSION TO SAVE AND SPREAD LOVE ACROSS THE UNIVERSE.

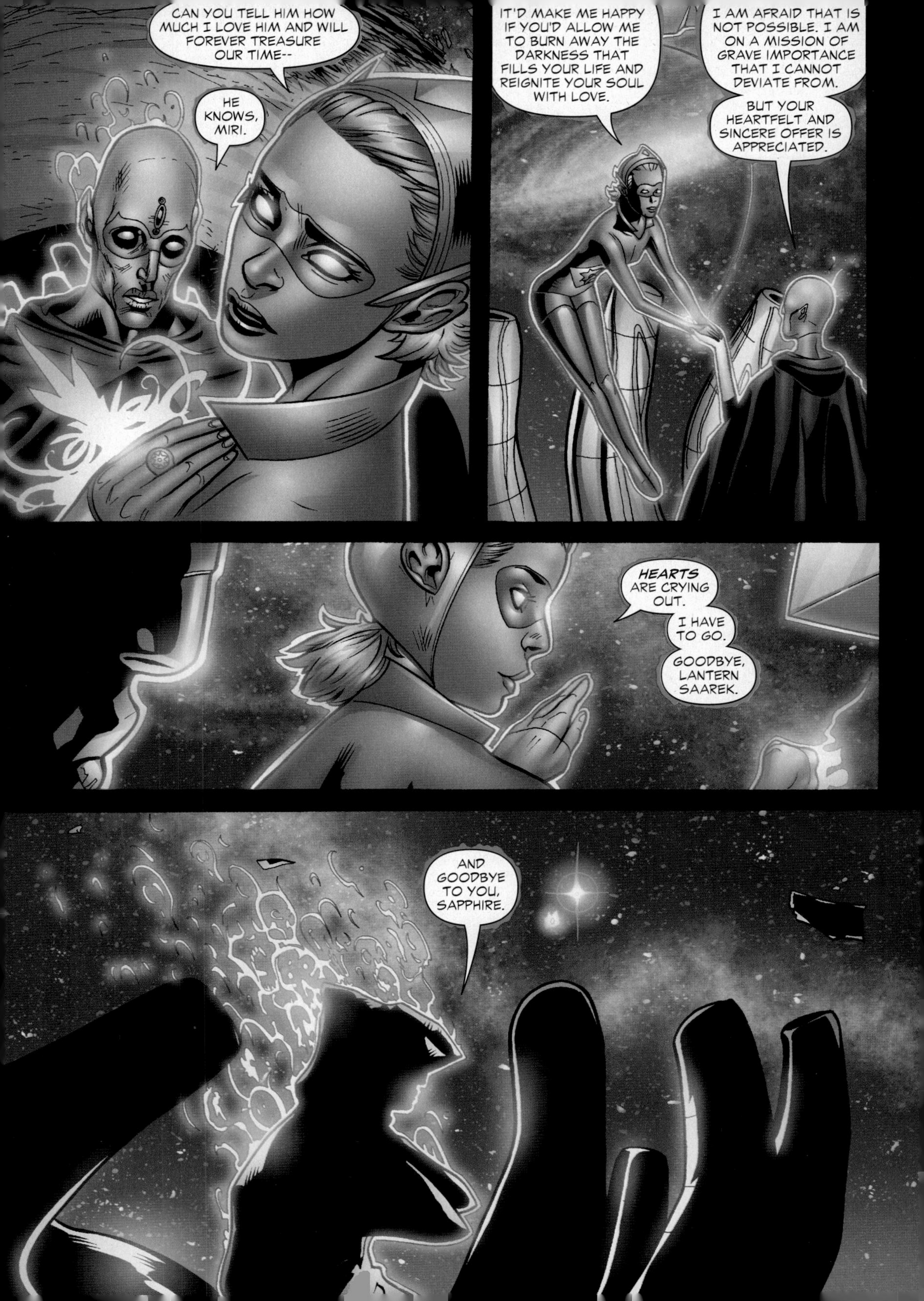
CAN YOU TELL HIM HOW MUCH I LOVE HIM AND WILL FOREVER TREASURE OUR TIME--
HE KNOWS, MIRI.
IT'D MAKE ME HAPPY IF YOU'D ALLOW ME TO BURN AWAY THE DARKNESS THAT FILLS YOUR LIFE AND REIGNITE YOUR SOUL WITH LOVE.
I AM AFRAID THAT IS NOT POSSIBLE. I AM ON A MISSION OF GRAVE IMPORTANCE THAT I CANNOT DEVIATE FROM.
BUT YOUR HEARTFELT AND SINCERE OFFER IS APPRECIATED.
HEARTS ARE CRYING OUT.
I HAVE TO GO.
GOODBYE, LANTERN SAAREK.
AND GOODBYE TO YOU, SAPPHIRE.

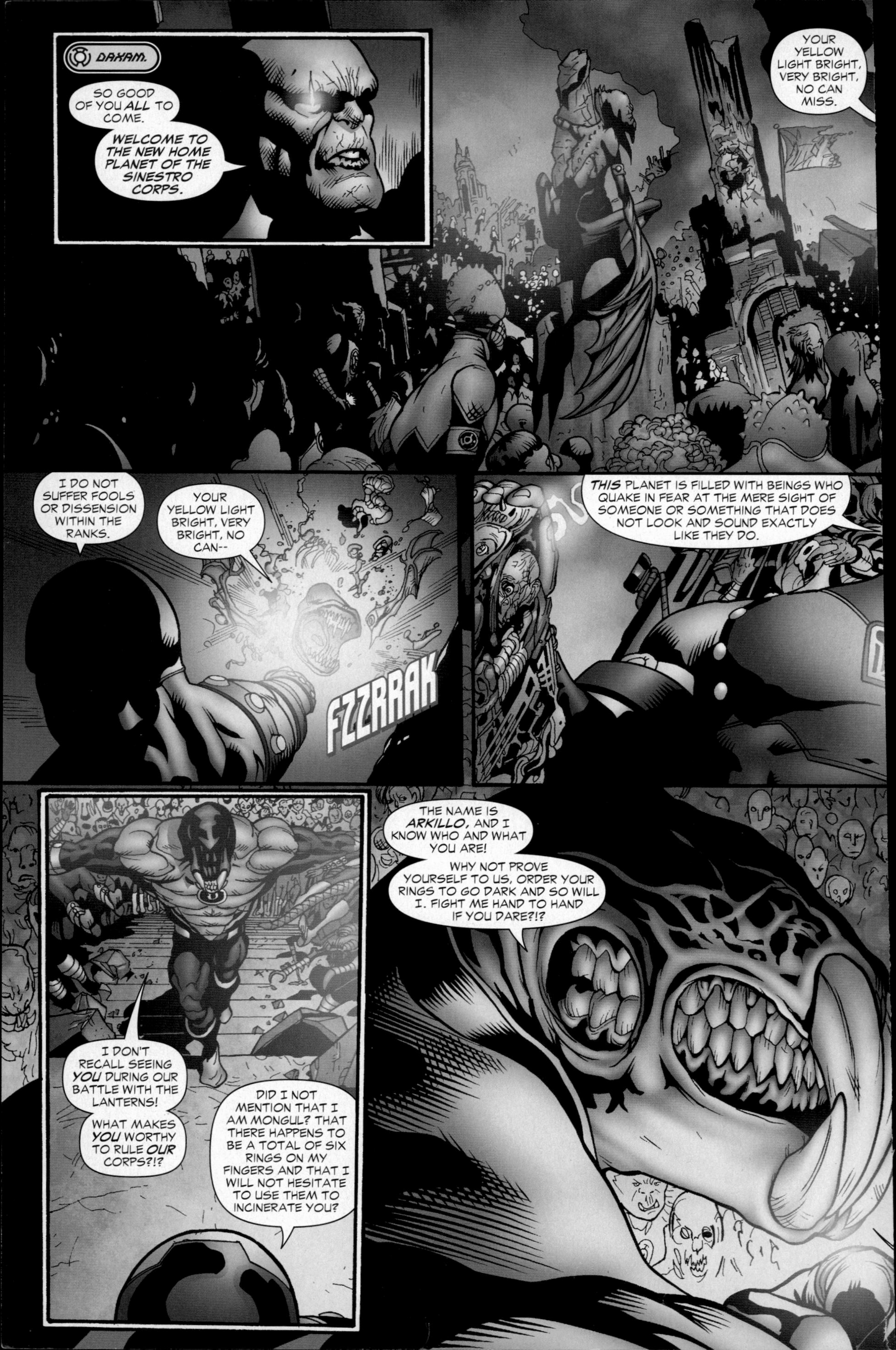
DAXAM.
SO GOOD OF YOU ALL TO COME.
WELCOME TO THE NEW HOME PLANET OF THE SINESTRO CORPS.
YOUR YELLOW LIGHT BRIGHT, VERY BRIGHT, NO CAN MISS.
I DO NOT SUFFER FOOLS OR DISSENSION WITHIN THE RANKS.
YOUR YELLOW LIGHT BRIGHT, VERY BRIGHT, NO CAN--
FZZRRAK
THIS PLANET IS FILLED WITH BEINGS WHO QUAKE IN FEAR AT THE MERE SIGHT OF SOMEONE OR SOMETHING THAT DOES NOT LOOK AND SOUND EXACTLY LIKE THEY DO.
I DON'T RECALL SEEING YOU DURING OUR BATTLE WITH THE LANTERNS!
WHAT MAKES YOU WORTHY TO RULE OUR CORPS?!?
DID I NOT MENTION THAT I AM MONGUL? THAT THERE HAPPENS TO BE A TOTAL OF SIX RINGS ON MY FINGERS AND THAT I WILL NOT HESITATE TO USE THEM TO INCINERATE YOU?
THE NAME IS ARKILLO, AND I KNOW WHO AND WHAT YOU ARE!
WHY NOT PROVE YOURSELF TO US, ORDER YOUR RINGS TO GO DARK AND SO WILL I. FIGHT ME HAND TO HAND IF YOU DARE?!?

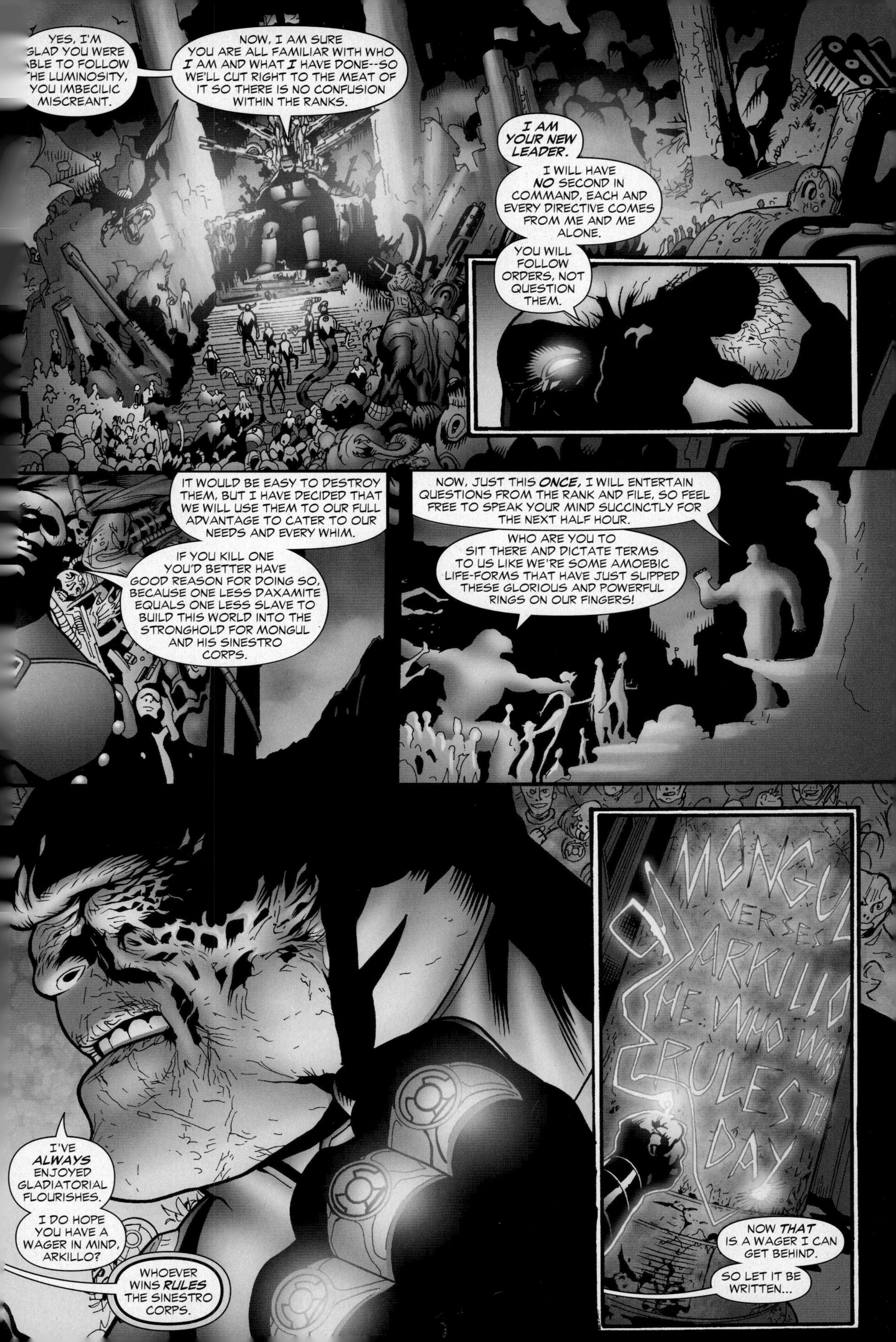
YES, I'M GLAD YOU WERE ABLE TO FOLLOW THE LUMINOSITY, YOU IMBECILIC MISCREANT.
NOW, I AM SURE YOU ARE ALL FAMILIAR WITH WHO I AM AND WHAT I HAVE DONE--SO WE'LL CUT RIGHT TO THE MEAT OF IT SO THERE IS NO CONFUSION WITHIN THE RANKS.
I AM YOUR NEW LEADER.
I WILL HAVE NO SECOND IN COMMAND, EACH AND EVERY DIRECTIVE COMES FROM ME AND ME ALONE.
YOU WILL FOLLOW ORDERS, NOT QUESTION THEM.
IT WOULD BE EASY TO DESTROY THEM, BUT I HAVE DECIDED THAT WE WILL USE THEM TO OUR FULL ADVANTAGE TO CATER TO OUR NEEDS AND EVERY WHIM.
IF YOU KILL ONE YOU'D BETTER HAVE GOOD REASON FOR DOING SO, BECAUSE ONE LESS DAXAMITE EQUALS ONE LESS SLAVE TO BUILD THIS WORLD INTO THE STRONGHOLD FOR MONGUL AND HIS SINESTRO CORPS.
NOW, JUST THIS ONCE, I WILL ENTERTAIN QUESTIONS FROM THE RANK AND FILE, SO FEEL FREE TO SPEAK YOUR MIND SUCCINCTLY FOR THE NEXT HALF HOUR.
WHO ARE YOU TO SIT THERE AND DICTATE TERMS TO US LIKE WE'RE SOME AMOEBIC LIFE-FORMS THAT HAVE JUST SLIPPED THESE GLORIOUS AND POWERFUL RINGS ON OUR FINGERS!
I'VE ALWAYS ENJOYED GLADIATORIAL FLOURISHES.
I DO HOPE YOU HAVE A WAGER IN MIND, ARKILLO?
WHOEVER WINS RULES THE SINESTRO CORPS.
MONGUL VERSES ARKILLO HE WHO WINS RULES TH DAY
NOW THAT IS A WAGER I CAN GET BEHIND.
SO LET IT BE WRITTEN...

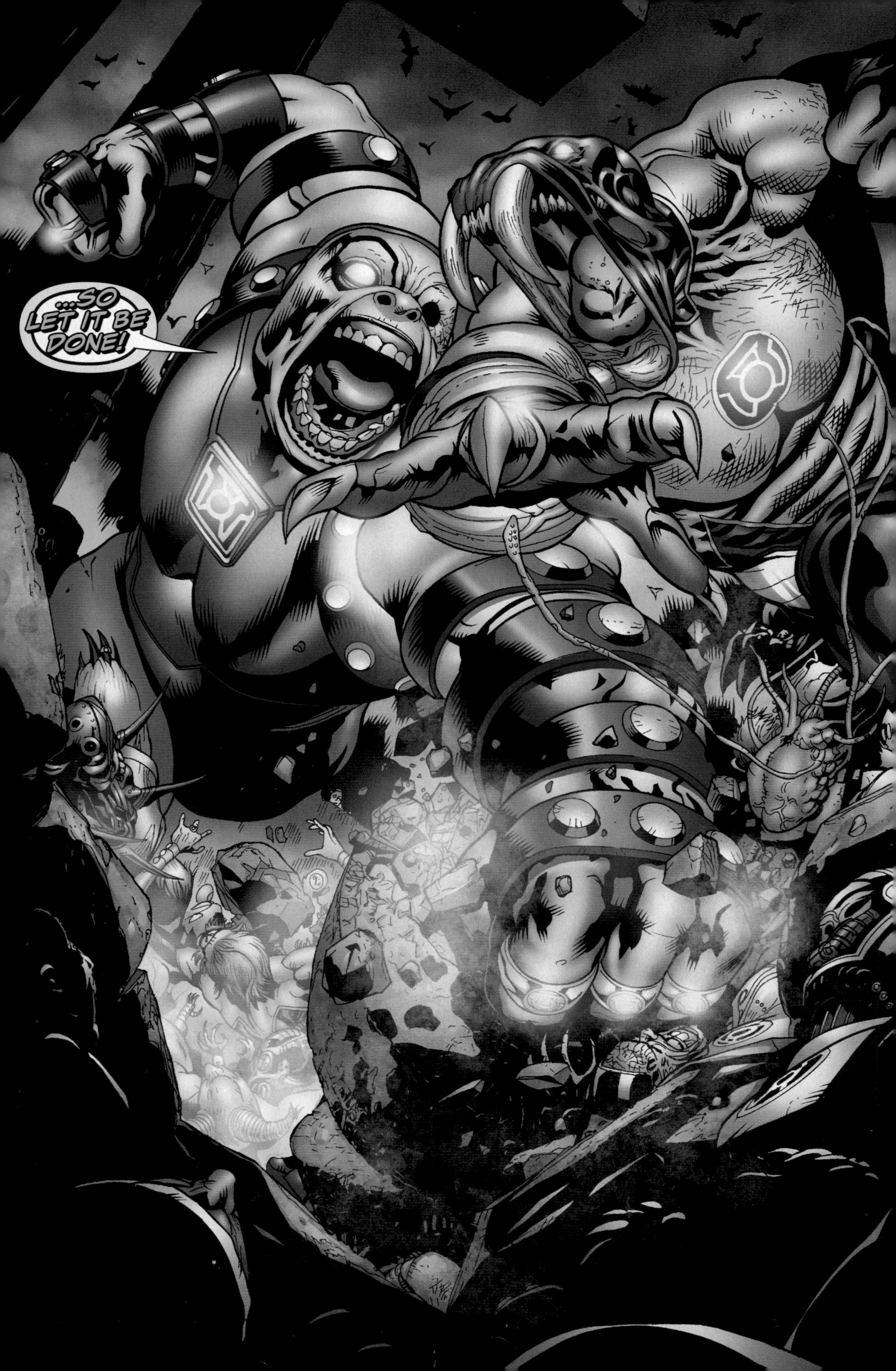
...SO LET IT BE DONE!

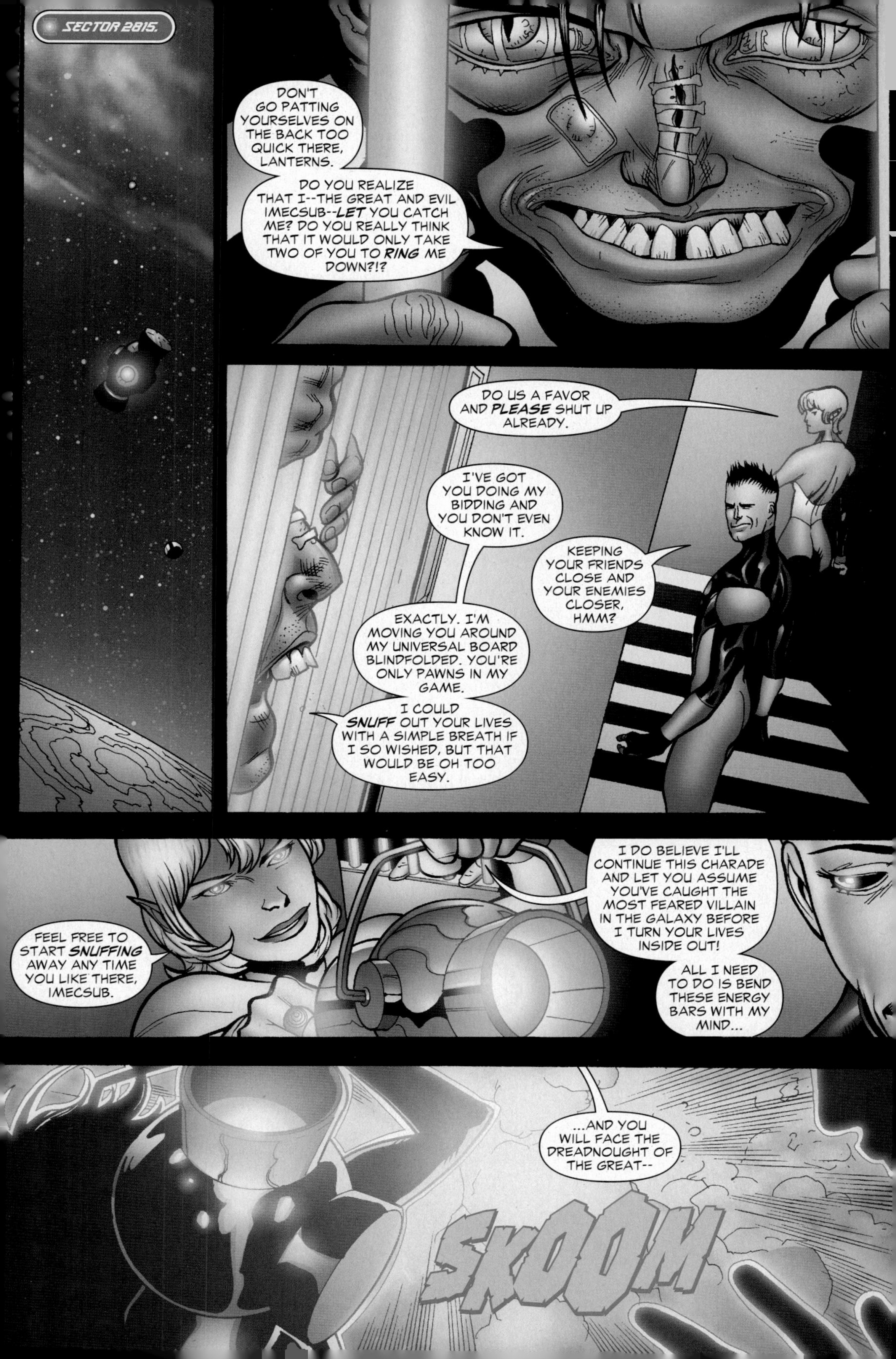
SECTOR 2815.
DON'T GO PATTING YOURSELVES ON THE BACK TOO QUICK THERE, LANTERNS.
DO YOU REALIZE THAT I--THE GREAT AND EVIL IMECSUB--LET YOU CATCH ME? DO YOU REALLY THINK THAT IT WOULD ONLY TAKE TWO OF YOU TO RING ME DOWN?!?
DO US A FAVOR AND PLEASE SHUT UP ALREADY.
I'VE GOT YOU DOING MY BIDDING AND YOU DON'T EVEN KNOW IT.
KEEPING YOUR FRIENDS CLOSE AND YOUR ENEMIES CLOSER, HMM?
EXACTLY. I'M MOVING YOU AROUND MY UNIVERSAL BOARD BLINDFOLDED. YOU'RE ONLY PAWNS IN MY GAME.
I COULD SNUFF OUT YOUR LIVES WITH A SIMPLE BREATH IF I SO WISHED, BUT THAT WOULD BE OH TOO EASY.
FEEL FREE TO START SNUFFING AWAY ANY TIME YOU LIKE THERE, IMECSUB.
I DO BELIEVE I'LL CONTINUE THIS CHARADE AND LET YOU ASSUME YOU'VE CAUGHT THE MOST FEARED VILLAIN IN THE GALAXY BEFORE I TURN YOUR LIVES INSIDE OUT!
ALL I NEED TO DO IS BEND THESE ENERGY BARS WITH MY MIND...
...AND YOU WILL FACE THE DREADNOUGHT OF THE GREAT--
SKOOM

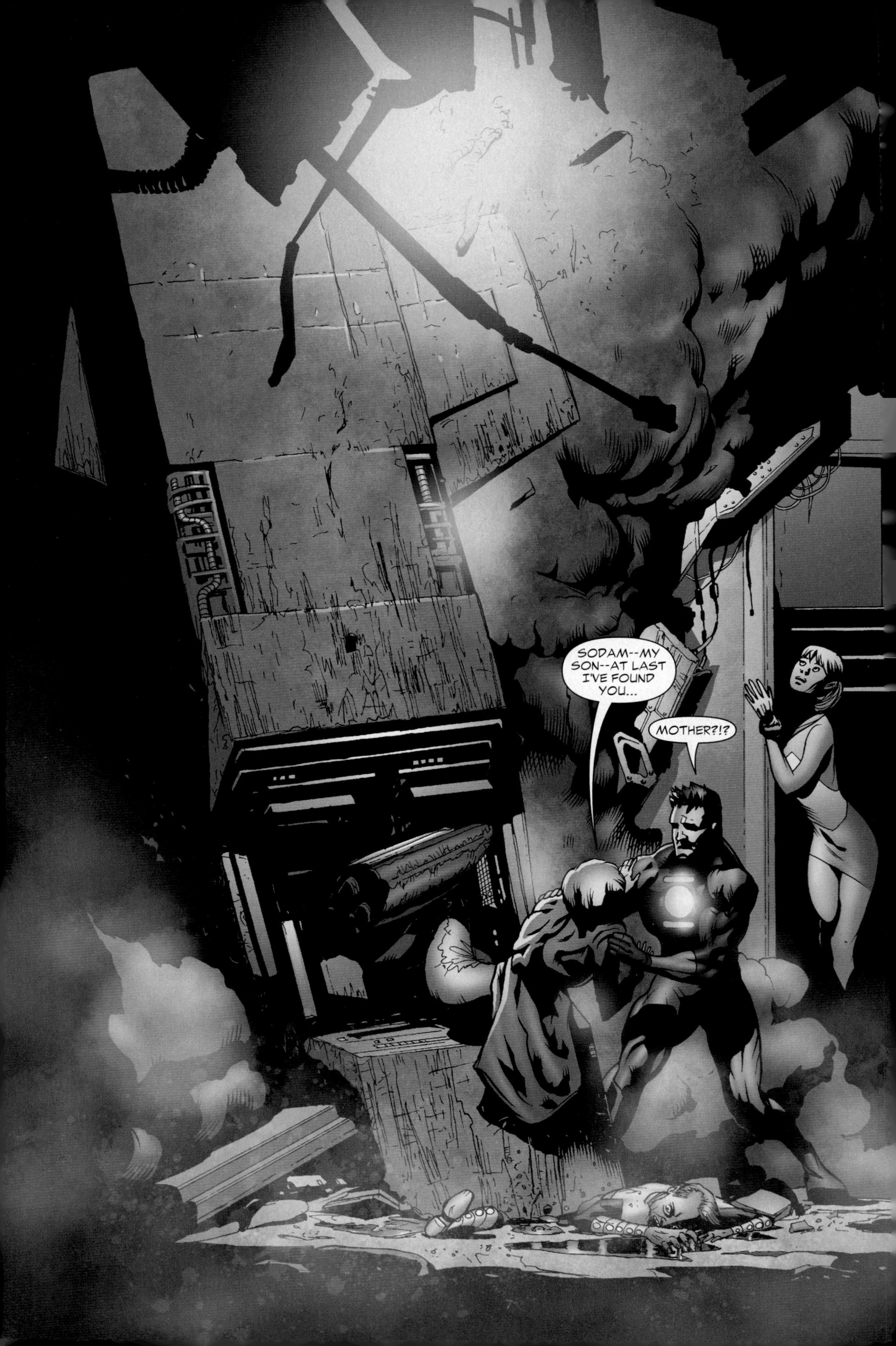
SODAM--MY SON--AT LAST I'VE FOUND YOU...
MOTHER?!?

GREEN LANTERN CORPS #34
Cover by Patrick Gleason, Rebecca Buchman & Nei Ruffino

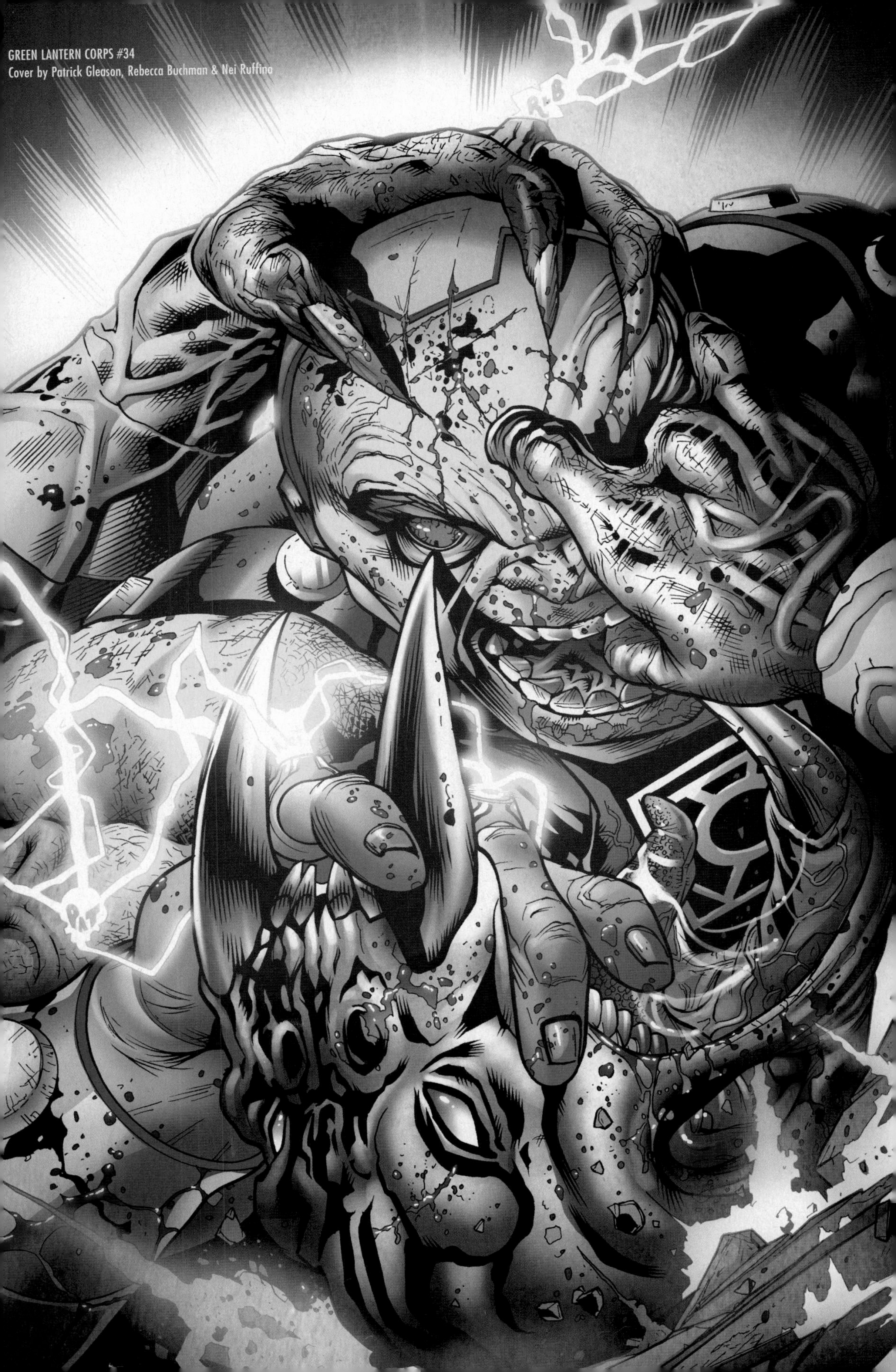

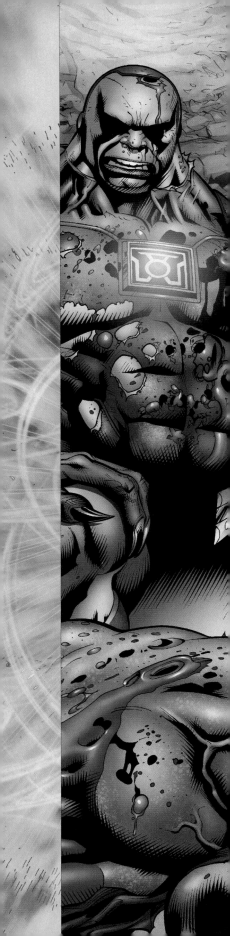

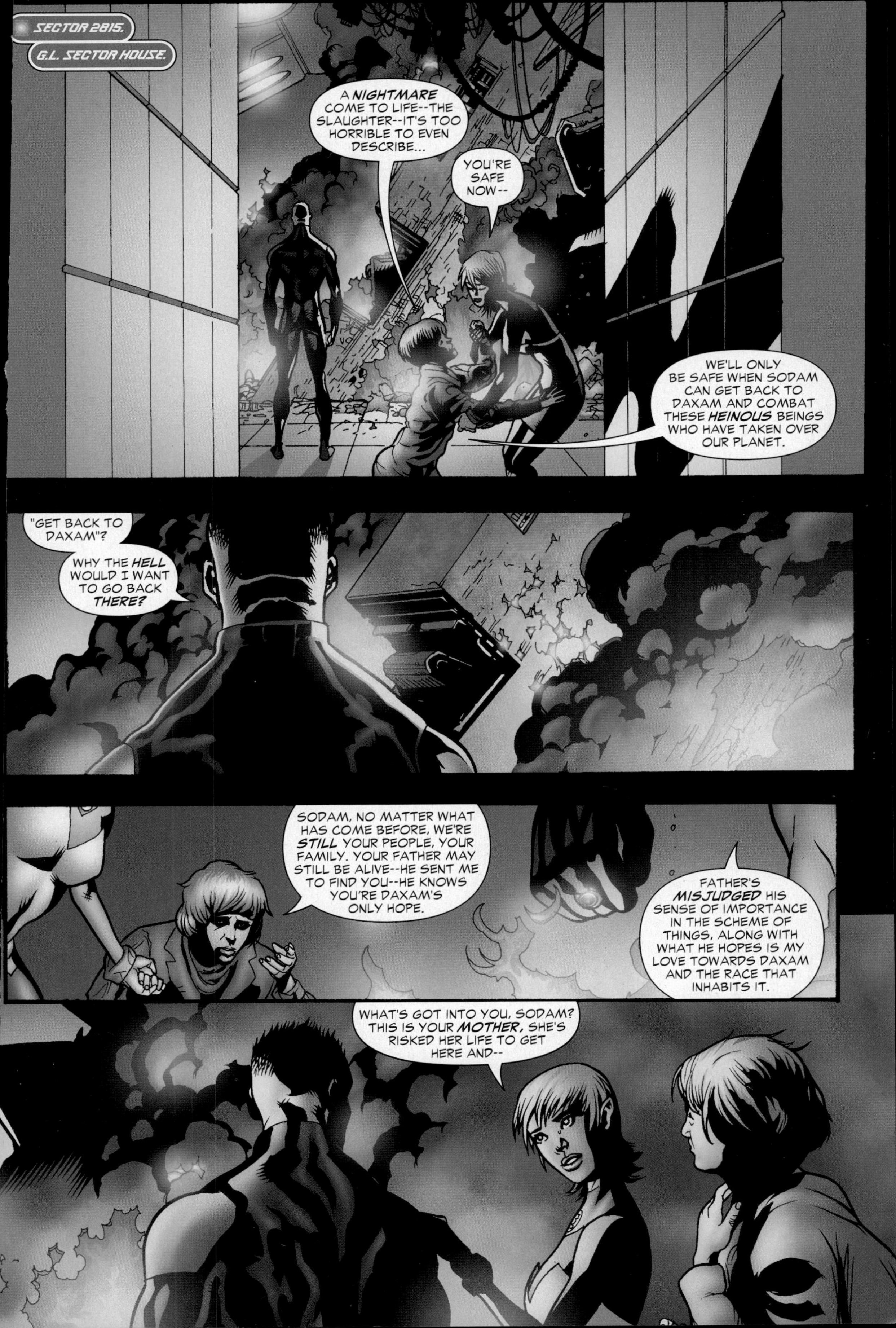
SECTOR 2815.
G.L. SECTOR HOUSE.
A NIGHTMARE COME TO LIFE--THE SLAUGHTER--IT'S TOO HORRIBLE TO EVEN DESCRIBE...
YOU'RE SAFE NOW--
WE'LL ONLY BE SAFE WHEN SODAM CAN GET BACK TO DAXAM AND COMBAT THESE HEINOUS BEINGS WHO HAVE TAKEN OVER OUR PLANET.
"GET BACK TO DAXAM"?
WHY THE HELL WOULD I WANT TO GO BACK THERE?
SODAM, NO MATTER WHAT HAS COME BEFORE, WE'RE STILL YOUR PEOPLE, YOUR FAMILY. YOUR FATHER MAY STILL BE ALIVE--HE SENT ME TO FIND YOU--HE KNOWS YOU'RE DAXAM'S ONLY HOPE.
FATHER'S MISJUDGED HIS SENSE OF IMPORTANCE IN THE SCHEME OF THINGS, ALONG WITH WHAT HE HOPES IS MY LOVE TOWARDS DAXAM AND THE RACE THAT INHABITS IT.
WHAT'S GOT INTO YOU, SODAM? THIS IS YOUR MOTHER, SHE'S RISKED HER LIFE TO GET HERE AND--

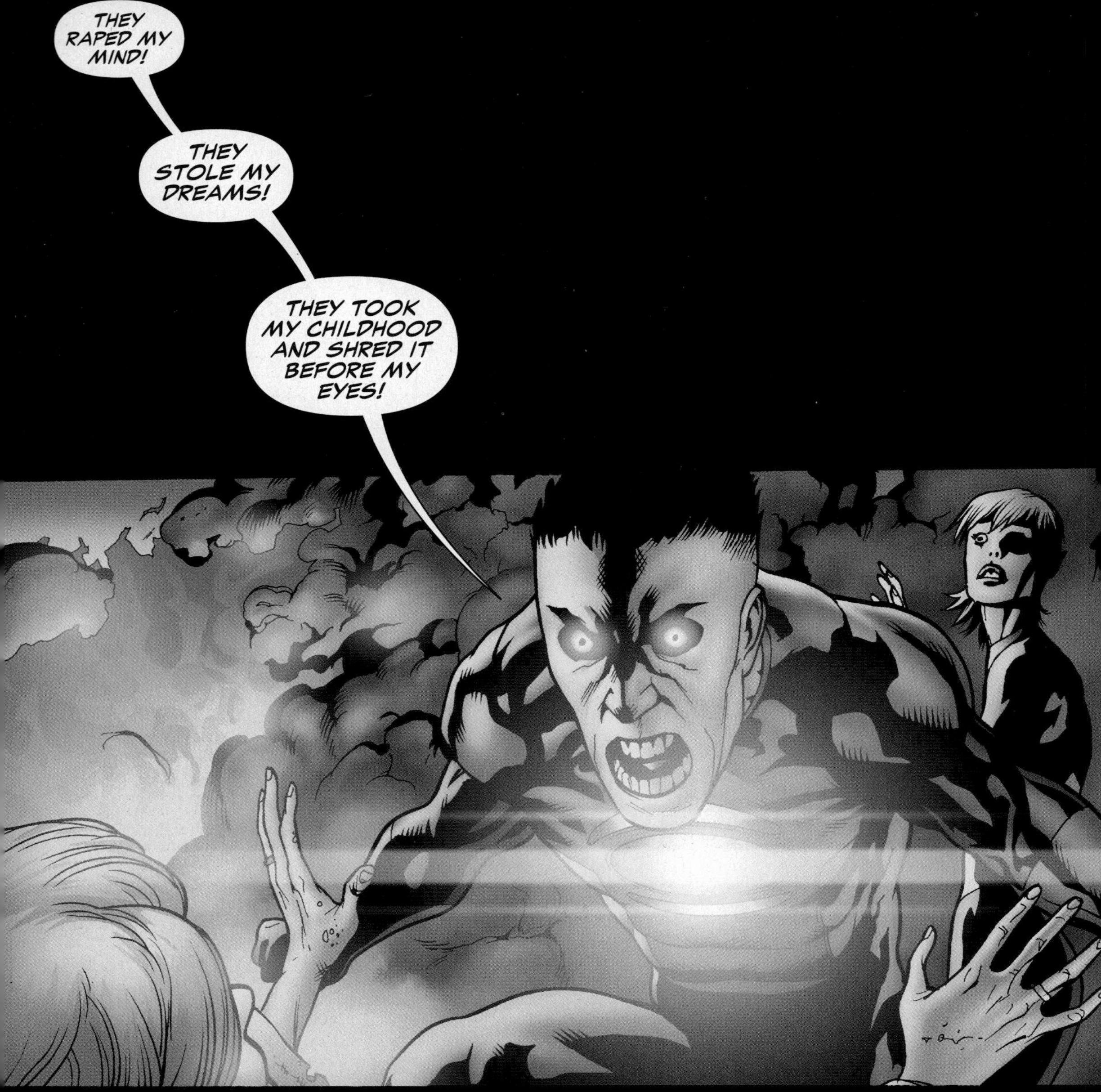
THEY RAPED MY MIND!
THEY STOLE MY DREAMS!
THEY TOOK MY CHILDHOOD AND SHRED IT BEFORE MY EYES!

EMERALD ECLIPSE
PART TWO

YOU'RE NO DIFFERENT FROM THE "HEINOUS BEINGS" YOU'RE RUNNING FROM!

MAYBE *THIS* WAS MEANT TO BE, MAYBE DAXAM IS *FINALLY* PAYING FOR ITS SINS, MOTHER.

YOU CAN'T MEAN THAT, SODAM.

I CAN AND I DO.

DAXAM IS A *HATE-FILLED PLACED*--HATING ANYTHING DIFFERENT--ANYTHING THAT DOESN'T FIT INTO THEIR LITTLE BOX.

THAT *LITTLE BOX* KEPT YOU SAFE FROM HARM. IT GAVE YOU A LIFE OF MEANS AND COMFORT--

STRAPPING ME INTO THAT CHAIR-- PUTTING THOUGHTS OF HATE THAT WEREN'T THERE BEFORE INTO MY--

YOUR FATHER AND I DID WHAT WE DID BECAUSE WE LOVED YOU.

YOU INVADED MY BRAIN! YOU TRIED TO *PROGRAM* ME TO EMBRACE THE PREJUDICE AND HATE THAT FILLED YOUR OWN HEARTS AND MINDS!

SODAM, YOU NEED TO RELAX, LET'S ATTEND TO YOUR MOTHER'S WOUNDS AND FIGURE OUT WHAT--

THERE'S *NOTHING* TO FIGURE OUT.

THEY *MURDERED* A FRIEND OF MINE--A FRIEND I HELPED NURSE BACK TO HEALTH--A FRIEND WHO SHOWED ME THAT THE DARKNESS OF SPACE WASN'T FILLED WITH HATE AND FEAR.

WHAT ARE YOU TALKING ABOUT, SODAM?

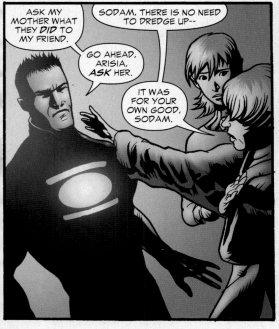

ASK MY MOTHER WHAT THEY *DID* TO MY FRIEND.

SODAM, THERE IS NO NEED TO DREDGE UP--

GO AHEAD, ARISIA, *ASK* HER.

IT WAS FOR YOUR OWN GOOD, SODAM.

YOU WERE A BOY WHOSE HEAD WAS ALWAYS IN THE CLOUDS, YOUR MIND FOREVER ELSEWHERE, AND WE NEEDED IT TO BE FOCUSED ON DAXAM AND ITS PEOPLE.

YOUR FATHER IS A SENATOR, HE HAS RESPONSIBILITIES-- RESPONSIBILITIES HE HOPED HIS ONLY SON WOULD ONE DAY TAKE ON.

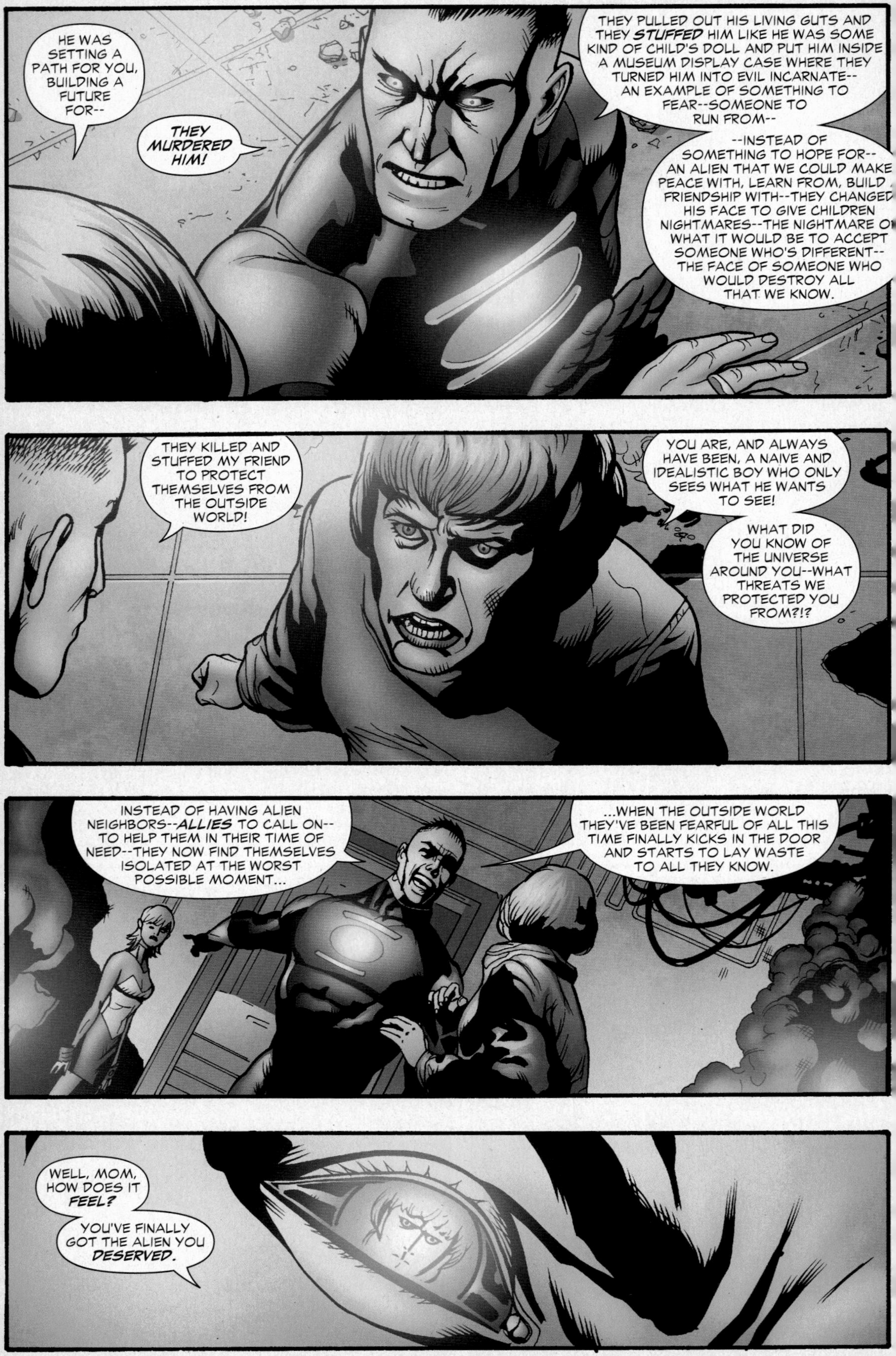
HE WAS SETTING A PATH FOR YOU, BUILDING A FUTURE FOR--
THEY MURDERED HIM!
THEY PULLED OUT HIS LIVING GUTS AND THEY STUFFED HIM LIKE HE WAS SOME KIND OF CHILD'S DOLL AND PUT HIM INSIDE A MUSEUM DISPLAY CASE WHERE THEY TURNED HIM INTO EVIL INCARNATE-- AN EXAMPLE OF SOMETHING TO FEAR--SOMEONE TO RUN FROM--
--INSTEAD OF SOMETHING TO HOPE FOR-- AN ALIEN THAT WE COULD MAKE PEACE WITH, LEARN FROM, BUILD A FRIENDSHIP WITH--THEY CHANGED HIS FACE TO GIVE CHILDREN NIGHTMARES--THE NIGHTMARE OF WHAT IT WOULD BE TO ACCEPT SOMEONE WHO'S DIFFERENT-- THE FACE OF SOMEONE WHO WOULD DESTROY ALL THAT WE KNOW.
THEY KILLED AND STUFFED MY FRIEND TO PROTECT THEMSELVES FROM THE OUTSIDE WORLD!
YOU ARE, AND ALWAYS HAVE BEEN, A NAIVE AND IDEALISTIC BOY WHO ONLY SEES WHAT HE WANTS TO SEE!
WHAT DID YOU KNOW OF THE UNIVERSE AROUND YOU--WHAT THREATS WE PROTECTED YOU FROM?!?
INSTEAD OF HAVING ALIEN NEIGHBORS--ALLIES TO CALL ON-- TO HELP THEM IN THEIR TIME OF NEED--THEY NOW FIND THEMSELVES ISOLATED AT THE WORST POSSIBLE MOMENT...
...WHEN THE OUTSIDE WORLD THEY'VE BEEN FEARFUL OF ALL THIS TIME FINALLY KICKS IN THE DOOR AND STARTS TO LAY WASTE TO ALL THEY KNOW.
WELL, MOM, HOW DOES IT FEEL?
YOU'VE FINALLY GOT THE ALIEN YOU DESERVED.

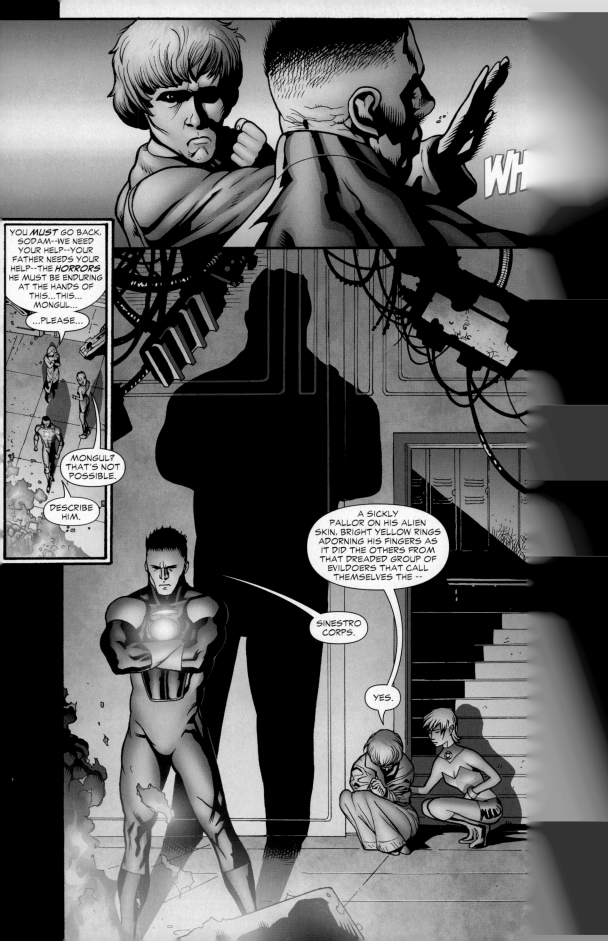

YOU **MUST** GO BACK, SODAM--WE NEED YOUR HELP--YOUR FATHER NEEDS YOUR HELP--THE **HORRORS** HE MUST BE ENDURING AT THE HANDS OF THIS...THIS... MONGUL...

...PLEASE...

MONGUL? THAT'S NOT POSSIBLE.

DESCRIBE HIM.

WH

A SICKLY PALLOR ON HIS ALIEN SKIN, BRIGHT YELLOW RINGS ADORNING HIS FINGERS AS IT DID THE OTHERS FROM THAT DREADED GROUP OF EVILDOERS THAT CALL THEMSELVES THE --

SINESTRO CORPS.

YES.

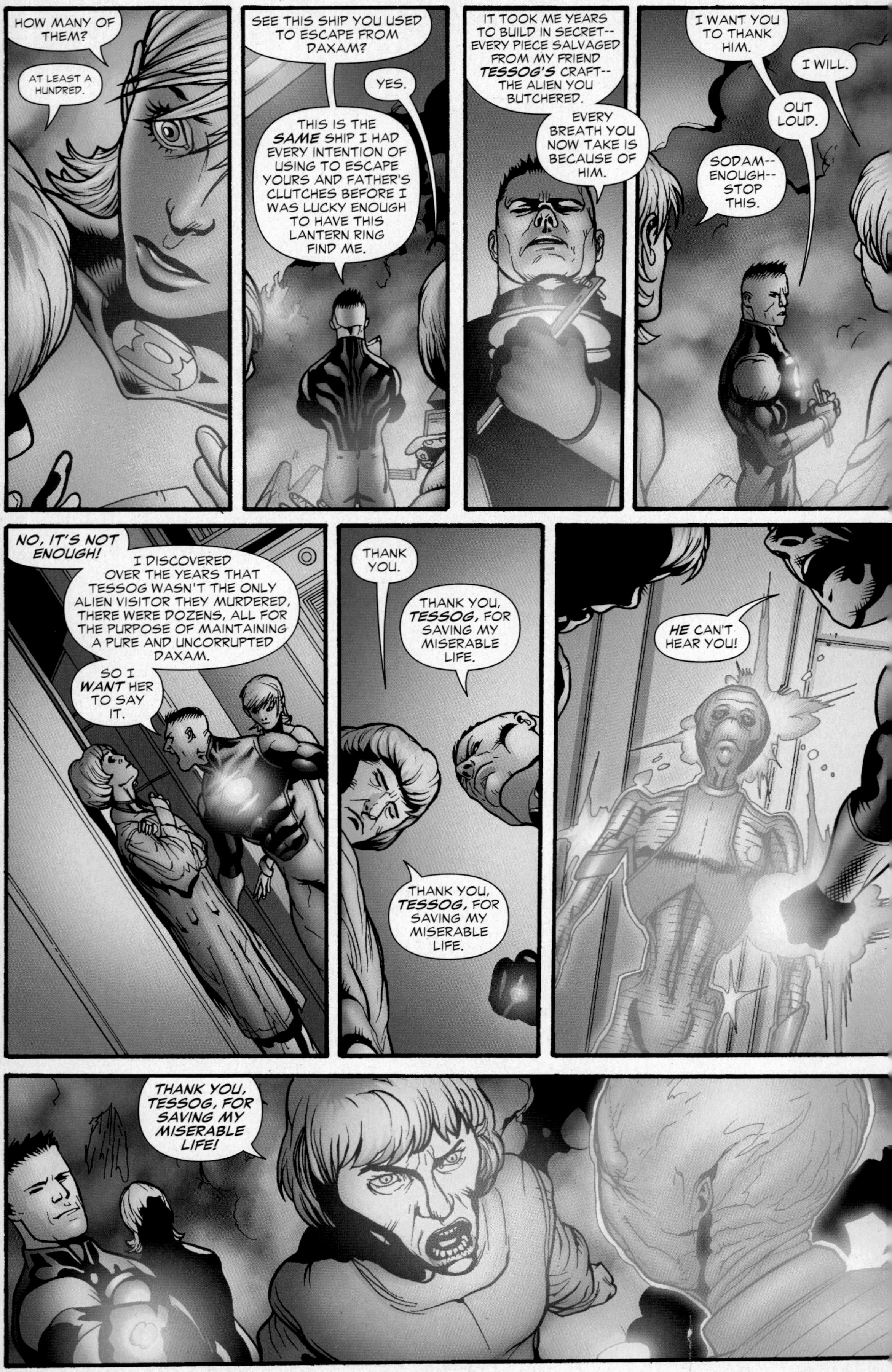
HOW MANY OF THEM?
AT LEAST A HUNDRED.
SEE THIS SHIP YOU USED TO ESCAPE FROM DAXAM?
YES.
THIS IS THE SAME SHIP I HAD EVERY INTENTION OF USING TO ESCAPE YOURS AND FATHER'S CLUTCHES BEFORE I WAS LUCKY ENOUGH TO HAVE THIS LANTERN RING FIND ME.
IT TOOK ME YEARS TO BUILD IN SECRET-- EVERY PIECE SALVAGED FROM MY FRIEND TESSOG'S CRAFT-- THE ALIEN YOU BUTCHERED.
EVERY BREATH YOU NOW TAKE IS BECAUSE OF HIM.
I WANT YOU TO THANK HIM.
I WILL.
OUT LOUD.
SODAM-- ENOUGH-- STOP THIS.
NO, IT'S NOT ENOUGH!
I DISCOVERED OVER THE YEARS THAT TESSOG WASN'T THE ONLY ALIEN VISITOR THEY MURDERED, THERE WERE DOZENS, ALL FOR THE PURPOSE OF MAINTAINING A PURE AND UNCORRUPTED DAXAM.
SO I WANT HER TO SAY IT.
THANK YOU.
THANK YOU, TESSOG, FOR SAVING MY MISERABLE LIFE.
THANK YOU, TESSOG, FOR SAVING MY MISERABLE LIFE.
HE CAN'T HEAR YOU!
THANK YOU, TESSOG, FOR SAVING MY MISERABLE LIFE!

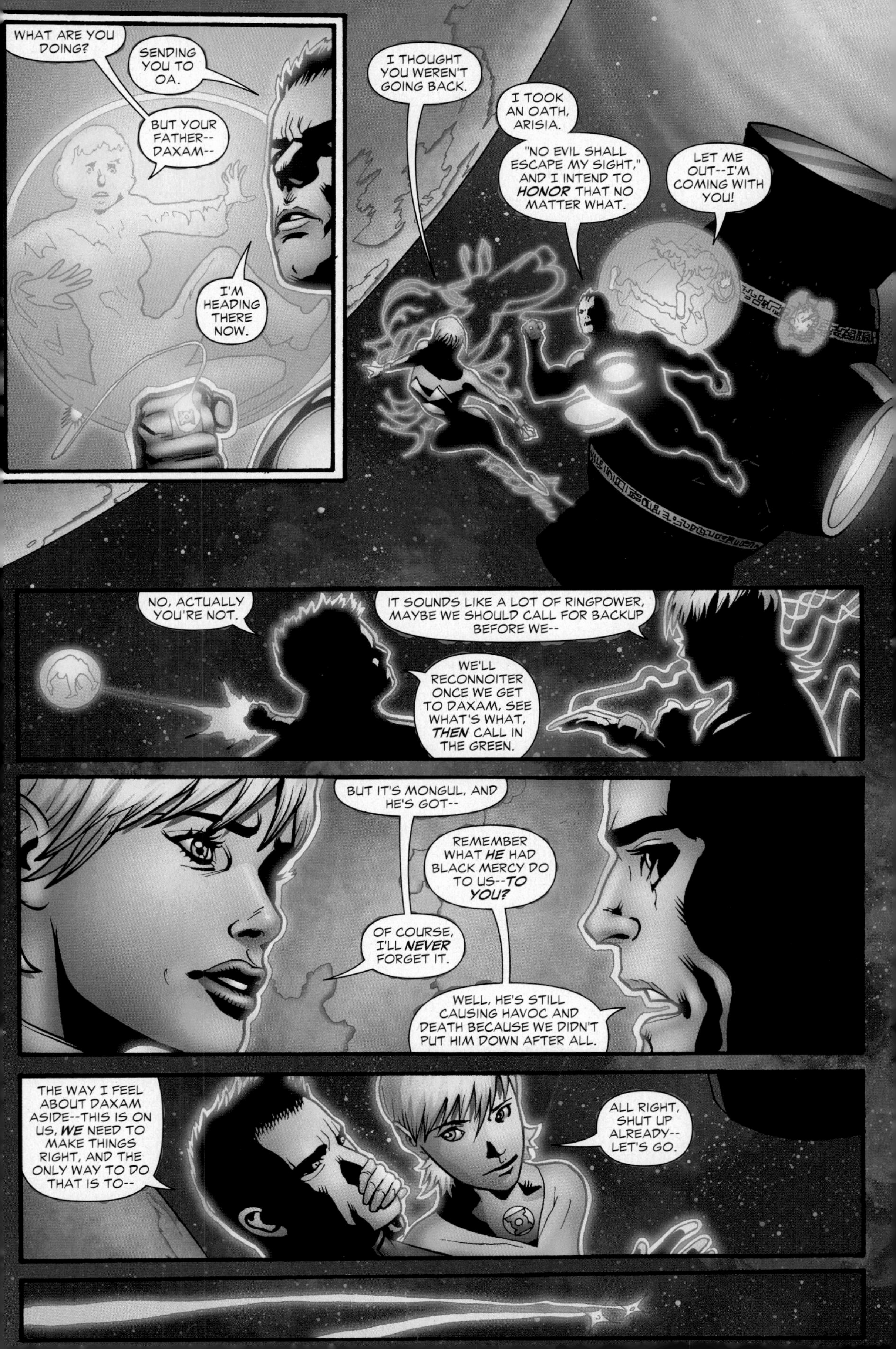
WHAT ARE YOU DOING?
SENDING YOU TO OA.
BUT YOUR FATHER--DAXAM--
I'M HEADING THERE NOW.
I THOUGHT YOU WEREN'T GOING BACK.
I TOOK AN OATH, ARISIA.
"NO EVIL SHALL ESCAPE MY SIGHT," AND I INTEND TO **HONOR** THAT NO MATTER WHAT.
LET ME OUT--I'M COMING WITH YOU!
NO, ACTUALLY YOU'RE NOT.
IT SOUNDS LIKE A LOT OF RINGPOWER, MAYBE WE SHOULD CALL FOR BACKUP BEFORE WE--
WE'LL RECONNOITER ONCE WE GET TO DAXAM, SEE WHAT'S WHAT, **THEN** CALL IN THE GREEN.
BUT IT'S MONGUL, AND HE'S GOT--
REMEMBER WHAT **HE** HAD BLACK MERCY DO TO US--**TO YOU?**
OF COURSE, I'LL **NEVER** FORGET IT.
WELL, HE'S STILL CAUSING HAVOC AND DEATH BECAUSE WE DIDN'T PUT HIM DOWN AFTER ALL.
THE WAY I FEEL ABOUT DAXAM ASIDE--THIS IS ON US, **WE** NEED TO MAKE THINGS RIGHT, AND THE ONLY WAY TO DO THAT IS TO--
ALL RIGHT, SHUT UP ALREADY--LET'S GO.

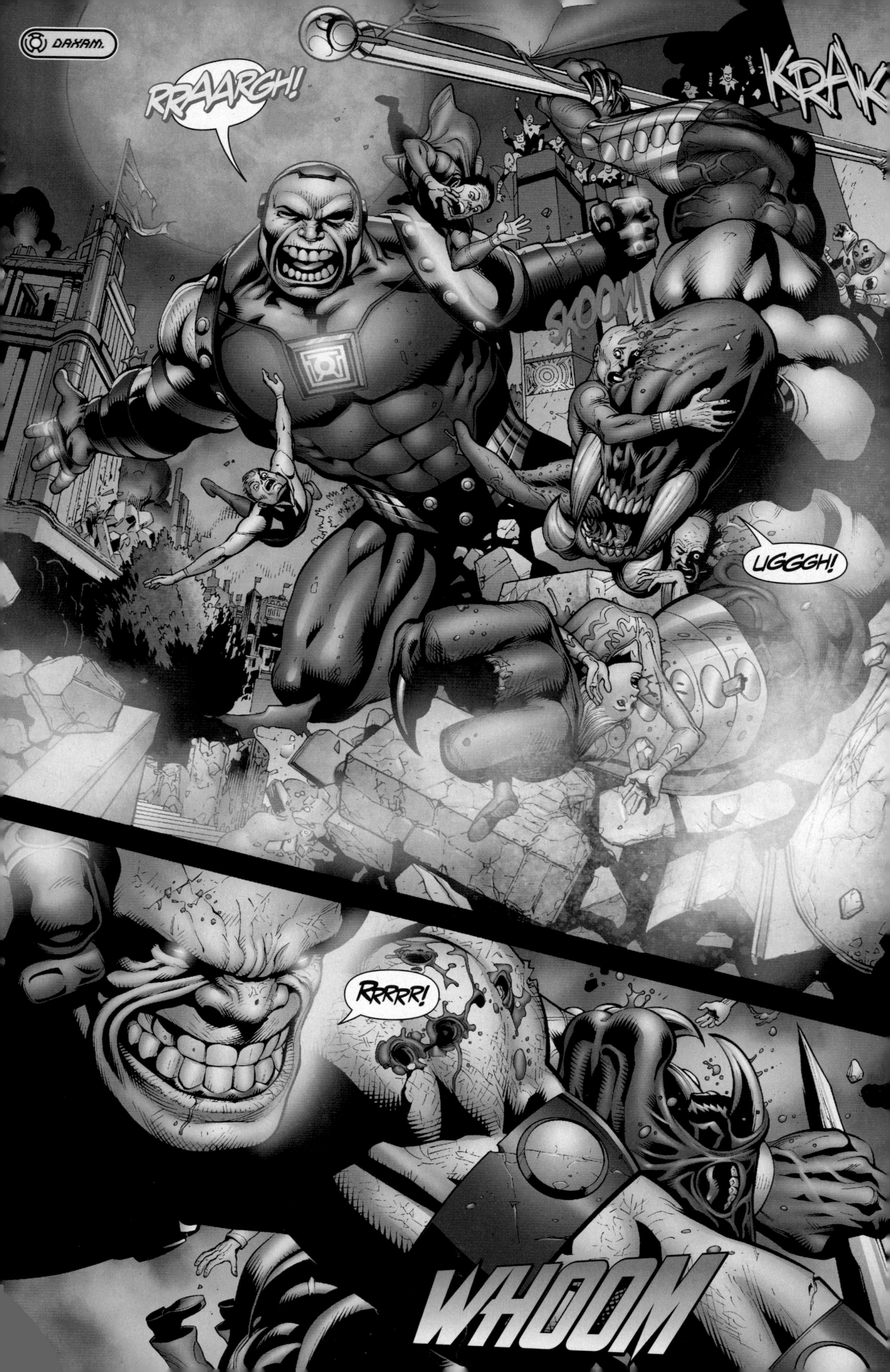
DAXAM.
RRAARGH!
KRAK
SKOOM
UGGGH!
RRRRR!
WHOOM

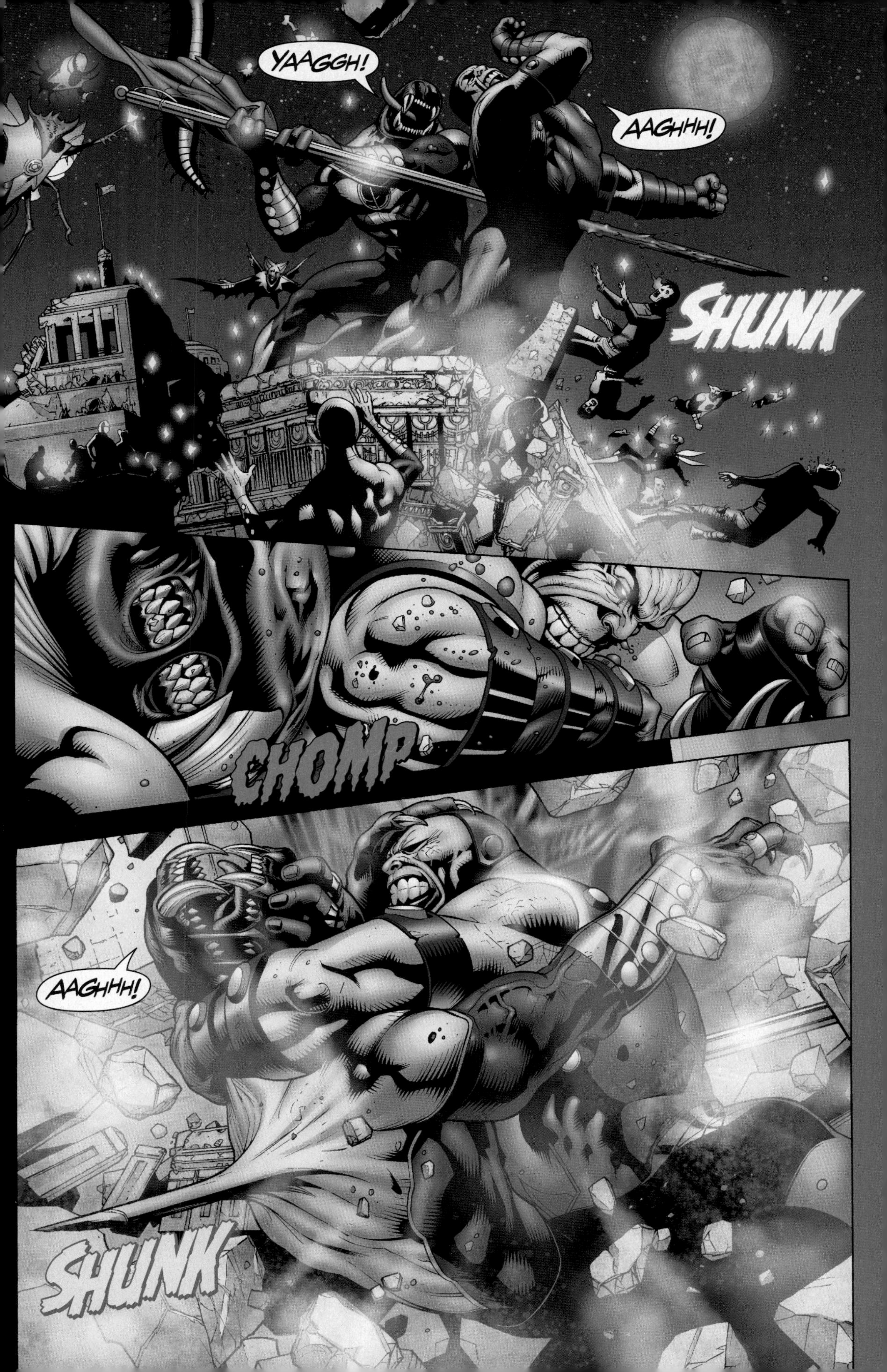
YAAGGH!
AAGHHH!
SHUNK
CHOMP
AAGHHH!
SHUNK

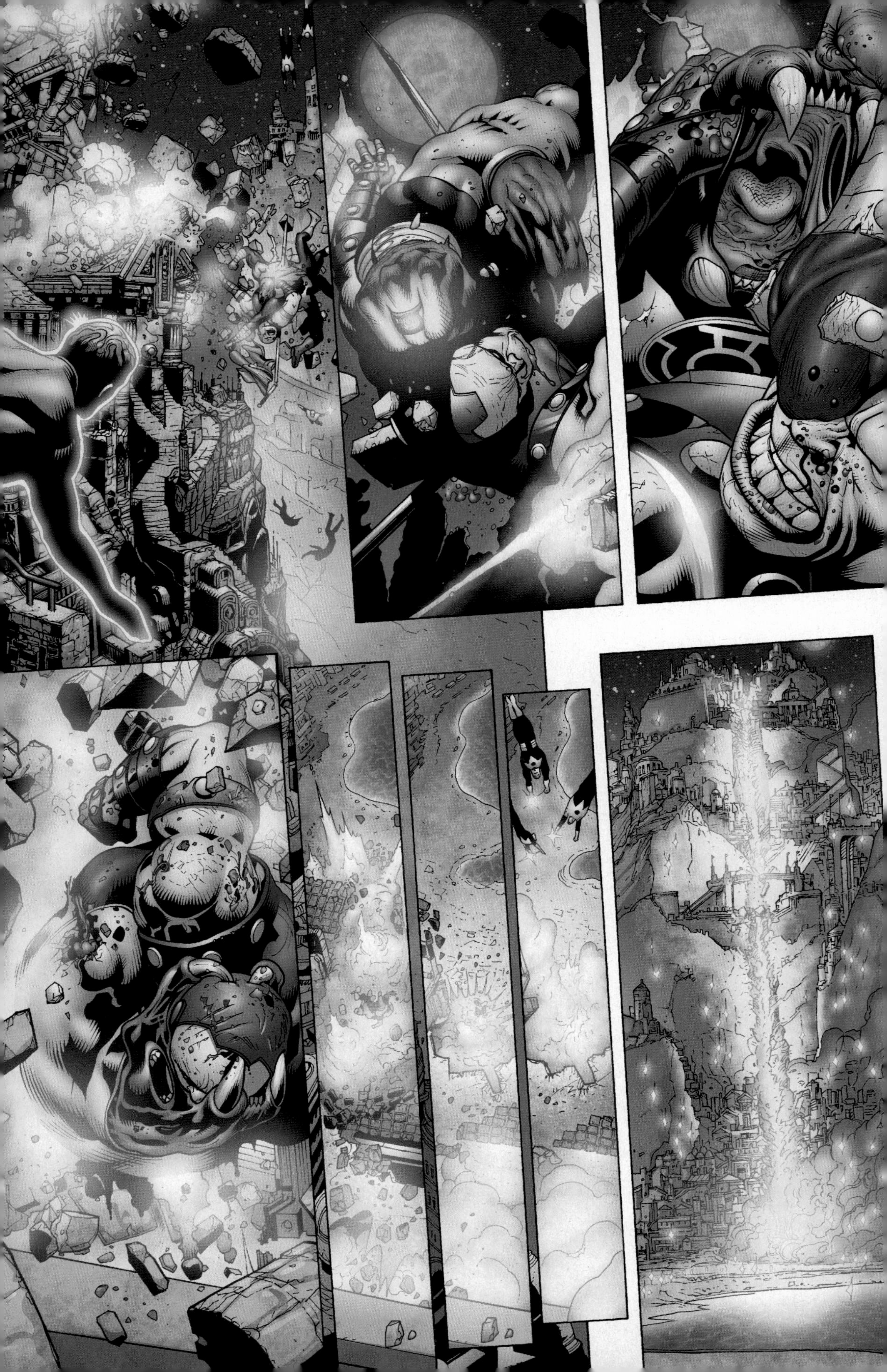

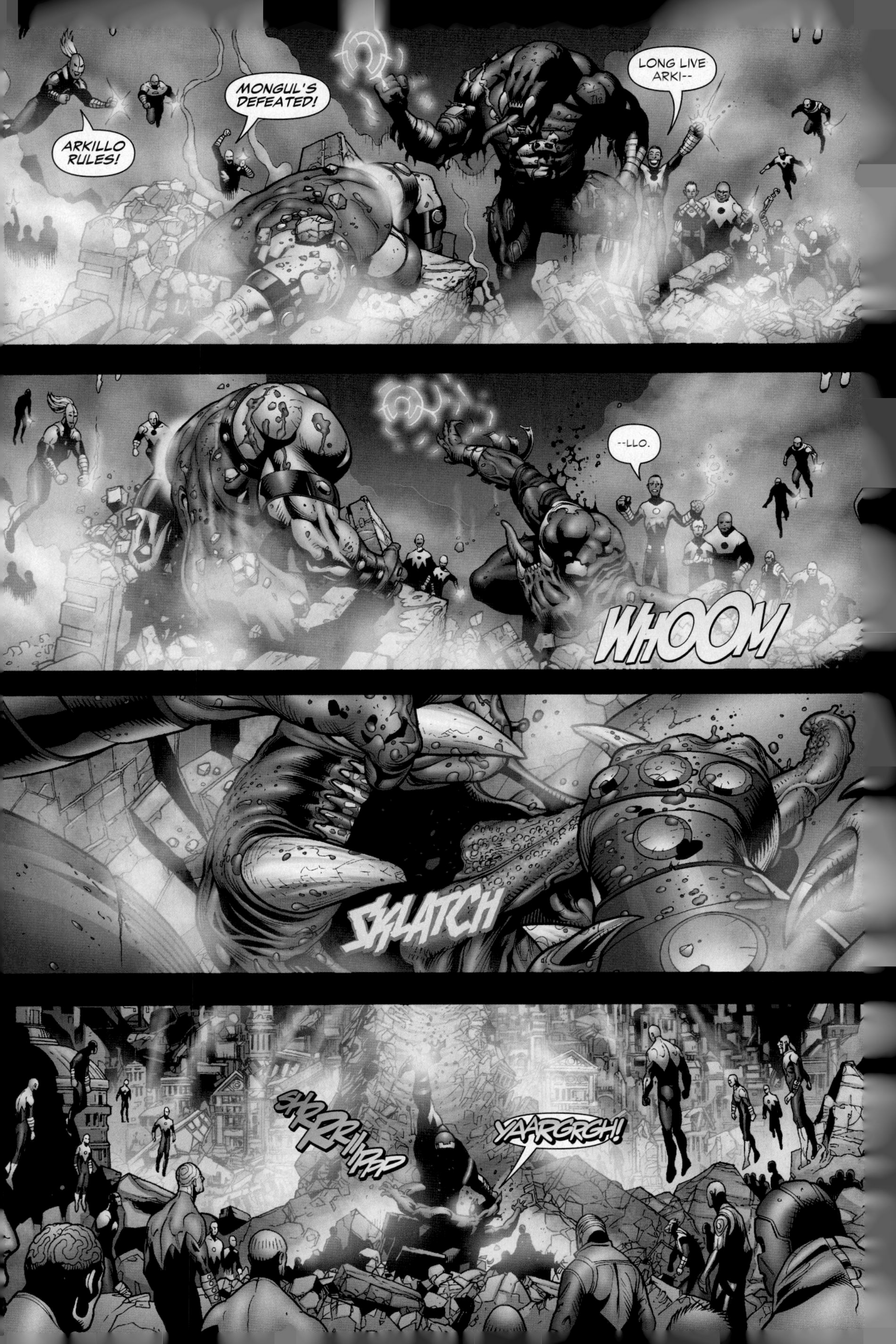
ARKILLO RULES!
MONGUL'S DEFEATED!
LONG LIVE ARKI--
--LLO.
WHOOM
SKLATCH
SHRRRIIPPP
YAARGRGH!

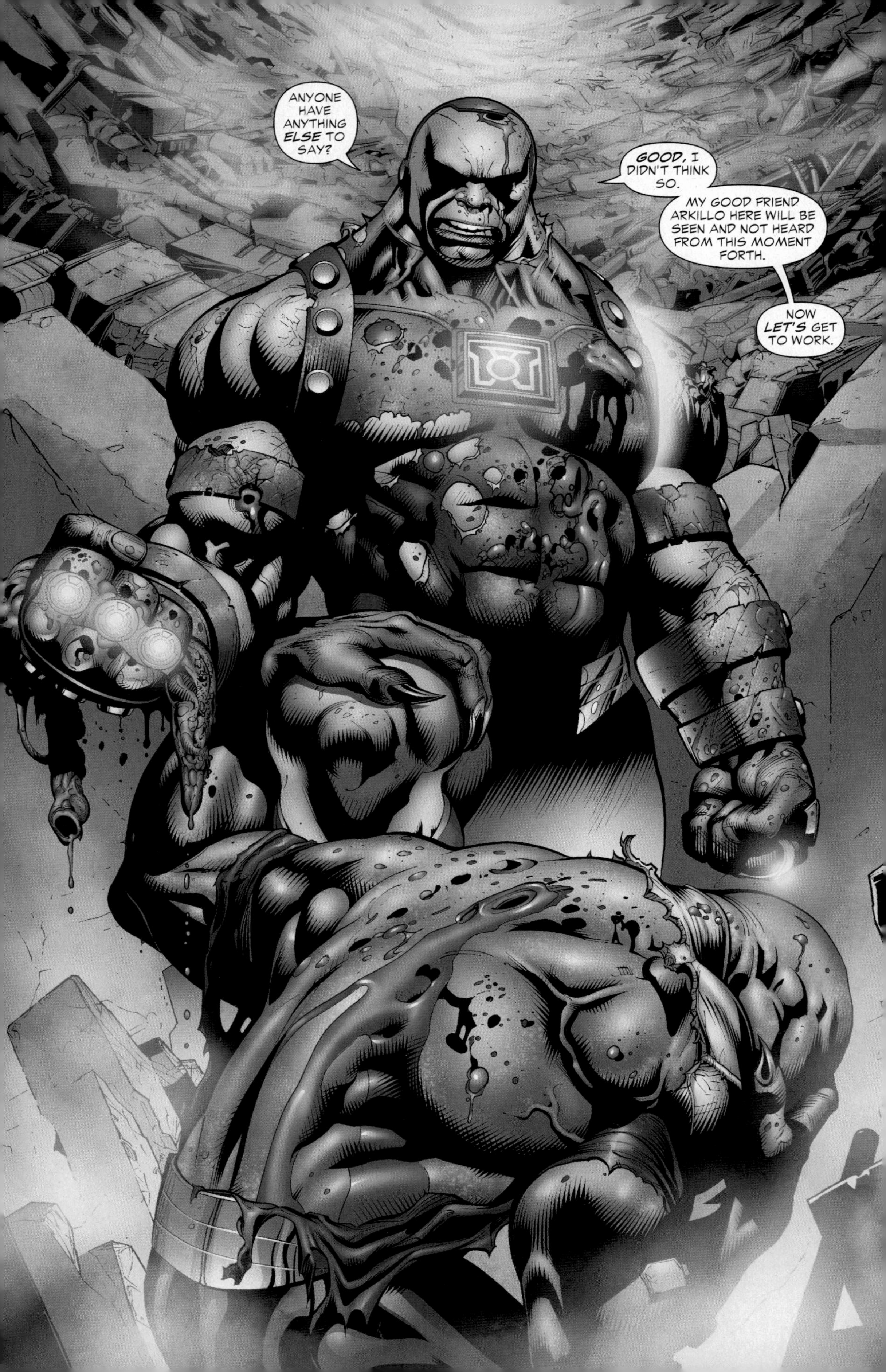
ANYONE HAVE ANYTHING ELSE TO SAY?
GOOD, I DIDN'T THINK SO.
MY GOOD FRIEND ARKILLO HERE WILL BE SEEN AND NOT HEARD FROM THIS MOMENT FORTH.
NOW LET'S GET TO WORK.

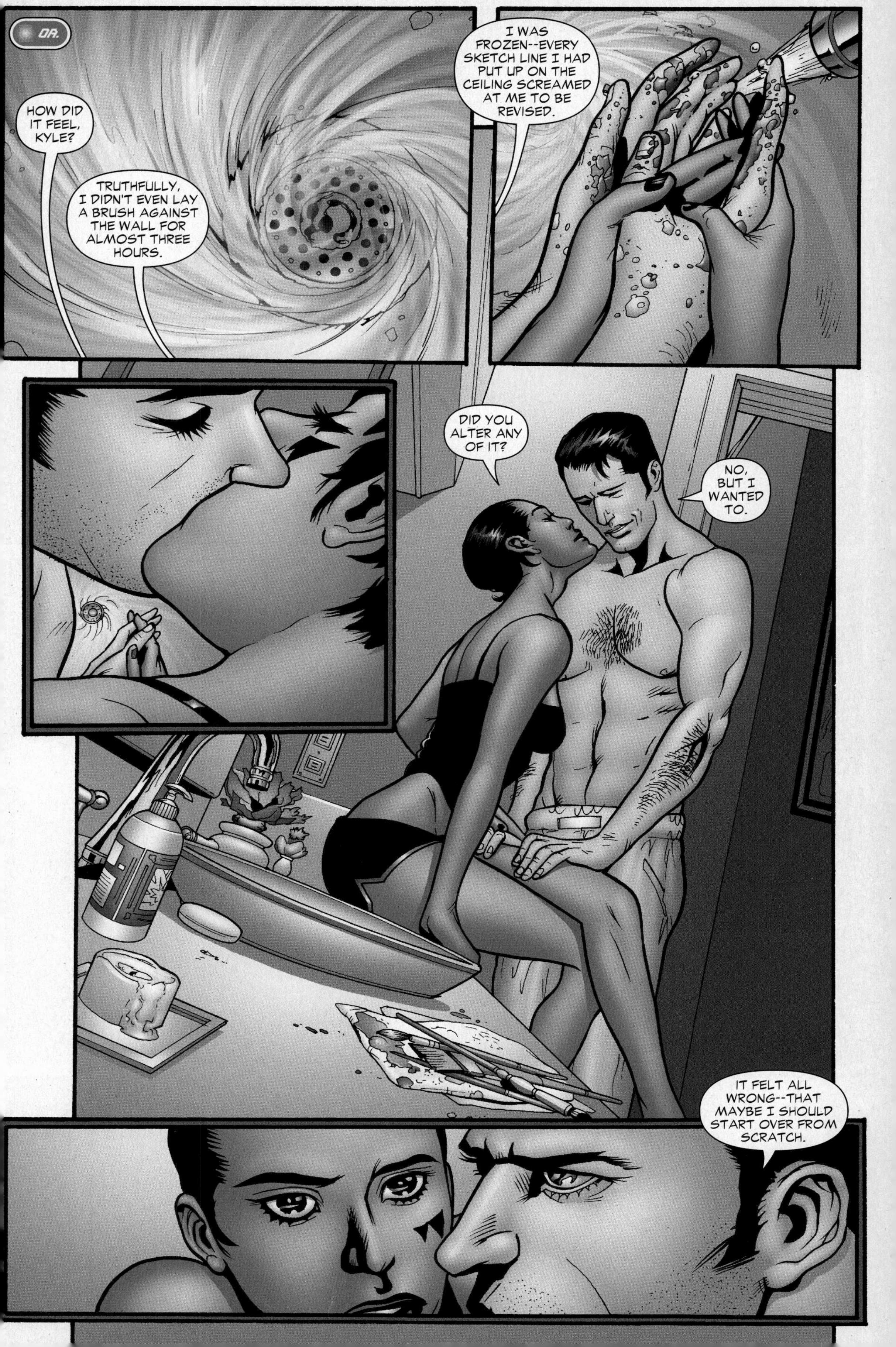
HOW DID IT FEEL, KYLE?
TRUTHFULLY, I DIDN'T EVEN LAY A BRUSH AGAINST THE WALL FOR ALMOST THREE HOURS.
I WAS FROZEN--EVERY SKETCH LINE I HAD PUT UP ON THE CEILING SCREAMED AT ME TO BE REVISED.
DID YOU ALTER ANY OF IT?
NO, BUT I WANTED TO.
IT FELT ALL WRONG--THAT MAYBE I SHOULD START OVER FROM SCRATCH.

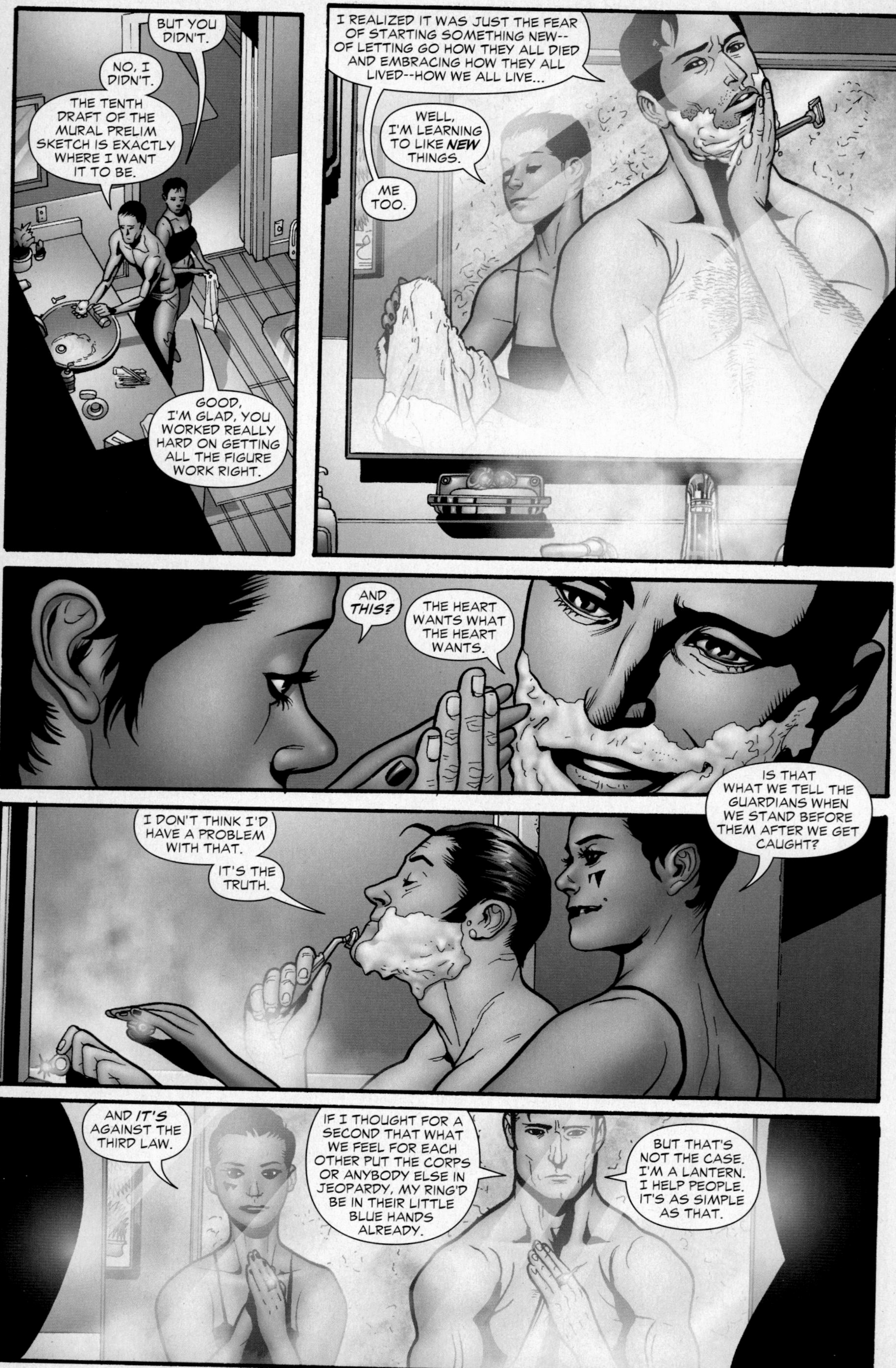
BUT YOU DIDN'T.
NO, I DIDN'T.
THE TENTH DRAFT OF THE MURAL PRELIM SKETCH IS EXACTLY WHERE I WANT IT TO BE.
GOOD, I'M GLAD, YOU WORKED REALLY HARD ON GETTING ALL THE FIGURE WORK RIGHT.
I REALIZED IT WAS JUST THE FEAR OF STARTING SOMETHING NEW-- OF LETTING GO HOW THEY ALL DIED AND EMBRACING HOW THEY ALL LIVED--HOW WE ALL LIVE...
WELL, I'M LEARNING TO LIKE NEW THINGS.
ME TOO.
AND THIS?
THE HEART WANTS WHAT THE HEART WANTS.
IS THAT WHAT WE TELL THE GUARDIANS WHEN WE STAND BEFORE THEM AFTER WE GET CAUGHT?
I DON'T THINK I'D HAVE A PROBLEM WITH THAT.
IT'S THE TRUTH.
AND IT'S AGAINST THE THIRD LAW.
IF I THOUGHT FOR A SECOND THAT WHAT WE FEEL FOR EACH OTHER PUT THE CORPS OR ANYBODY ELSE IN JEOPARDY, MY RING'D BE IN THEIR LITTLE BLUE HANDS ALREADY.
BUT THAT'S NOT THE CASE. I'M A LANTERN. I HELP PEOPLE. IT'S AS SIMPLE AS THAT.

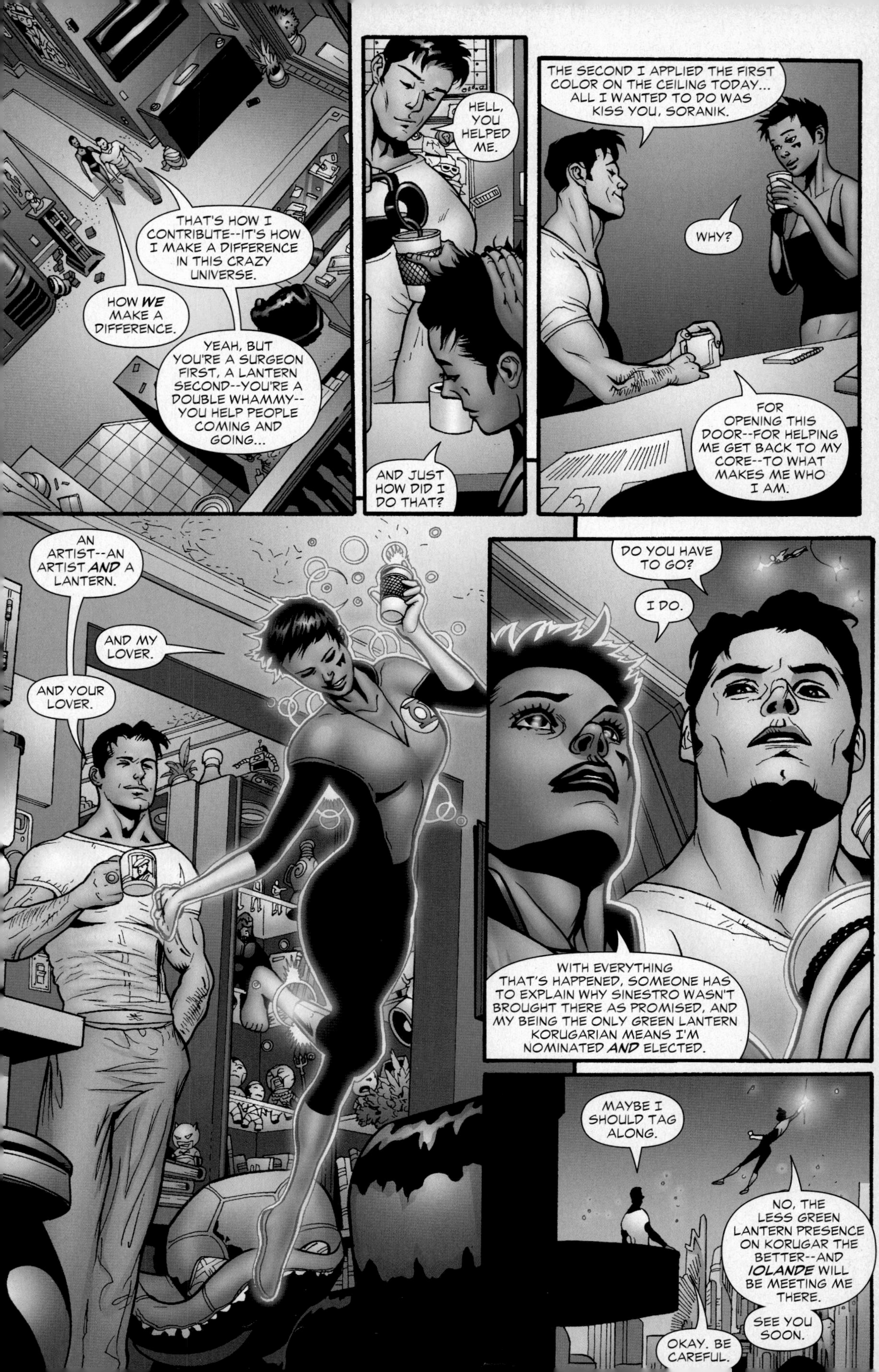
THAT'S HOW I CONTRIBUTE--IT'S HOW I MAKE A DIFFERENCE IN THIS CRAZY UNIVERSE.
HOW WE MAKE A DIFFERENCE.
YEAH, BUT YOU'RE A SURGEON FIRST, A LANTERN SECOND--YOU'RE A DOUBLE WHAMMY--YOU HELP PEOPLE COMING AND GOING...
HELL, YOU HELPED ME.
AND JUST HOW DID I DO THAT?
THE SECOND I APPLIED THE FIRST COLOR ON THE CEILING TODAY... ALL I WANTED TO DO WAS KISS YOU, SORANIK.
WHY?
FOR OPENING THIS DOOR--FOR HELPING ME GET BACK TO MY CORE--TO WHAT MAKES ME WHO I AM.
AN ARTIST--AN ARTIST AND A LANTERN.
AND MY LOVER.
AND YOUR LOVER.
DO YOU HAVE TO GO?
I DO.
WITH EVERYTHING THAT'S HAPPENED, SOMEONE HAS TO EXPLAIN WHY SINESTRO WASN'T BROUGHT THERE AS PROMISED, AND MY BEING THE ONLY GREEN LANTERN KORUGARIAN MEANS I'M NOMINATED AND ELECTED.
MAYBE I SHOULD TAG ALONG.
NO, THE LESS GREEN LANTERN PRESENCE ON KORUGAR THE BETTER--AND IOLANDE WILL BE MEETING ME THERE.
SEE YOU SOON.
OKAY. BE CAREFUL.

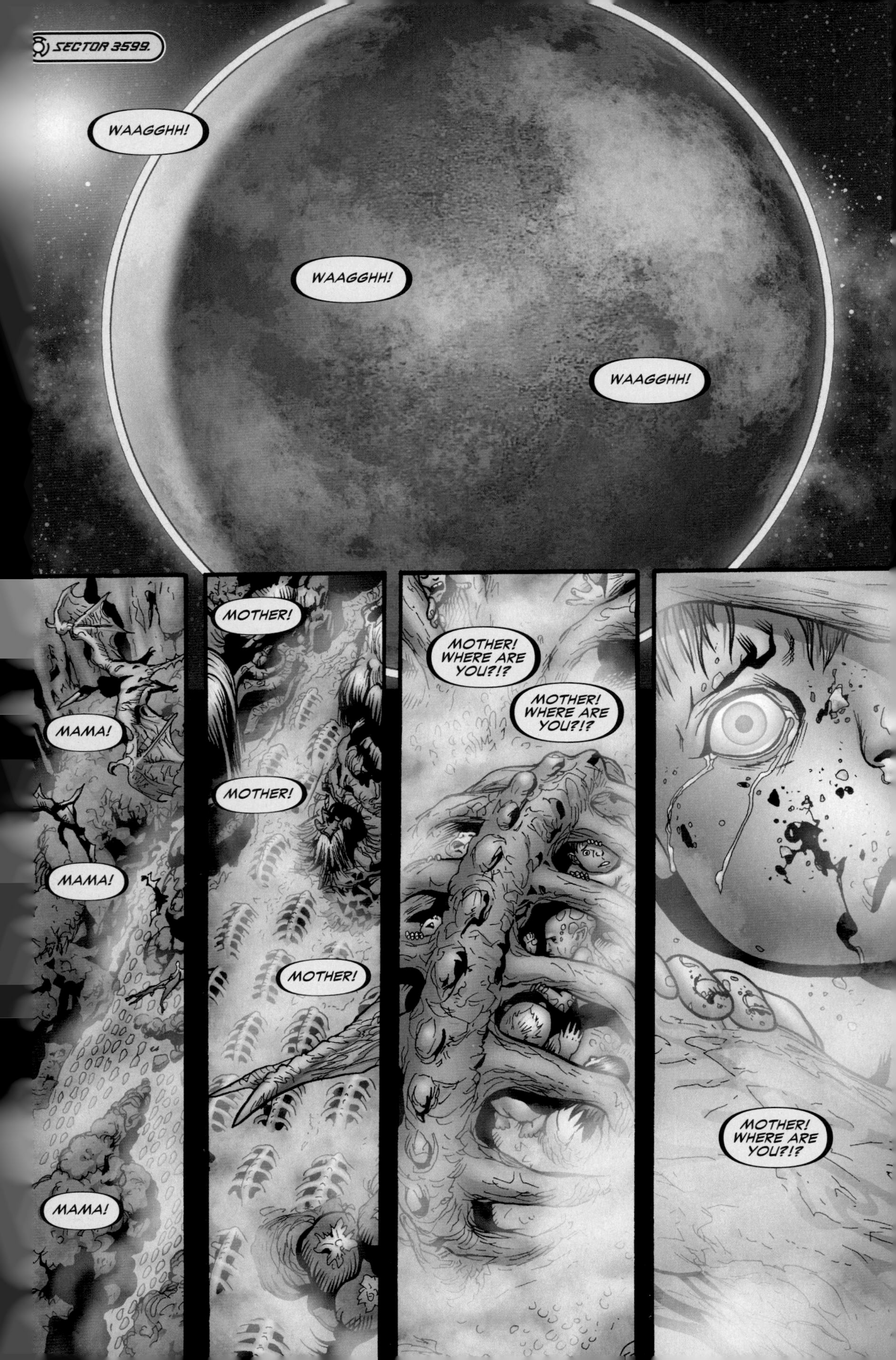
SECTOR 3599.
WAAGGHH!
WAAGGHH!
WAAGGHH!
MAMA!
MAMA!
MAMA!
MOTHER!
MOTHER!
MOTHER!
MOTHER! WHERE ARE YOU?!?
MOTHER! WHERE ARE YOU?!?
MOTHER! WHERE ARE YOU?!?

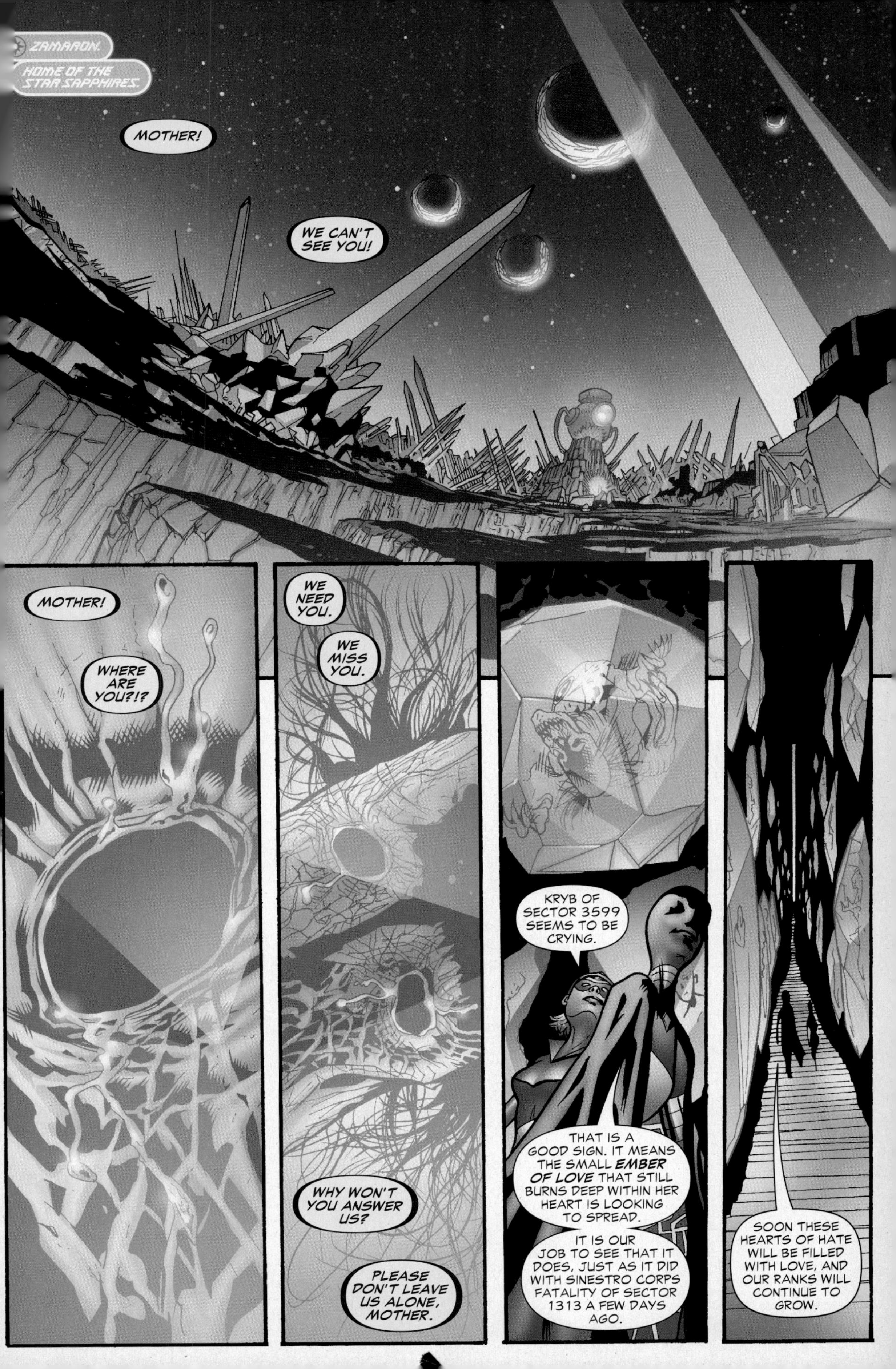
ZAMARON.
HOME OF THE STAR SAPPHIRES.
MOTHER!
WE CAN'T SEE YOU!
MOTHER!
WHERE ARE YOU?!?
WE NEED YOU.
WE MISS YOU.
WHY WON'T YOU ANSWER US?
PLEASE DON'T LEAVE US ALONE, MOTHER.
KRYB OF SECTOR 3599 SEEMS TO BE CRYING.
THAT IS A GOOD SIGN. IT MEANS THE SMALL EMBER OF LOVE THAT STILL BURNS DEEP WITHIN HER HEART IS LOOKING TO SPREAD.
IT IS OUR JOB TO SEE THAT IT DOES, JUST AS IT DID WITH SINESTRO CORPS FATALITY OF SECTOR 1313 A FEW DAYS AGO.
SOON THESE HEARTS OF HATE WILL BE FILLED WITH LOVE, AND OUR RANKS WILL CONTINUE TO GROW.

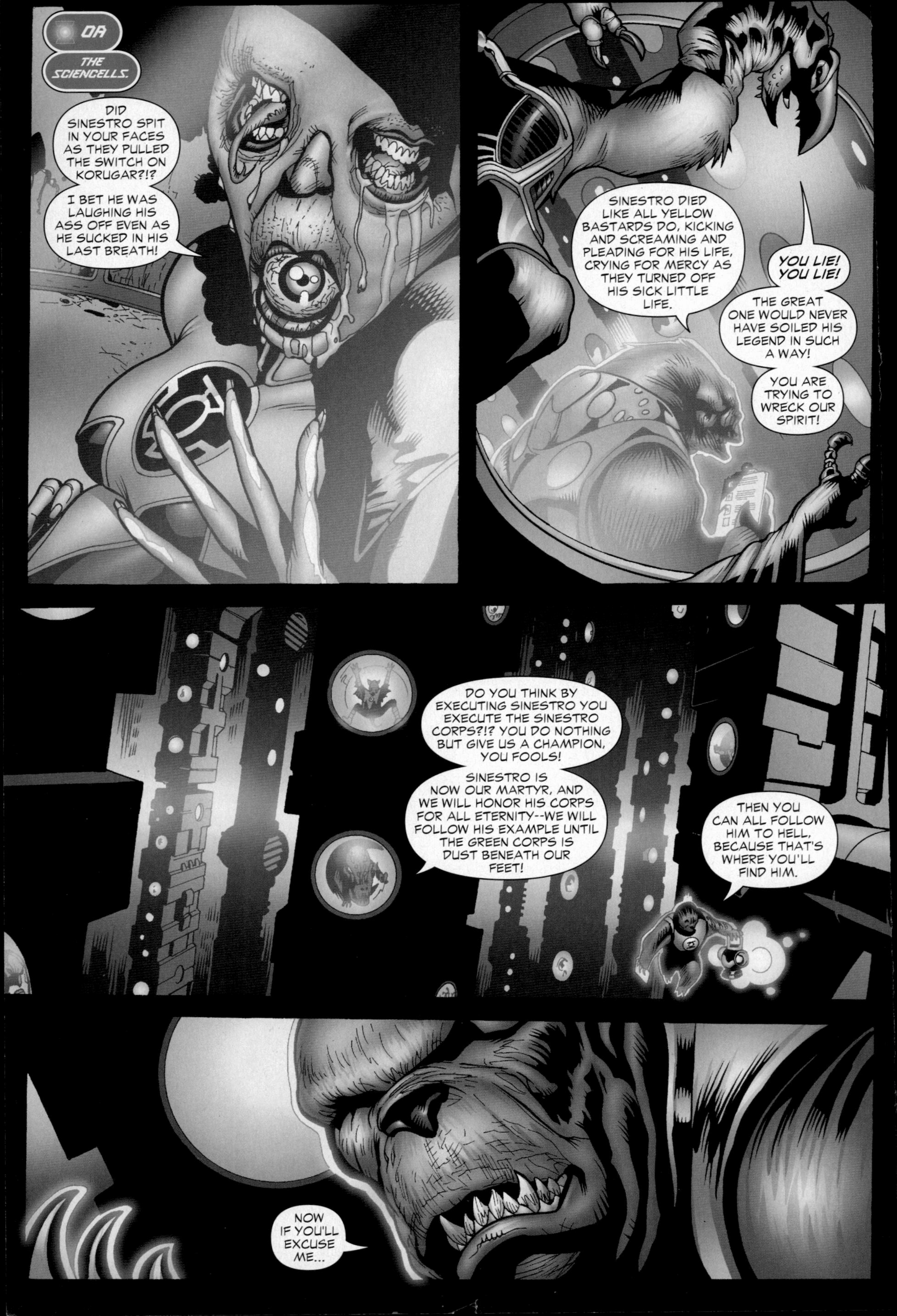
OA
THE SCIENCELLS.
DID SINESTRO SPIT IN YOUR FACES AS THEY PULLED THE SWITCH ON KORUGAR?!?
I BET HE WAS LAUGHING HIS ASS OFF EVEN AS HE SUCKED IN HIS LAST BREATH!
SINESTRO DIED LIKE ALL YELLOW BASTARDS DO, KICKING AND SCREAMING AND PLEADING FOR HIS LIFE, CRYING FOR MERCY AS THEY TURNED OFF HIS SICK LITTLE LIFE.
YOU LIE! YOU LIE!
THE GREAT ONE WOULD NEVER HAVE SOILED HIS LEGEND IN SUCH A WAY!
YOU ARE TRYING TO WRECK OUR SPIRIT!
DO YOU THINK BY EXECUTING SINESTRO YOU EXECUTE THE SINESTRO CORPS?!? YOU DO NOTHING BUT GIVE US A CHAMPION, YOU FOOLS!
SINESTRO IS NOW OUR MARTYR, AND WE WILL HONOR HIS CORPS FOR ALL ETERNITY--WE WILL FOLLOW HIS EXAMPLE UNTIL THE GREEN CORPS IS DUST BENEATH OUR FEET!
THEN YOU CAN ALL FOLLOW HIM TO HELL, BECAUSE THAT'S WHERE YOU'LL FIND HIM.
NOW IF YOU'LL EXCUSE ME...

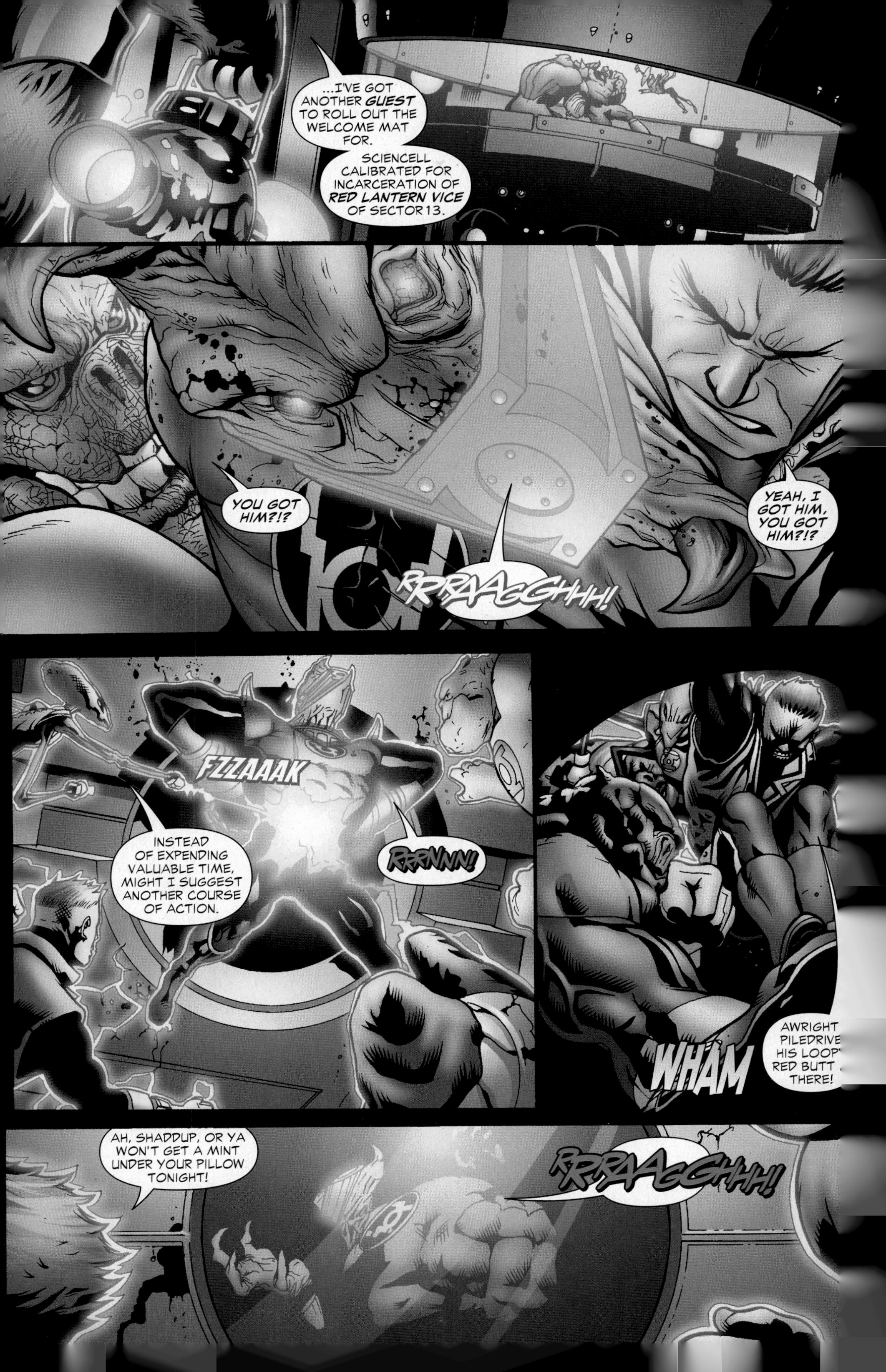

...I'VE GOT ANOTHER GUEST TO ROLL OUT THE WELCOME MAT FOR.
SCIENCELL CALIBRATED FOR INCARCERATION OF RED LANTERN VICE OF SECTOR 13.
YOU GOT HIM?!?
YEAH, I GOT HIM, YOU GOT HIM?!?
RRRAAGGHHH!
FZZAAAK
INSTEAD OF EXPENDING VALUABLE TIME, MIGHT I SUGGEST ANOTHER COURSE OF ACTION.
RRRNNN!
WHAM
AH, SHADDUP, OR YA WON'T GET A MINT UNDER YOUR PILLOW TONIGHT!
RRRAAGGHHH!

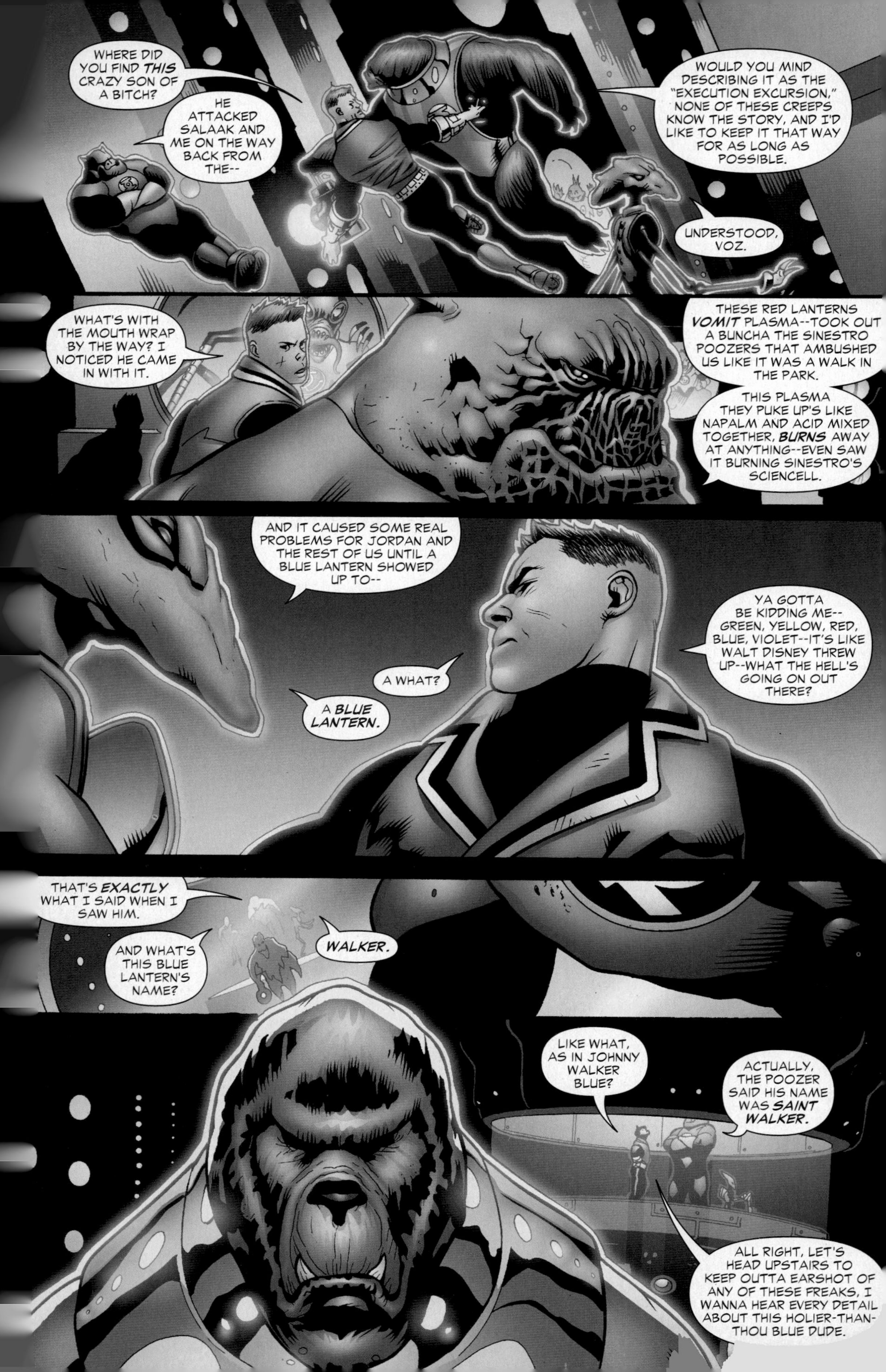

WHERE DID YOU FIND THIS CRAZY SON OF A BITCH?
HE ATTACKED SALAAK AND ME ON THE WAY BACK FROM THE--
WOULD YOU MIND DESCRIBING IT AS THE "EXECUTION EXCURSION," NONE OF THESE CREEPS KNOW THE STORY, AND I'D LIKE TO KEEP IT THAT WAY FOR AS LONG AS POSSIBLE.
UNDERSTOOD, VOZ.
WHAT'S WITH THE MOUTH WRAP BY THE WAY? I NOTICED HE CAME IN WITH IT.
THESE RED LANTERNS VOMIT PLASMA--TOOK OUT A BUNCHA THE SINESTRO POOZERS THAT AMBUSHED US LIKE IT WAS A WALK IN THE PARK.
THIS PLASMA THEY PUKE UP'S LIKE NAPALM AND ACID MIXED TOGETHER, BURNS AWAY AT ANYTHING--EVEN SAW IT BURNING SINESTRO'S SCIENCELL.
AND IT CAUSED SOME REAL PROBLEMS FOR JORDAN AND THE REST OF US UNTIL A BLUE LANTERN SHOWED UP TO--
A WHAT?
A BLUE LANTERN.
YA GOTTA BE KIDDING ME--GREEN, YELLOW, RED, BLUE, VIOLET--IT'S LIKE WALT DISNEY THREW UP--WHAT THE HELL'S GOING ON OUT THERE?
THAT'S EXACTLY WHAT I SAID WHEN I SAW HIM.
AND WHAT'S THIS BLUE LANTERN'S NAME?
WALKER.
LIKE WHAT, AS IN JOHNNY WALKER BLUE?
ACTUALLY, THE POOZER SAID HIS NAME WAS SAINT WALKER.
ALL RIGHT, LET'S HEAD UPSTAIRS TO KEEP OUTTA EARSHOT OF ANY OF THESE FREAKS, I WANNA HEAR EVERY DETAIL ABOUT THIS HOLIER-THAN-THOU BLUE DUDE.

HOW DOES SOMEONE LIKE YOU EXIST?

WHERE DOES ALL THIS EVIL COME FROM?

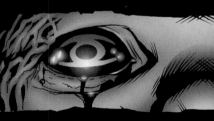

DEEP IN THE DEPTHS OF OA.

THE TIME HAS COME.

A *FISSURE* IS NEEDED...

...IF WE ARE TO TEAR OA ASUNDER.

AND IT SHALL EGIN WHERE ALL THE RAGE AND FEAR RESIDES ON OA...

...THE SCIENCELLS.

RRMMM!

SKRAK!

HRRUM?

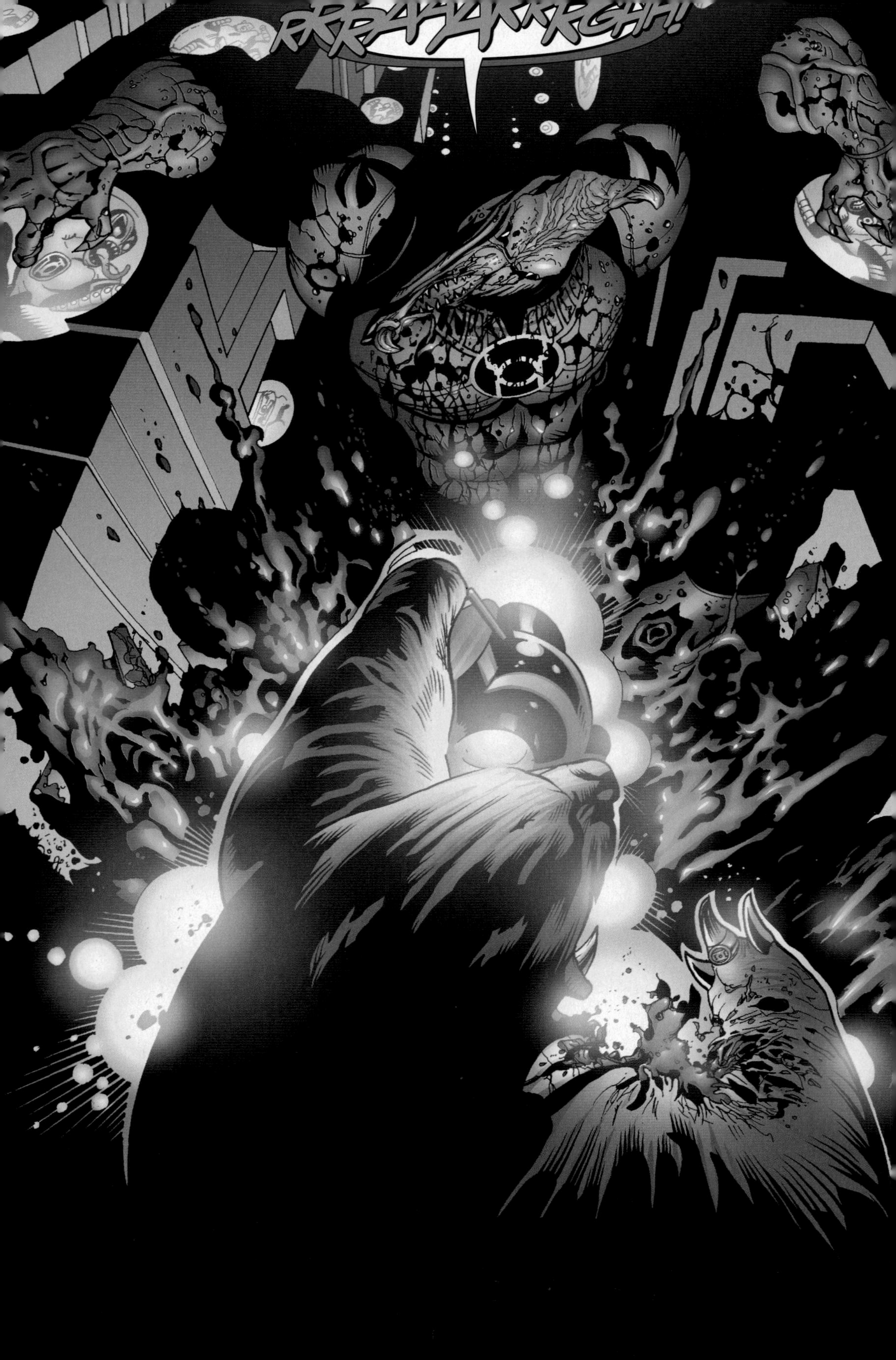
RRRAAAHRRRGHH!

REEN LANTERN CORPS #35
over by Patrick Gleason, Rebecca Buchman & Nei Ruffino

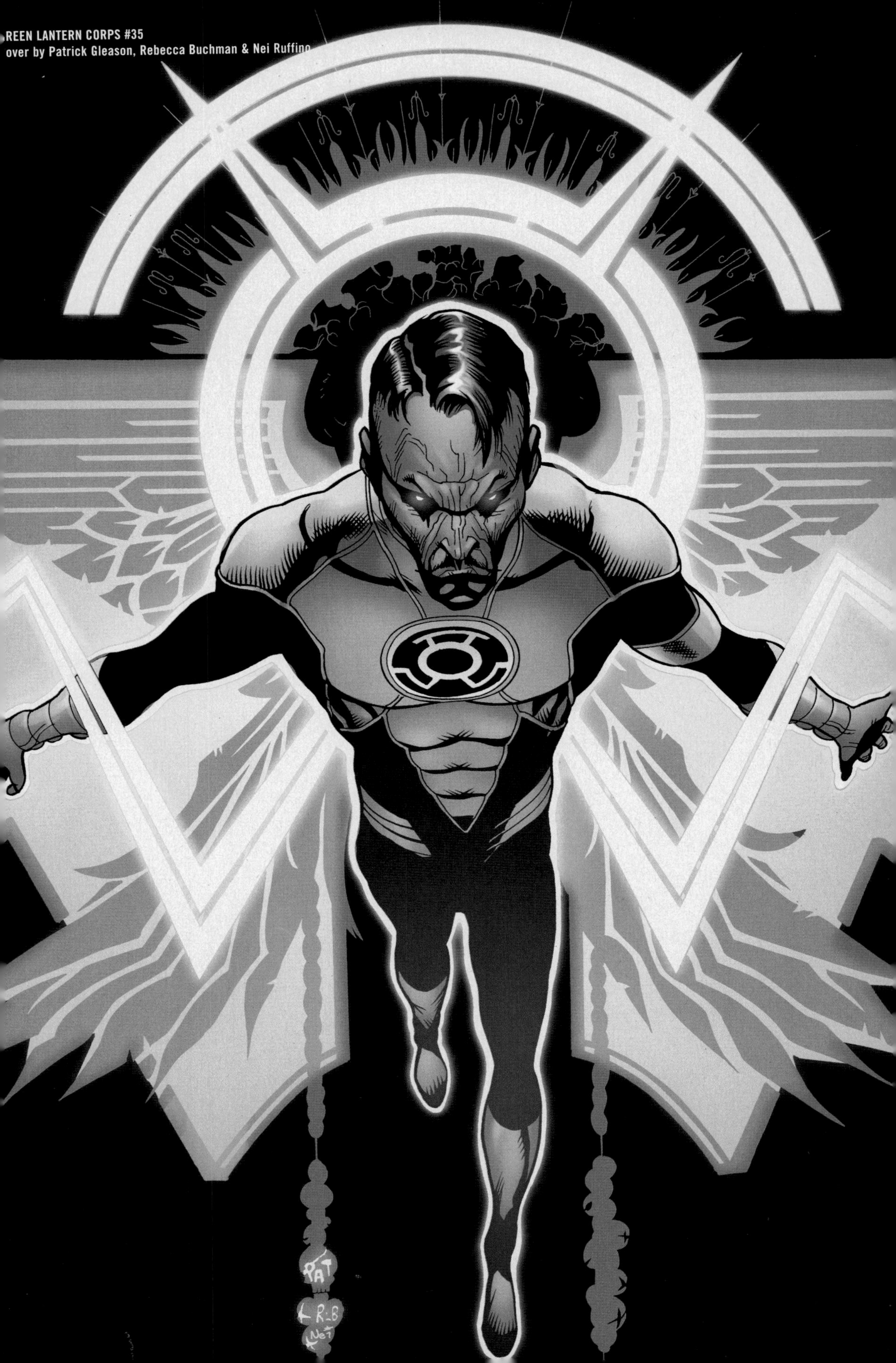

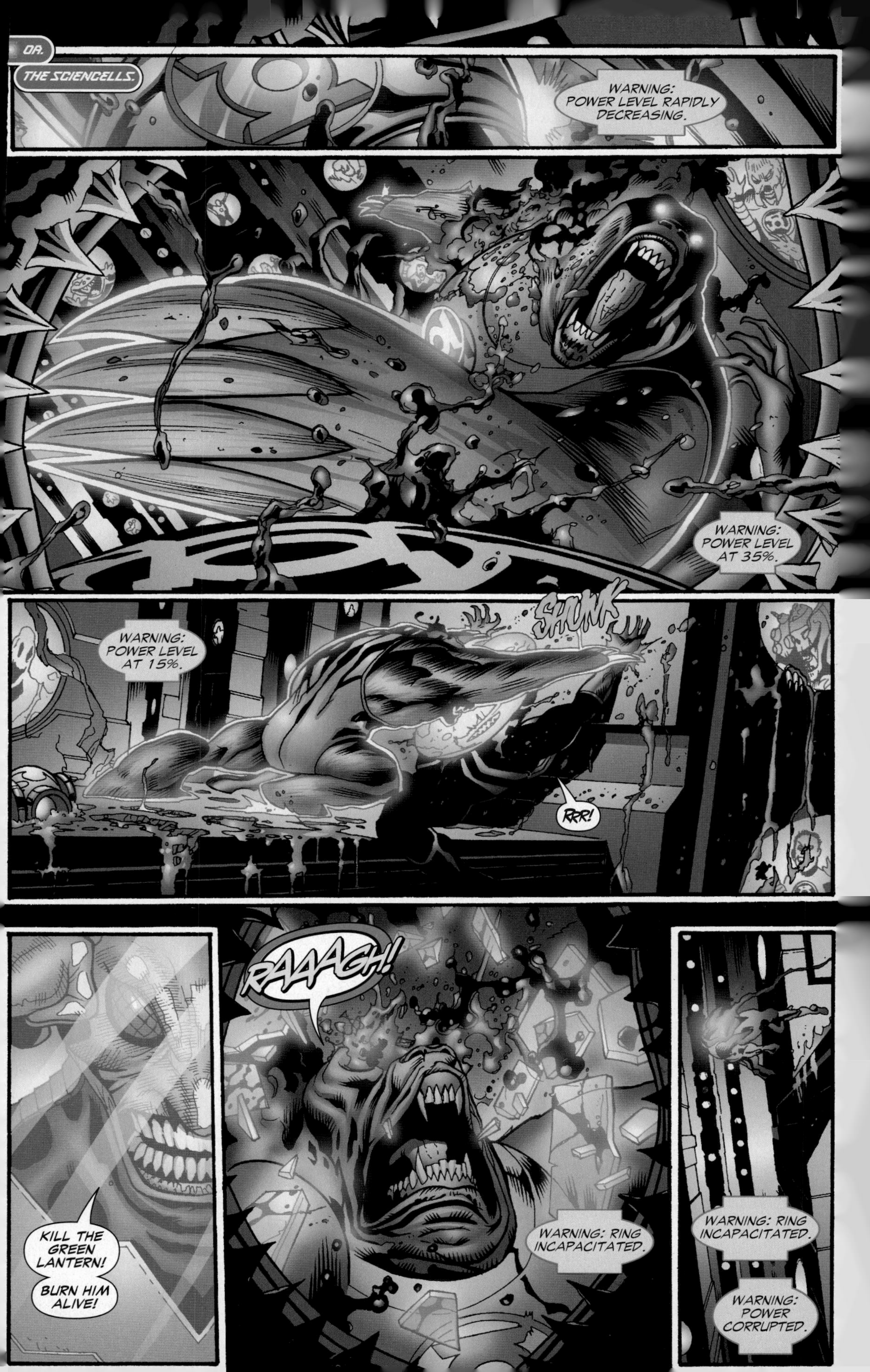
OA.
THE SCIENCELLS.
WARNING: POWER LEVEL RAPIDLY DECREASING.
WARNING: POWER LEVEL AT 35%.
WARNING: POWER LEVEL AT 15%.
SHUNK
RRR!
RAAAGH!
KILL THE GREEN LANTERN!
BURN HIM ALIVE!
WARNING: RING INCAPACITATED.
WARNING: RING INCAPACITATED.
WARNING: POWER CORRUPTED.

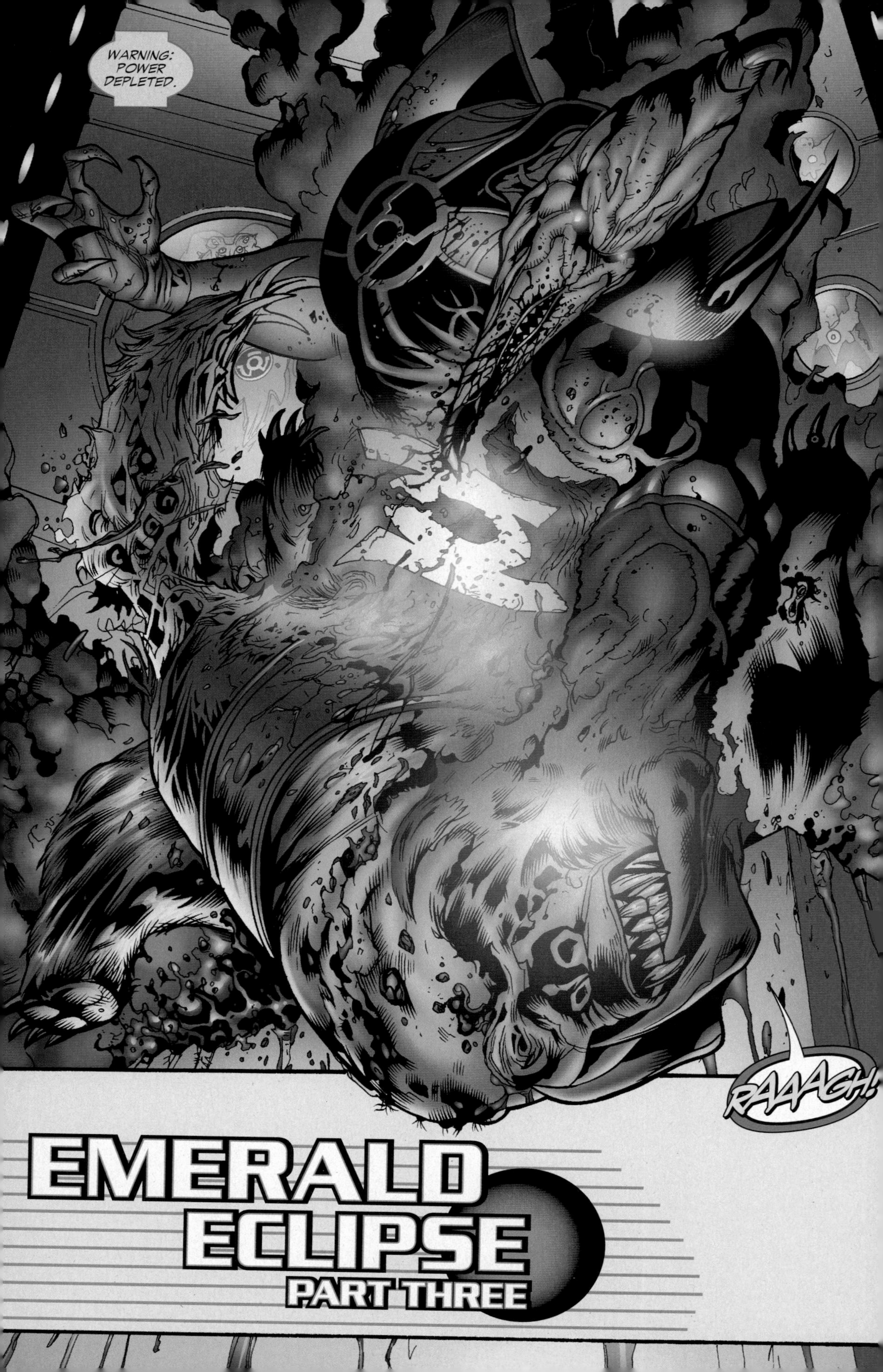
WARNING: POWER DEPLETED.
RAAAGH!
EMERALD ECLIPSE
PART THREE

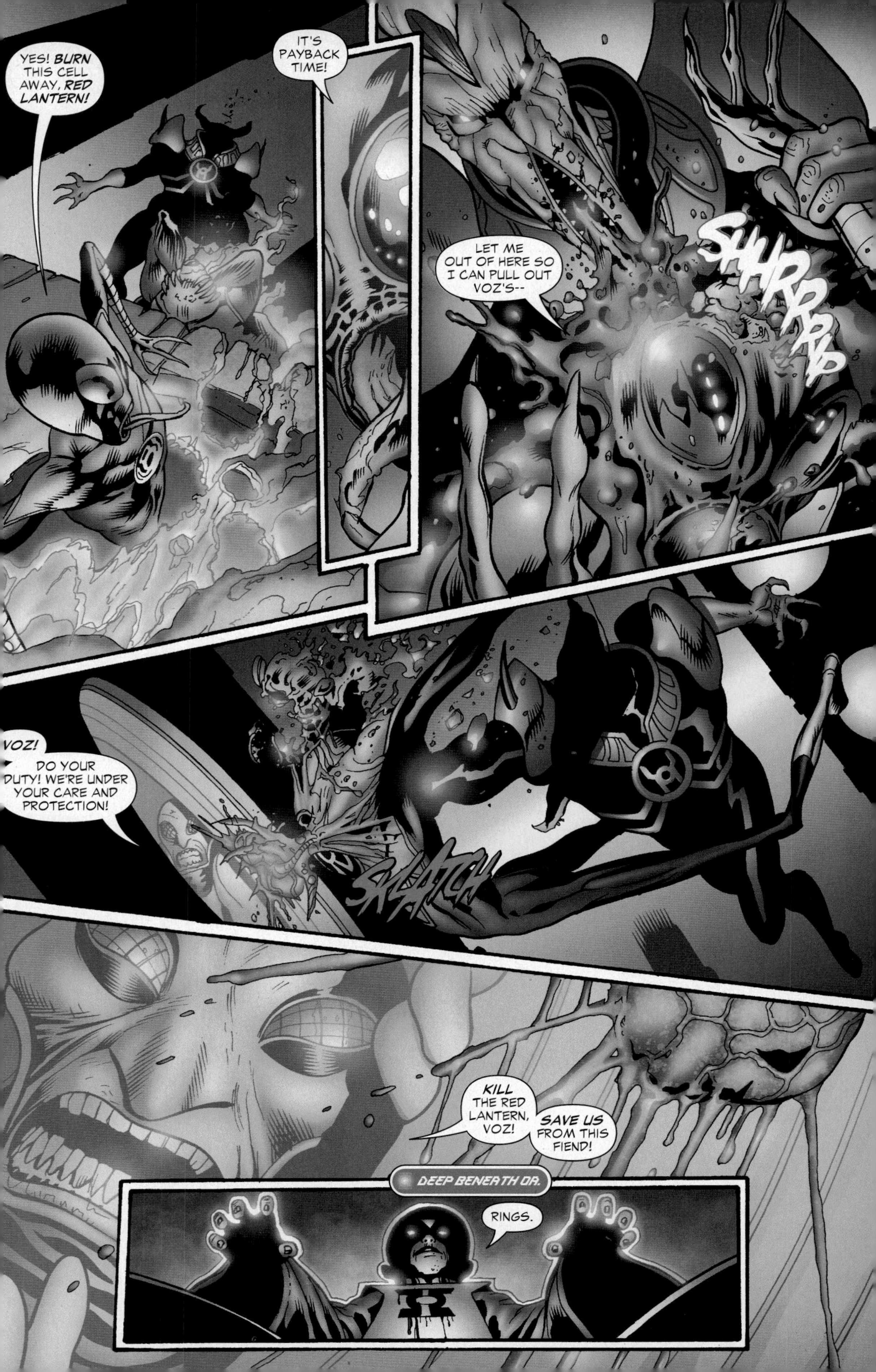
YES! BURN THIS CELL AWAY, RED LANTERN!
IT'S PAYBACK TIME!
LET ME OUT OF HERE SO I CAN PULL OUT VOZ'S--
SHHRRRRB
VOZ!
DO YOUR DUTY! WE'RE UNDER YOUR CARE AND PROTECTION!
SKLATCH
KILL THE RED LANTERN, VOZ!
SAVE US FROM THIS FIEND!
DEEP BENEATH OA.
RINGS.

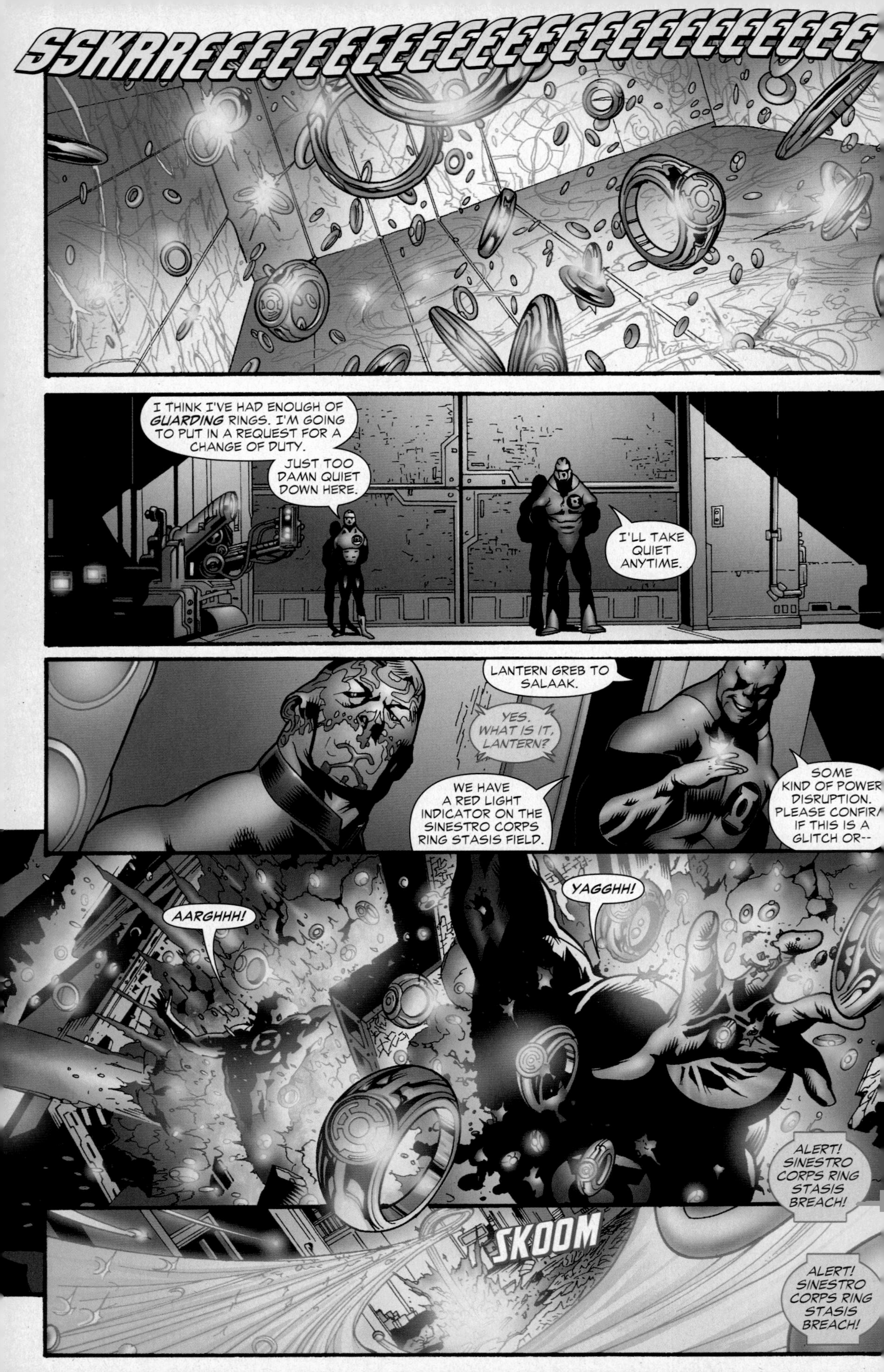
SSKRREEEEEEEEEEEEEEEEEEEEEE
I THINK I'VE HAD ENOUGH OF GUARDING RINGS. I'M GOING TO PUT IN A REQUEST FOR A CHANGE OF DUTY.
JUST TOO DAMN QUIET DOWN HERE.
I'LL TAKE QUIET ANYTIME.
LANTERN GREB TO SALAAK.
YES. WHAT IS IT, LANTERN?
WE HAVE A RED LIGHT INDICATOR ON THE SINESTRO CORPS RING STASIS FIELD.
SOME KIND OF POWER DISRUPTION. PLEASE CONFIRM IF THIS IS A GLITCH OR--
AARGHHH!
YAGGHH!
ALERT! SINESTRO CORPS RING STASIS BREACH!
SKOOM
ALERT! SINESTRO CORPS RING STASIS BREACH!

ATTENTION--ALL RST LINE DEFENSE LANTERNS REPORT TO SCIENCELLS!

YEAH, THIS IS NOT A DRILL--REPEAT--THIS IS *NOT* A FREAKIN' DRILL!

SINCE WE HAVEN'T HEARD FROM VOZ, WE HAVE TO ASSUME HE'S BEEN KILLED WHICH MEANS GOD ONLY KNOWS WHAT WE'RE FLYING INTO.

IF THOSE RINGS GET INTO THE SCIENCELLS WE'RE GOING TO NEED THE GUARDIANS TO--

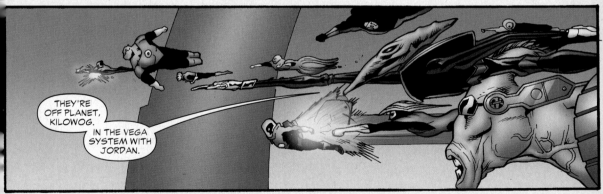

THEY'RE OFF PLANET, KILOWOG. IN THE VEGA SYSTEM WITH JORDAN.

YEAH, WELL, THAT FIGURES, SALAAK, WHEN YA *ACTUALLY* NEED THE *BLUE MAN GROUP* THEY'RE NOT AROUND!

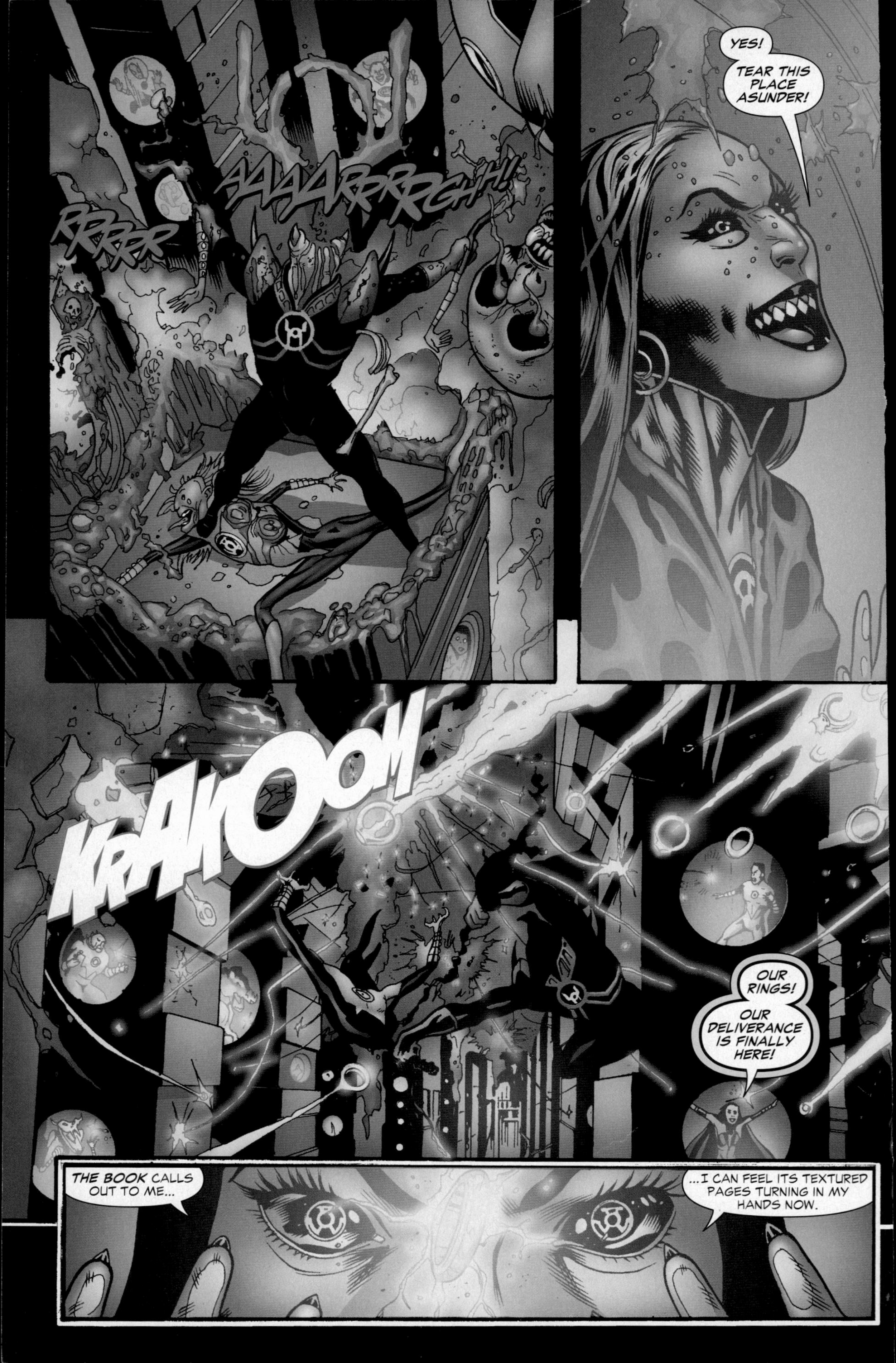
AAAAARRRRGH!!
RRRRR
YES!
TEAR THIS PLACE ASUNDER!
KRAKOOM
OUR RINGS!
OUR DELIVERANCE IS FINALLY HERE!
THE BOOK CALLS OUT TO ME...
...I CAN FEEL ITS TEXTURED PAGES TURNING IN MY HANDS NOW.

THEY'LL PROBABLY BE EXPECTING US TO COME RIGHT THROUGH THE FRONT DOOR.

RING, GIMME A SCHEMATIC OF THE SCIENCELLS.

THIS TUNNEL WILL BRING US UP FROM THE BOTTOM OF THE SCIENCELLS AND HOPEFULLY GIVE US A SECOND OR TWO TO GET THE DROP ON 'EM.

KILOWOG AND I JUST HAD FIRSTHAND EXPERIENCE AGAINST THE RED LANTERNS WHEN WE WERE AMBUSHED BRINGING SINESTRO TO KORUGAR.

THIS RED LANTERN'S AN X-FACTOR. I'VE UPLOADED EVERYONE'S RINGS WITH THE RECENT ACTION REPORT SO YOU CAN EXPECT THE UNEXPECTED.

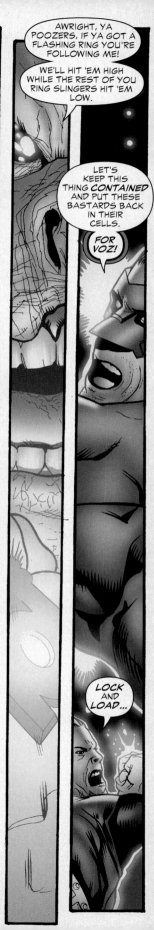

AWRIGHT, YA POOZERS, IF YA GOT A FLASHING RING YOU'RE FOLLOWING ME!

WE'LL HIT 'EM HIGH WHILE THE REST OF YOU RING SLINGERS HIT 'EM LOW.

LET'S KEEP THIS THING CONTAINED AND PUT THESE BASTARDS BACK IN THEIR CELLS.

FOR VOZ!

LOCK AND LOAD...

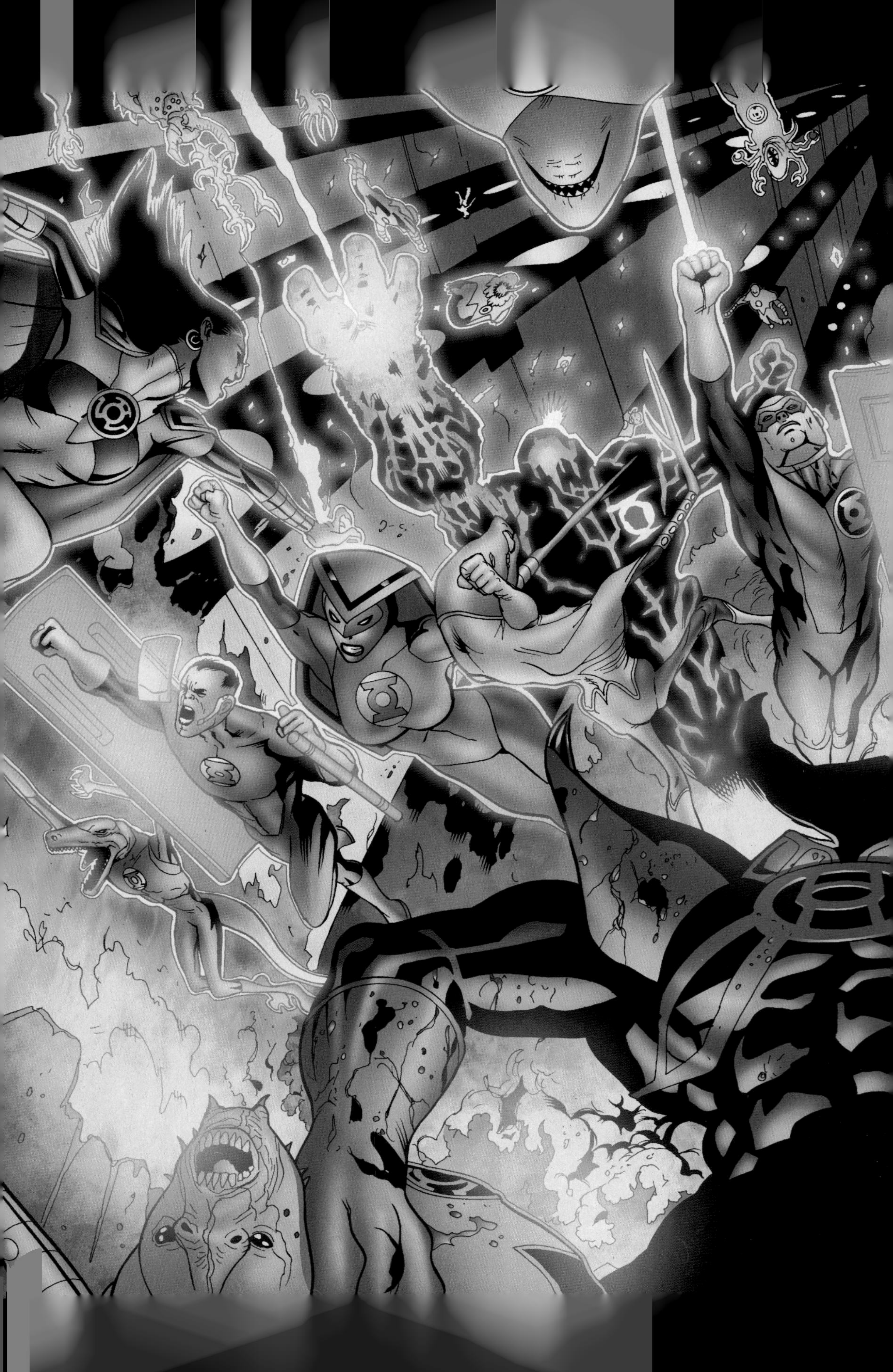

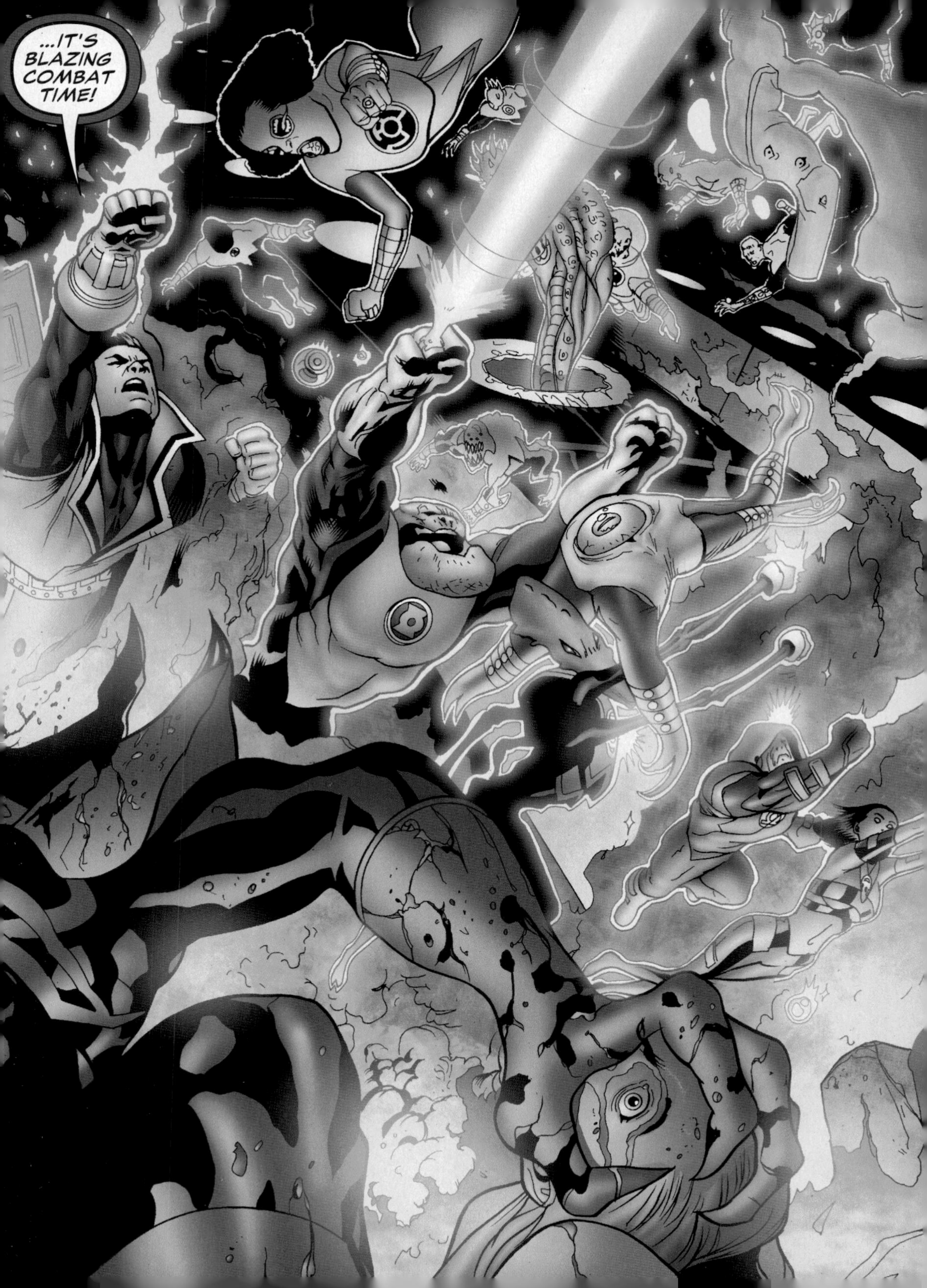
...IT'S BLAZING COMBAT TIME!

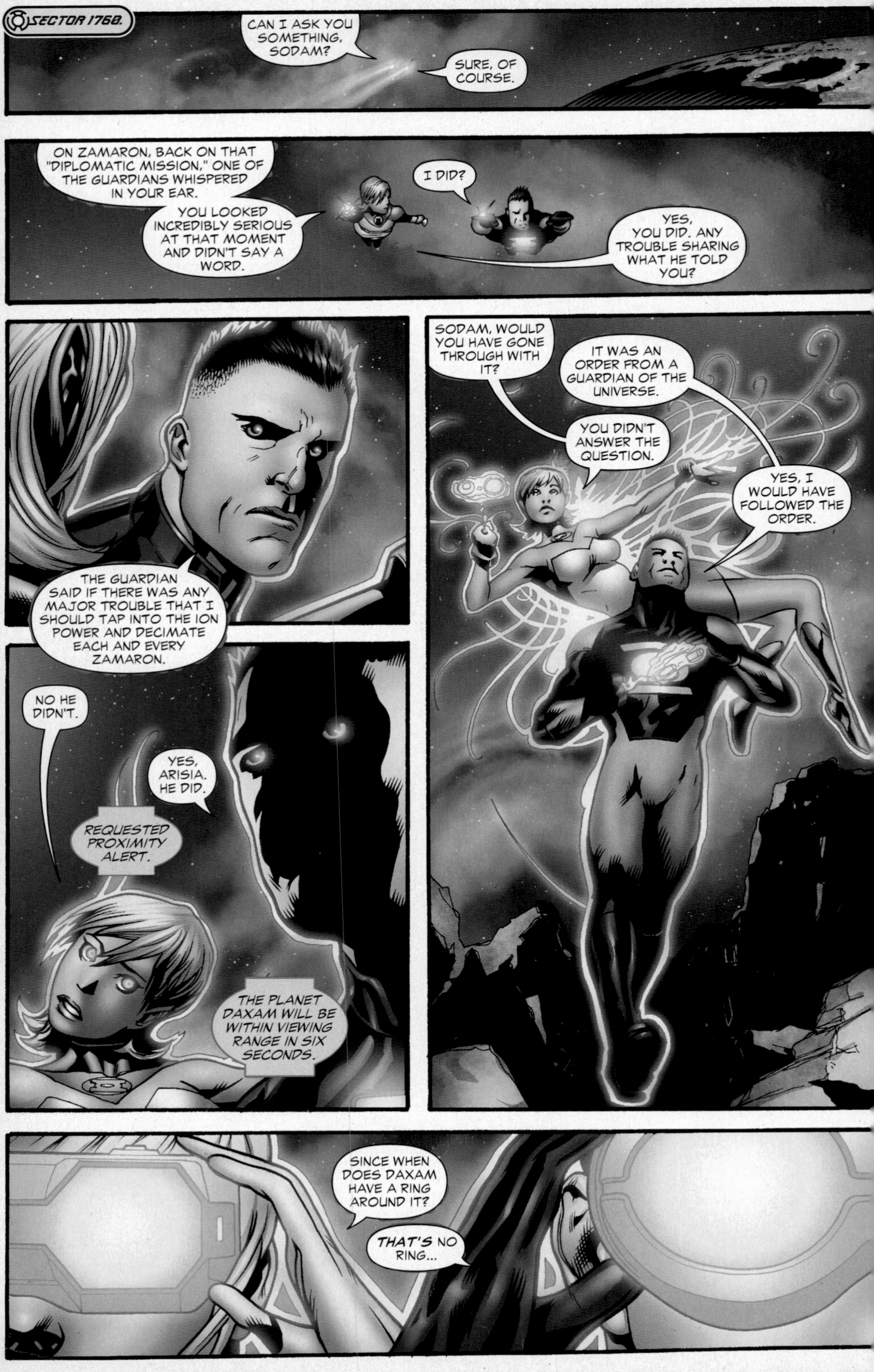
SECTOR 1760.
CAN I ASK YOU SOMETHING, SODAM?
SURE, OF COURSE.
ON ZAMARON, BACK ON THAT "DIPLOMATIC MISSION," ONE OF THE GUARDIANS WHISPERED IN YOUR EAR.
YOU LOOKED INCREDIBLY SERIOUS AT THAT MOMENT AND DIDN'T SAY A WORD.
I DID?
YES, YOU DID. ANY TROUBLE SHARING WHAT HE TOLD YOU?
THE GUARDIAN SAID IF THERE WAS ANY MAJOR TROUBLE THAT I SHOULD TAP INTO THE ION POWER AND DECIMATE EACH AND EVERY ZAMARON.
NO HE DIDN'T.
YES, ARISIA. HE DID.
REQUESTED PROXIMITY ALERT.
THE PLANET DAXAM WILL BE WITHIN VIEWING RANGE IN SIX SECONDS.
SODAM, WOULD YOU HAVE GONE THROUGH WITH IT?
IT WAS AN ORDER FROM A GUARDIAN OF THE UNIVERSE.
YOU DIDN'T ANSWER THE QUESTION.
YES, I WOULD HAVE FOLLOWED THE ORDER.
SINCE WHEN DOES DAXAM HAVE A RING AROUND IT?
THAT'S NO RING...

...THAT'S A *SINESTRO CORPS SENTRY.*

AND IT LOOKS PRETTY HUNGRY.

WHICH MEANS MONGUL'S *SOLIDIFIED* HIS POSITION ON DAXAM AND DOESN'T WANT ANY VISITORS.

IT ALSO MEANS HE HAS HIS HANDS FULL RULING THE PLANET AND KEEPING THE SINESTRO CORPS IN LINE.

IF WE STAND ANY CHANCE AT ALL, WE'VE GOT TO GET DOWN THERE WITHOUT BEING NOTICED.

THE ELEMENT OF *SURPRISE* IS ALL WE HAVE.

AND JUST HOW DO YOU EXPECT US TO SURPRISE THEM, BY LOOKING FOR A SIGN FROM THE STARS?

I WAS A BIT OF AN *ASTRONOMER* BACK WHEN I WAS A KID. MY FATHER LIKED TO SHATTER MY TELESCOPES AND LENSES, KEEP MY EYES FROM THE SKIES, BUT THERE WAS NO GETTING AROUND IT...

...DAXAM ALWAYS SEEMED TO BE A MAGNET FOR *METEORITES.*

OKAY, SO HOW DOES *THAT* HELP US EXACTLY?

I HAVE AN IDEA.

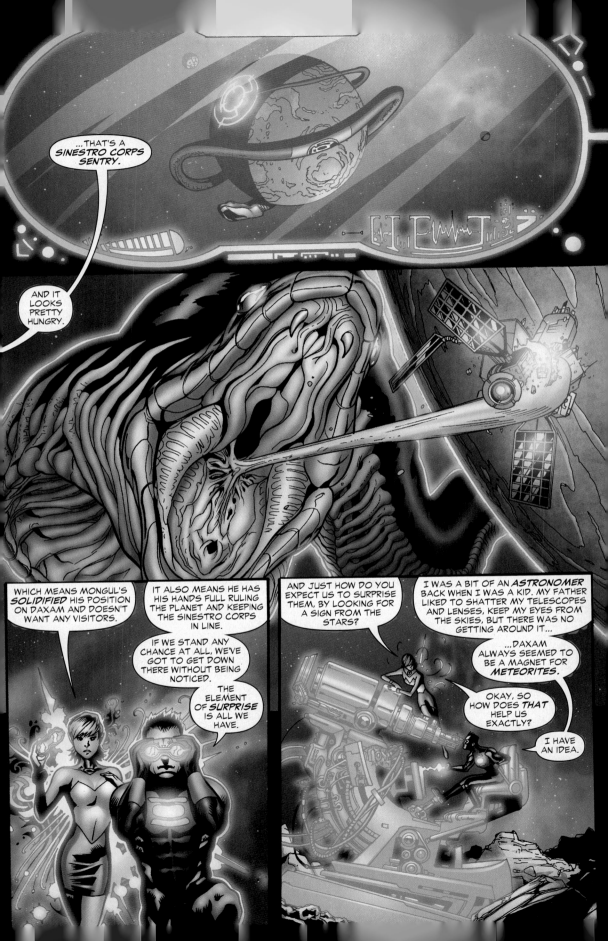

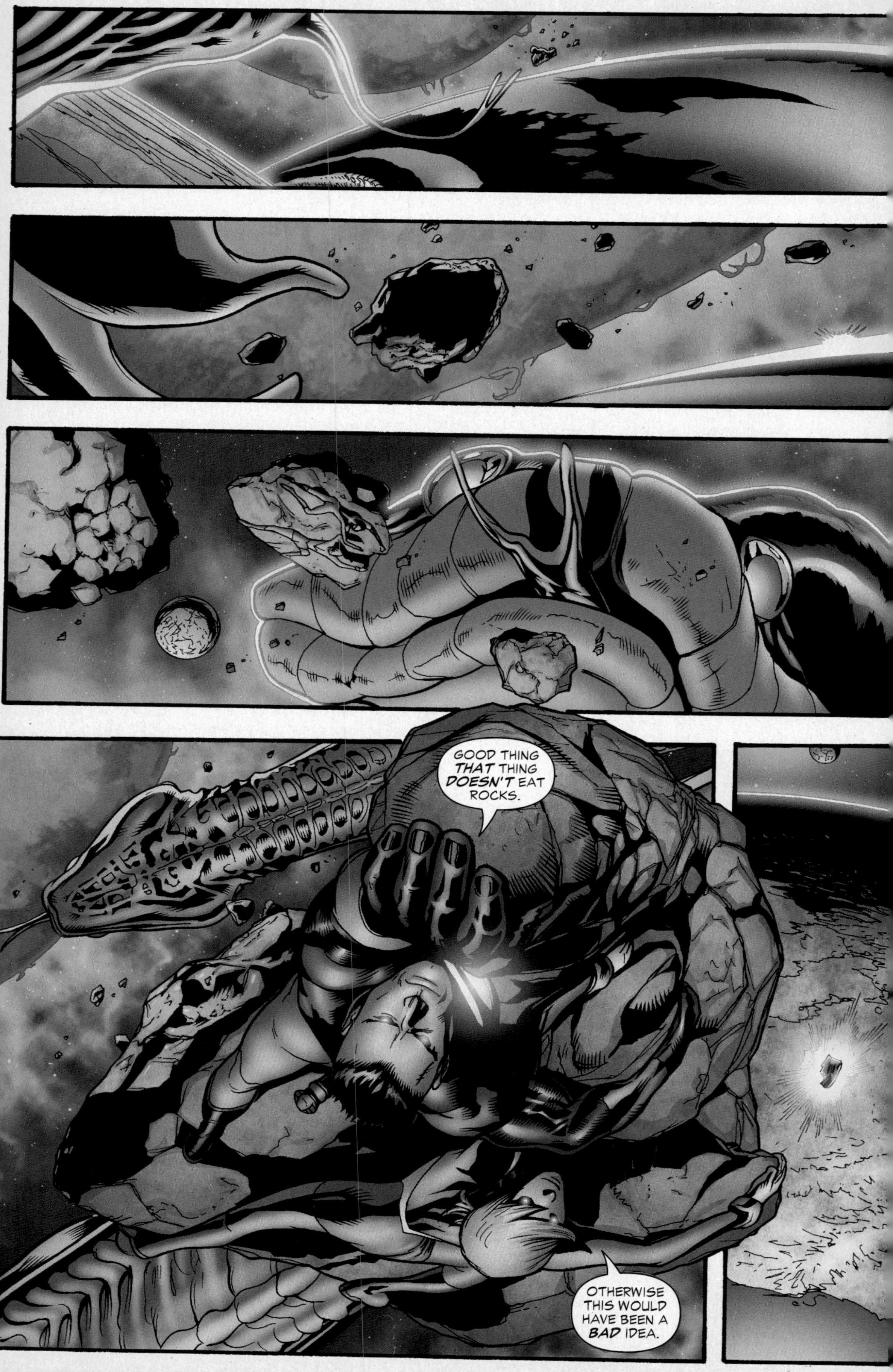
GOOD THING THAT THING DOESN'T EAT ROCKS.
OTHERWISE THIS WOULD HAVE BEEN A BAD IDEA.

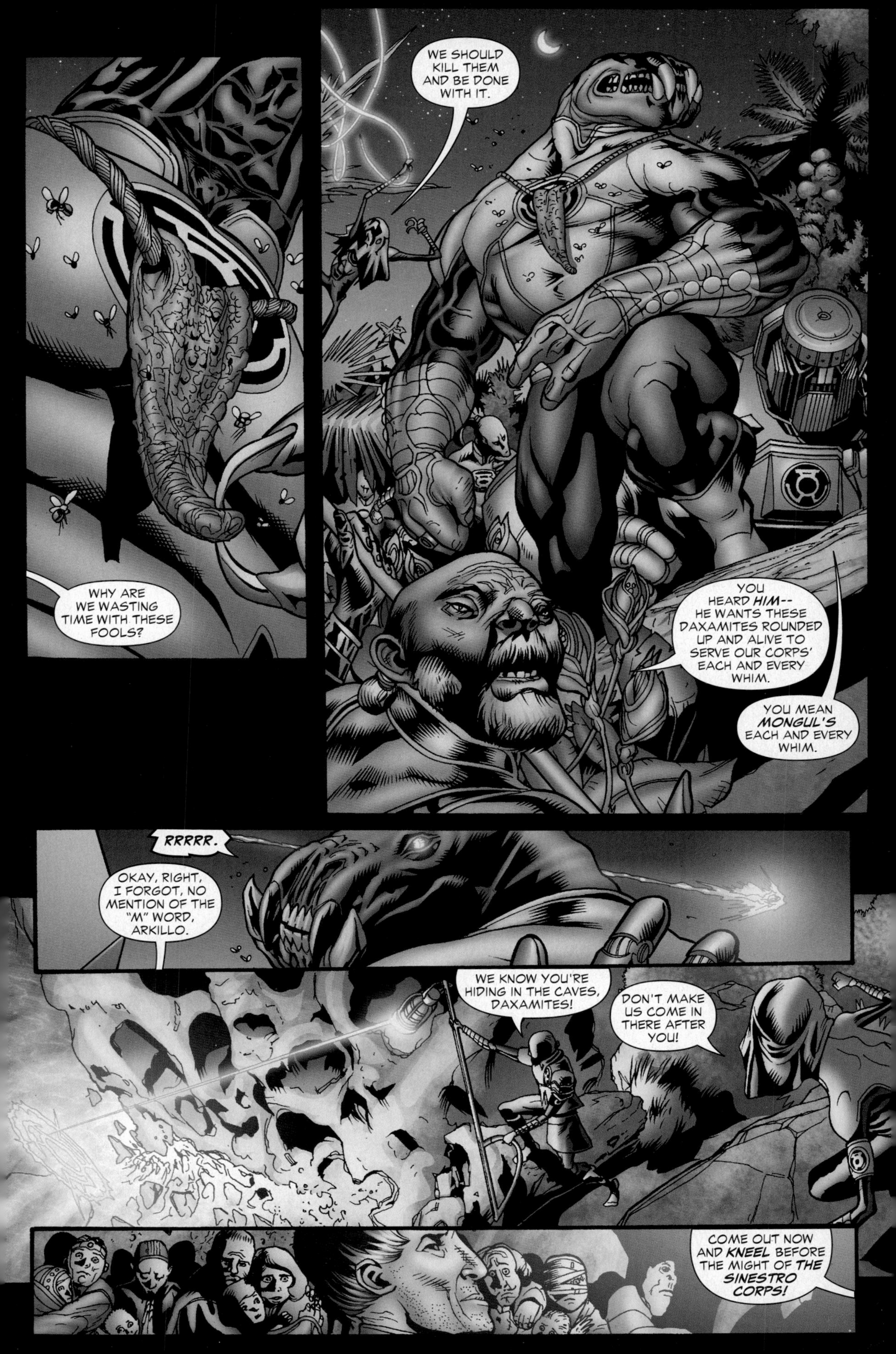
WE SHOULD KILL THEM AND BE DONE WITH IT.
WHY ARE WE WASTING TIME WITH THESE FOOLS?
YOU HEARD HIM-- HE WANTS THESE DAXAMITES ROUNDED UP AND ALIVE TO SERVE OUR CORPS' EACH AND EVERY WHIM.
YOU MEAN MONGUL'S EACH AND EVERY WHIM.
RRRRR.
OKAY, RIGHT, I FORGOT, NO MENTION OF THE "M" WORD, ARKILLO.
WE KNOW YOU'RE HIDING IN THE CAVES, DAXAMITES!
DON'T MAKE US COME IN THERE AFTER YOU!
COME OUT NOW AND KNEEL BEFORE THE MIGHT OF THE SINESTRO CORPS!

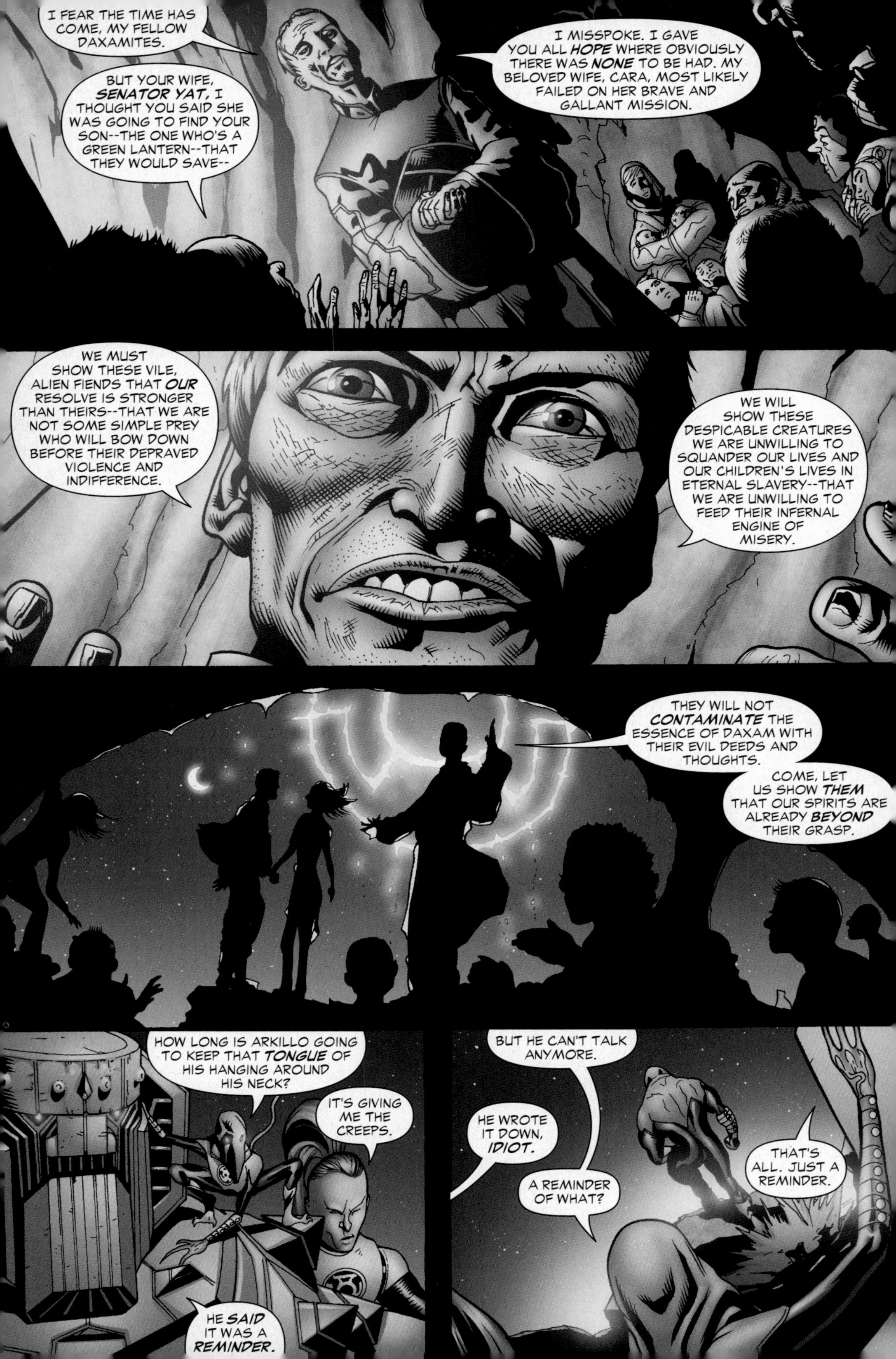
I FEAR THE TIME HAS COME, MY FELLOW DAXAMITES.
BUT YOUR WIFE, SENATOR YAT, I THOUGHT YOU SAID SHE WAS GOING TO FIND YOUR SON--THE ONE WHO'S A GREEN LANTERN--THAT THEY WOULD SAVE--
I MISSPOKE. I GAVE YOU ALL HOPE WHERE OBVIOUSLY THERE WAS NONE TO BE HAD. MY BELOVED WIFE, CARA, MOST LIKELY FAILED ON HER BRAVE AND GALLANT MISSION.
WE MUST SHOW THESE VILE, ALIEN FIENDS THAT OUR RESOLVE IS STRONGER THAN THEIRS--THAT WE ARE NOT SOME SIMPLE PREY WHO WILL BOW DOWN BEFORE THEIR DEPRAVED VIOLENCE AND INDIFFERENCE.
WE WILL SHOW THESE DESPICABLE CREATURES WE ARE UNWILLING TO SQUANDER OUR LIVES AND OUR CHILDREN'S LIVES IN ETERNAL SLAVERY--THAT WE ARE UNWILLING TO FEED THEIR INFERNAL ENGINE OF MISERY.
THEY WILL NOT CONTAMINATE THE ESSENCE OF DAXAM WITH THEIR EVIL DEEDS AND THOUGHTS.
COME, LET US SHOW THEM THAT OUR SPIRITS ARE ALREADY BEYOND THEIR GRASP.
HOW LONG IS ARKILLO GOING TO KEEP THAT TONGUE OF HIS HANGING AROUND HIS NECK?
IT'S GIVING ME THE CREEPS.
HE SAID IT WAS A REMINDER.
BUT HE CAN'T TALK ANYMORE.
HE WROTE IT DOWN, IDIOT.
A REMINDER OF WHAT?
THAT'S ALL. JUST A REMINDER.

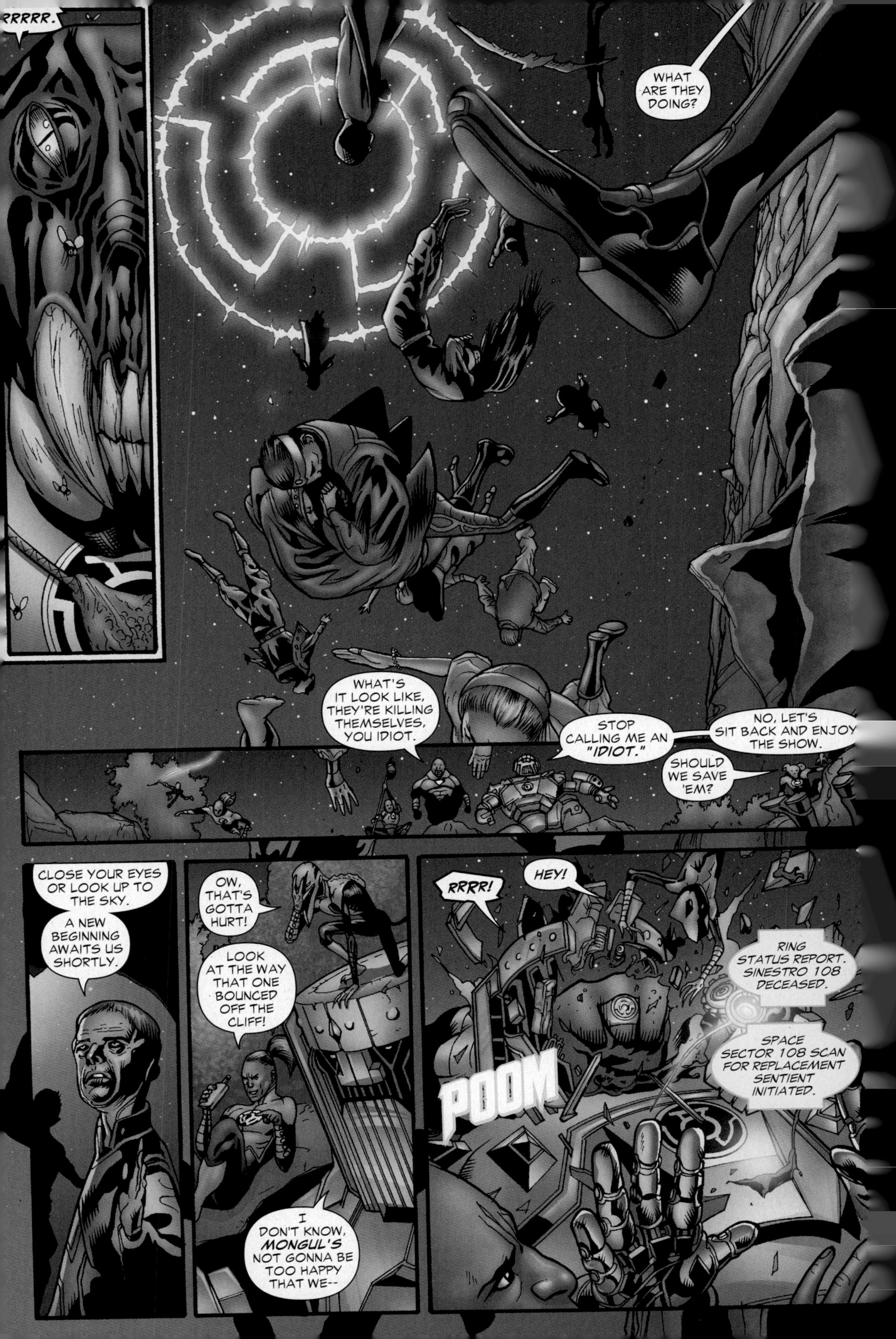
RRRRR.
WHAT ARE THEY DOING?
WHAT'S IT LOOK LIKE, THEY'RE KILLING THEMSELVES, YOU IDIOT.
STOP CALLING ME AN "IDIOT."
NO, LET'S SIT BACK AND ENJOY THE SHOW.
SHOULD WE SAVE 'EM?
CLOSE YOUR EYES OR LOOK UP TO THE SKY.
A NEW BEGINNING AWAITS US SHORTLY.
OW, THAT'S GOTTA HURT!
LOOK AT THE WAY THAT ONE BOUNCED OFF THE CLIFF!
I DON'T KNOW, MONGUL'S NOT GONNA BE TOO HAPPY THAT WE--
RRRR!
HEY!
POOM
RING STATUS REPORT. SINESTRO 108 DECEASED.
SPACE SECTOR 108 SCAN FOR REPLACEMENT SENTIENT INITIATED.

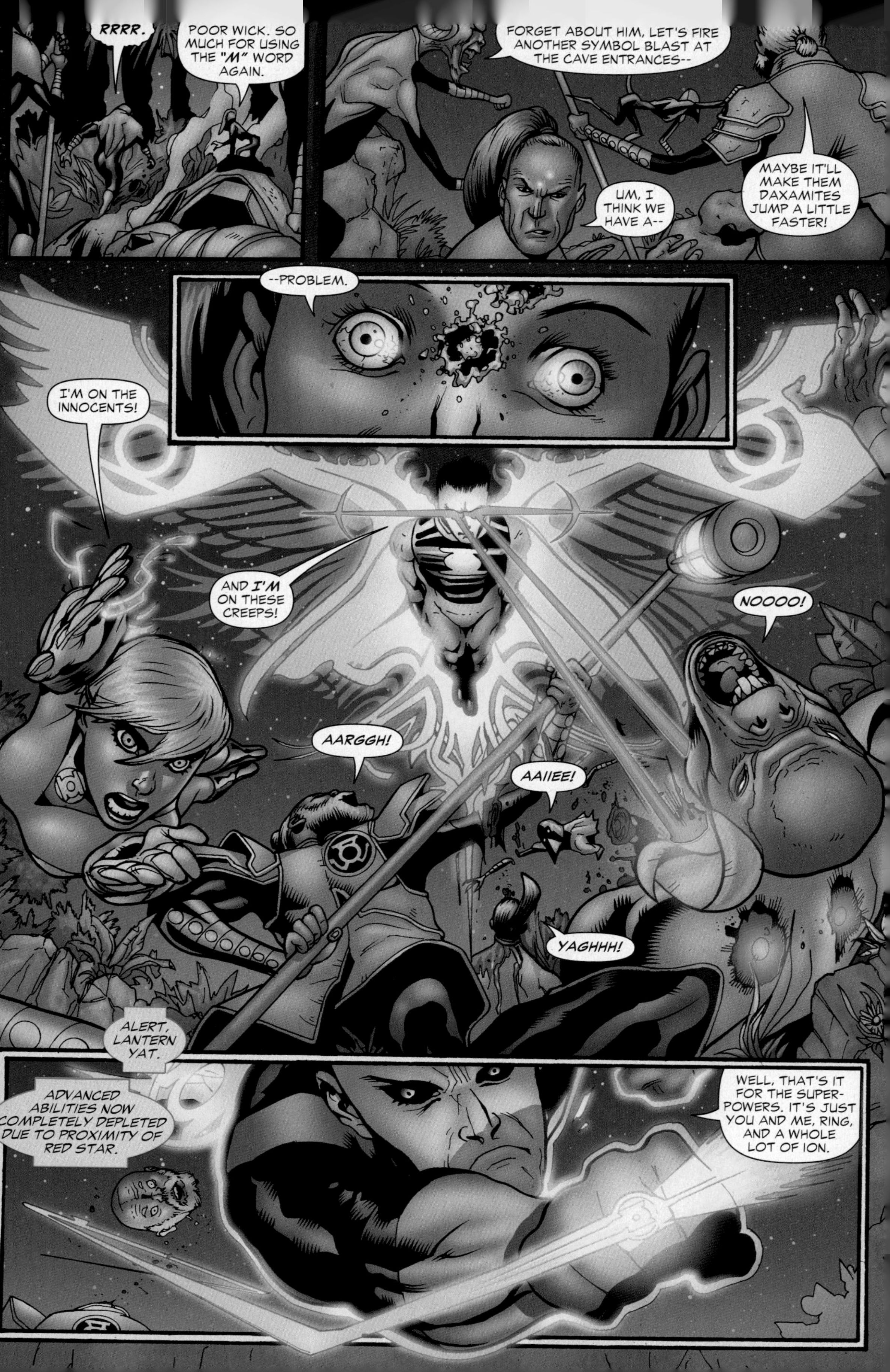
RRRR.
POOR WICK. SO MUCH FOR USING THE "M" WORD AGAIN.
FORGET ABOUT HIM, LET'S FIRE ANOTHER SYMBOL BLAST AT THE CAVE ENTRANCES--
MAYBE IT'LL MAKE THEM DAXAMITES JUMP A LITTLE FASTER!
UM, I THINK WE HAVE A--
--PROBLEM.
I'M ON THE INNOCENTS!
AND I'M ON THESE CREEPS!
NOOOO!
AARGGH!
AAIIEE!
YAGHHH!
ALERT, LANTERN YAT.
ADVANCED ABILITIES NOW COMPLETELY DEPLETED DUE TO PROXIMITY OF RED STAR.
WELL, THAT'S IT FOR THE SUPER-POWERS. IT'S JUST YOU AND ME, RING, AND A WHOLE LOT OF ION.

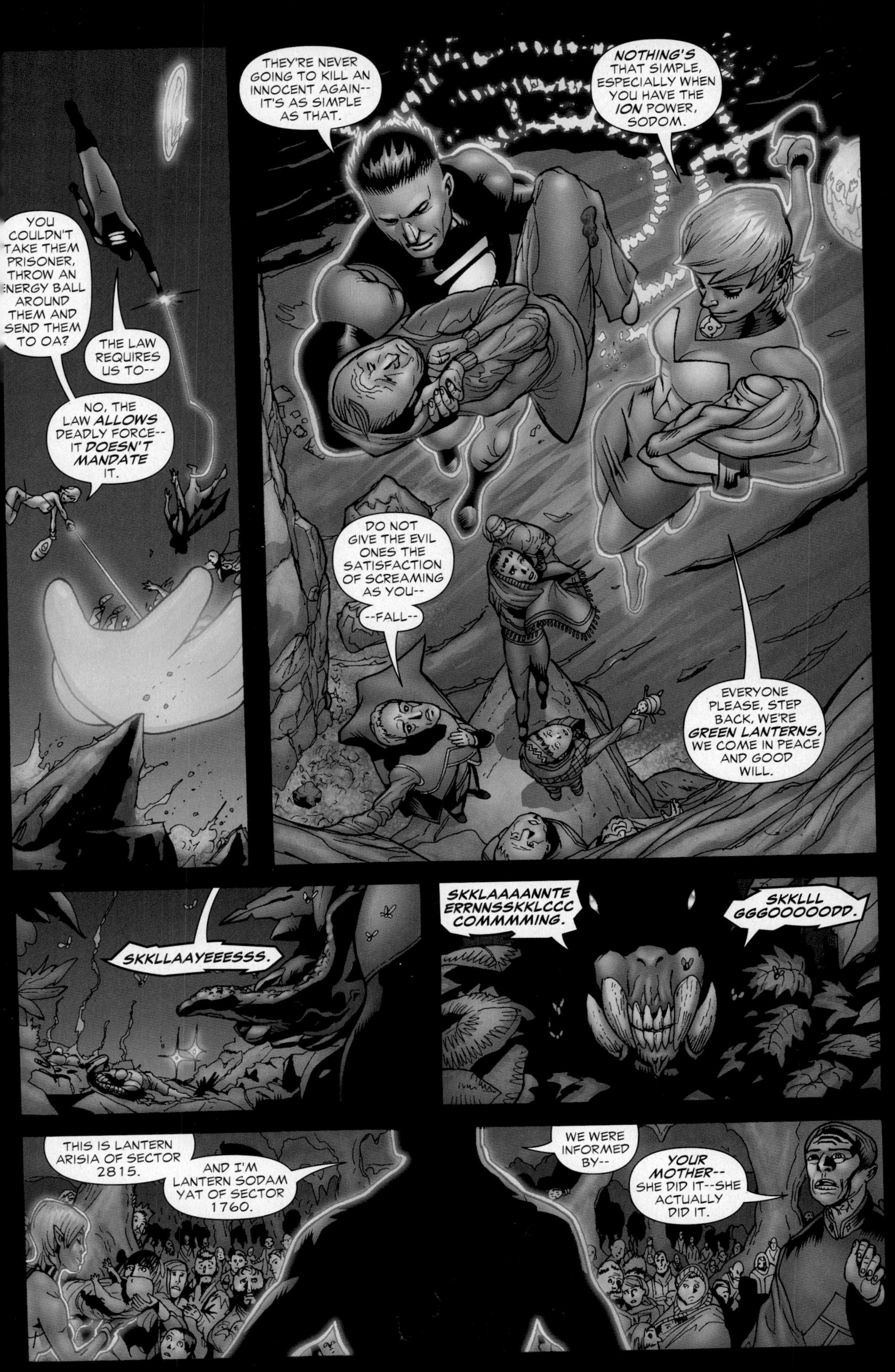
YOU COULDN'T TAKE THEM PRISONER, THROW AN ENERGY BALL AROUND THEM AND SEND THEM TO OA?
THE LAW REQUIRES US TO--
NO, THE LAW ALLOWS DEADLY FORCE-- IT DOESN'T MANDATE IT.
THEY'RE NEVER GOING TO KILL AN INNOCENT AGAIN-- IT'S AS SIMPLE AS THAT.
NOTHING'S THAT SIMPLE, ESPECIALLY WHEN YOU HAVE THE ION POWER, SODOM.
DO NOT GIVE THE EVIL ONES THE SATISFACTION OF SCREAMING AS YOU--
--FALL--
EVERYONE PLEASE, STEP BACK, WE'RE GREEN LANTERNS, WE COME IN PEACE AND GOOD WILL.
SKKLLAAYEEESSS.
SKKLAAAANNTE ERRNNSSKKLCCC COMMMMING.
SKKLLL GGGOOOOODD.
THIS IS LANTERN ARISIA OF SECTOR 2815.
AND I'M LANTERN SODAM YAT OF SECTOR 1760.
WE WERE INFORMED BY--
YOUR MOTHER-- SHE DID IT--SHE ACTUALLY DID IT.

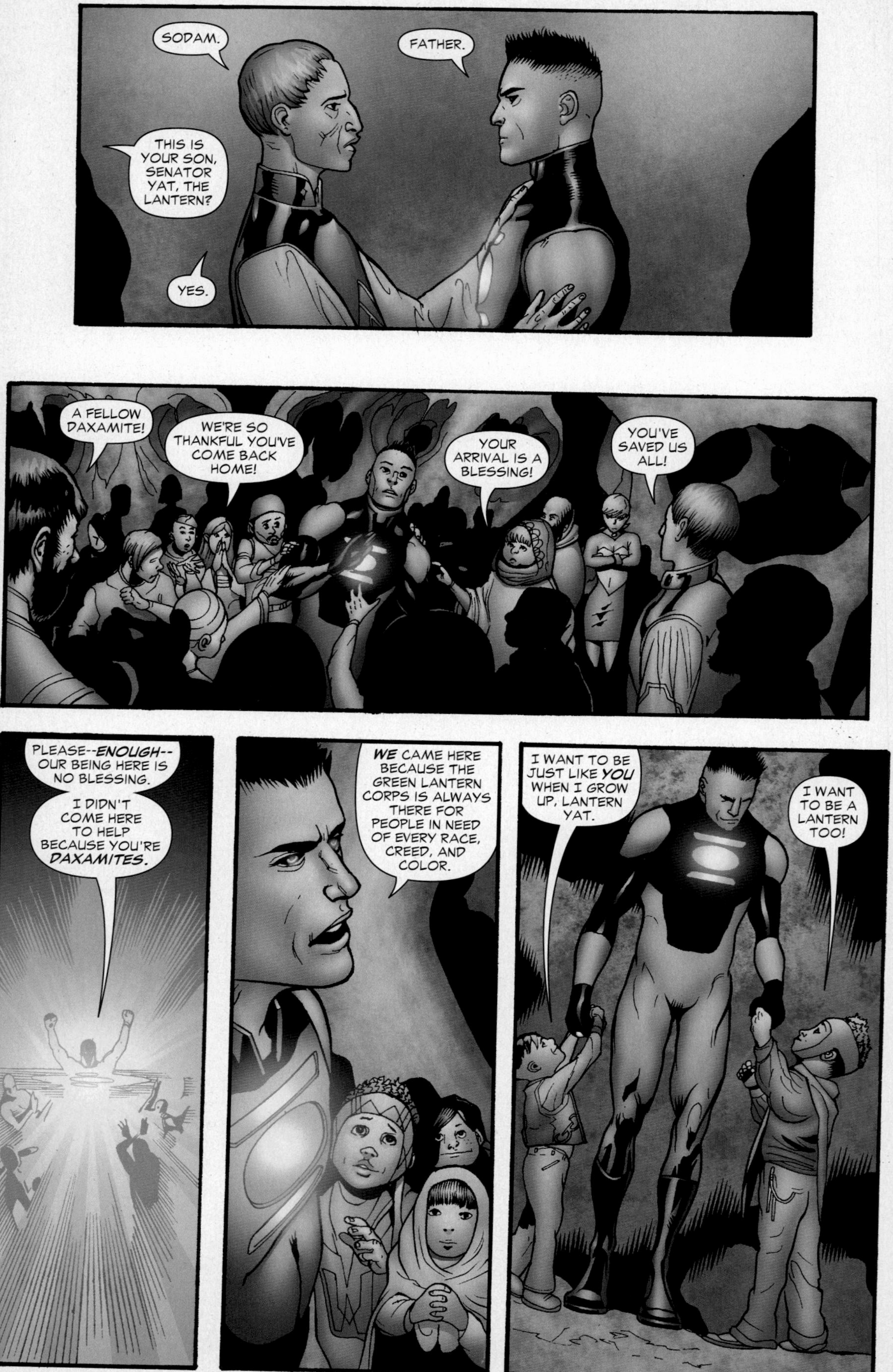
SODAM.
FATHER.
THIS IS YOUR SON, SENATOR YAT, THE LANTERN?
YES.
A FELLOW DAXAMITE!
WE'RE SO THANKFUL YOU'VE COME BACK HOME!
YOUR ARRIVAL IS A BLESSING!
YOU'VE SAVED US ALL!
PLEASE--*ENOUGH*--OUR BEING HERE IS NO BLESSING.
I DIDN'T COME HERE TO HELP BECAUSE YOU'RE *DAXAMITES.*
WE CAME HERE BECAUSE THE GREEN LANTERN CORPS IS ALWAYS THERE FOR PEOPLE IN NEED OF EVERY RACE, CREED, AND COLOR.
I WANT TO BE JUST LIKE *YOU* WHEN I GROW UP, LANTERN YAT.
I WANT TO BE A LANTERN TOO!

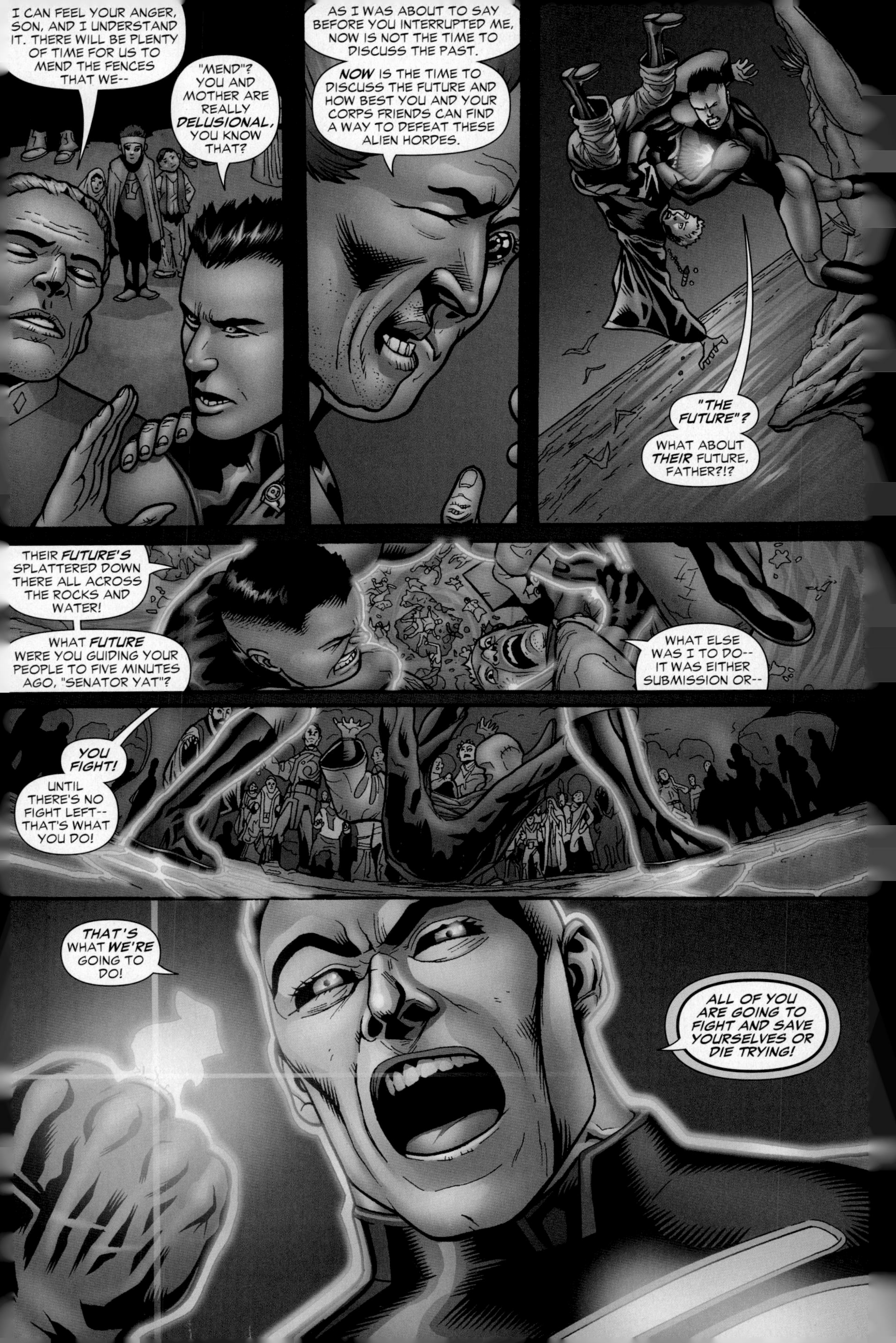
I CAN FEEL YOUR ANGER, SON, AND I UNDERSTAND IT. THERE WILL BE PLENTY OF TIME FOR US TO MEND THE FENCES THAT WE--
"MEND"? YOU AND MOTHER ARE REALLY DELUSIONAL, YOU KNOW THAT?
AS I WAS ABOUT TO SAY BEFORE YOU INTERRUPTED ME, NOW IS NOT THE TIME TO DISCUSS THE PAST.
NOW IS THE TIME TO DISCUSS THE FUTURE AND HOW BEST YOU AND YOUR CORPS FRIENDS CAN FIND A WAY TO DEFEAT THESE ALIEN HORDES.
"THE FUTURE"?
WHAT ABOUT THEIR FUTURE, FATHER?!?
THEIR FUTURE'S SPLATTERED DOWN THERE ALL ACROSS THE ROCKS AND WATER!
WHAT FUTURE WERE YOU GUIDING YOUR PEOPLE TO FIVE MINUTES AGO, "SENATOR YAT"?
WHAT ELSE WAS I TO DO-- IT WAS EITHER SUBMISSION OR--
YOU FIGHT!
UNTIL THERE'S NO FIGHT LEFT-- THAT'S WHAT YOU DO!
THAT'S WHAT WE'RE GOING TO DO!
ALL OF YOU ARE GOING TO FIGHT AND SAVE YOURSELVES OR DIE TRYING!

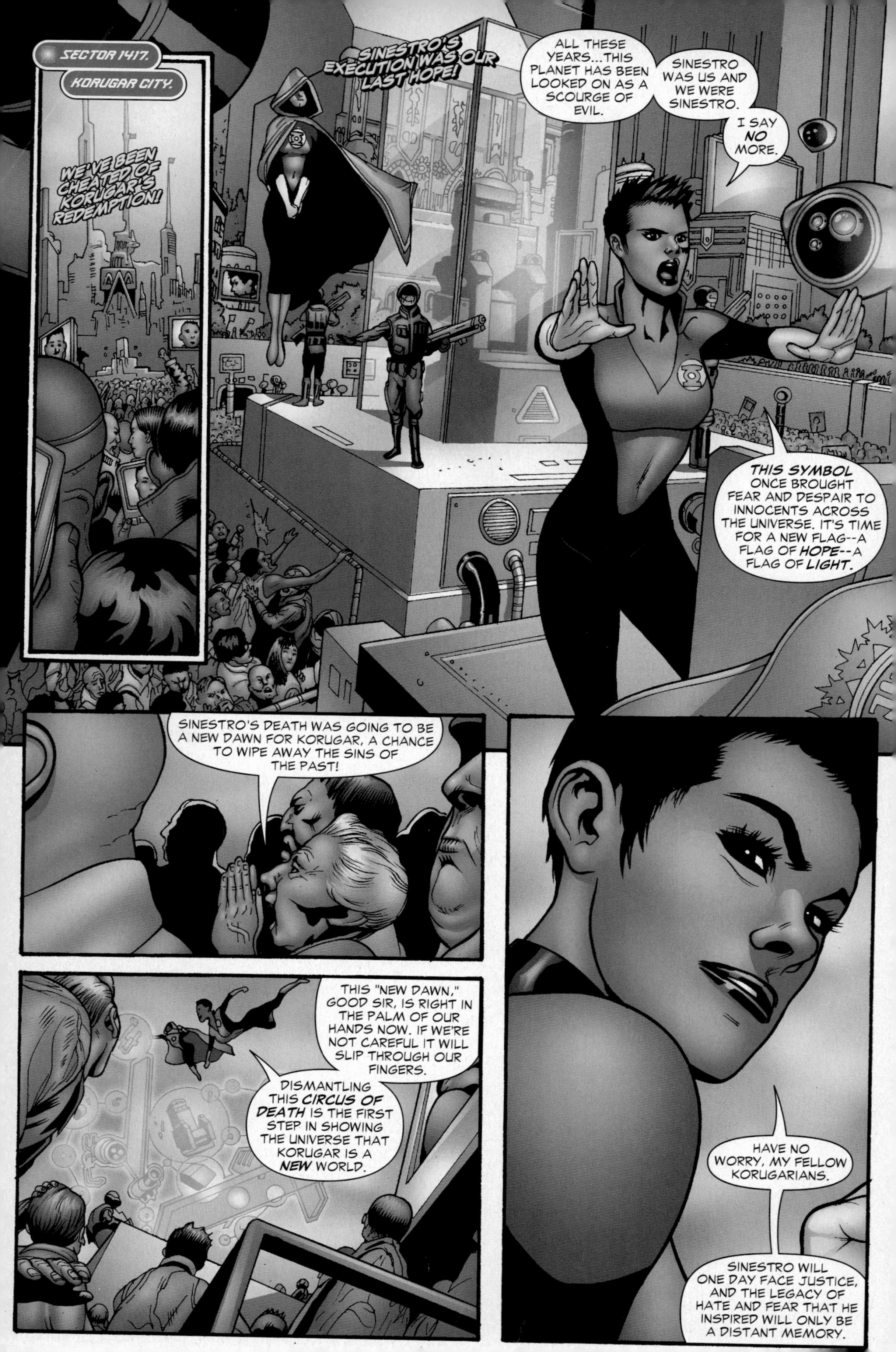

SECTOR 1417.
KORUGAR CITY.
WE'VE BEEN CHEATED OF KORUGAR'S REDEMPTION!
SINESTRO'S EXECUTION WAS OUR LAST HOPE!
ALL THESE YEARS... THIS PLANET HAS BEEN LOOKED ON AS A SCOURGE OF EVIL.
SINESTRO WAS US AND WE WERE SINESTRO.
I SAY NO MORE.
THIS SYMBOL ONCE BROUGHT FEAR AND DESPAIR TO INNOCENTS ACROSS THE UNIVERSE. IT'S TIME FOR A NEW FLAG--A FLAG OF HOPE--A FLAG OF LIGHT.
SINESTRO'S DEATH WAS GOING TO BE A NEW DAWN FOR KORUGAR, A CHANCE TO WIPE AWAY THE SINS OF THE PAST!
THIS "NEW DAWN," GOOD SIR, IS RIGHT IN THE PALM OF OUR HANDS NOW. IF WE'RE NOT CAREFUL IT WILL SLIP THROUGH OUR FINGERS.
DISMANTLING THIS CIRCUS OF DEATH IS THE FIRST STEP IN SHOWING THE UNIVERSE THAT KORUGAR IS A NEW WORLD.
HAVE NO WORRY, MY FELLOW KORUGARIANS.
SINESTRO WILL ONE DAY FACE JUSTICE, AND THE LEGACY OF HATE AND FEAR THAT HE INSPIRED WILL ONLY BE A DISTANT MEMORY.

...WELL, I'M JUST HAPPY WE CAN PUT AWAY THESE INSTRUMENTS OF DEATH FOR THE TIME BEING, IOLANDE.

THE *BLOODLUST* IN THAT CROWD WAS QUITE PALPABLE, SORANIK.

THE WAY YOU REASSURED THEM WAS IMPRESSIVE.

THANKS, IOLANDE.

I JUST SAID WHAT WAS IN MY HEART.

AS DID THEY, I'M AFRAID, SORANIK.

WHAT IS *THAT* SUPPOSED TO MEAN?

HONESTLY--AND I DON'T MEAN TO HURT YOUR FEELINGS--I THINK THE ONLY WAY YOUR PLANET WILL EVER MOVE FORWARD IS TO HAVE THAT BLOODLUST SATIATED.

THEY WANT SINESTRO TO PAY--THEY *NEED* SINESTRO TO PAY FOR HIS SINS AND THEIRS, OTHERWISE A DARK, MALIGNANT SPOT WILL ALWAYS REMAIN--EATING AWAY AT YOUR PEOPLE'S SPIRITS, ALWAYS READY TO UNDO WHATEVER FUTURE THEY BEGIN TO BUILD FOR THEMSELVES.

ONLY *SINESTRO'S DEATH* WILL FREE THEM.

HOW CAN YOU *CONDONE* THE DEATH PENALTY AFTER WATCHING YOUR OWN BROTHER BE BEHEADED BACK ON BETRASSUS?

MY BROTHER, RAGNAR, COMMITTED EVIL DEEDS--NOT JUST AGAINST HIS OWN FAMILY, BUT AGAINST HIS OWN PEOPLE. HE EVEN TOOK THE LIFE OF MYRRT, YOUR OLD PARTNER.

DID I LOVE RAGNAR? YES, OF COURSE, BUT HE WAS A BLIGHT ON OUR RACE AND PLANET.

HIS *SANCTIONED* DEATH SERVED THE GREATER GOOD AND--

ZZRAP

IOLANDE?

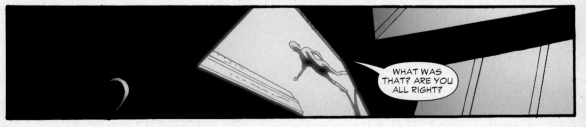

WHAT WAS THAT? ARE YOU ALL RIGHT?

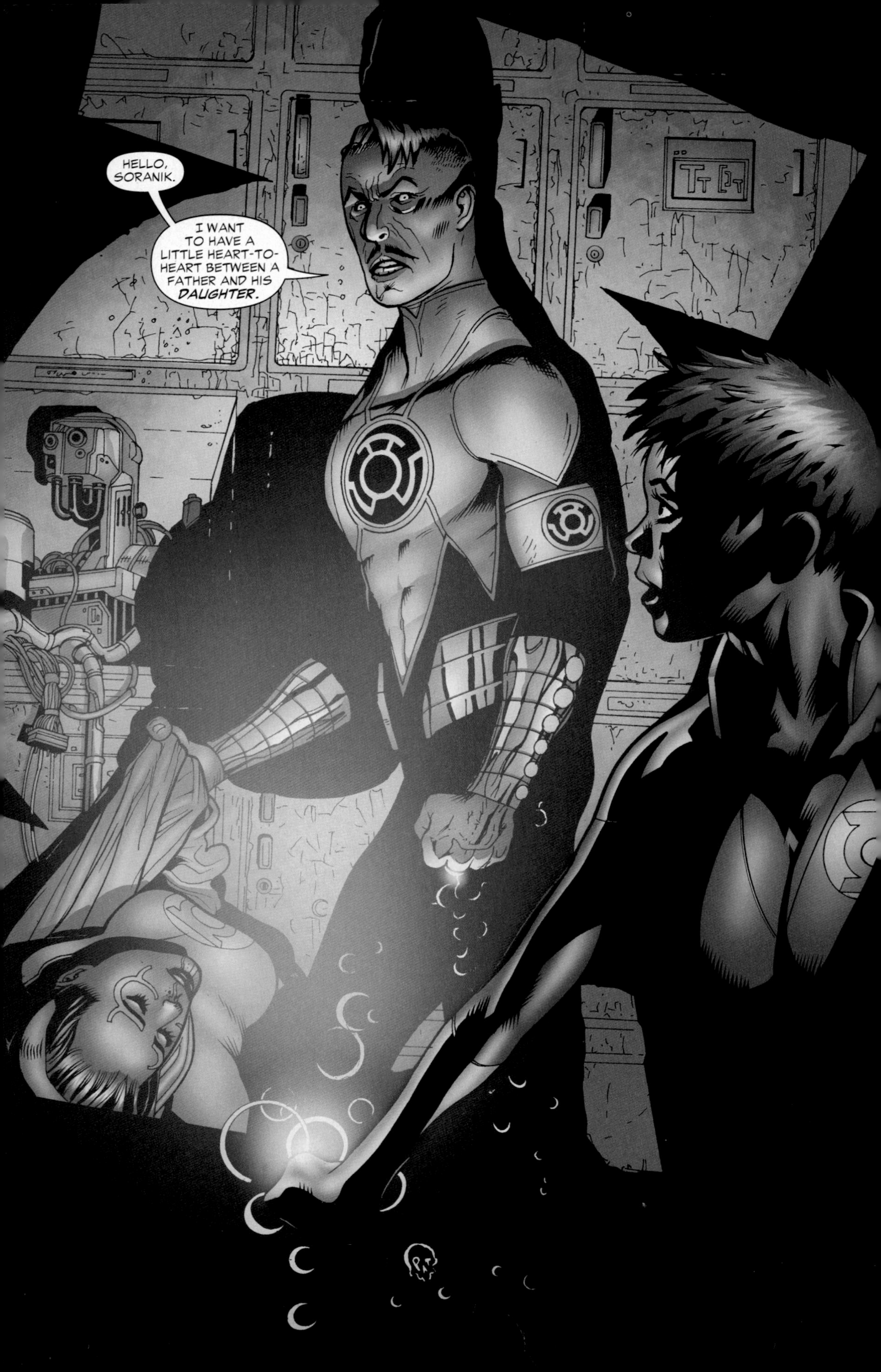
HELLO, SORANIK.
I WANT TO HAVE A LITTLE HEART-TO-HEART BETWEEN A FATHER AND HIS *DAUGHTER*.

GREEN LANTERN CORPS #36
Cover by Patrick Gleason, Rebecca Buchman & Randy Mayor

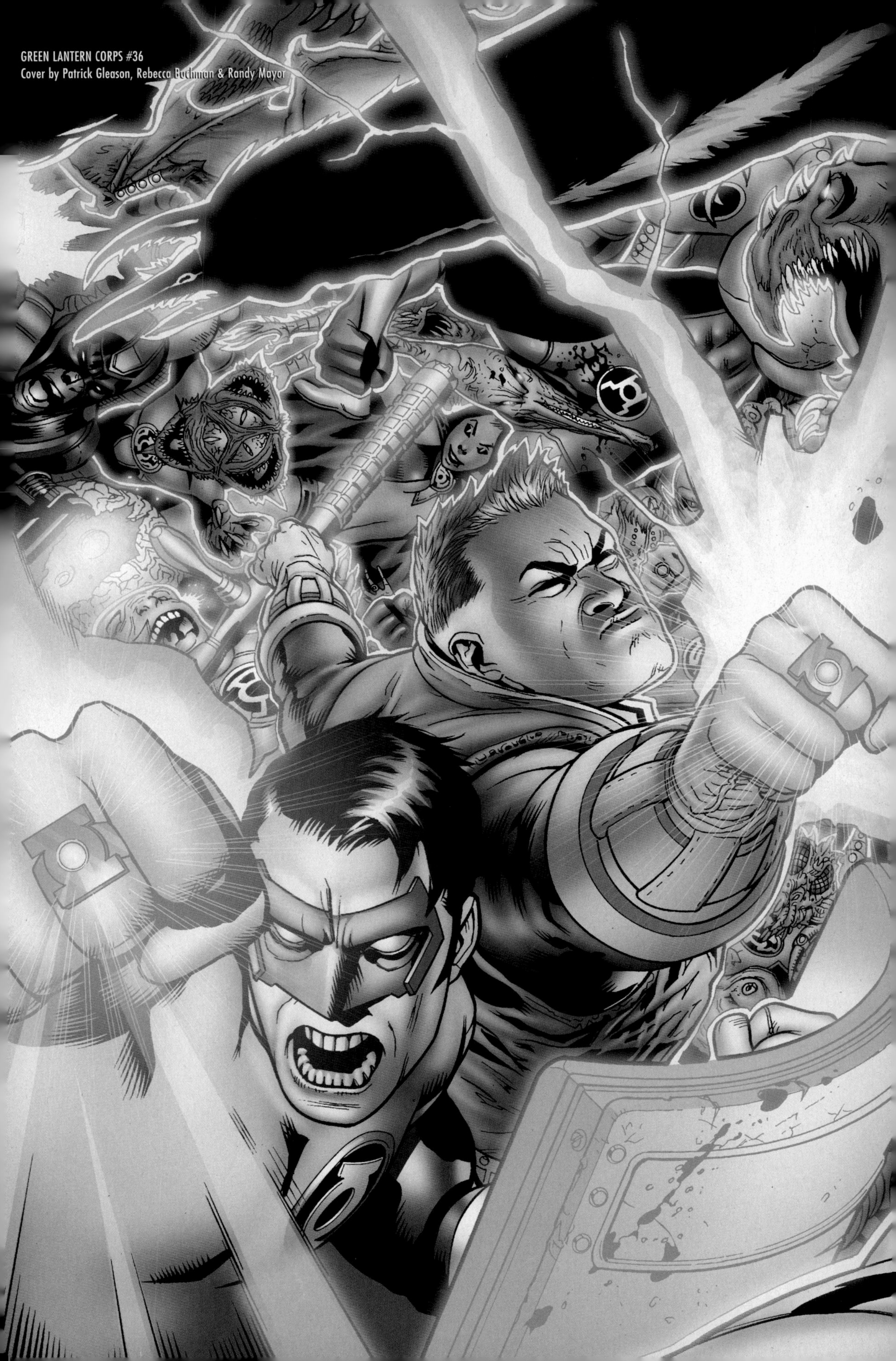

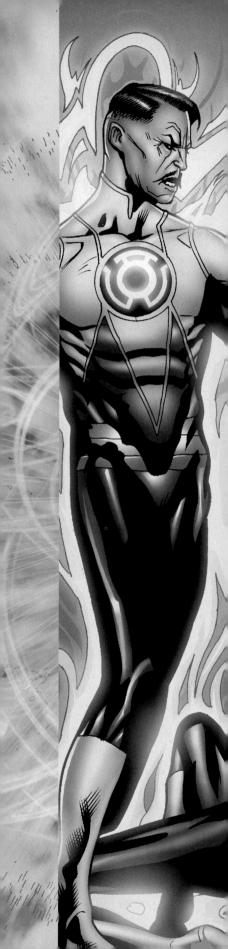

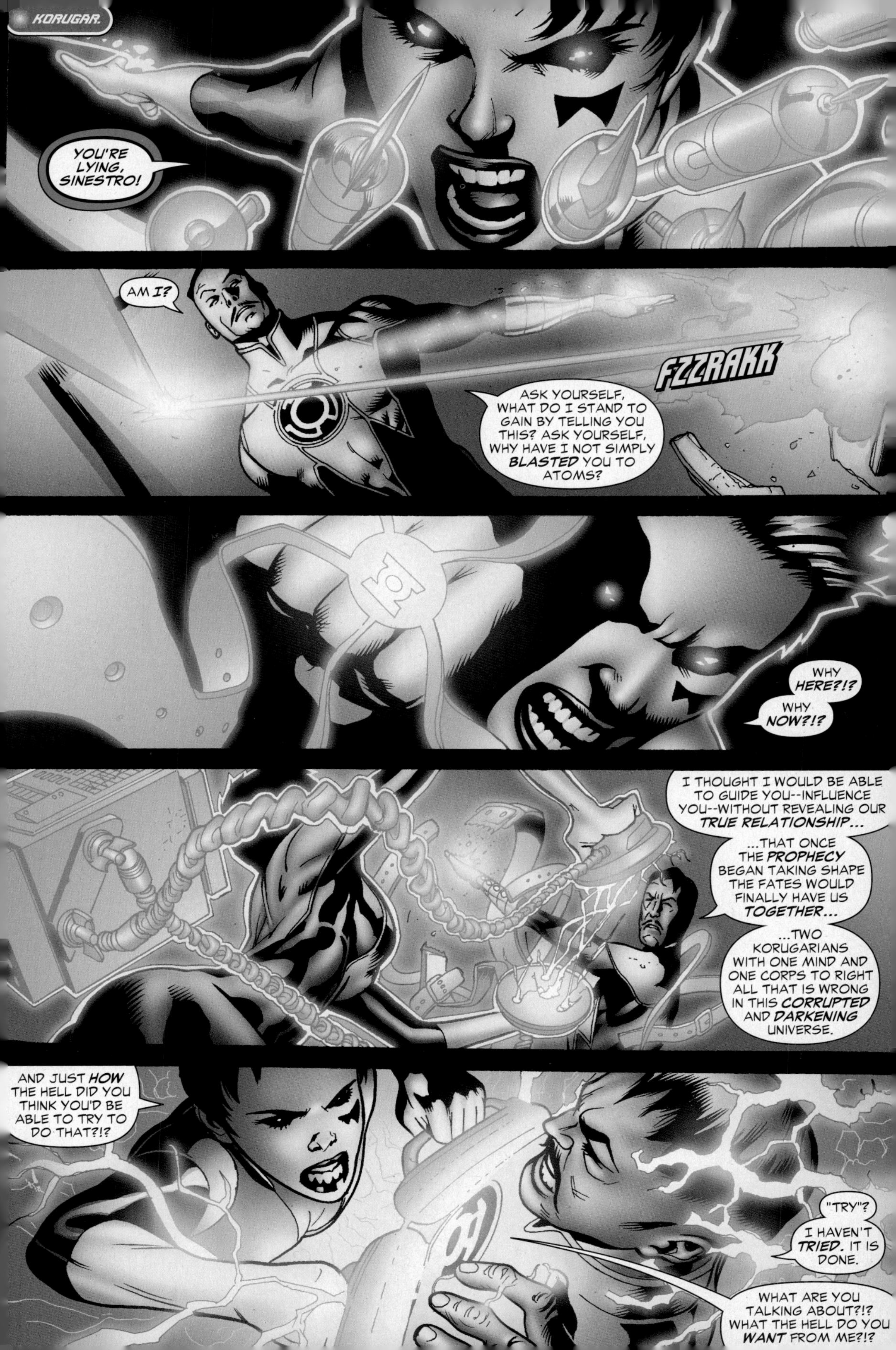
KORUGAR.
YOU'RE LYING, SINESTRO!
AM I?
FZZRAKK
ASK YOURSELF, WHAT DO I STAND TO GAIN BY TELLING YOU THIS? ASK YOURSELF, WHY HAVE I NOT SIMPLY BLASTED YOU TO ATOMS?
WHY HERE?!?
WHY NOW?!?
I THOUGHT I WOULD BE ABLE TO GUIDE YOU--INFLUENCE YOU--WITHOUT REVEALING OUR TRUE RELATIONSHIP...
...THAT ONCE THE PROPHECY BEGAN TAKING SHAPE THE FATES WOULD FINALLY HAVE US TOGETHER...
...TWO KORUGARIANS WITH ONE MIND AND ONE CORPS TO RIGHT ALL THAT IS WRONG IN THIS CORRUPTED AND DARKENING UNIVERSE.
AND JUST HOW THE HELL DID YOU THINK YOU'D BE ABLE TO TRY TO DO THAT?!?
"TRY"?
I HAVEN'T TRIED. IT IS DONE.
WHAT ARE YOU TALKING ABOUT?!? WHAT THE HELL DO YOU WANT FROM ME?!?

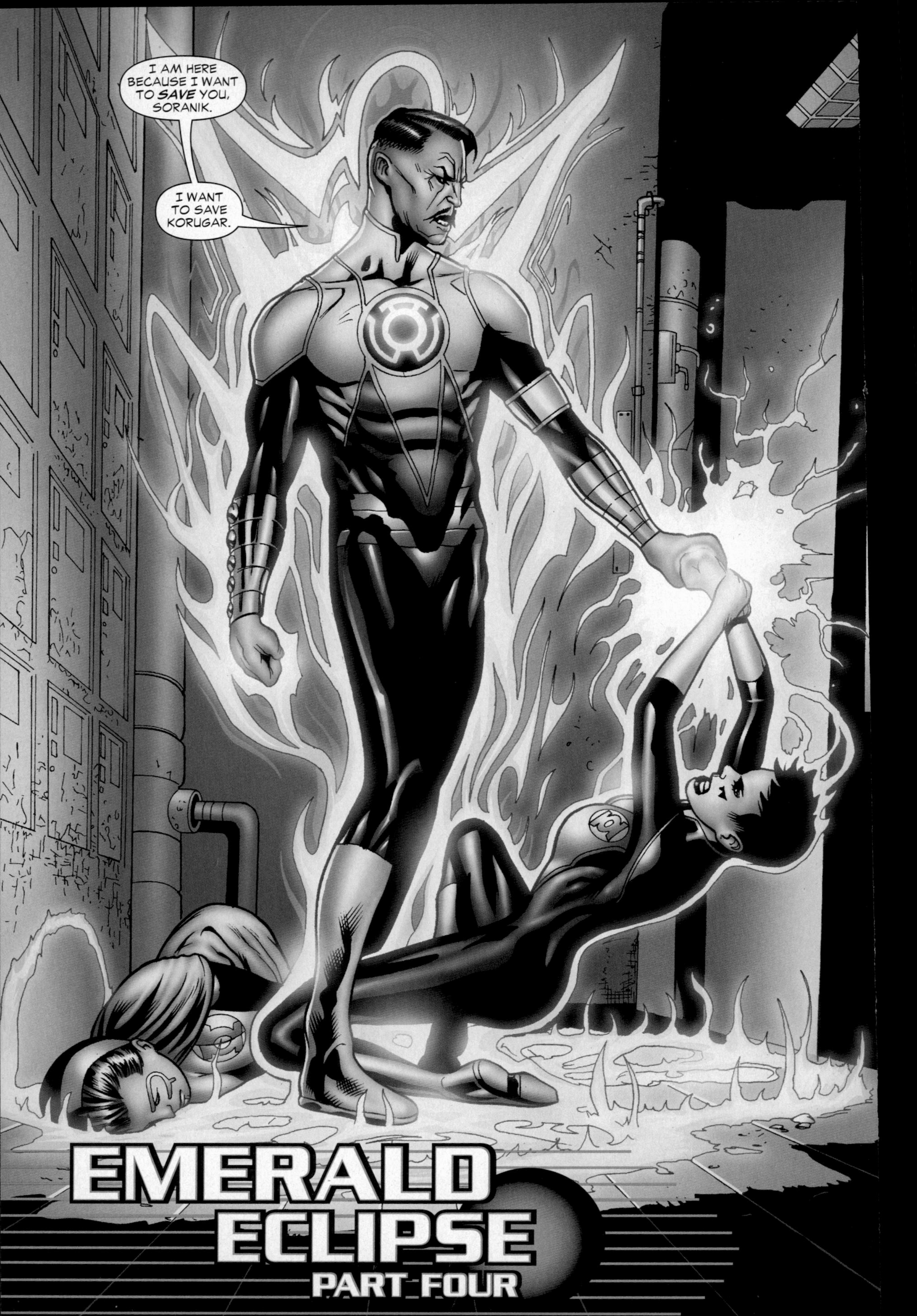
I AM HERE BECAUSE I WANT TO SAVE YOU, SORANIK.
I WANT TO SAVE KORUGAR.
EMERALD ECLIPSE
PART FOUR

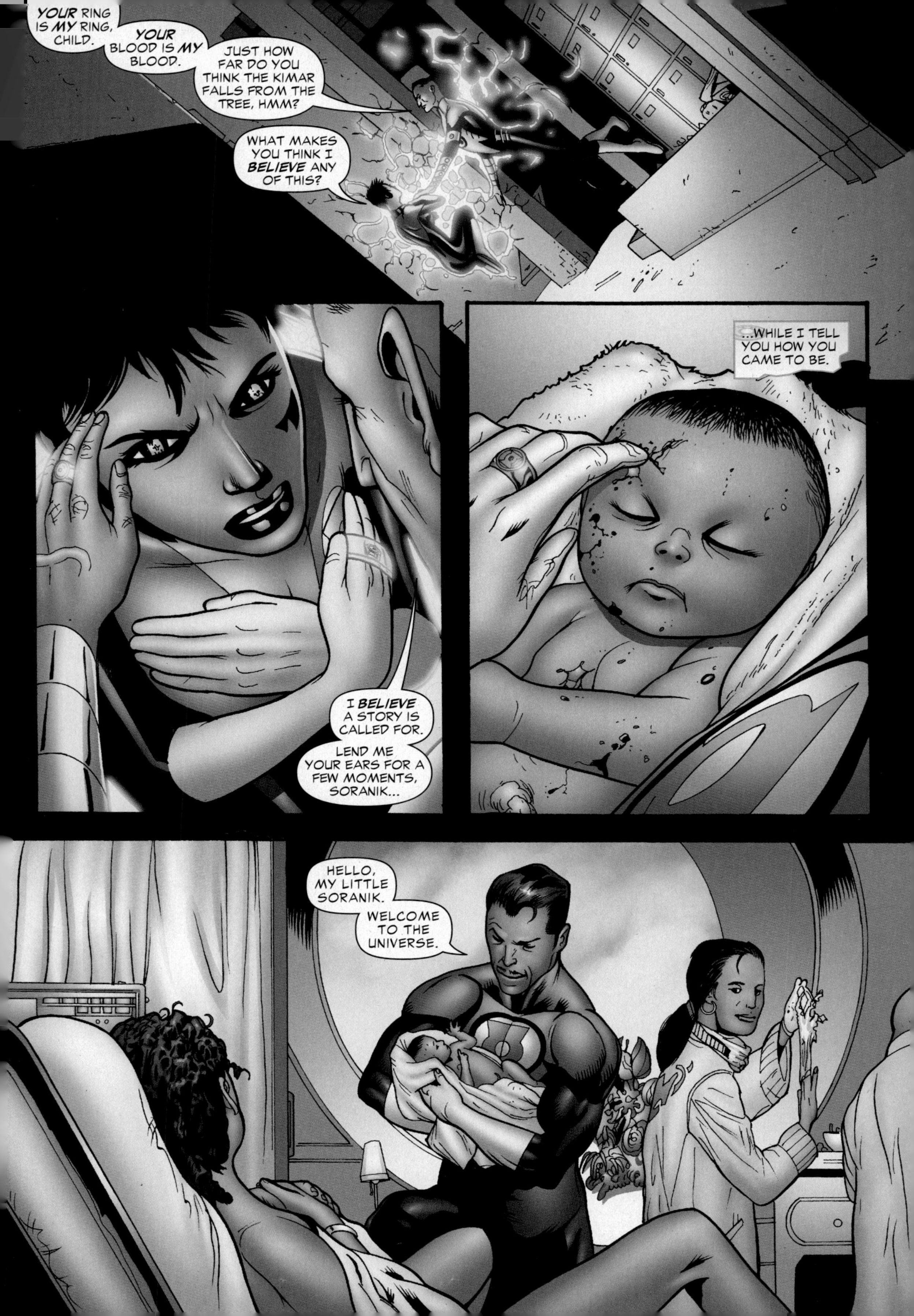
YOUR RING IS MY RING, CHILD.
YOUR BLOOD IS MY BLOOD.
JUST HOW FAR DO YOU THINK THE KIMAR FALLS FROM THE TREE, HMM?
WHAT MAKES YOU THINK I BELIEVE ANY OF THIS?
I BELIEVE A STORY IS CALLED FOR.
LEND ME YOUR EARS FOR A FEW MOMENTS, SORANIK...
...WHILE I TELL YOU HOW YOU CAME TO BE.
HELLO, MY LITTLE SORANIK.
WELCOME TO THE UNIVERSE.

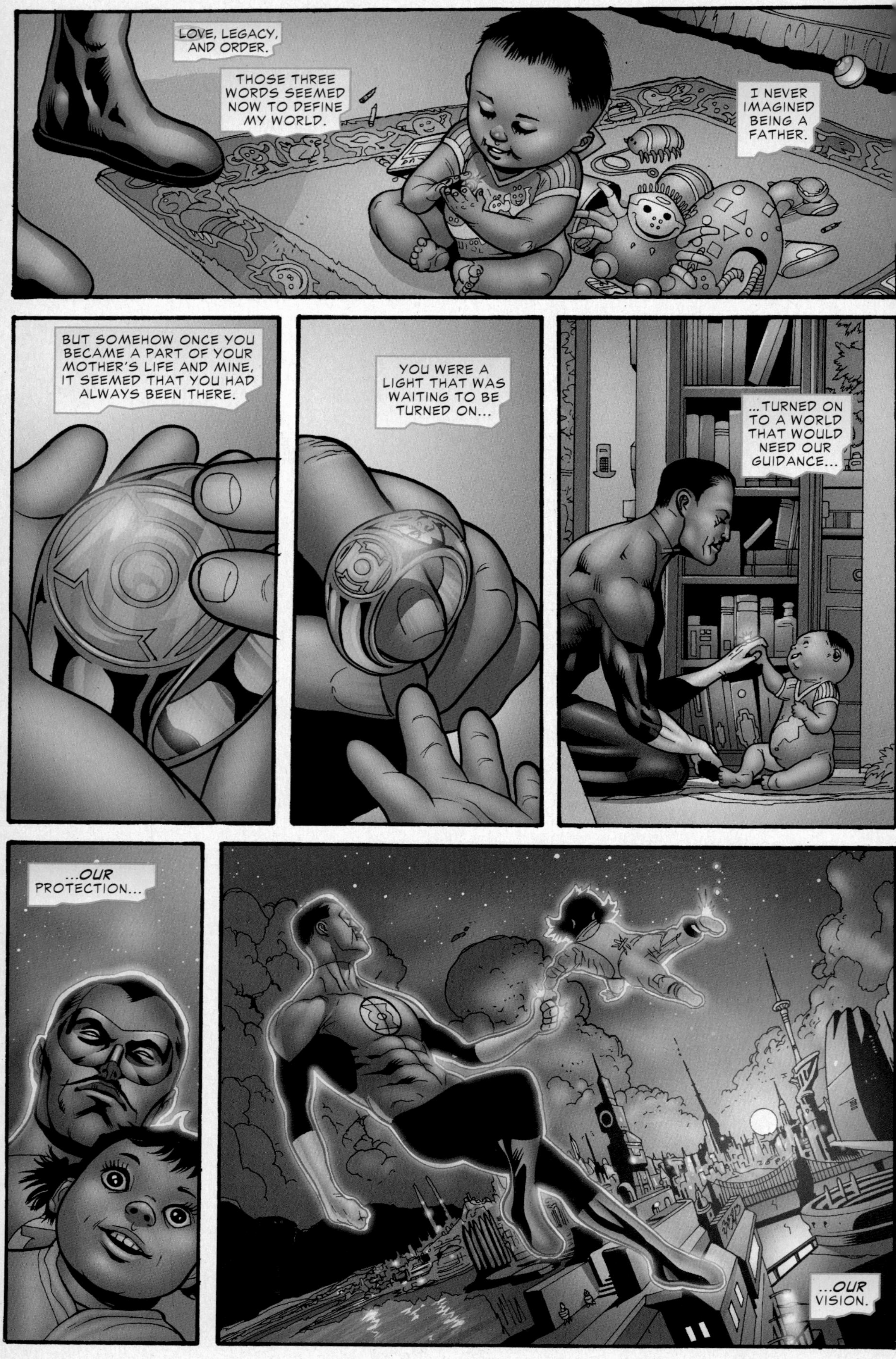

LOVE, LEGACY, AND ORDER.
THOSE THREE WORDS SEEMED NOW TO DEFINE MY WORLD.
I NEVER IMAGINED BEING A FATHER.
BUT SOMEHOW ONCE YOU BECAME A PART OF YOUR MOTHER'S LIFE AND MINE, IT SEEMED THAT YOU HAD ALWAYS BEEN THERE.
YOU WERE A LIGHT THAT WAS WAITING TO BE TURNED ON...
...TURNED ON TO A WORLD THAT WOULD NEED OUR GUIDANCE...
...*OUR* PROTECTION...
...*OUR* VISION.

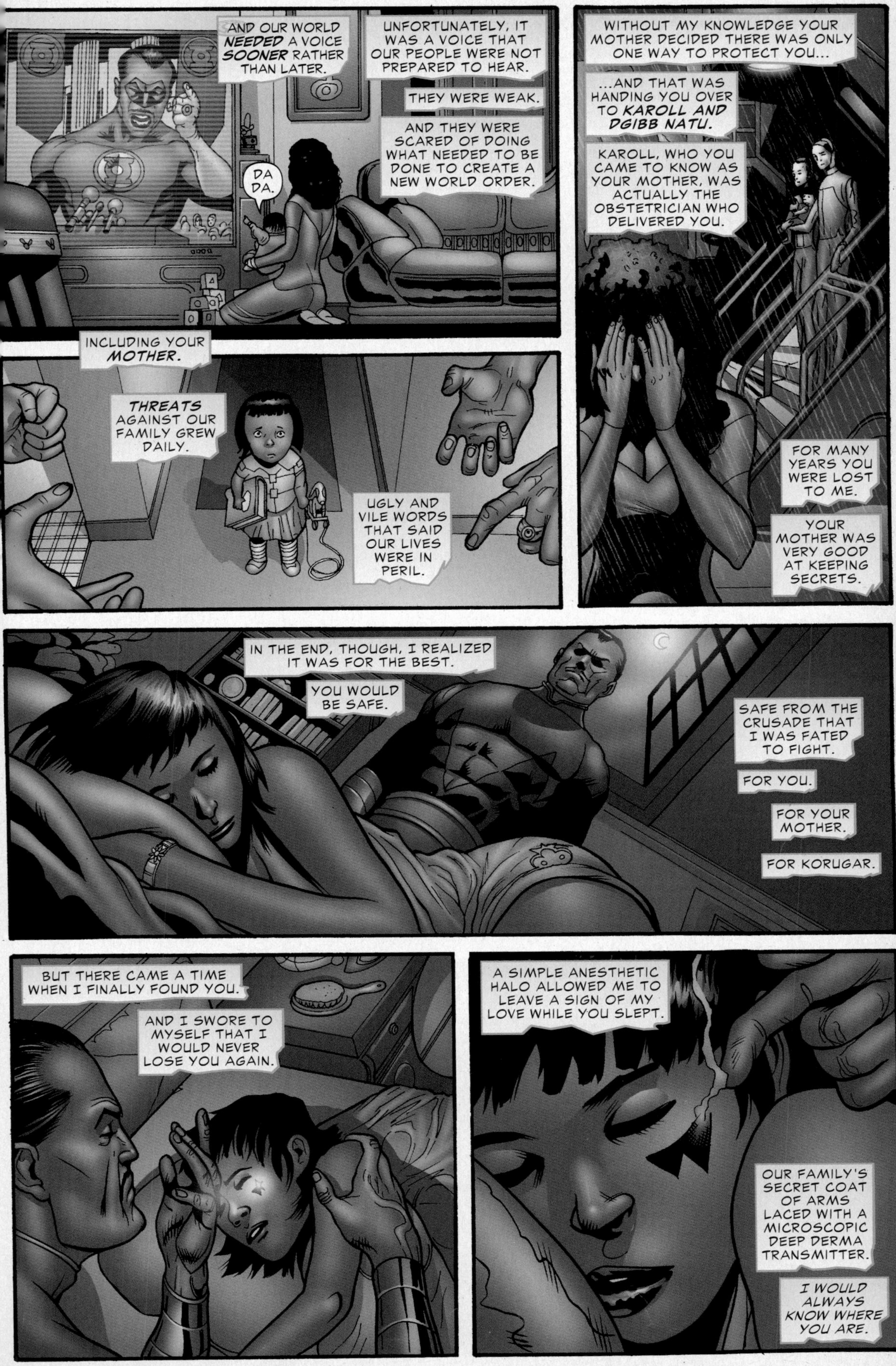
AND OUR WORLD NEEDED A VOICE SOONER RATHER THAN LATER.
UNFORTUNATELY, IT WAS A VOICE THAT OUR PEOPLE WERE NOT PREPARED TO HEAR.
THEY WERE WEAK.
AND THEY WERE SCARED OF DOING WHAT NEEDED TO BE DONE TO CREATE A NEW WORLD ORDER.
DA DA.
INCLUDING YOUR MOTHER.
THREATS AGAINST OUR FAMILY GREW DAILY.
UGLY AND VILE WORDS THAT SAID OUR LIVES WERE IN PERIL.
WITHOUT MY KNOWLEDGE YOUR MOTHER DECIDED THERE WAS ONLY ONE WAY TO PROTECT YOU...
...AND THAT WAS HANDING YOU OVER TO KAROLL AND DGIBB NATU.
KAROLL, WHO YOU CAME TO KNOW AS YOUR MOTHER, WAS ACTUALLY THE OBSTETRICIAN WHO DELIVERED YOU.
FOR MANY YEARS YOU WERE LOST TO ME.
YOUR MOTHER WAS VERY GOOD AT KEEPING SECRETS.
IN THE END, THOUGH, I REALIZED IT WAS FOR THE BEST.
YOU WOULD BE SAFE.
SAFE FROM THE CRUSADE THAT I WAS FATED TO FIGHT.
FOR YOU.
FOR YOUR MOTHER.
FOR KORUGAR.
BUT THERE CAME A TIME WHEN I FINALLY FOUND YOU.
AND I SWORE TO MYSELF THAT I WOULD NEVER LOSE YOU AGAIN.
A SIMPLE ANESTHETIC HALO ALLOWED ME TO LEAVE A SIGN OF MY LOVE WHILE YOU SLEPT.
OUR FAMILY'S SECRET COAT OF ARMS LACED WITH A MICROSCOPIC DEEP DERMA TRANSMITTER.
I WOULD ALWAYS KNOW WHERE YOU ARE.

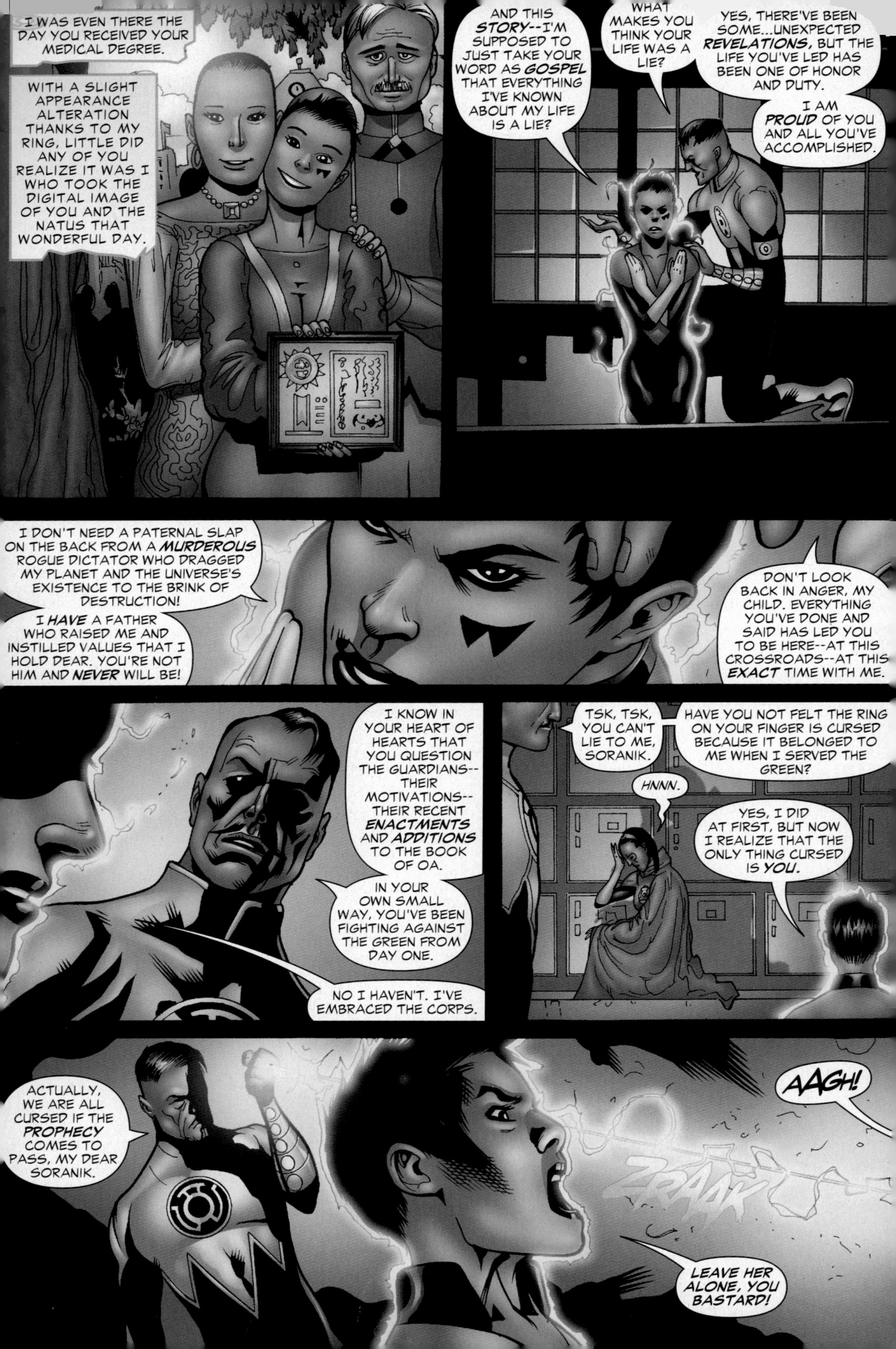

I WAS EVEN THERE THE DAY YOU RECEIVED YOUR MEDICAL DEGREE.
WITH A SLIGHT APPEARANCE ALTERATION THANKS TO MY RING, LITTLE DID ANY OF YOU REALIZE IT WAS I WHO TOOK THE DIGITAL IMAGE OF YOU AND THE NATUS THAT WONDERFUL DAY.
AND THIS STORY--I'M SUPPOSED TO JUST TAKE YOUR WORD AS GOSPEL THAT EVERYTHING I'VE KNOWN ABOUT MY LIFE IS A LIE?
WHAT MAKES YOU THINK YOUR LIFE WAS A LIE?
YES, THERE'VE BEEN SOME...UNEXPECTED REVELATIONS, BUT THE LIFE YOU'VE LED HAS BEEN ONE OF HONOR AND DUTY.
I AM PROUD OF YOU AND ALL YOU'VE ACCOMPLISHED.
I DON'T NEED A PATERNAL SLAP ON THE BACK FROM A MURDEROUS ROGUE DICTATOR WHO DRAGGED MY PLANET AND THE UNIVERSE'S EXISTENCE TO THE BRINK OF DESTRUCTION!
I HAVE A FATHER WHO RAISED ME AND INSTILLED VALUES THAT I HOLD DEAR. YOU'RE NOT HIM AND NEVER WILL BE!
DON'T LOOK BACK IN ANGER, MY CHILD. EVERYTHING YOU'VE DONE AND SAID HAS LED YOU TO BE HERE--AT THIS CROSSROADS--AT THIS EXACT TIME WITH ME.
I KNOW IN YOUR HEART OF HEARTS THAT YOU QUESTION THE GUARDIANS--THEIR MOTIVATIONS--THEIR RECENT ENACTMENTS AND ADDITIONS TO THE BOOK OF OA.
IN YOUR OWN SMALL WAY, YOU'VE BEEN FIGHTING AGAINST THE GREEN FROM DAY ONE.
NO I HAVEN'T. I'VE EMBRACED THE CORPS.
TSK, TSK, YOU CAN'T LIE TO ME, SORANIK.
HAVE YOU NOT FELT THE RING ON YOUR FINGER IS CURSED BECAUSE IT BELONGED TO ME WHEN I SERVED THE GREEN?
HNNN.
YES, I DID AT FIRST, BUT NOW I REALIZE THAT THE ONLY THING CURSED IS YOU.
ACTUALLY, WE ARE ALL CURSED IF THE PROPHECY COMES TO PASS, MY DEAR SORANIK.
AAGH!
ZZAAK
LEAVE HER ALONE, YOU BASTARD!

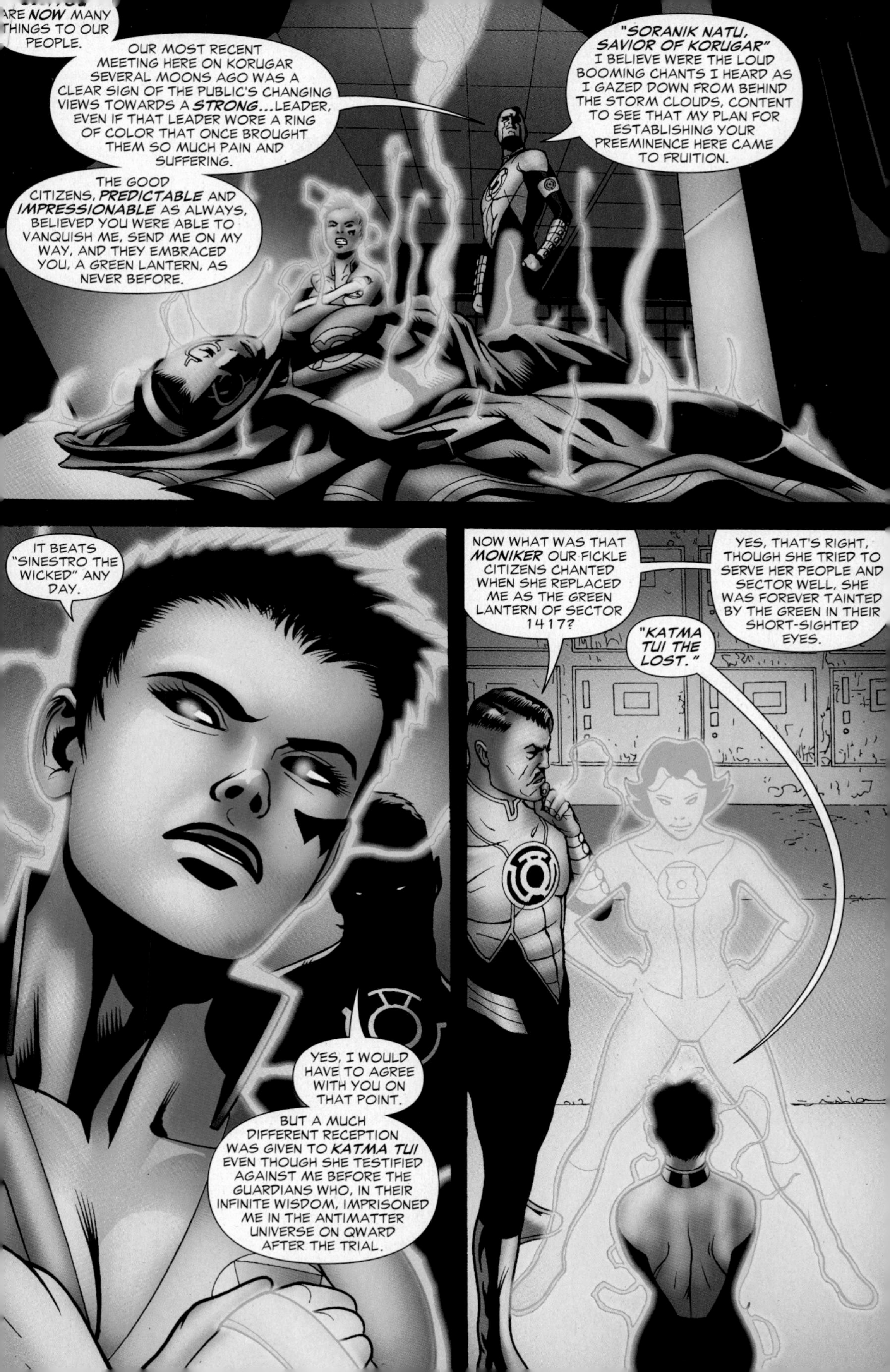
ARE NOW MANY THINGS TO OUR PEOPLE.
OUR MOST RECENT MEETING HERE ON KORUGAR SEVERAL MOONS AGO WAS A CLEAR SIGN OF THE PUBLIC'S CHANGING VIEWS TOWARDS A STRONG... LEADER, EVEN IF THAT LEADER WORE A RING OF COLOR THAT ONCE BROUGHT THEM SO MUCH PAIN AND SUFFERING.
THE GOOD CITIZENS, PREDICTABLE AND IMPRESSIONABLE AS ALWAYS, BELIEVED YOU WERE ABLE TO VANQUISH ME, SEND ME ON MY WAY, AND THEY EMBRACED YOU, A GREEN LANTERN, AS NEVER BEFORE.
"SORANIK NATU, SAVIOR OF KORUGAR" I BELIEVE WERE THE LOUD BOOMING CHANTS I HEARD AS I GAZED DOWN FROM BEHIND THE STORM CLOUDS, CONTENT TO SEE THAT MY PLAN FOR ESTABLISHING YOUR PREEMINENCE HERE CAME TO FRUITION.
IT BEATS "SINESTRO THE WICKED" ANY DAY.
YES, I WOULD HAVE TO AGREE WITH YOU ON THAT POINT.
BUT A MUCH DIFFERENT RECEPTION WAS GIVEN TO KATMA TUI EVEN THOUGH SHE TESTIFIED AGAINST ME BEFORE THE GUARDIANS WHO, IN THEIR INFINITE WISDOM, IMPRISONED ME IN THE ANTIMATTER UNIVERSE ON QWARD AFTER THE TRIAL.
NOW WHAT WAS THAT MONIKER OUR FICKLE CITIZENS CHANTED WHEN SHE REPLACED ME AS THE GREEN LANTERN OF SECTOR 1417?
"KATMA TUI THE LOST."
YES, THAT'S RIGHT, THOUGH SHE TRIED TO SERVE HER PEOPLE AND SECTOR WELL, SHE WAS FOREVER TAINTED BY THE GREEN IN THEIR SHORT-SIGHTED EYES.

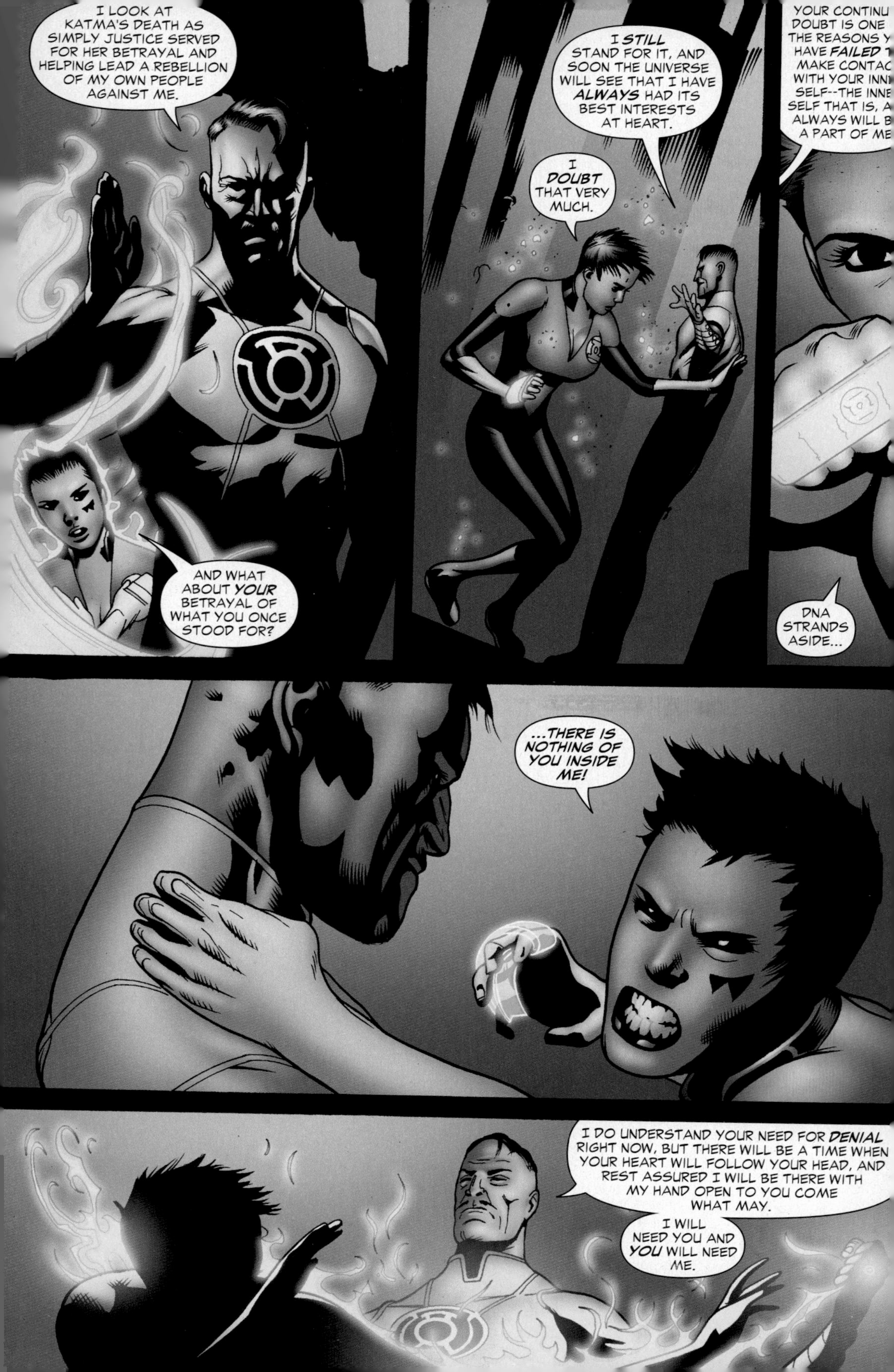
I LOOK AT KATMA'S DEATH AS SIMPLY JUSTICE SERVED FOR HER BETRAYAL AND HELPING LEAD A REBELLION OF MY OWN PEOPLE AGAINST ME.
AND WHAT ABOUT YOUR BETRAYAL OF WHAT YOU ONCE STOOD FOR?
I STILL STAND FOR IT, AND SOON THE UNIVERSE WILL SEE THAT I HAVE ALWAYS HAD ITS BEST INTERESTS AT HEART.
I DOUBT THAT VERY MUCH.
YOUR CONTINU DOUBT IS ONE THE REASONS Y HAVE FAILED T MAKE CONTAC WITH YOUR INN SELF--THE INNE SELF THAT IS, A ALWAYS WILL B A PART OF ME
DNA STRANDS ASIDE...
...THERE IS NOTHING OF YOU INSIDE ME!
I DO UNDERSTAND YOUR NEED FOR DENIAL RIGHT NOW, BUT THERE WILL BE A TIME WHEN YOUR HEART WILL FOLLOW YOUR HEAD, AND REST ASSURED I WILL BE THERE WITH MY HAND OPEN TO YOU COME WHAT MAY.
I WILL NEED YOU AND YOU WILL NEED ME.

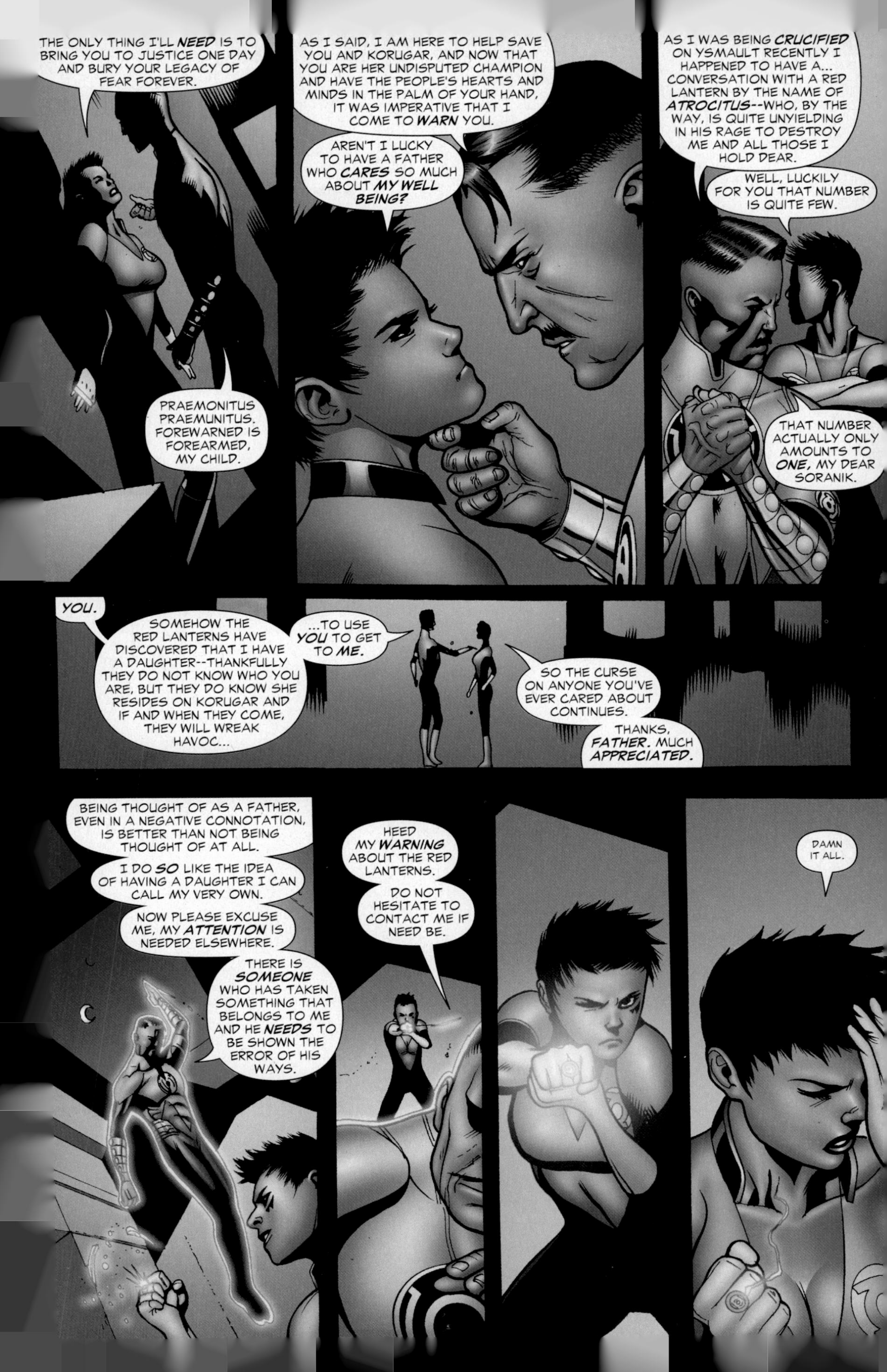
THE ONLY THING I'LL NEED IS TO BRING YOU TO JUSTICE ONE DAY AND BURY YOUR LEGACY OF FEAR FOREVER.
PRAEMONITUS PRAEMUNITUS. FOREWARNED IS FOREARMED, MY CHILD.
AS I SAID, I AM HERE TO HELP SAVE YOU AND KORUGAR, AND NOW THAT YOU ARE HER UNDISPUTED CHAMPION AND HAVE THE PEOPLE'S HEARTS AND MINDS IN THE PALM OF YOUR HAND, IT WAS IMPERATIVE THAT I COME TO WARN YOU.
AREN'T I LUCKY TO HAVE A FATHER WHO CARES SO MUCH ABOUT MY WELL BEING?
AS I WAS BEING CRUCIFIED ON YSMAULT RECENTLY I HAPPENED TO HAVE A... CONVERSATION WITH A RED LANTERN BY THE NAME OF ATROCITUS--WHO, BY THE WAY, IS QUITE UNYIELDING IN HIS RAGE TO DESTROY ME AND ALL THOSE I HOLD DEAR.
WELL, LUCKILY FOR YOU THAT NUMBER IS QUITE FEW.
THAT NUMBER ACTUALLY ONLY AMOUNTS TO ONE, MY DEAR SORANIK.
YOU.
SOMEHOW THE RED LANTERNS HAVE DISCOVERED THAT I HAVE A DAUGHTER--THANKFULLY THEY DO NOT KNOW WHO YOU ARE, BUT THEY DO KNOW SHE RESIDES ON KORUGAR AND IF AND WHEN THEY COME, THEY WILL WREAK HAVOC...
...TO USE YOU TO GET TO ME.
SO THE CURSE ON ANYONE YOU'VE EVER CARED ABOUT CONTINUES.
THANKS, FATHER. MUCH APPRECIATED.
BEING THOUGHT OF AS A FATHER, EVEN IN A NEGATIVE CONNOTATION, IS BETTER THAN NOT BEING THOUGHT OF AT ALL.
I DO SO LIKE THE IDEA OF HAVING A DAUGHTER I CAN CALL MY VERY OWN.
NOW PLEASE EXCUSE ME, MY ATTENTION IS NEEDED ELSEWHERE.
THERE IS SOMEONE WHO HAS TAKEN SOMETHING THAT BELONGS TO ME AND HE NEEDS TO BE SHOWN THE ERROR OF HIS WAYS.
HEED MY WARNING ABOUT THE RED LANTERNS.
DO NOT HESITATE TO CONTACT ME IF NEED BE.
DAMN IT ALL.

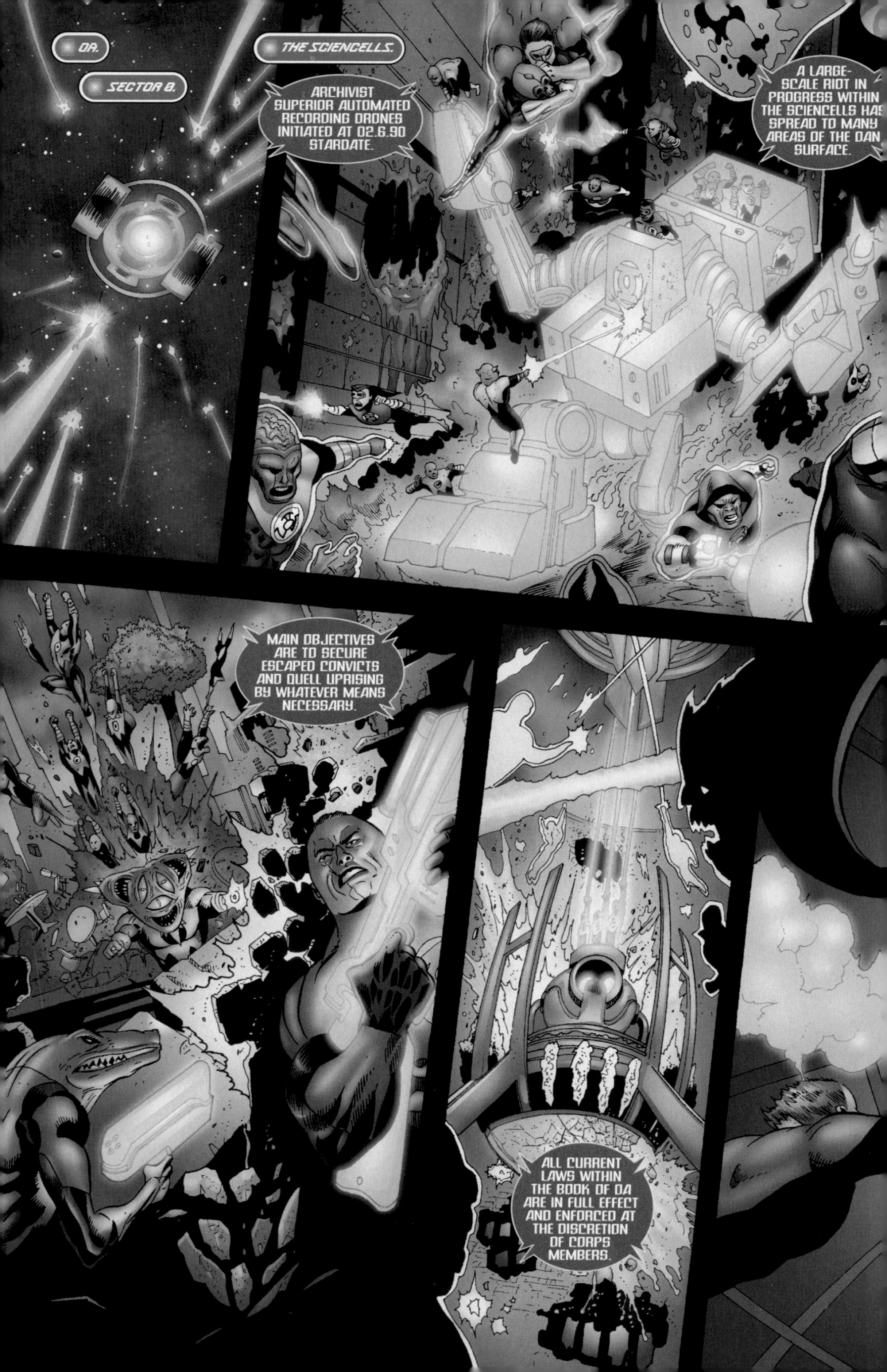
OA.
SECTOR 0.
THE SCIENCELLS.
ARCHIVIST SUPERIOR AUTOMATED RECORDING DRONES INITIATED AT 02.6.90 STARDATE.
A LARGE-SCALE RIOT IN PROGRESS WITHIN THE SCIENCELLS HAS SPREAD TO MANY AREAS OF THE OAN SURFACE.
MAIN OBJECTIVES ARE TO SECURE ESCAPED CONVICTS AND QUELL UPRISING BY WHATEVER MEANS NECESSARY.
ALL CURRENT LAWS WITHIN THE BOOK OF OA ARE IN FULL EFFECT AND ENFORCED AT THE DISCRETION OF CORPS MEMBERS.

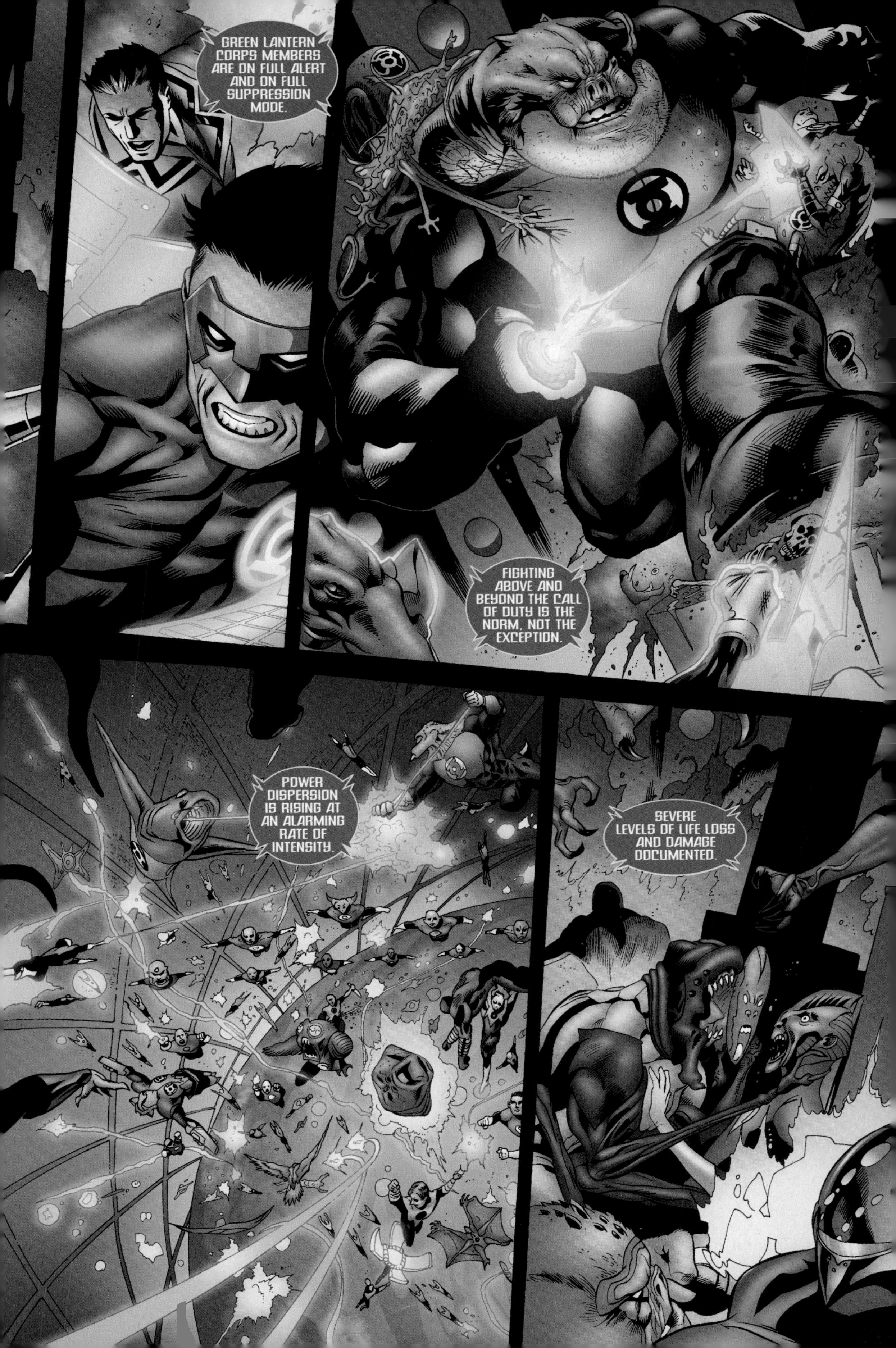
GREEN LANTERN CORPS MEMBERS ARE ON FULL ALERT AND ON FULL SUPPRESSION MODE.
FIGHTING ABOVE AND BEYOND THE CALL OF DUTY IS THE NORM, NOT THE EXCEPTION.
POWER DISPERSION IS RISING AT AN ALARMING RATE OF INTENSITY.
SEVERE LEVELS OF LIFE LOSS AND DAMAGE DOCUMENTED.

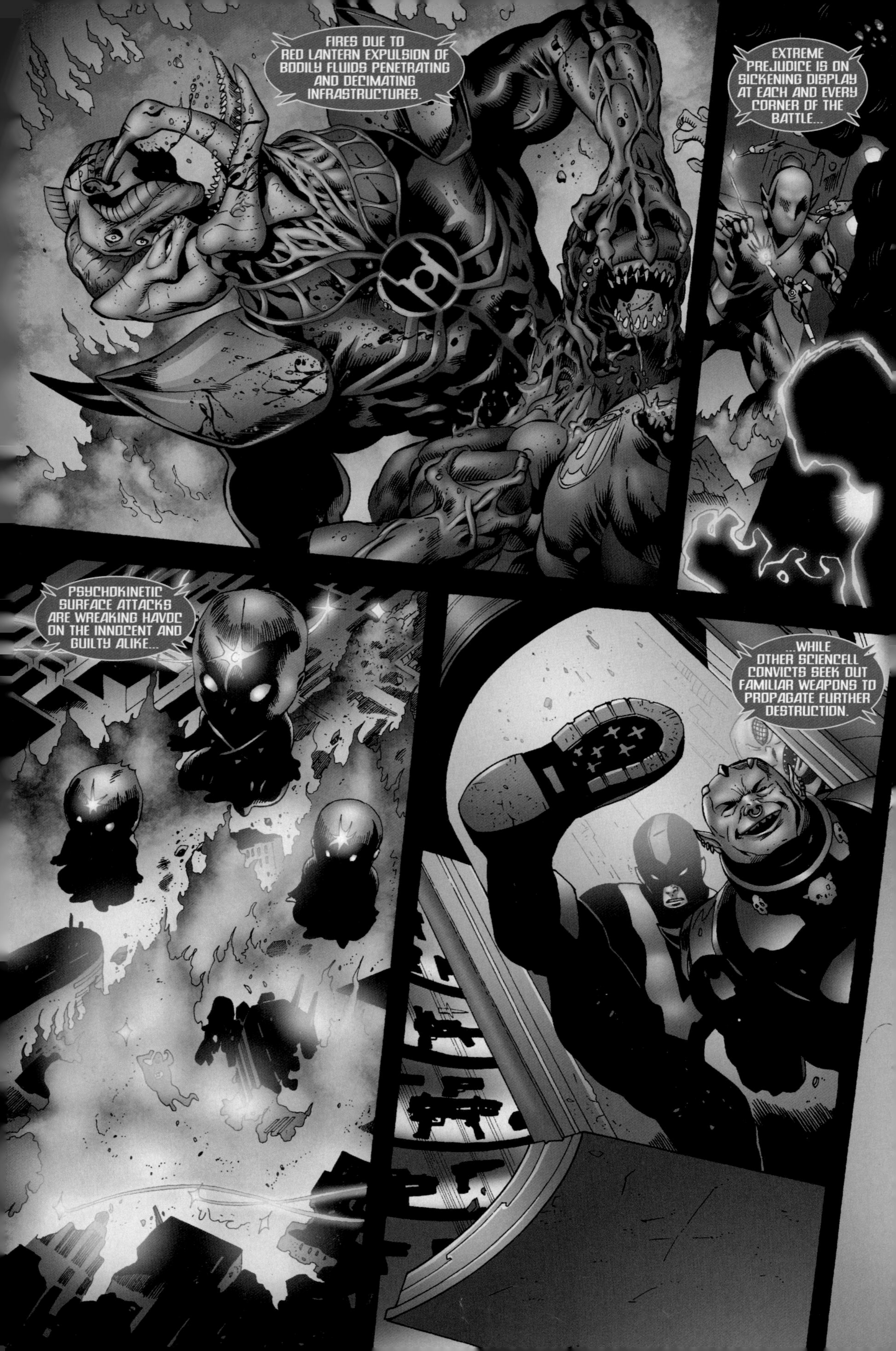
FIRES DUE TO RED LANTERN EXPULSION OF BODILY FLUIDS PENETRATING AND DECIMATING INFRASTRUCTURES.
EXTREME PREJUDICE IS ON SICKENING DISPLAY AT EACH AND EVERY CORNER OF THE BATTLE...
PSYCHOKINETIC SURFACE ATTACKS ARE WREAKING HAVOC ON THE INNOCENT AND GUILTY ALIKE...
...WHILE OTHER SCIENCELL CONVICTS SEEK OUT FAMILIAR WEAPONS TO PROPAGATE FURTHER DESTRUCTION.

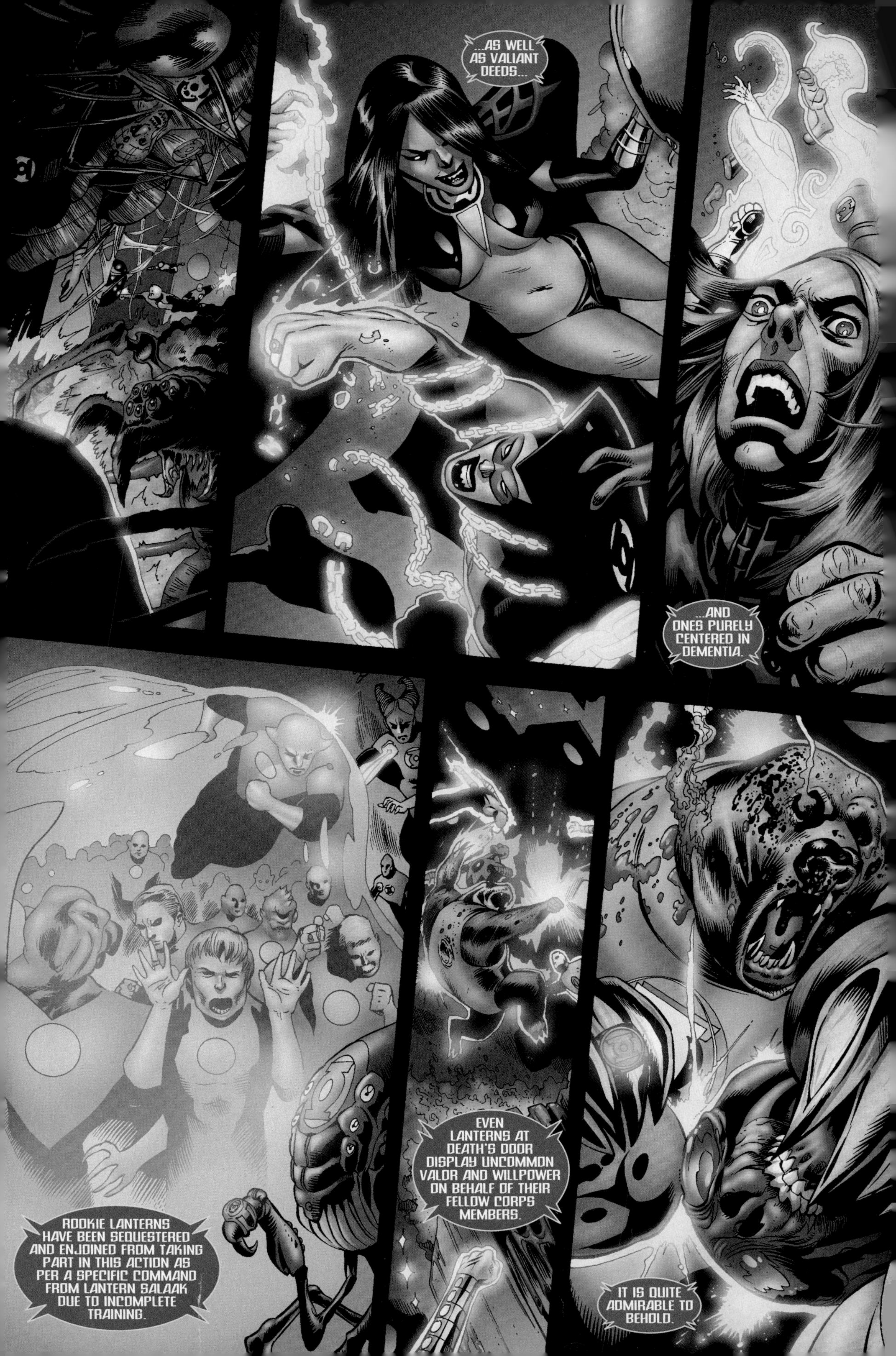
...AS WELL AS VALIANT DEEDS...
...AND ONES PURELY CENTERED IN DEMENTIA.
ROOKIE LANTERNS HAVE BEEN SEQUESTERED AND ENJOINED FROM TAKING PART IN THIS ACTION AS PER A SPECIFIC COMMAND FROM LANTERN SALAAK DUE TO INCOMPLETE TRAINING.
EVEN LANTERNS AT DEATH'S DOOR DISPLAY UNCOMMON VALOR AND WILLPOWER ON BEHALF OF THEIR FELLOW CORPS MEMBERS.
IT IS QUITE ADMIRABLE TO BEHOLD.

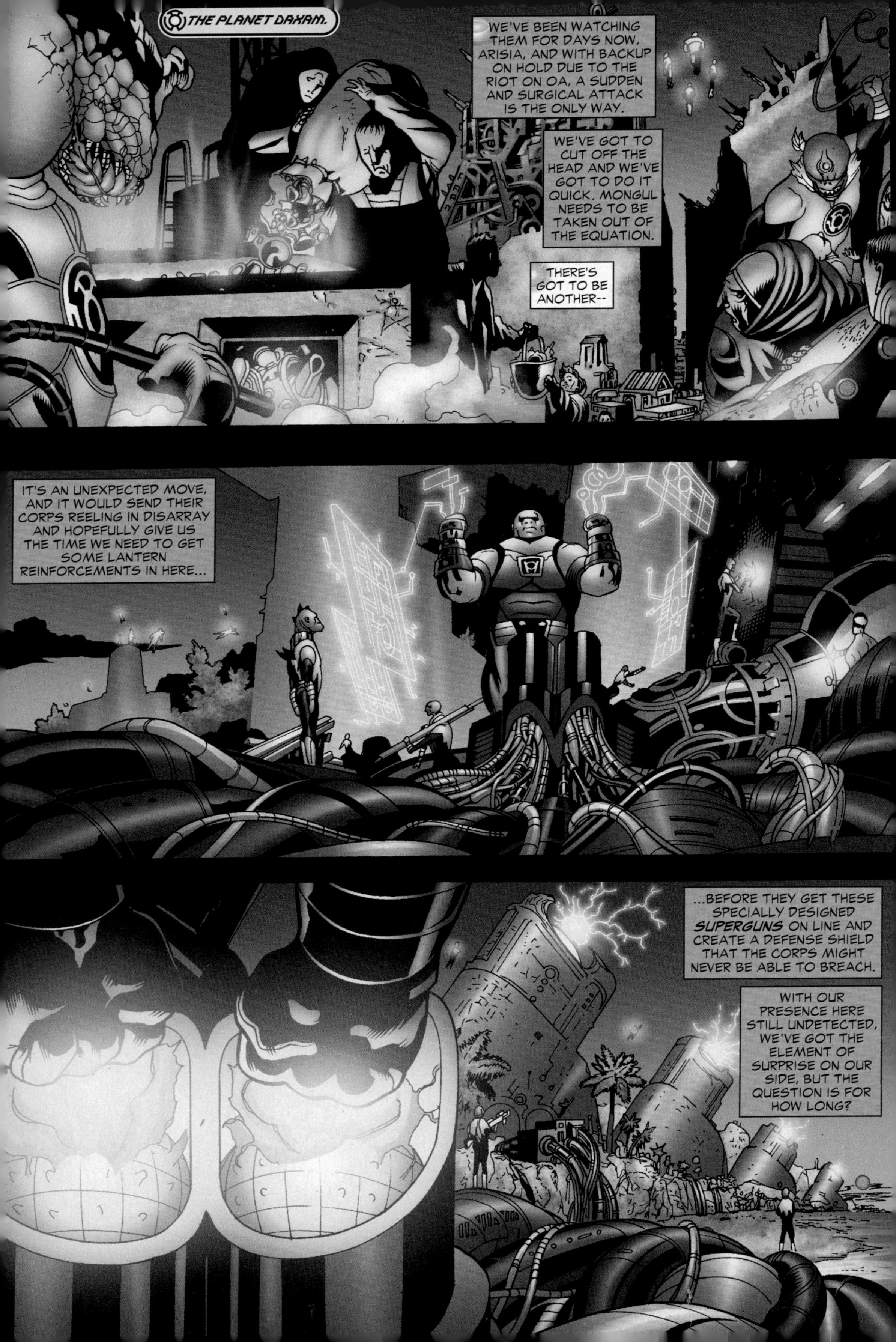
THE PLANET DAXAM.
WE'VE BEEN WATCHING THEM FOR DAYS NOW, ARISIA, AND WITH BACKUP ON HOLD DUE TO THE RIOT ON OA, A SUDDEN AND SURGICAL ATTACK IS THE ONLY WAY.
WE'VE GOT TO CUT OFF THE HEAD AND WE'VE GOT TO DO IT QUICK. MONGUL NEEDS TO BE TAKEN OUT OF THE EQUATION.
THERE'S GOT TO BE ANOTHER--
IT'S AN UNEXPECTED MOVE, AND IT WOULD SEND THEIR CORPS REELING IN DISARRAY AND HOPEFULLY GIVE US THE TIME WE NEED TO GET SOME LANTERN REINFORCEMENTS IN HERE...
...BEFORE THEY GET THESE SPECIALLY DESIGNED SUPERGUNS ON LINE AND CREATE A DEFENSE SHIELD THAT THE CORPS MIGHT NEVER BE ABLE TO BREACH.
WITH OUR PRESENCE HERE STILL UNDETECTED, WE'VE GOT THE ELEMENT OF SURPRISE ON OUR SIDE, BUT THE QUESTION IS FOR HOW LONG?

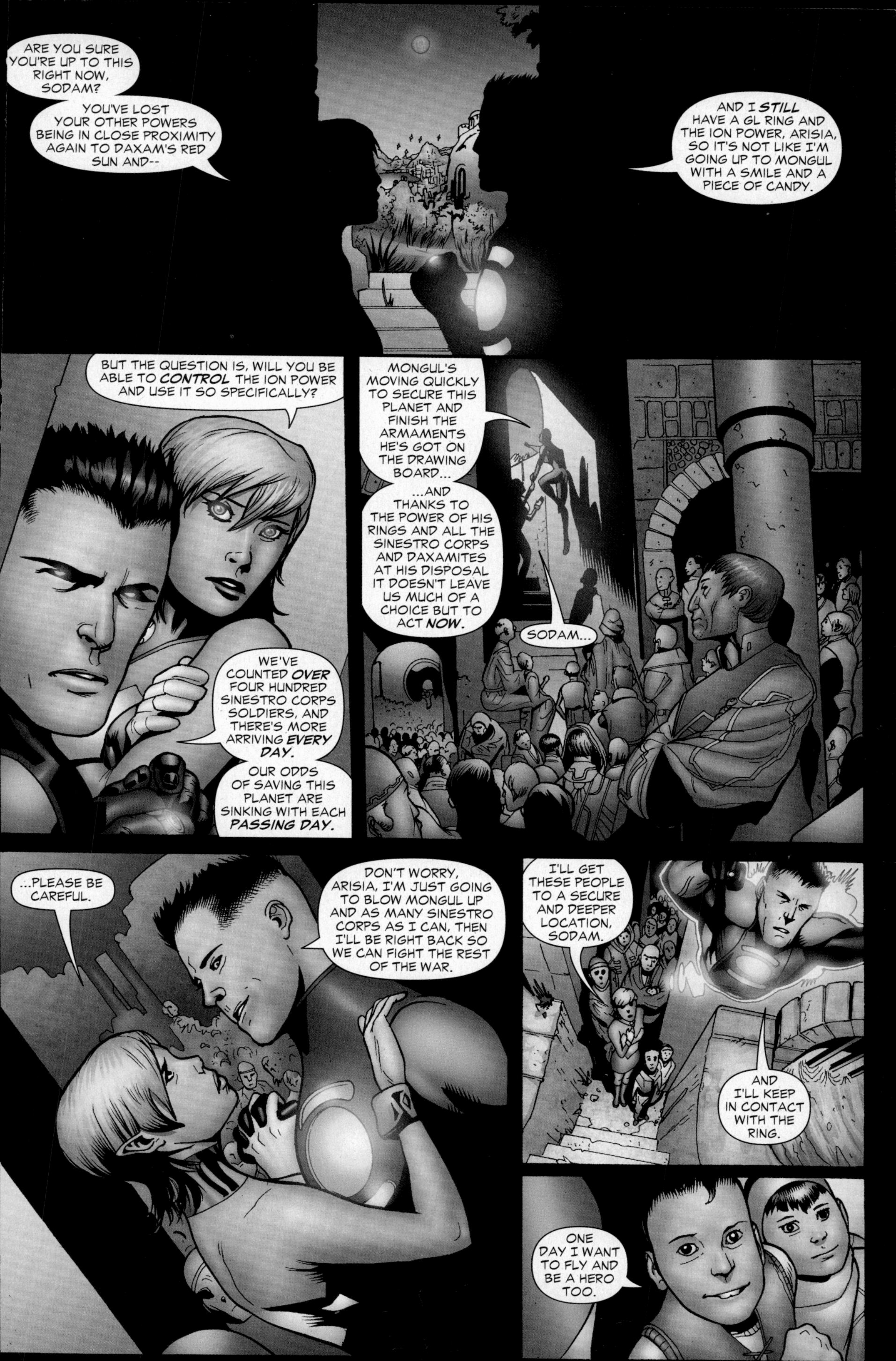
ARE YOU SURE YOU'RE UP TO THIS RIGHT NOW, SODAM?
YOU'VE LOST YOUR OTHER POWERS BEING IN CLOSE PROXIMITY AGAIN TO DAXAM'S RED SUN AND--
AND I STILL HAVE A GL RING AND THE ION POWER, ARISIA, SO IT'S NOT LIKE I'M GOING UP TO MONGUL WITH A SMILE AND A PIECE OF CANDY.
BUT THE QUESTION IS, WILL YOU BE ABLE TO CONTROL THE ION POWER AND USE IT SO SPECIFICALLY?
WE'VE COUNTED OVER FOUR HUNDRED SINESTRO CORPS SOLDIERS, AND THERE'S MORE ARRIVING EVERY DAY.
OUR ODDS OF SAVING THIS PLANET ARE SINKING WITH EACH PASSING DAY.
MONGUL'S MOVING QUICKLY TO SECURE THIS PLANET AND FINISH THE ARMAMENTS HE'S GOT ON THE DRAWING BOARD...
...AND THANKS TO THE POWER OF HIS RINGS AND ALL THE SINESTRO CORPS AND DAXAMITES AT HIS DISPOSAL IT DOESN'T LEAVE US MUCH OF A CHOICE BUT TO ACT NOW.
SODAM...
...PLEASE BE CAREFUL.
DON'T WORRY, ARISIA, I'M JUST GOING TO BLOW MONGUL UP AND AS MANY SINESTRO CORPS AS I CAN, THEN I'LL BE RIGHT BACK SO WE CAN FIGHT THE REST OF THE WAR.
I'LL GET THESE PEOPLE TO A SECURE AND DEEPER LOCATION, SODAM.
AND I'LL KEEP IN CONTACT WITH THE RING.
ONE DAY I WANT TO FLY AND BE A HERO TOO.

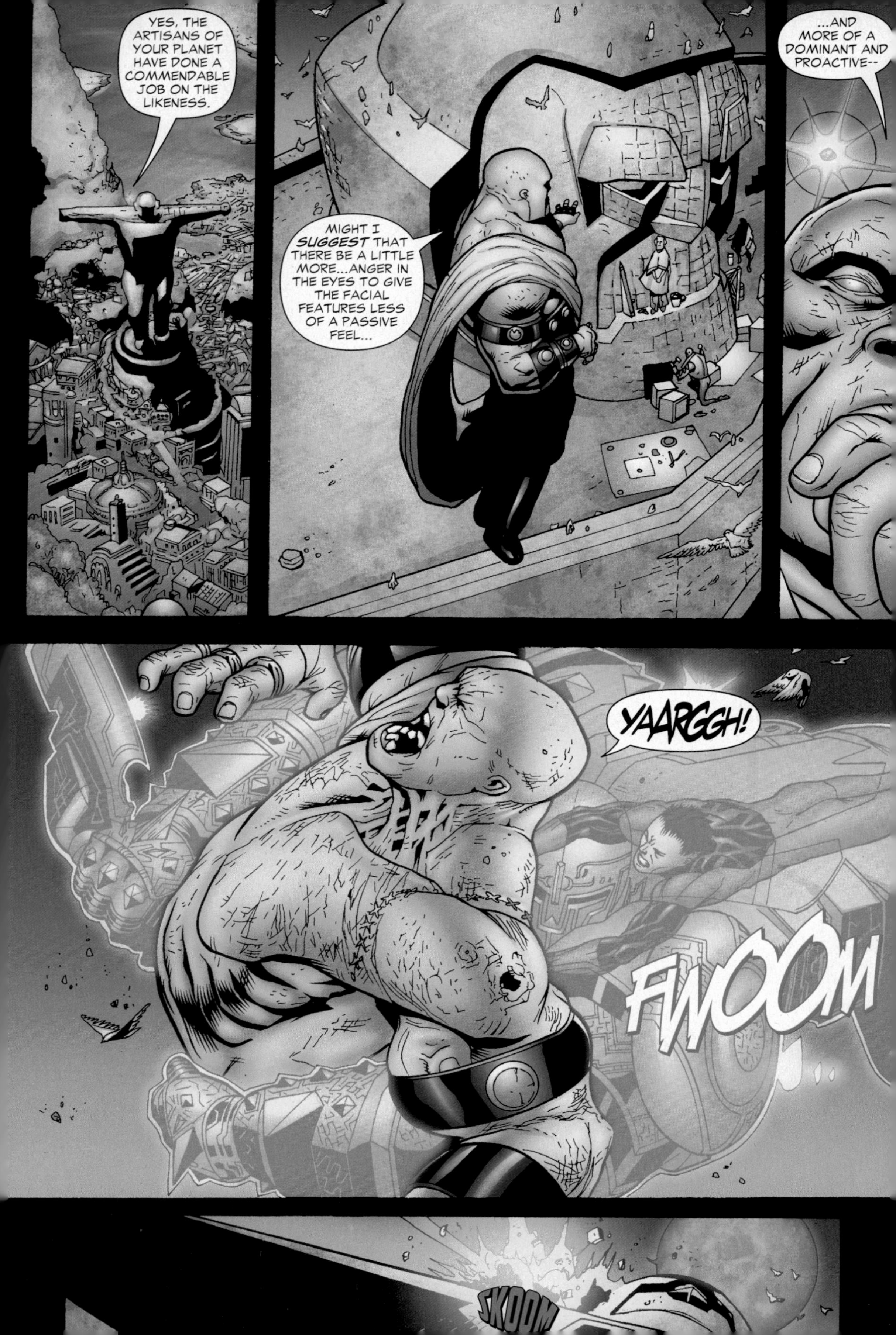
YES, THE ARTISANS OF YOUR PLANET HAVE DONE A COMMENDABLE JOB ON THE LIKENESS.
MIGHT I SUGGEST THAT THERE BE A LITTLE MORE...ANGER IN THE EYES TO GIVE THE FACIAL FEATURES LESS OF A PASSIVE FEEL...
...AND MORE OF A DOMINANT AND PROACTIVE--
YAARGGH!
FWOOM
SKOOM

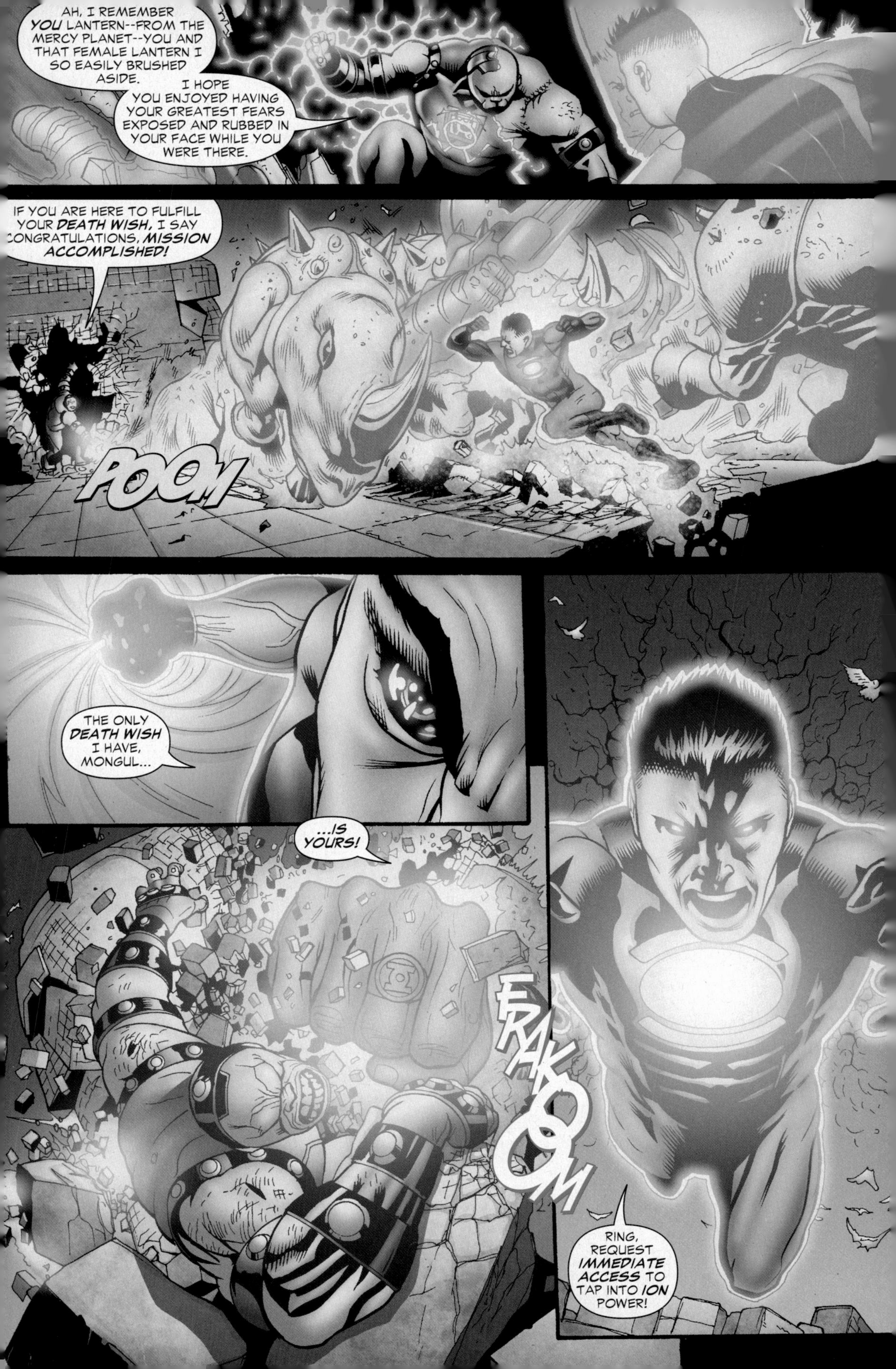
AH, I REMEMBER YOU LANTERN--FROM THE MERCY PLANET--YOU AND THAT FEMALE LANTERN I SO EASILY BRUSHED ASIDE.
I HOPE YOU ENJOYED HAVING YOUR GREATEST FEARS EXPOSED AND RUBBED IN YOUR FACE WHILE YOU WERE THERE.
IF YOU ARE HERE TO FULFILL YOUR DEATH WISH, I SAY CONGRATULATIONS, MISSION ACCOMPLISHED!
POOM
THE ONLY DEATH WISH I HAVE, MONGUL...
...IS YOURS!
FRAKOOM
RING, REQUEST IMMEDIATE ACCESS TO TAP INTO ION POWER!

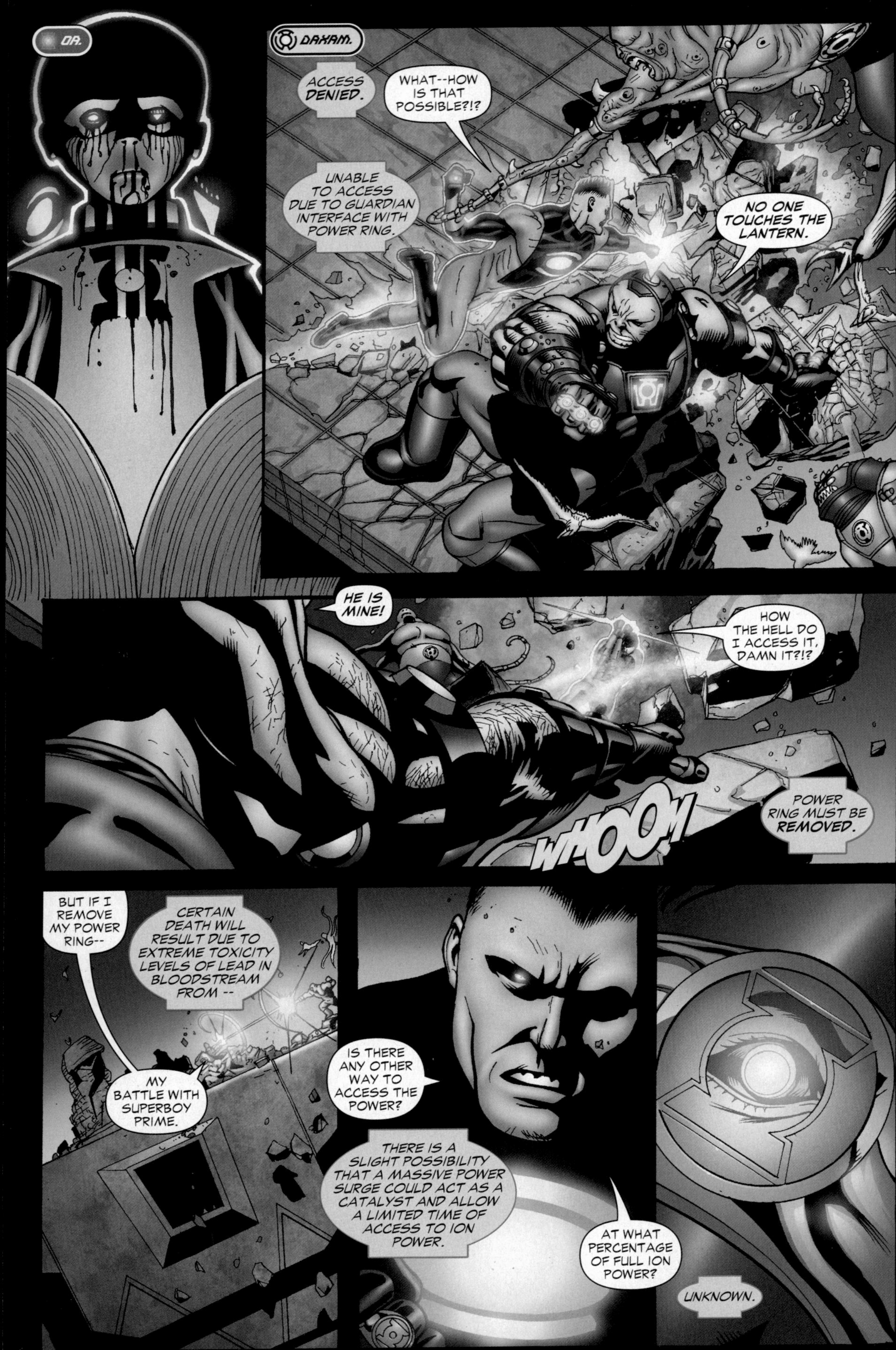
OA.
DAXAM.
ACCESS DENIED.
WHAT--HOW IS THAT POSSIBLE?!?
UNABLE TO ACCESS DUE TO GUARDIAN INTERFACE WITH POWER RING.
NO ONE TOUCHES THE LANTERN.
HE IS MINE!
HOW THE HELL DO I ACCESS IT, DAMN IT?!?
WHOOM
POWER RING MUST BE REMOVED.
BUT IF I REMOVE MY POWER RING--
CERTAIN DEATH WILL RESULT DUE TO EXTREME TOXICITY LEVELS OF LEAD IN BLOODSTREAM FROM --
MY BATTLE WITH SUPERBOY PRIME.
IS THERE ANY OTHER WAY TO ACCESS THE POWER?
THERE IS A SLIGHT POSSIBILITY THAT A MASSIVE POWER SURGE COULD ACT AS A CATALYST AND ALLOW A LIMITED TIME OF ACCESS TO ION POWER.
AT WHAT PERCENTAGE OF FULL ION POWER?
UNKNOWN.

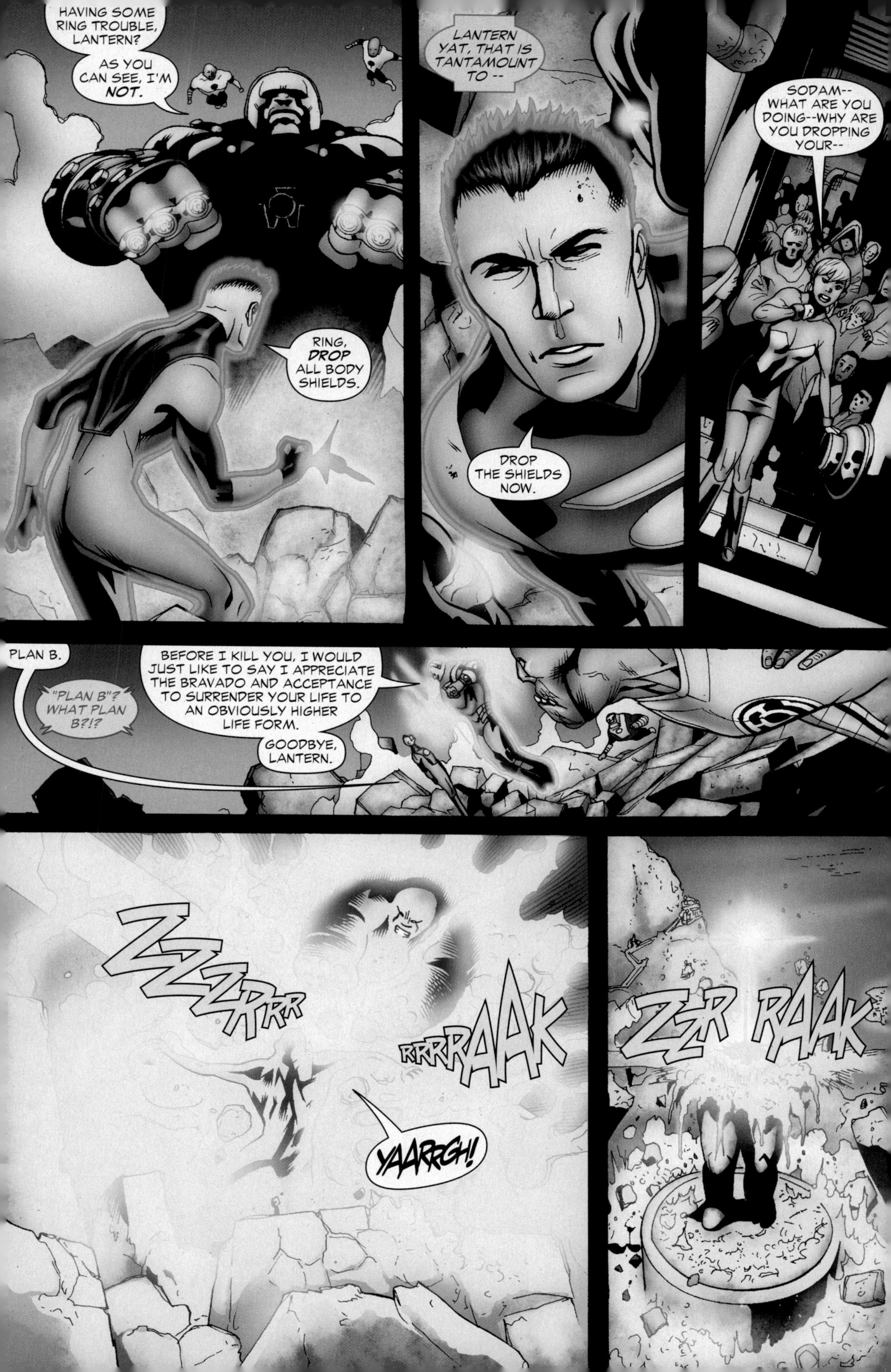
HAVING SOME RING TROUBLE, LANTERN?
AS YOU CAN SEE, I'M NOT.
RING, DROP ALL BODY SHIELDS.
LANTERN YAT, THAT IS TANTAMOUNT TO --
DROP THE SHIELDS NOW.
SODAM-- WHAT ARE YOU DOING--WHY ARE YOU DROPPING YOUR--
PLAN B.
"PLAN B"? WHAT PLAN B?!?
BEFORE I KILL YOU, I WOULD JUST LIKE TO SAY I APPRECIATE THE BRAVADO AND ACCEPTANCE TO SURRENDER YOUR LIFE TO AN OBVIOUSLY HIGHER LIFE FORM.
GOODBYE, LANTERN.
ZZZZRRRR
RRRRRAAAK
YAARRGH!
ZZR
RAAK

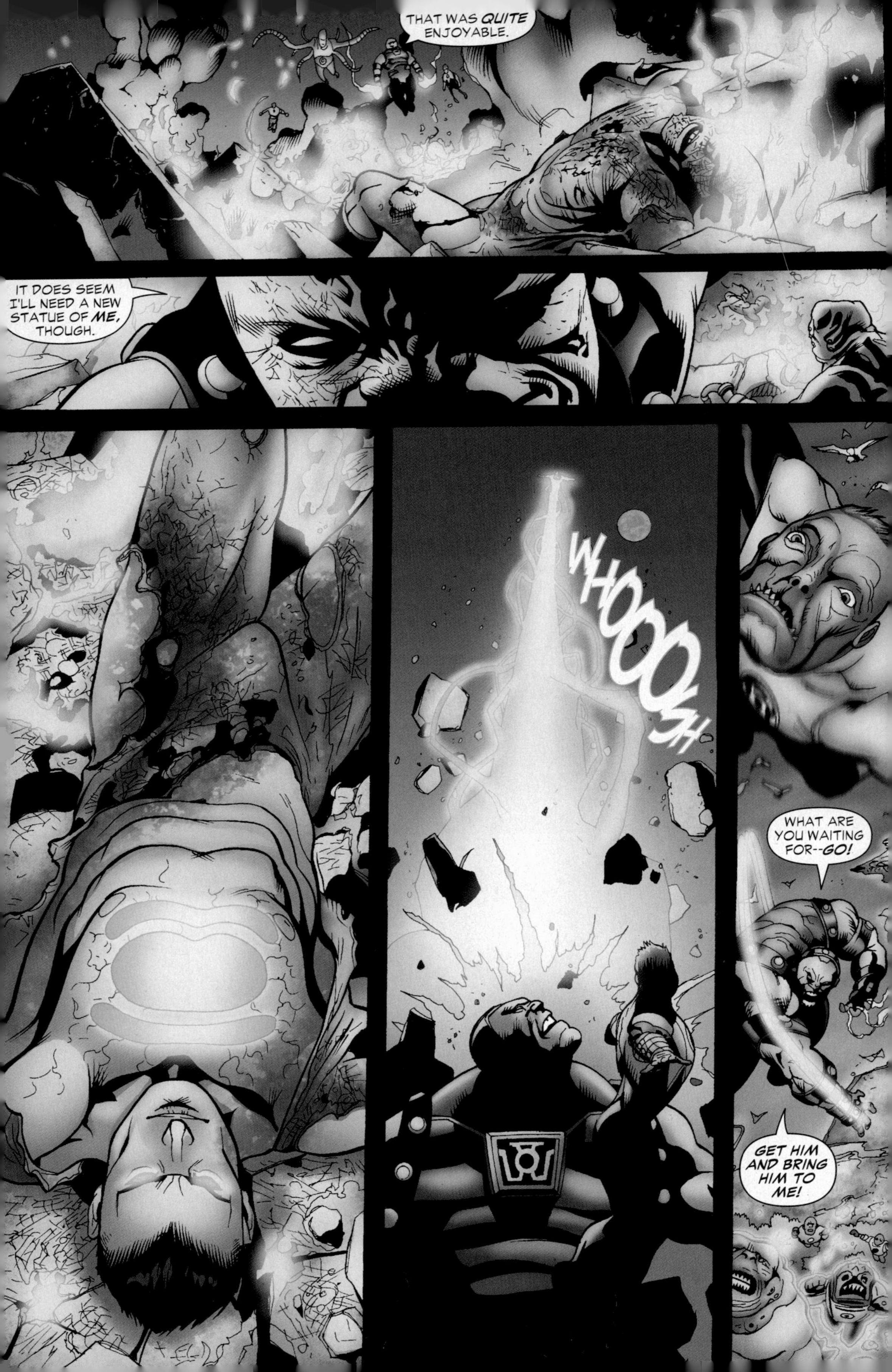
THAT WAS QUITE ENJOYABLE.
IT DOES SEEM I'LL NEED A NEW STATUE OF ME, THOUGH.
WHOOOOM
WHAT ARE YOU WAITING FOR--GO!
GET HIM AND BRING HIM TO ME!

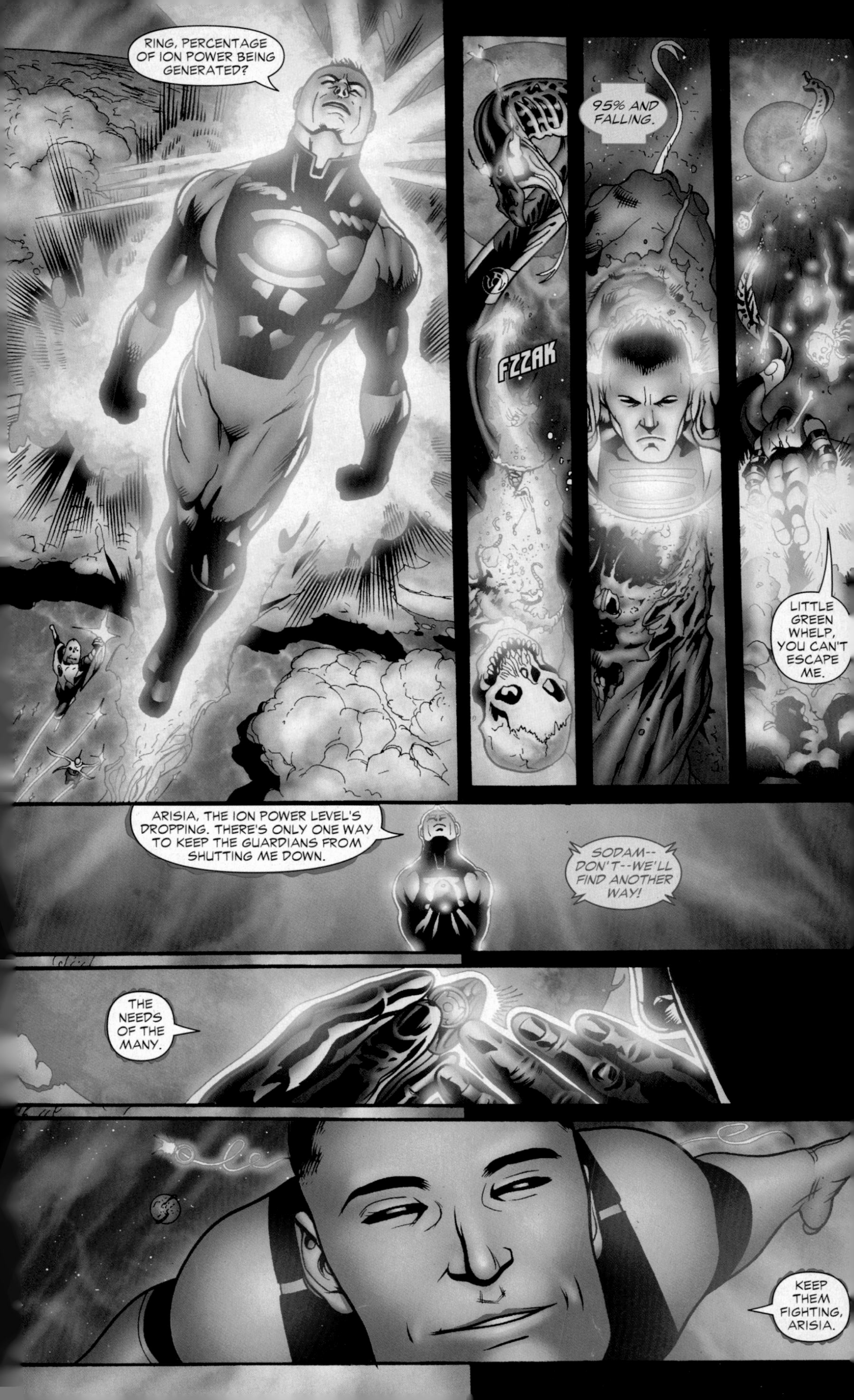
RING, PERCENTAGE OF ION POWER BEING GENERATED?
FZZAK
95% AND FALLING.
LITTLE GREEN WHELP, YOU CAN'T ESCAPE ME.
ARISIA, THE ION POWER LEVEL'S DROPPING. THERE'S ONLY ONE WAY TO KEEP THE GUARDIANS FROM SHUTTING ME DOWN.
SODAM-- DON'T--WE'LL FIND ANOTHER WAY!
THE NEEDS OF THE MANY.
KEEP THEM FIGHTING, ARISIA.

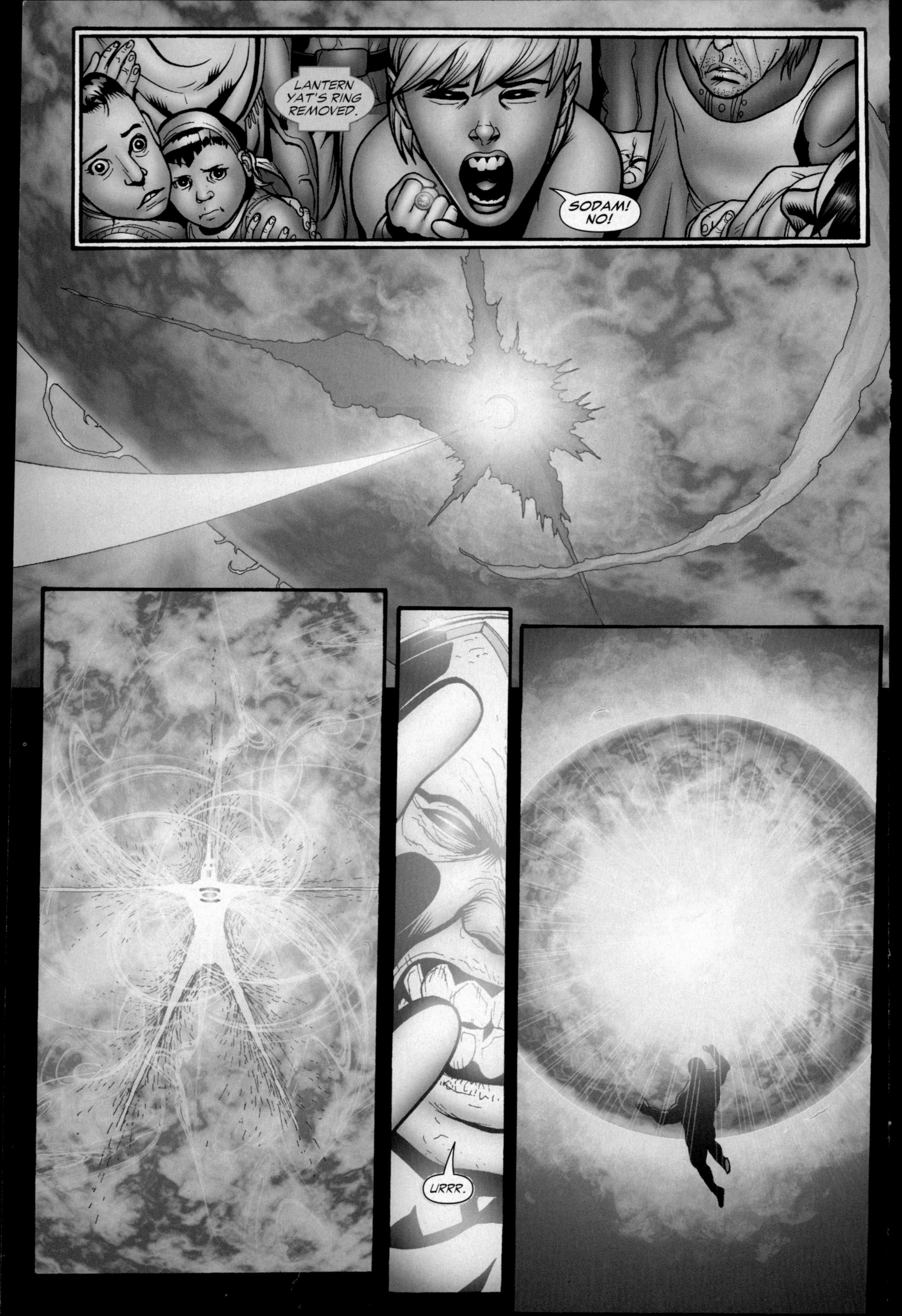
LANTERN YAT'S RING REMOVED.
SODAM! NO!
URRR.

GREEN LANTERN CORPS #37
Cover by Patrick Gleason, Rebecca Buchman & Randy Mayor

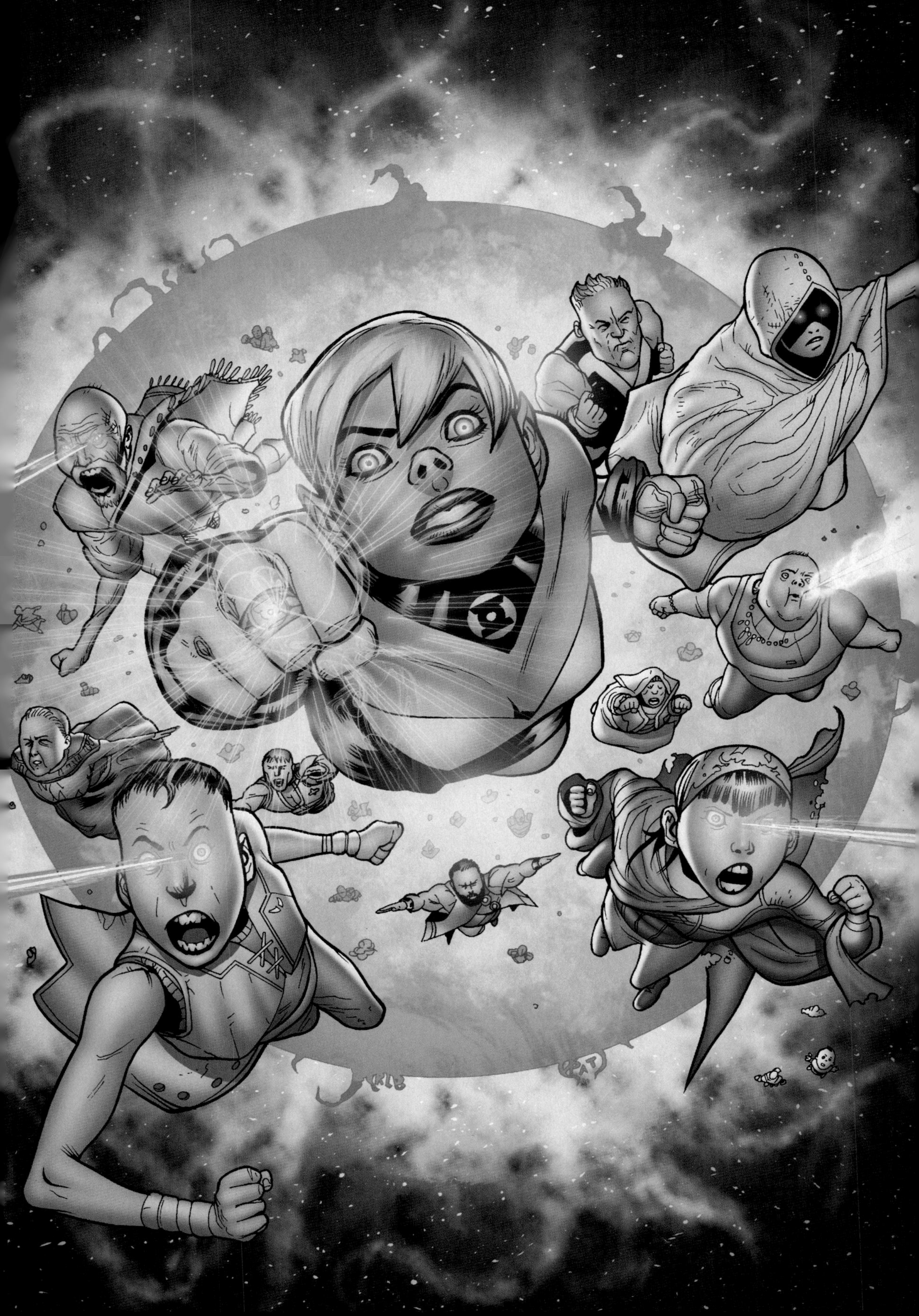

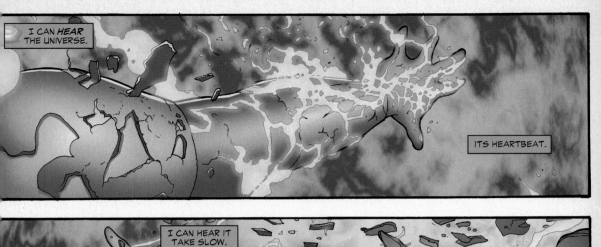

I CAN *HEAR* THE UNIVERSE.

ITS HEARTBEAT.

I CAN HEAR IT TAKE SLOW, DEEP BREATHS.

I CAN HEAR IT LAUGHING.

I CAN HEAR IT CRYING.

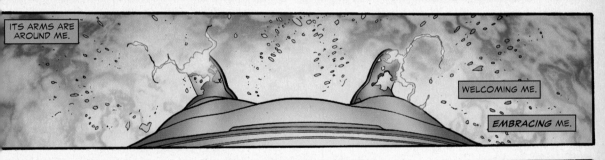

ITS ARMS ARE AROUND ME.

WELCOMING ME.

EMBRACING ME.

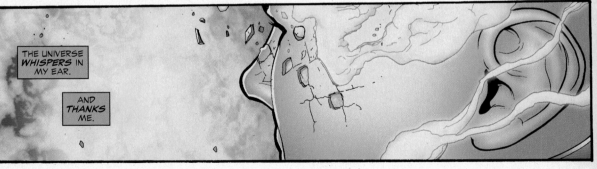

THE UNIVERSE *WHISPERS* IN MY EAR.

AND *THANKS* ME.

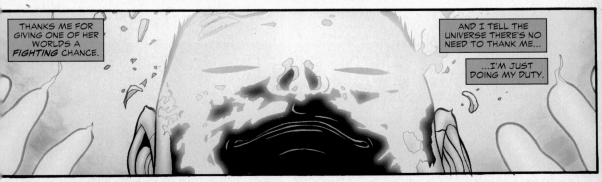

THANKS ME FOR GIVING ONE OF HER WORLDS A *FIGHTING* CHANCE.

AND I TELL THE UNIVERSE THERE'S NO NEED TO THANK ME...

...I'M JUST DOING MY DUTY.

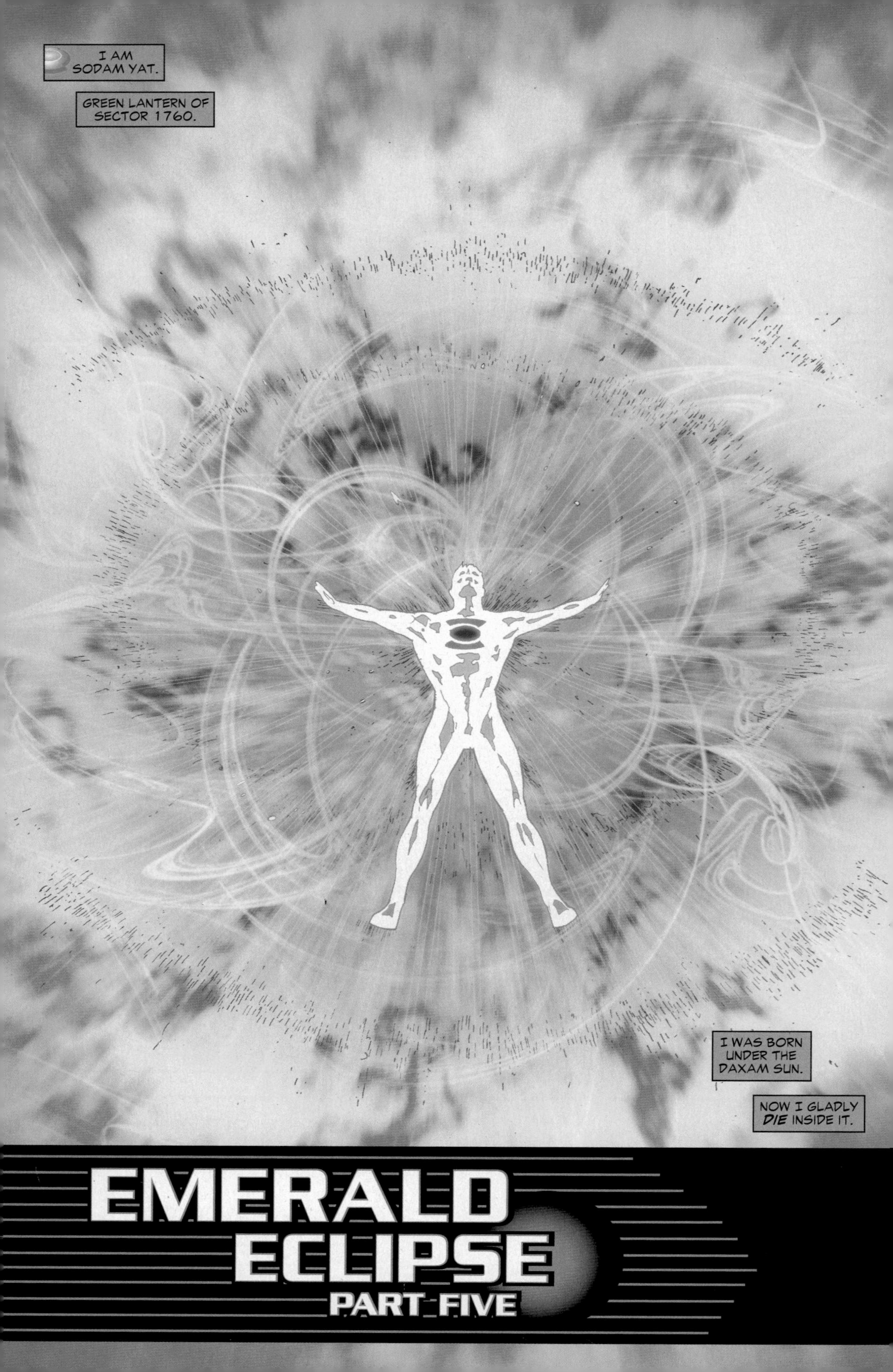

I AM SODAM YAT.
GREEN LANTERN OF SECTOR 1760.
I WAS BORN UNDER THE DAXAM SUN.
NOW I GLADLY DIE INSIDE IT.
EMERALD ECLIPSE PART FIVE

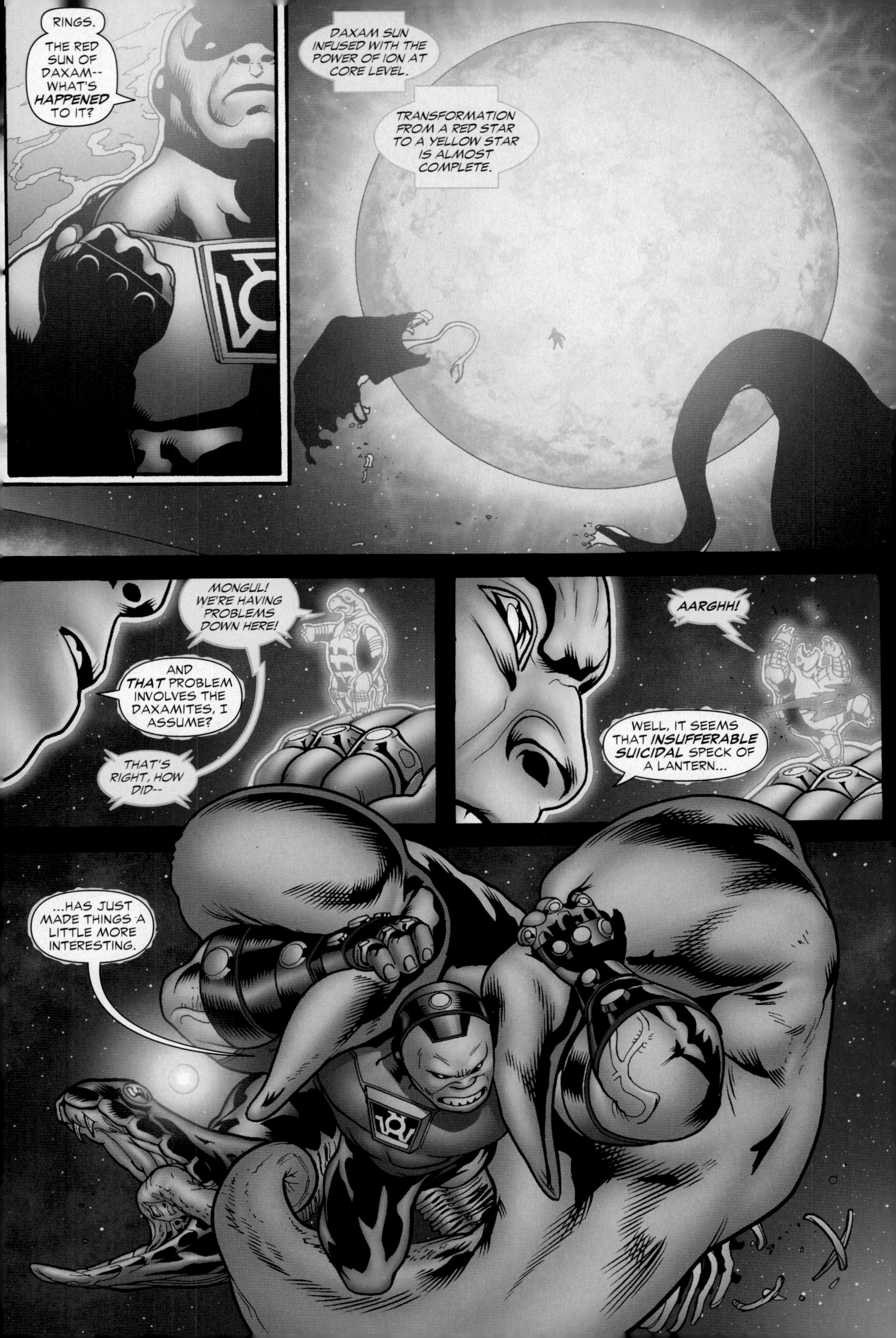
RINGS.
THE RED SUN OF DAXAM-- WHAT'S HAPPENED TO IT?
DAXAM SUN INFUSED WITH THE POWER OF ION AT CORE LEVEL.
TRANSFORMATION FROM A RED STAR TO A YELLOW STAR IS ALMOST COMPLETE.
MONGUL! WE'RE HAVING PROBLEMS DOWN HERE!
AND THAT PROBLEM INVOLVES THE DAXAMITES, I ASSUME?
THAT'S RIGHT, HOW DID--
AARGHH!
WELL, IT SEEMS THAT INSUFFERABLE SUICIDAL SPECK OF A LANTERN...
...HAS JUST MADE THINGS A LITTLE MORE INTERESTING.

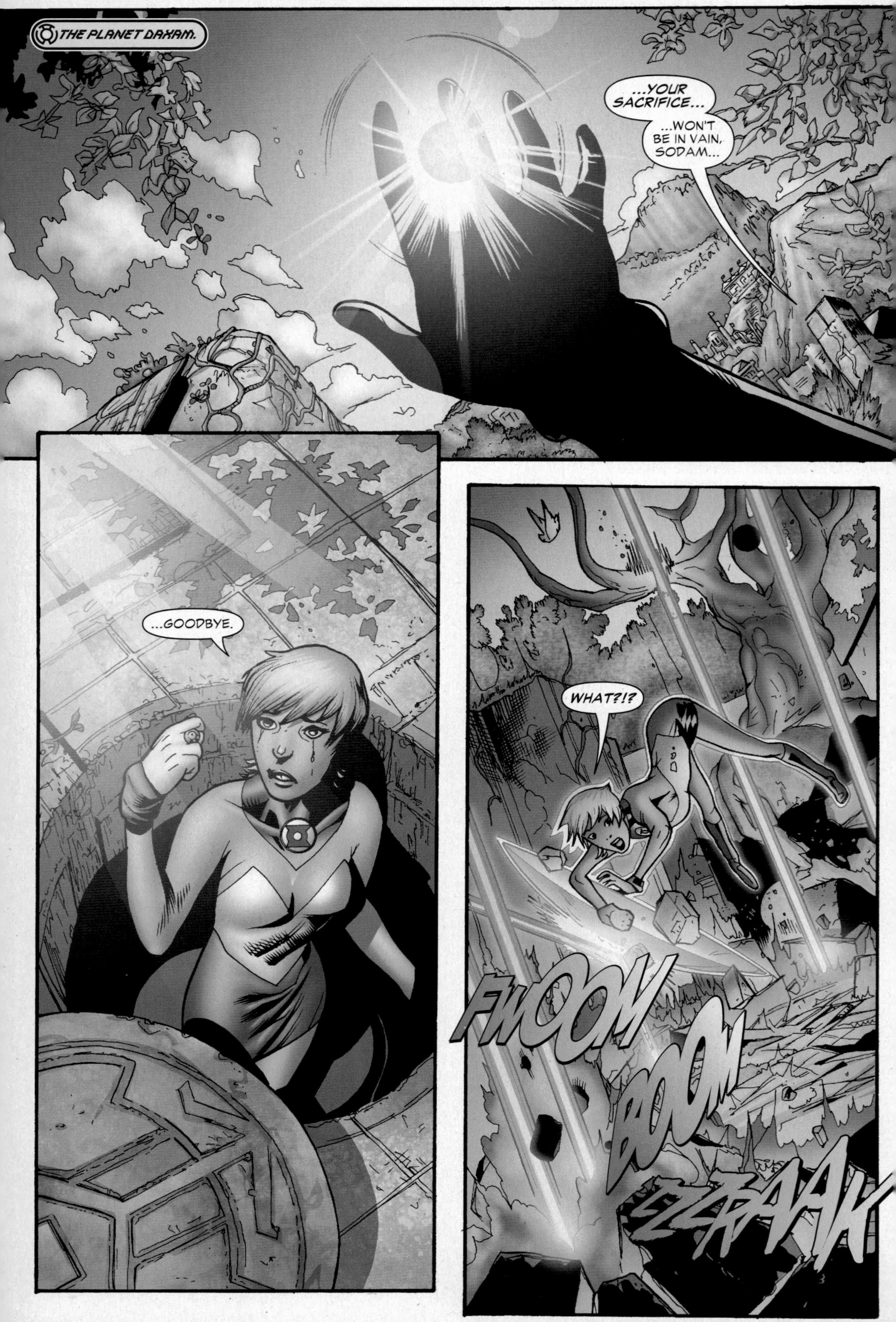
THE PLANET DAXAM.
...YOUR SACRIFICE...
...WON'T BE IN VAIN, SODAM...
...GOODBYE.
WHAT?!?
FWOOM
BOOM
SZRAAK

CALM DOWN! WE *KNEW* THIS WOULD HAPPEN ONCE SODAM TURNED THE SUN YELLOW!

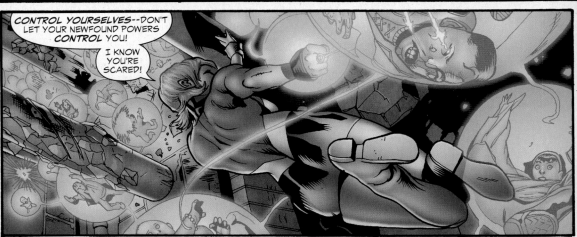

CONTROL YOURSELVES--DON'T LET YOUR NEWFOUND POWERS *CONTROL* YOU!

I KNOW YOU'RE SCARED!

I KNOW YOUR BODIES ARE DOING THINGS YOU COULD *NEVER* IMAGINE!

YOU MAY BE IN SOME *INITIAL* PAIN--BUT THAT'LL *FADE* AS YOUR PHYSIOLOGY GETS ACCLIMATED TO YOUR SPECIFIC ABILITY!

BUT YOU DON'T HAVE TO BE AFRAID ANYMORE!

DON'T LET YOUR EMOTIONS--

DON'T TELL US HOW TO FEEL, ALIEN! AND DON'T *PRESUME* TO TREAT US LIKE CHILDREN!

THANKS TO *MY SON,* WE HAVE THE POWER TO *TAKE* BACK OUR PLANET FROM THE SINESTRO CORPS AND SEEK *RETRIBUTION* FOR THE PERSECUTION OF OUR PEOPLE!

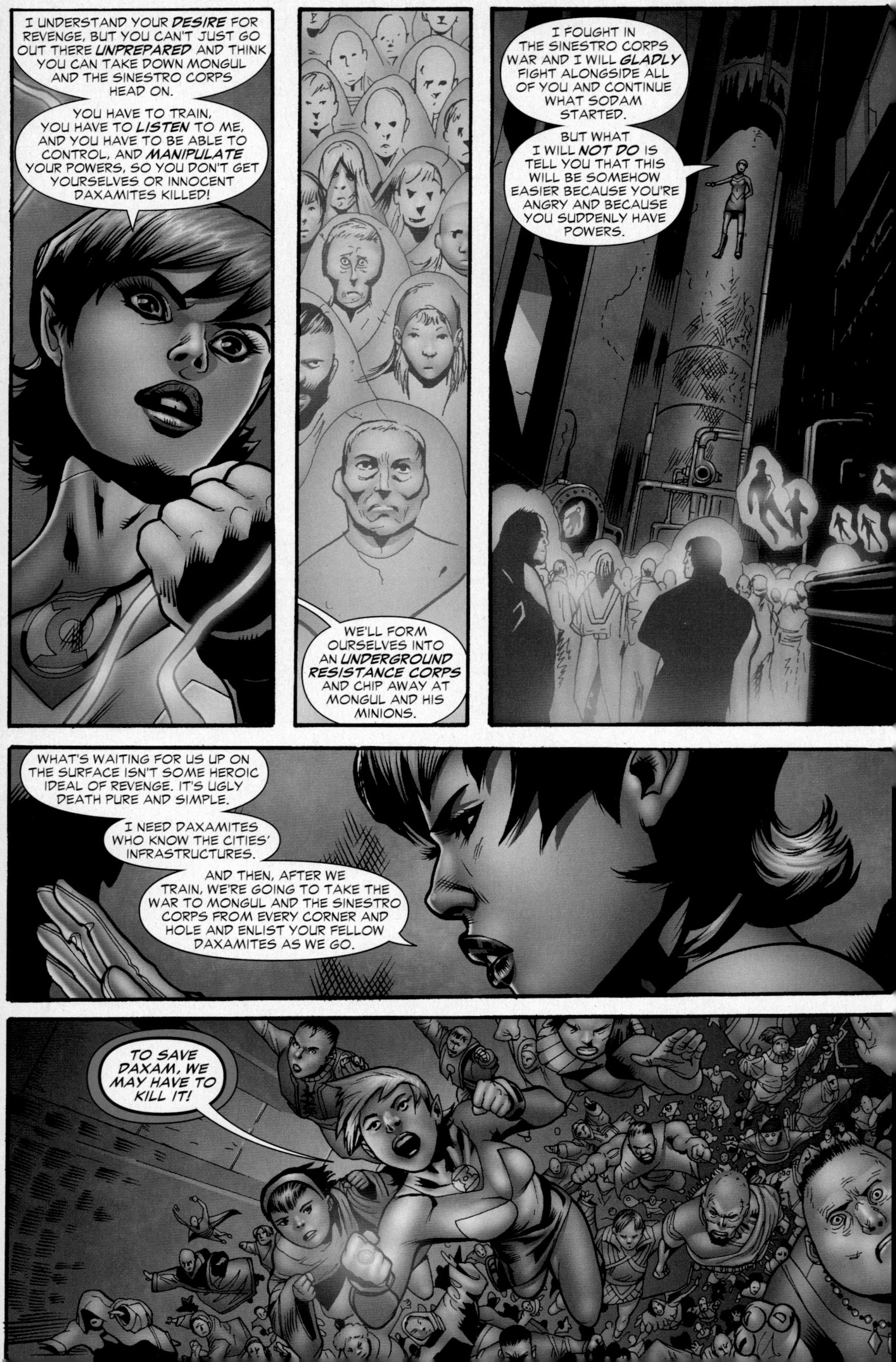

I UNDERSTAND YOUR DESIRE FOR REVENGE, BUT YOU CAN'T JUST GO OUT THERE UNPREPARED AND THINK YOU CAN TAKE DOWN MONGUL AND THE SINESTRO CORPS HEAD ON.
YOU HAVE TO TRAIN, YOU HAVE TO LISTEN TO ME, AND YOU HAVE TO BE ABLE TO CONTROL, AND MANIPULATE YOUR POWERS, SO YOU DON'T GET YOURSELVES OR INNOCENT DAXAMITES KILLED!
WE'LL FORM OURSELVES INTO AN UNDERGROUND RESISTANCE CORPS AND CHIP AWAY AT MONGUL AND HIS MINIONS.
I FOUGHT IN THE SINESTRO CORPS WAR AND I WILL GLADLY FIGHT ALONGSIDE ALL OF YOU AND CONTINUE WHAT SODAM STARTED.
BUT WHAT I WILL NOT DO IS TELL YOU THAT THIS WILL BE SOMEHOW EASIER BECAUSE YOU'RE ANGRY AND BECAUSE YOU SUDDENLY HAVE POWERS.
WHAT'S WAITING FOR US UP ON THE SURFACE ISN'T SOME HEROIC IDEAL OF REVENGE. IT'S UGLY DEATH PURE AND SIMPLE.
I NEED DAXAMITES WHO KNOW THE CITIES' INFRASTRUCTURES.
AND THEN, AFTER WE TRAIN, WE'RE GOING TO TAKE THE WAR TO MONGUL AND THE SINESTRO CORPS FROM EVERY CORNER AND HOLE AND ENLIST YOUR FELLOW DAXAMITES AS WE GO.
TO SAVE DAXAM, WE MAY HAVE TO KILL IT!

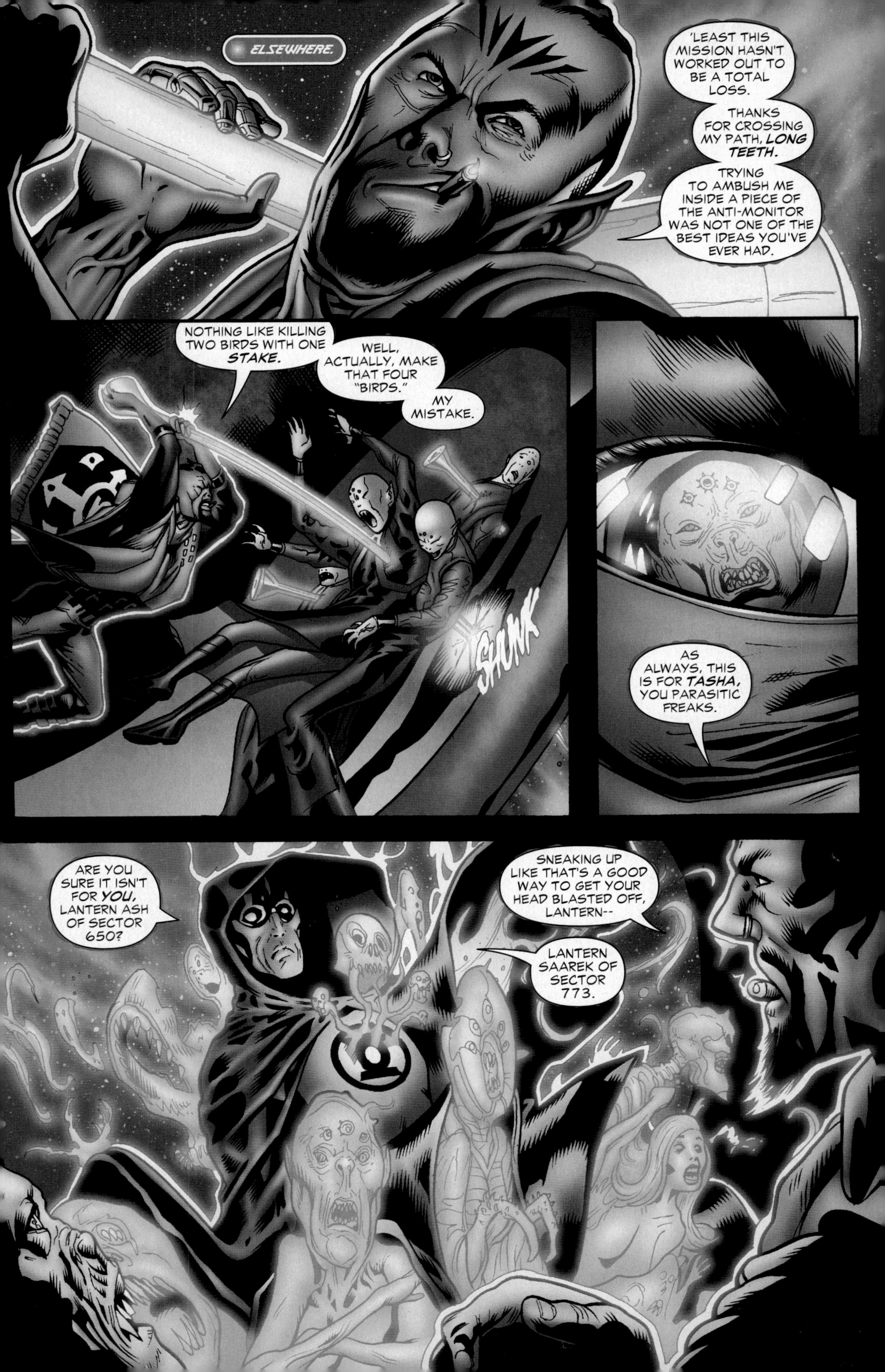
ELSEWHERE.
'LEAST THIS MISSION HASN'T WORKED OUT TO BE A TOTAL LOSS.
THANKS FOR CROSSING MY PATH, LONG TEETH.
TRYING TO AMBUSH ME INSIDE A PIECE OF THE ANTI-MONITOR WAS NOT ONE OF THE BEST IDEAS YOU'VE EVER HAD.
NOTHING LIKE KILLING TWO BIRDS WITH ONE STAKE.
WELL, ACTUALLY, MAKE THAT FOUR "BIRDS."
MY MISTAKE.
SHUNK
AS ALWAYS, THIS IS FOR TASHA, YOU PARASITIC FREAKS.
ARE YOU SURE IT ISN'T FOR YOU, LANTERN ASH OF SECTOR 650?
SNEAKING UP LIKE THAT'S A GOOD WAY TO GET YOUR HEAD BLASTED OFF, LANTERN--
LANTERN SAAREK OF SECTOR 773.

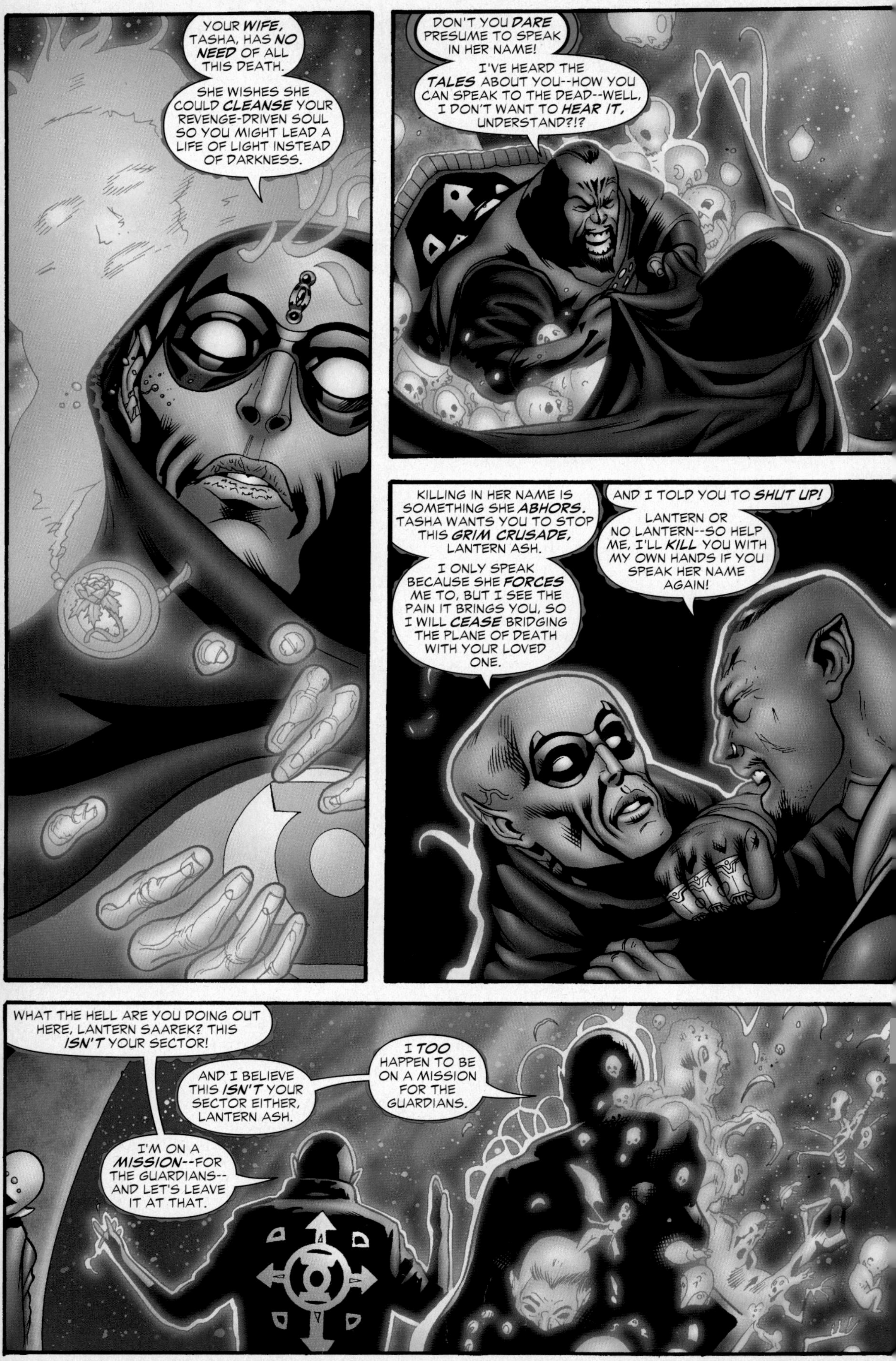

YOUR WIFE, TASHA, HAS NO NEED OF ALL THIS DEATH.
SHE WISHES SHE COULD CLEANSE YOUR REVENGE-DRIVEN SOUL SO YOU MIGHT LEAD A LIFE OF LIGHT INSTEAD OF DARKNESS.
DON'T YOU DARE PRESUME TO SPEAK IN HER NAME!
I'VE HEARD THE TALES ABOUT YOU--HOW YOU CAN SPEAK TO THE DEAD--WELL, I DON'T WANT TO HEAR IT, UNDERSTAND?!?
KILLING IN HER NAME IS SOMETHING SHE ABHORS. TASHA WANTS YOU TO STOP THIS GRIM CRUSADE, LANTERN ASH.
I ONLY SPEAK BECAUSE SHE FORCES ME TO, BUT I SEE THE PAIN IT BRINGS YOU, SO I WILL CEASE BRIDGING THE PLANE OF DEATH WITH YOUR LOVED ONE.
AND I TOLD YOU TO SHUT UP!
LANTERN OR NO LANTERN--SO HELP ME, I'LL KILL YOU WITH MY OWN HANDS IF YOU SPEAK HER NAME AGAIN!
WHAT THE HELL ARE YOU DOING OUT HERE, LANTERN SAAREK? THIS ISN'T YOUR SECTOR!
I'M ON A MISSION--FOR THE GUARDIANS--AND LET'S LEAVE IT AT THAT.
AND I BELIEVE THIS ISN'T YOUR SECTOR EITHER, LANTERN ASH.
I TOO HAPPEN TO BE ON A MISSION FOR THE GUARDIANS.

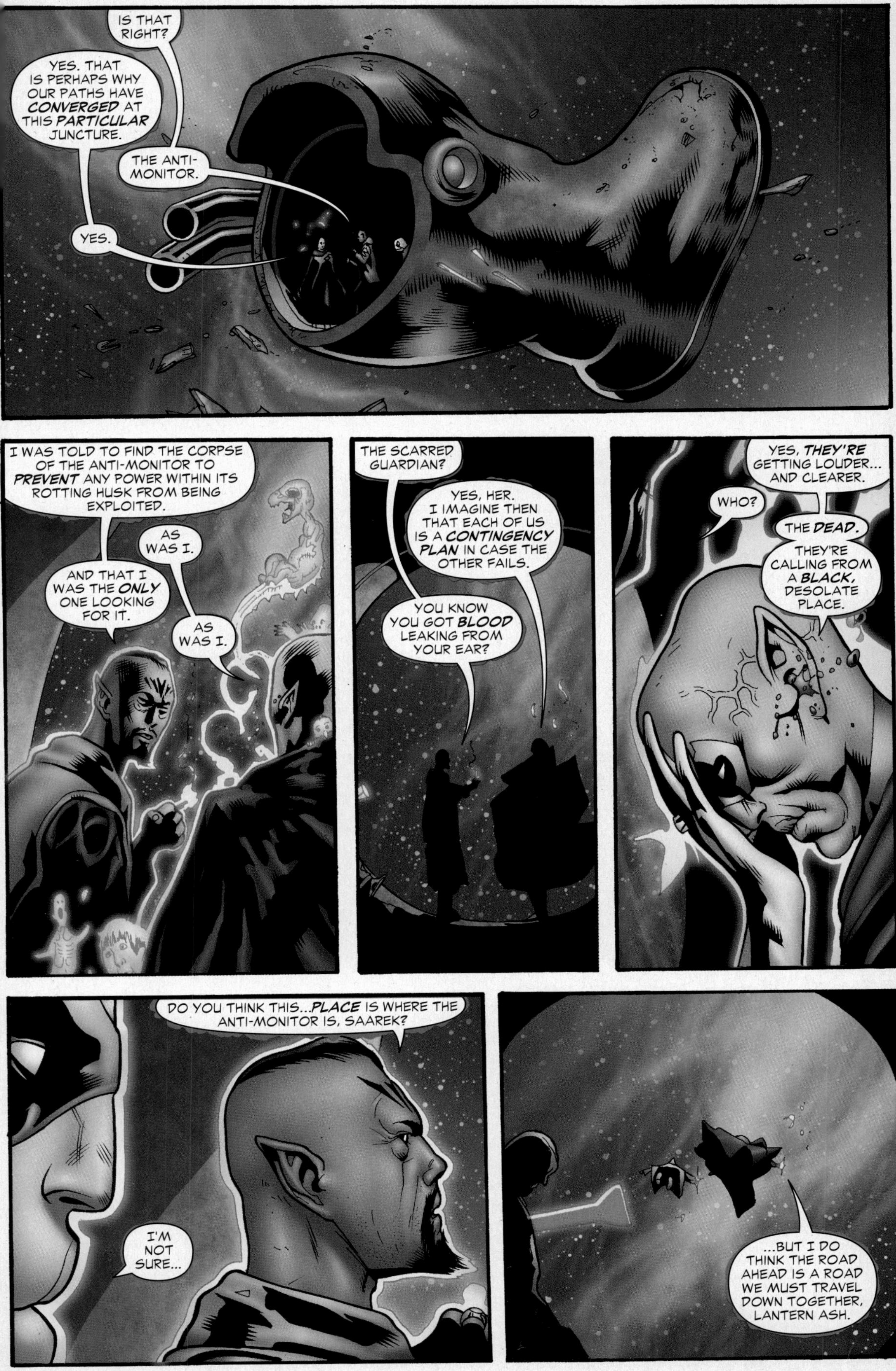
IS THAT RIGHT?
YES. THAT IS PERHAPS WHY OUR PATHS HAVE **CONVERGED** AT THIS **PARTICULAR** JUNCTURE.
THE ANTI-MONITOR.
YES.
I WAS TOLD TO FIND THE CORPSE OF THE ANTI-MONITOR TO **PREVENT** ANY POWER WITHIN ITS ROTTING HUSK FROM BEING EXPLOITED.
AS WAS I.
AND THAT I WAS THE **ONLY** ONE LOOKING FOR IT.
AS WAS I.
THE SCARRED GUARDIAN?
YES, HER. I IMAGINE THEN THAT EACH OF US IS A **CONTINGENCY PLAN** IN CASE THE OTHER FAILS.
YOU KNOW YOU GOT **BLOOD** LEAKING FROM YOUR EAR?
YES, **THEY'RE** GETTING LOUDER... AND CLEARER.
WHO?
THE **DEAD**.
THEY'RE CALLING FROM A **BLACK**, DESOLATE PLACE.
DO YOU THINK THIS...**PLACE** IS WHERE THE ANTI-MONITOR IS, SAAREK?
I'M NOT SURE...
...BUT I DO THINK THE ROAD AHEAD IS A ROAD WE MUST TRAVEL DOWN TOGETHER, LANTERN ASH.

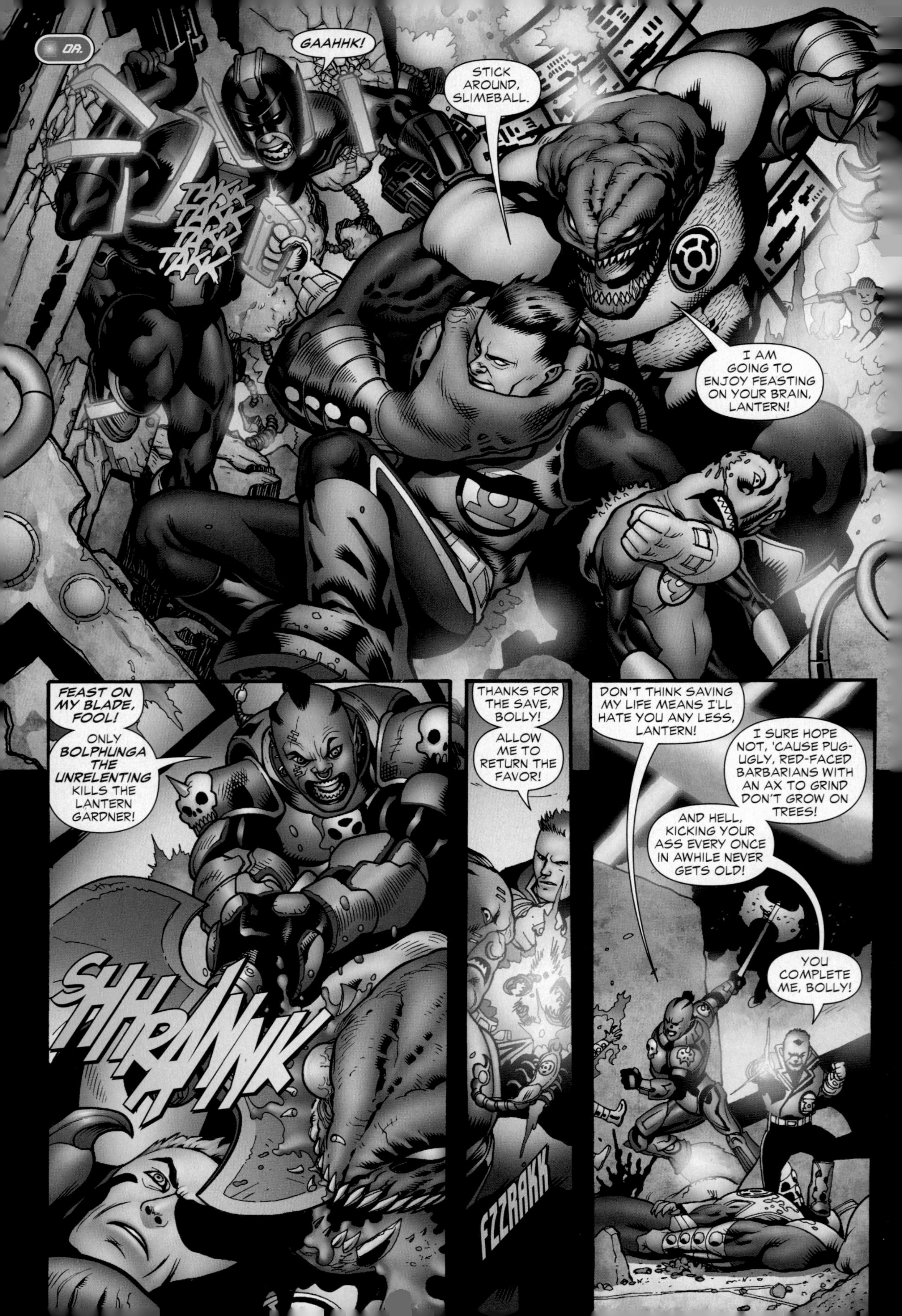
GAAHHK!
TAKK TAKK TAKK TAKK
STICK AROUND, SLIMEBALL.
I AM GOING TO ENJOY FEASTING ON YOUR BRAIN, LANTERN!
FEAST ON MY BLADE, FOOL!
ONLY BOLPHUNGA THE UNRELENTING KILLS THE LANTERN GARDNER!
SHHRANK
THANKS FOR THE SAVE, BOLLY!
ALLOW ME TO RETURN THE FAVOR!
FZZRAKK
DON'T THINK SAVING MY LIFE MEANS I'LL HATE YOU ANY LESS, LANTERN!
I SURE HOPE NOT, 'CAUSE PUG-UGLY, RED-FACED BARBARIANS WITH AN AX TO GRIND DON'T GROW ON TREES!
AND HELL, KICKING YOUR ASS EVERY ONCE IN AWHILE NEVER GETS OLD!
YOU COMPLETE ME, BOLLY!

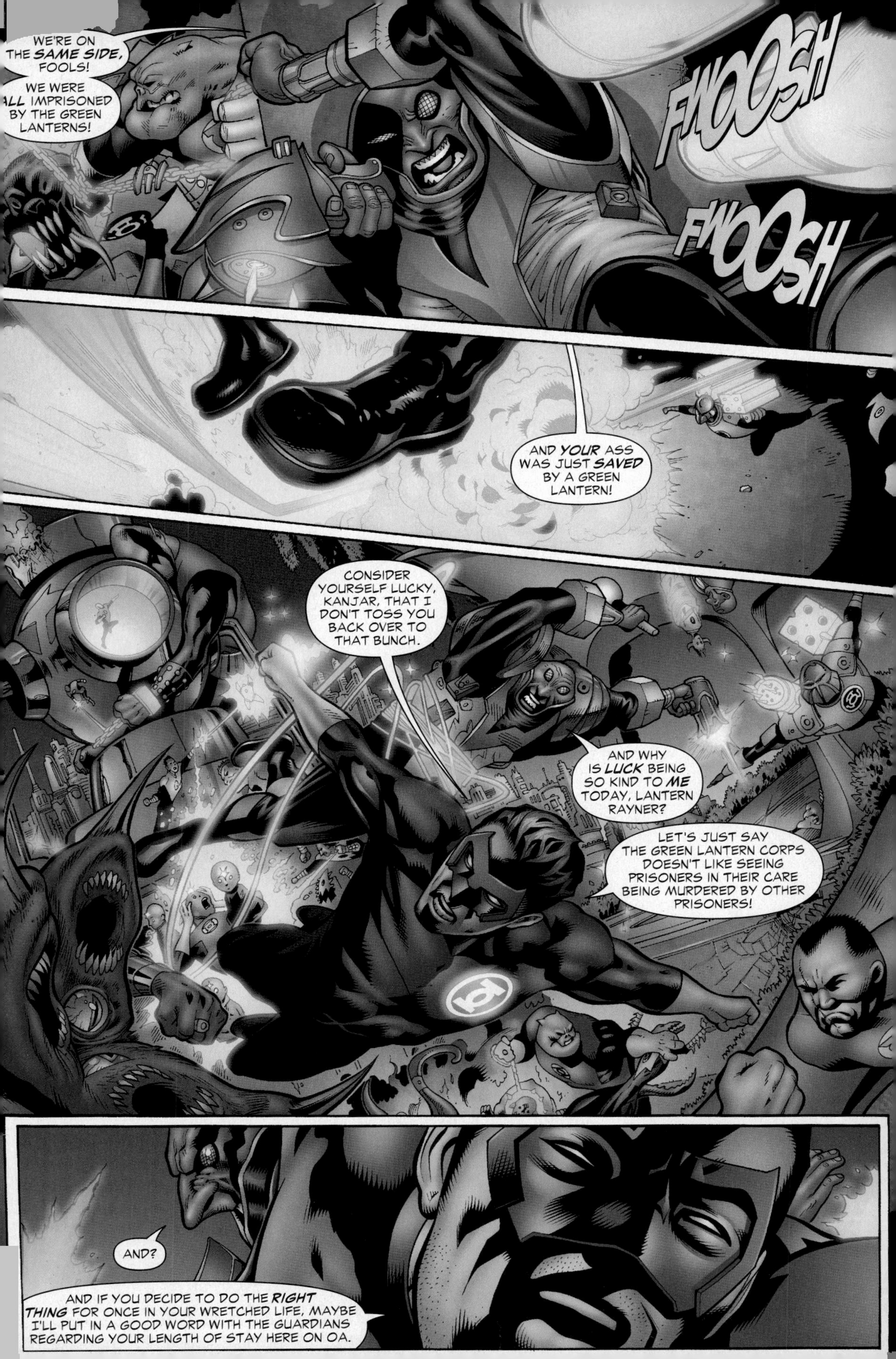
WE'RE ON THE SAME SIDE, FOOLS!
WE WERE ALL IMPRISONED BY THE GREEN LANTERNS!
FWOOSH
FWOOSH
AND YOUR ASS WAS JUST SAVED BY A GREEN LANTERN!
CONSIDER YOURSELF LUCKY, KANJAR, THAT I DON'T TOSS YOU BACK OVER TO THAT BUNCH.
AND WHY IS LUCK BEING SO KIND TO ME TODAY, LANTERN RAYNER?
LET'S JUST SAY THE GREEN LANTERN CORPS DOESN'T LIKE SEEING PRISONERS IN THEIR CARE BEING MURDERED BY OTHER PRISONERS!
AND?
AND IF YOU DECIDE TO DO THE RIGHT THING FOR ONCE IN YOUR WRETCHED LIFE, MAYBE I'LL PUT IN A GOOD WORD WITH THE GUARDIANS REGARDING YOUR LENGTH OF STAY HERE ON OA.

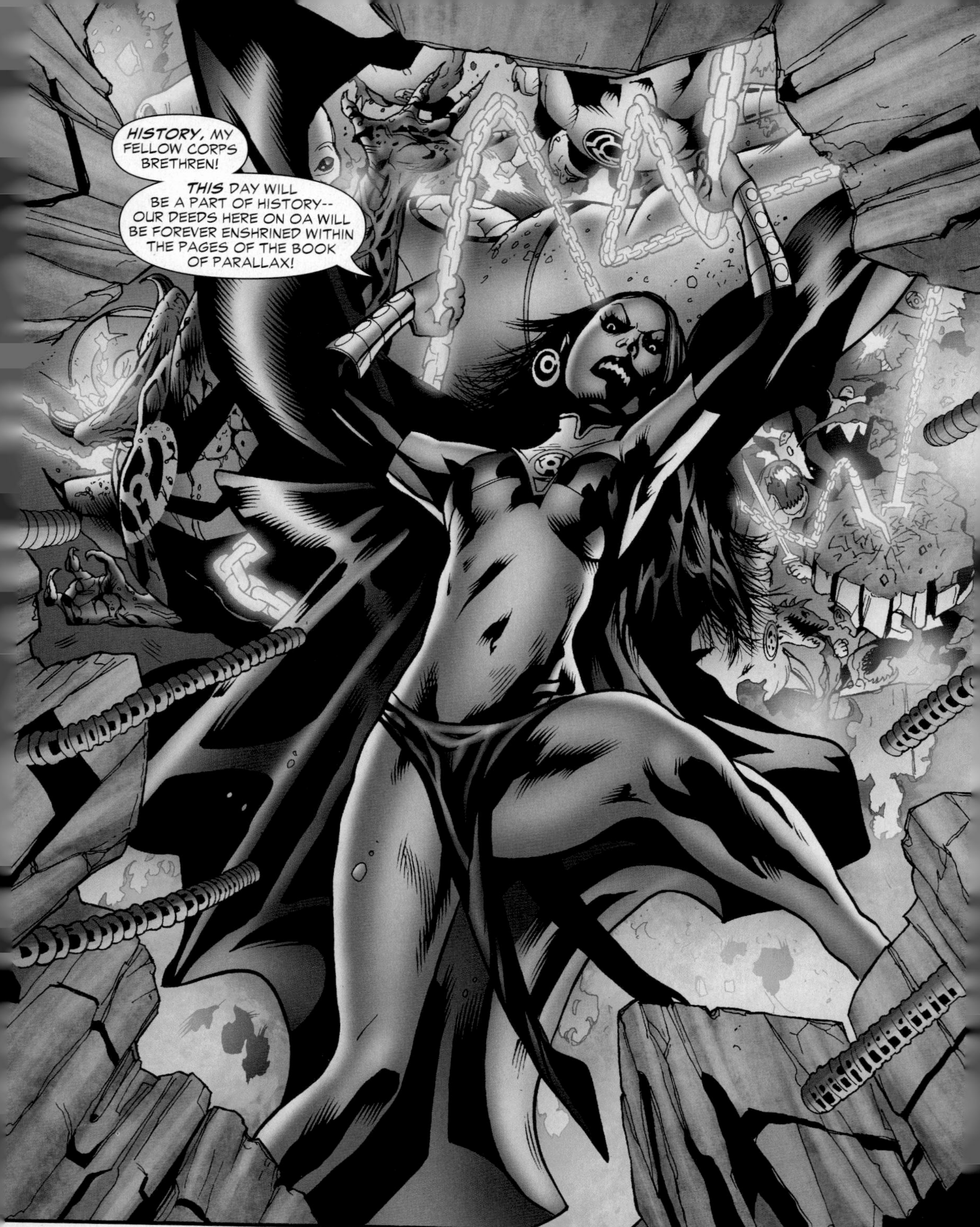
HISTORY, MY FELLOW CORPS BRETHREN!
THIS DAY WILL BE A PART OF HISTORY-- OUR DEEDS HERE ON OA WILL BE FOREVER ENSHRINED WITHIN THE PAGES OF THE BOOK OF PARALLAX!
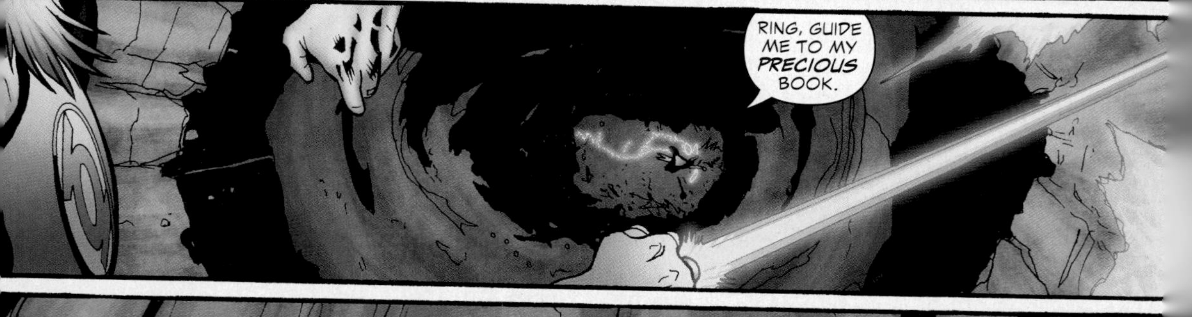
RING, GUIDE ME TO MY PRECIOUS BOOK.

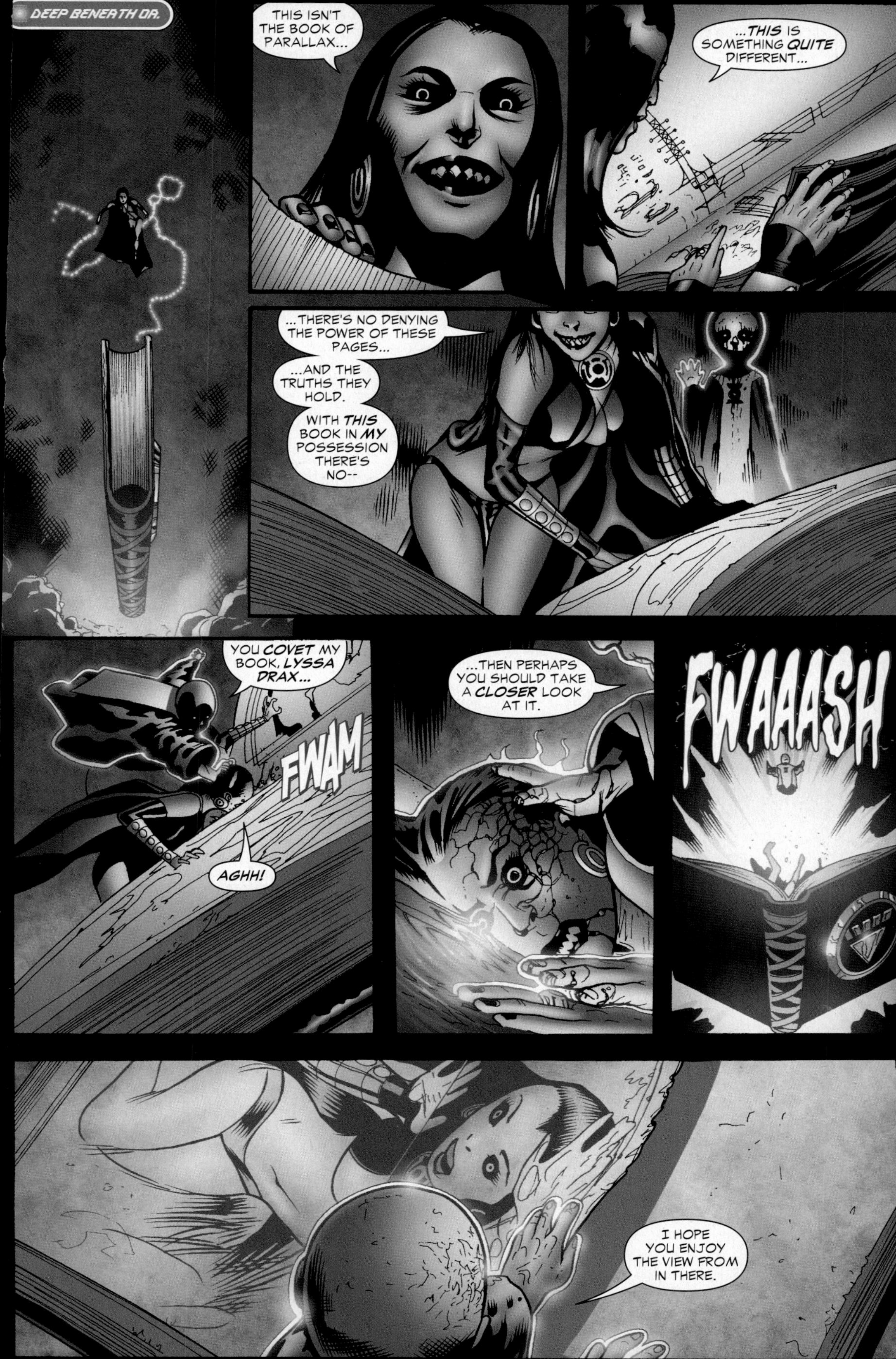
DEEP BENEATH OA.
THIS ISN'T THE BOOK OF PARALLAX...
...THIS IS SOMETHING QUITE DIFFERENT...
...THERE'S NO DENYING THE POWER OF THESE PAGES...
...AND THE TRUTHS THEY HOLD.
WITH THIS BOOK IN MY POSSESSION THERE'S NO--
YOU COVET MY BOOK, LYSSA DRAX...
FWAM
AGHH!
...THEN PERHAPS YOU SHOULD TAKE A CLOSER LOOK AT IT.
FWAAASH
I HOPE YOU ENJOY THE VIEW FROM IN THERE.

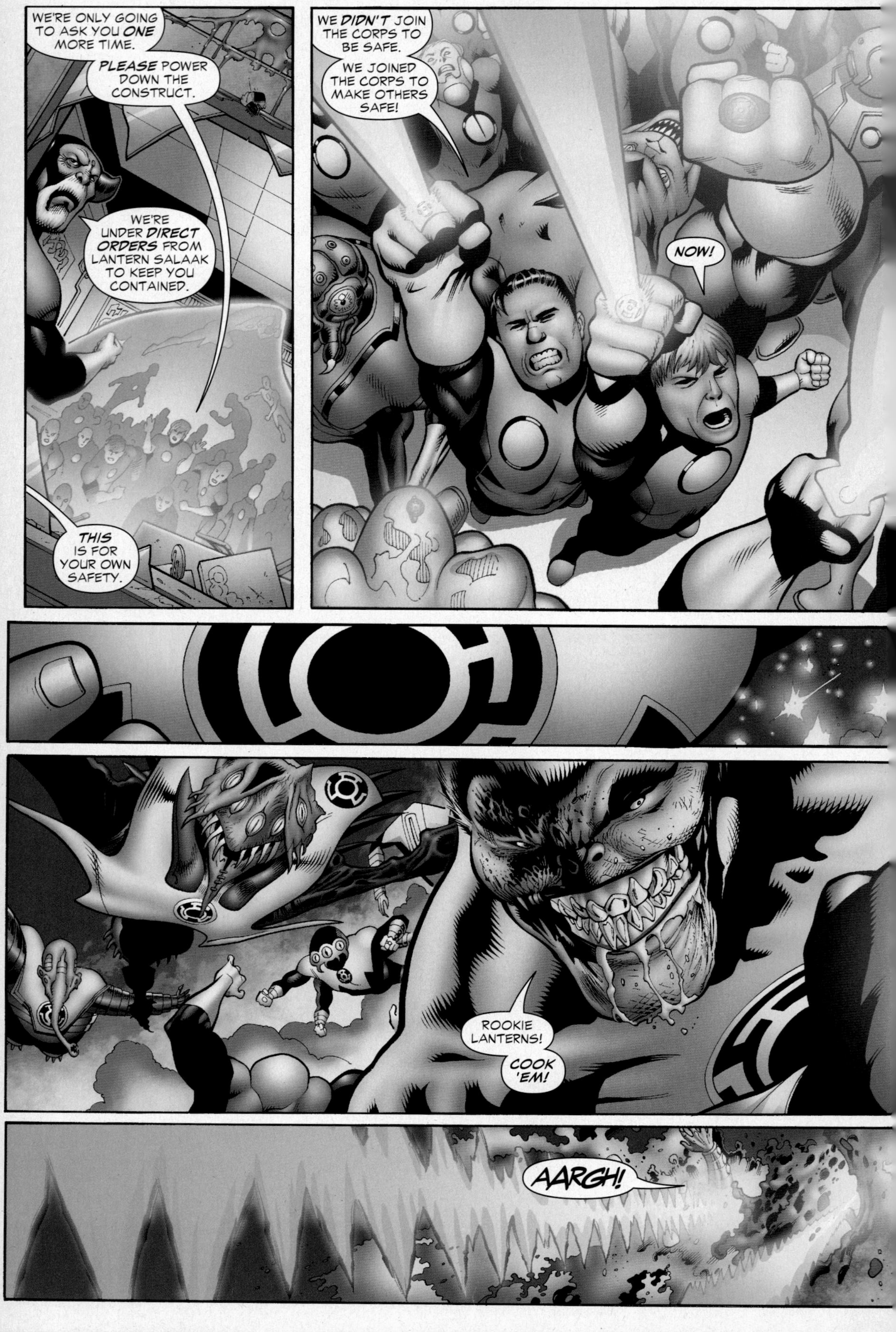
WE'RE ONLY GOING TO ASK YOU ONE MORE TIME.
PLEASE POWER DOWN THE CONSTRUCT.
WE'RE UNDER DIRECT ORDERS FROM LANTERN SALAAK TO KEEP YOU CONTAINED.
THIS IS FOR YOUR OWN SAFETY.
WE DIDN'T JOIN THE CORPS TO BE SAFE.
WE JOINED THE CORPS TO MAKE OTHERS SAFE!
NOW!
ROOKIE LANTERNS!
COOK 'EM!
AARGH!

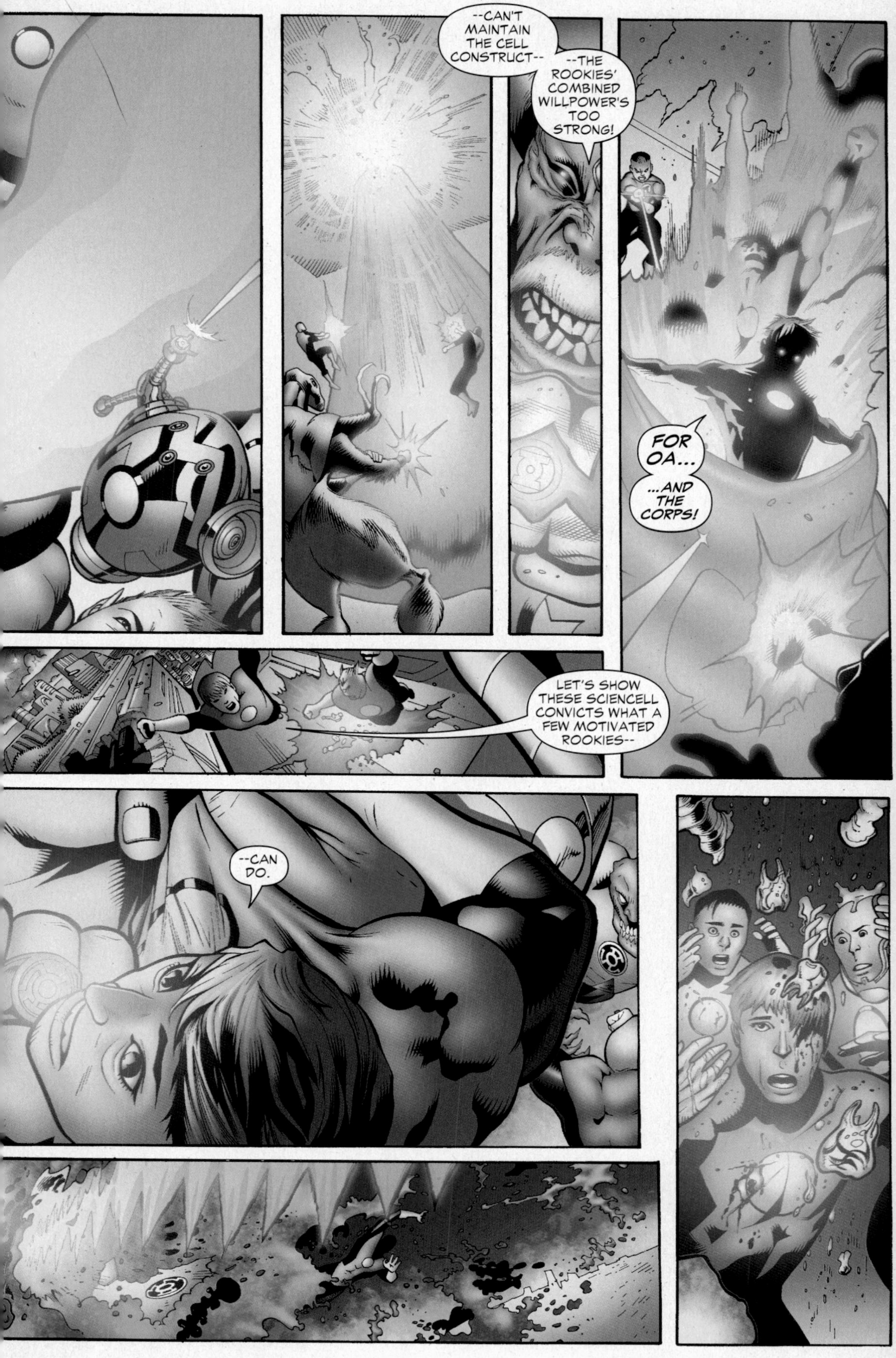
--CAN'T MAINTAIN THE CELL CONSTRUCT--
--THE ROOKIES' COMBINED WILLPOWER'S TOO STRONG!
FOR OA...
...AND THE CORPS!
LET'S SHOW THESE SCIENCELL CONVICTS WHAT A FEW MOTIVATED ROOKIES--
--CAN DO.

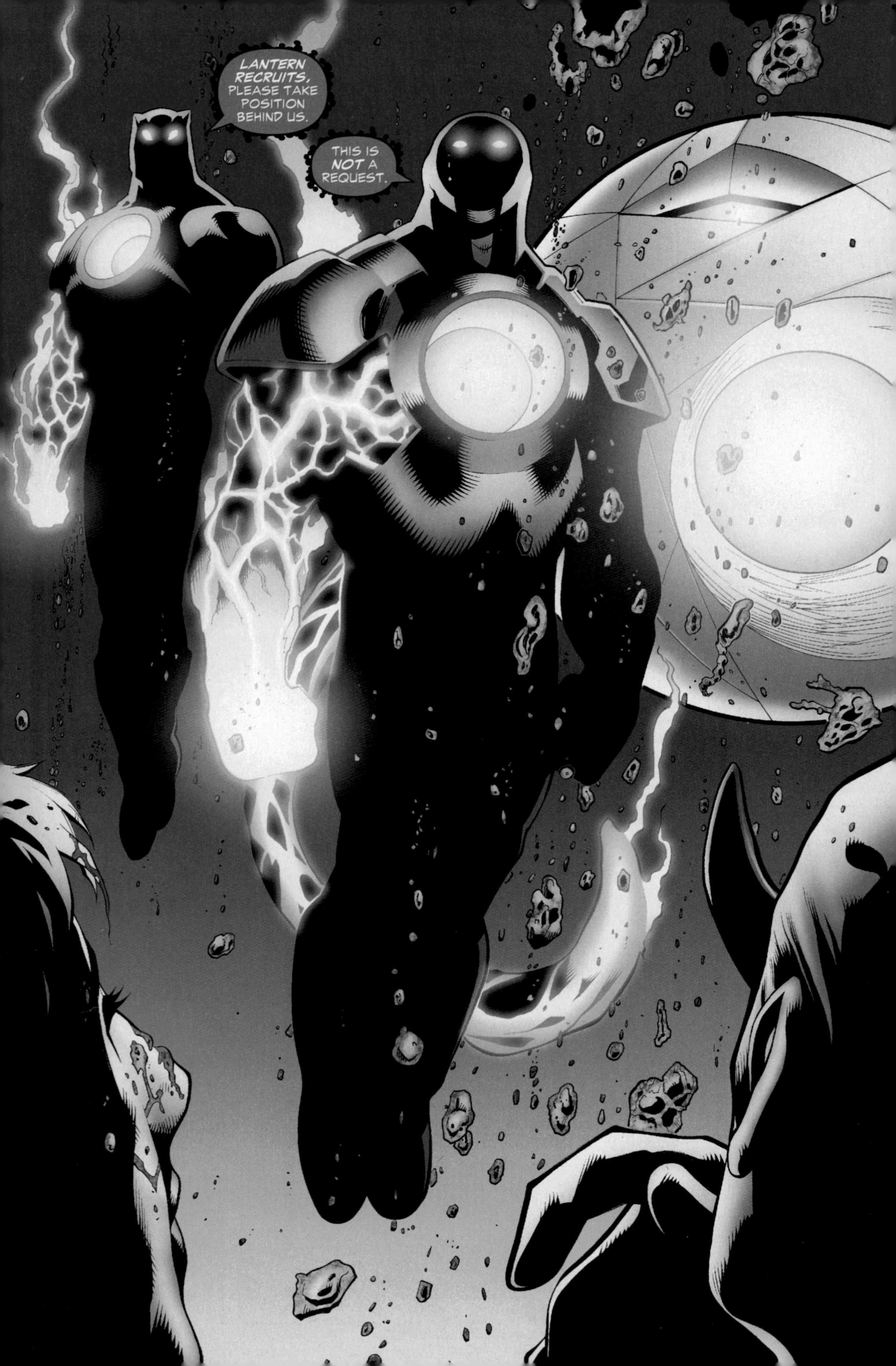
LANTERN RECRUITS, PLEASE TAKE POSITION BEHIND US.
THIS IS NOT A REQUEST.

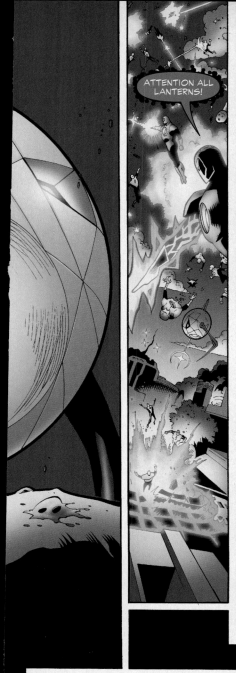

ATTENTION ALL LANTERNS!

ATTENTION ALL LANTERNS!

INITIATE *PHALANX DIRECTIVE* FROM QUADRANTS ZERO ONE AND ZERO FOUR!

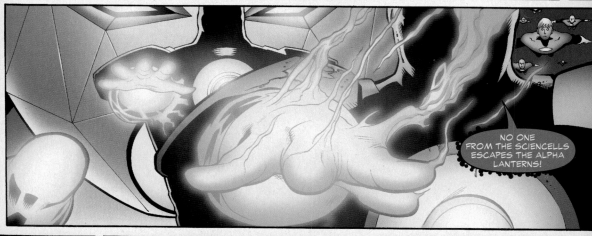

NO ONE FROM THE SCIENCELLS ESCAPES THE ALPHA LANTERNS!

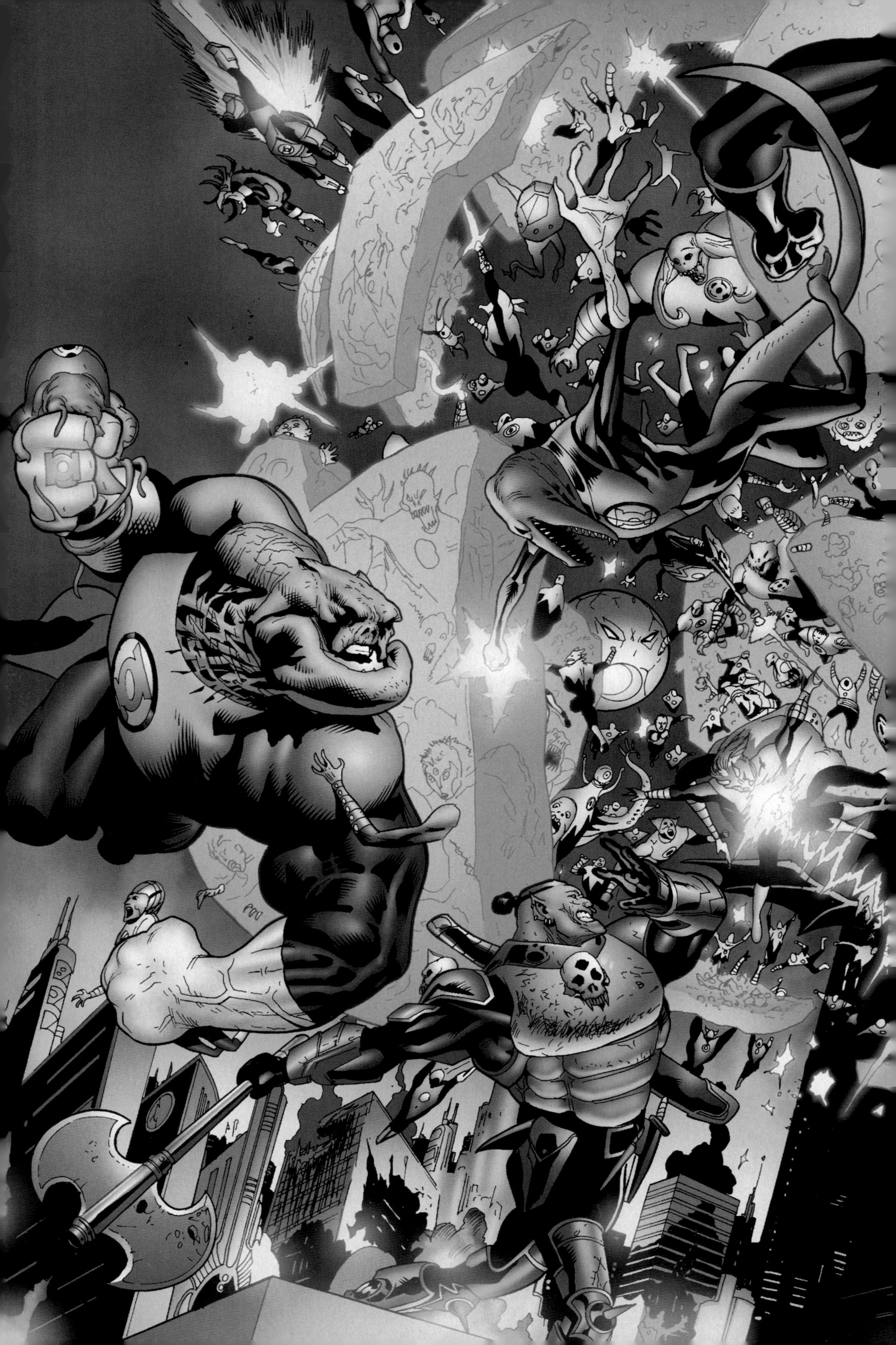

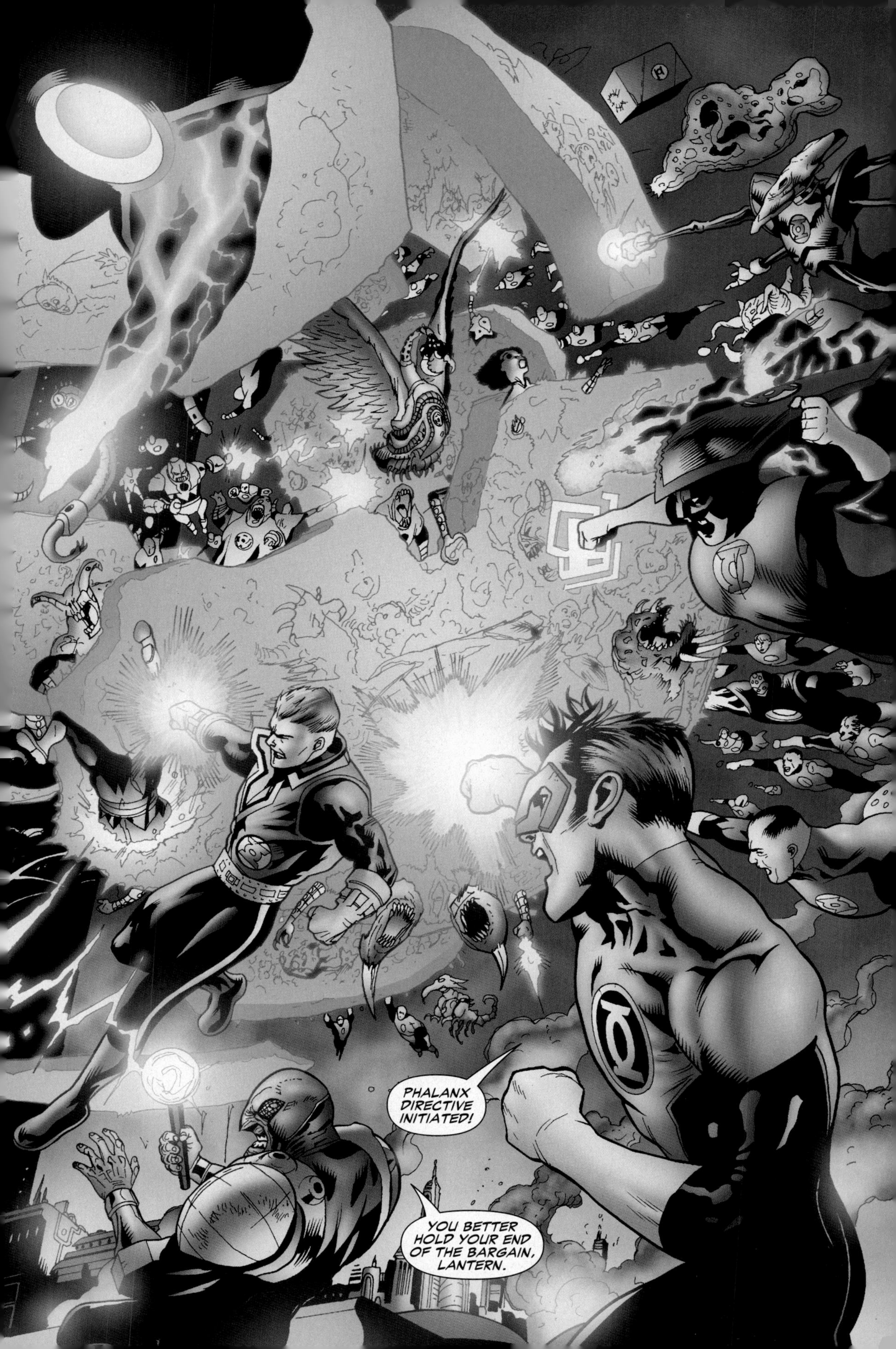
PHALANX DIRECTIVE INITIATED!
YOU BETTER HOLD YOUR END OF THE BARGAIN, LANTERN.

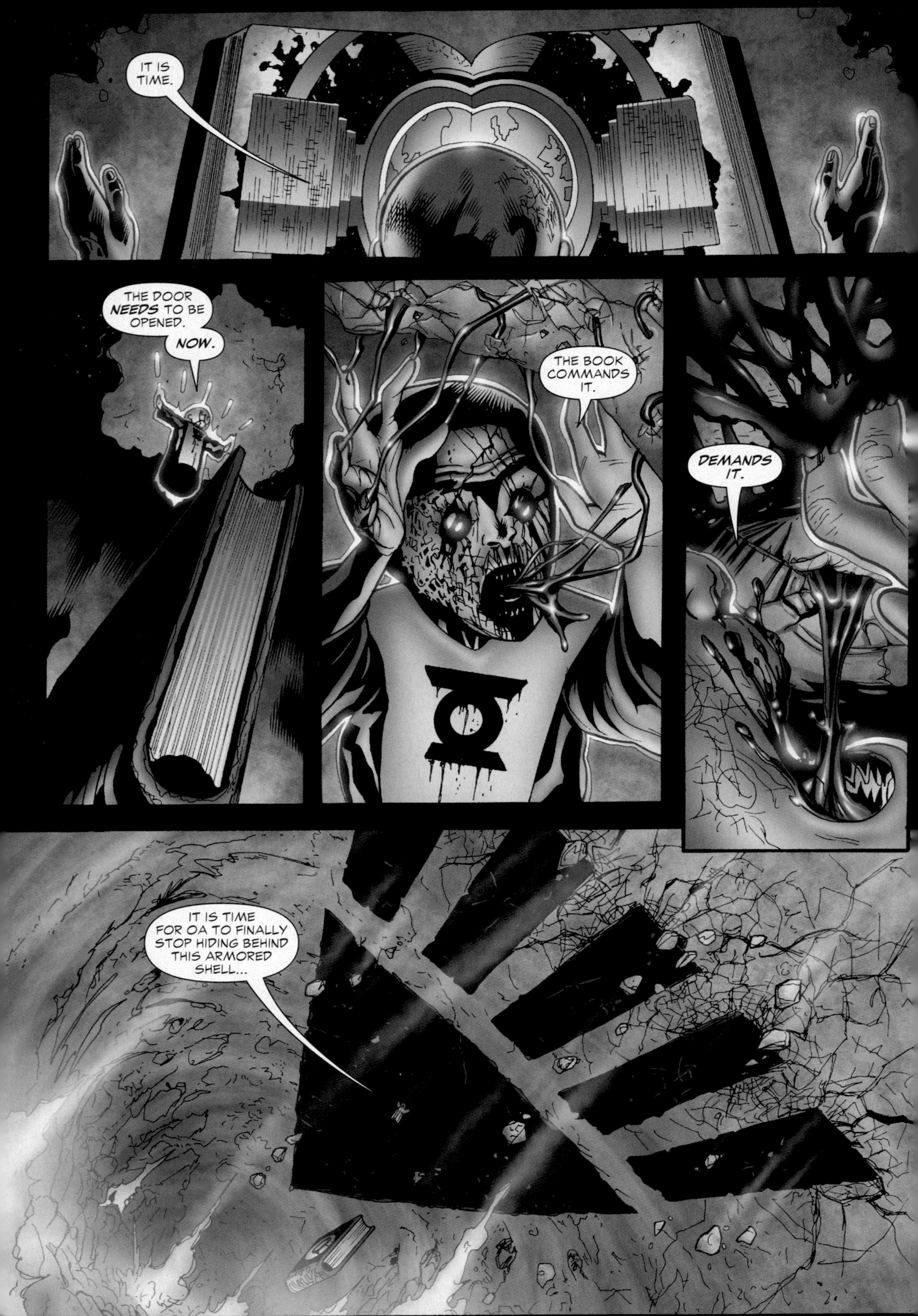
IT IS TIME.
THE DOOR NEEDS TO BE OPENED.
NOW.
THE BOOK COMMANDS IT.
DEMANDS IT.
IT IS TIME FOR OA TO FINALLY STOP HIDING BEHIND THIS ARMORED SHELL...

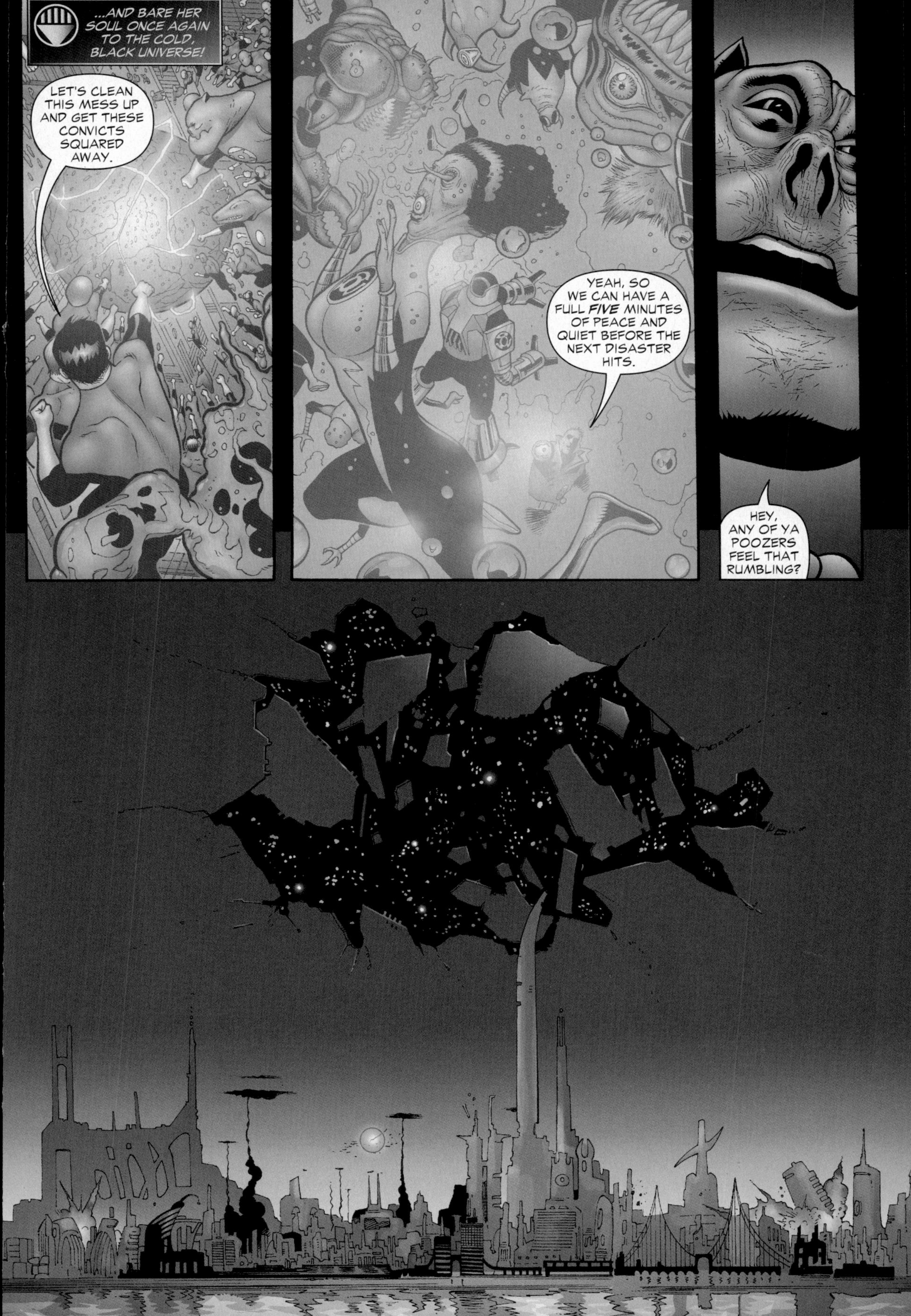
...AND BARE HER SOUL ONCE AGAIN TO THE COLD, BLACK UNIVERSE!
LET'S CLEAN THIS MESS UP AND GET THESE CONVICTS SQUARED AWAY.
YEAH, SO WE CAN HAVE A FULL *FIVE* MINUTES OF PEACE AND QUIET BEFORE THE NEXT DISASTER HITS.
HEY, ANY OF YA POOZERS FEEL THAT RUMBLING?

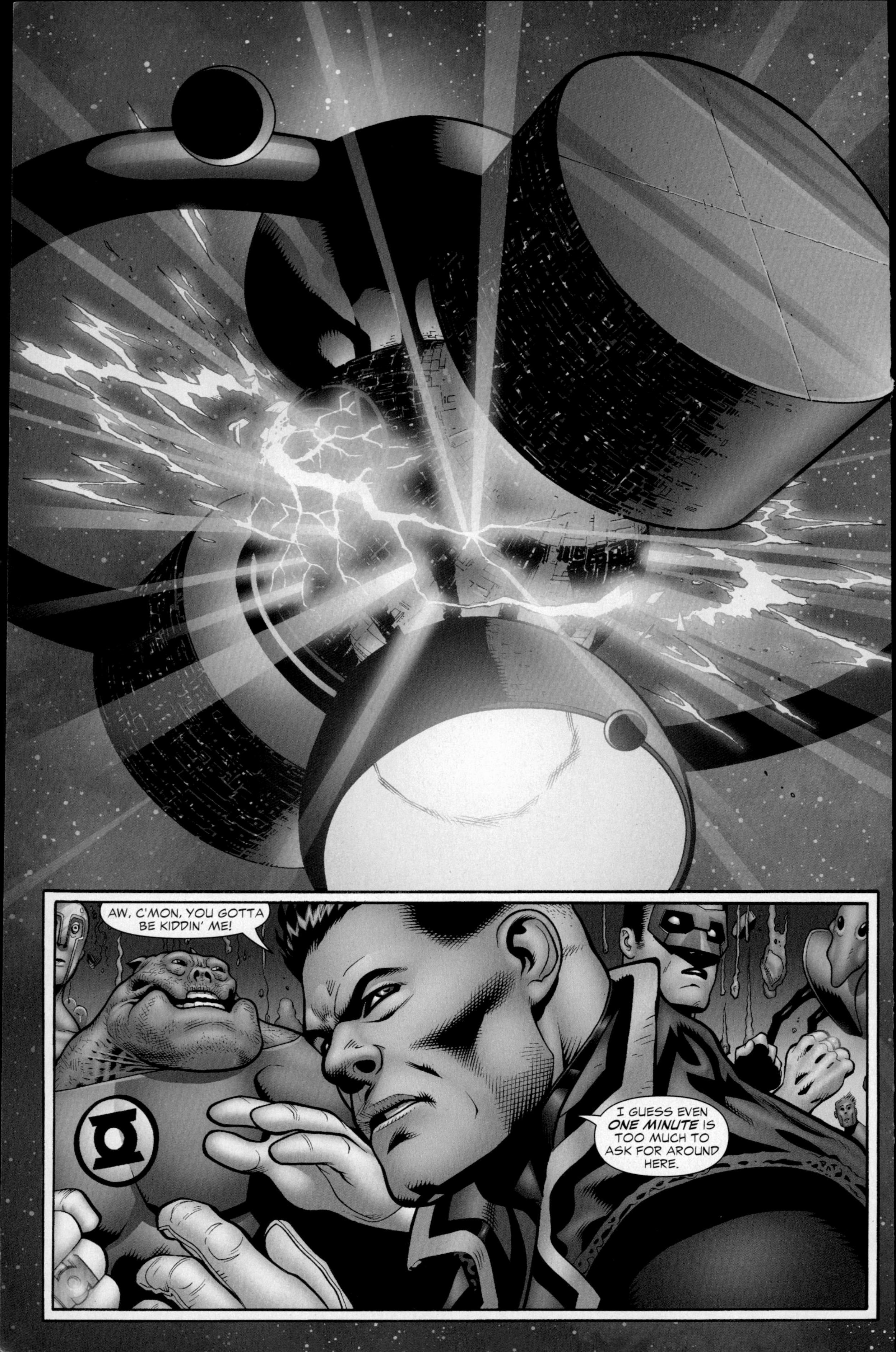
AW, C'MON, YOU GOTTA BE KIDDIN' ME!
I GUESS EVEN *ONE MINUTE* IS TOO MUCH TO ASK FOR AROUND HERE.

GREEN LANTERN CORPS #38
Cover by Patrick Gleason, Rebecca Buchman & Pete Pantazis

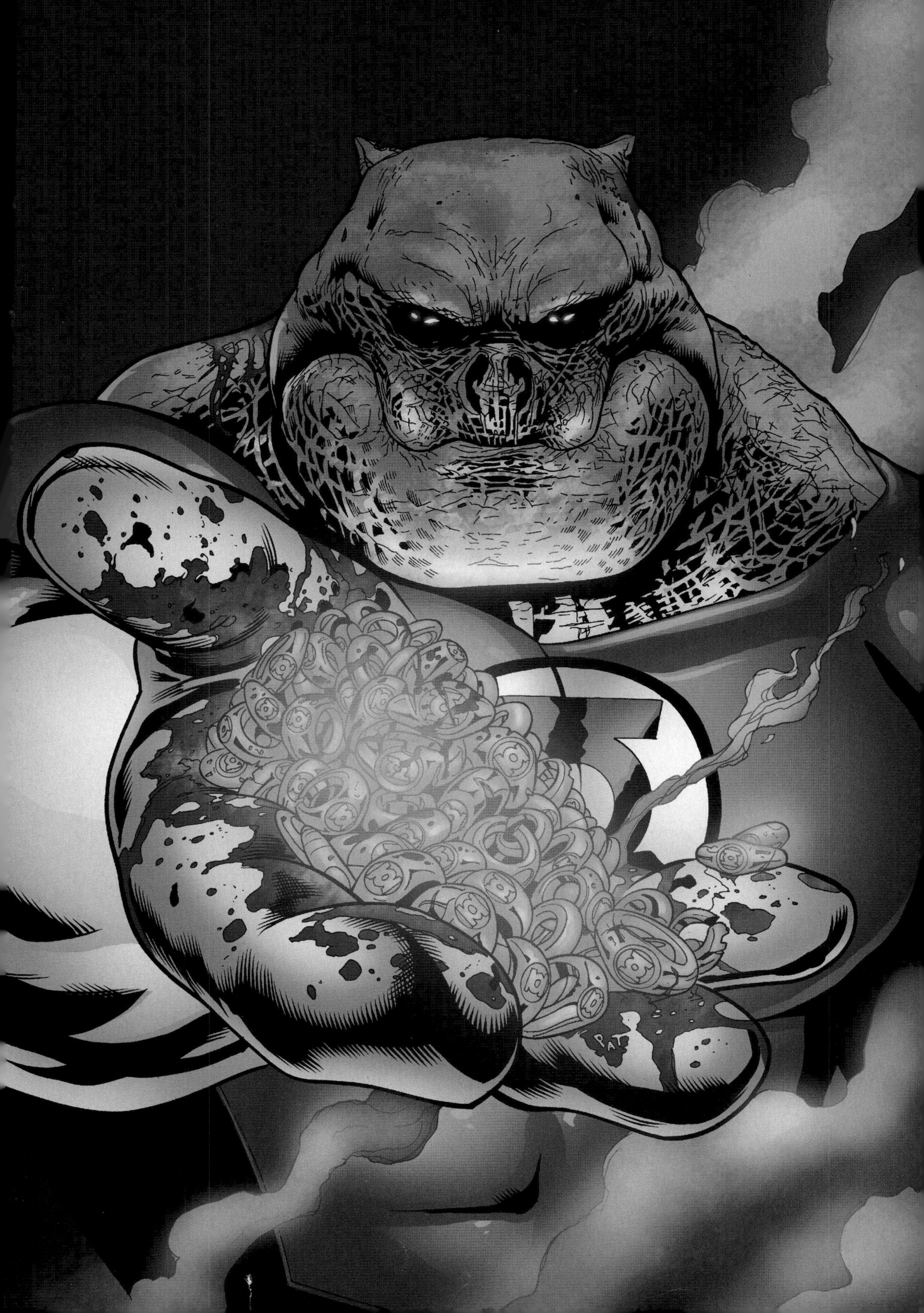

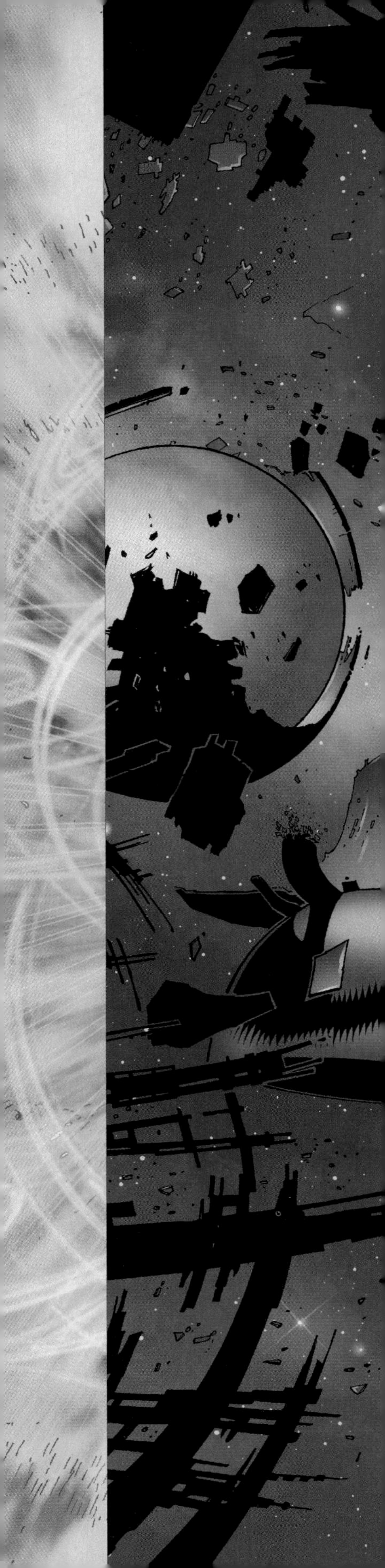

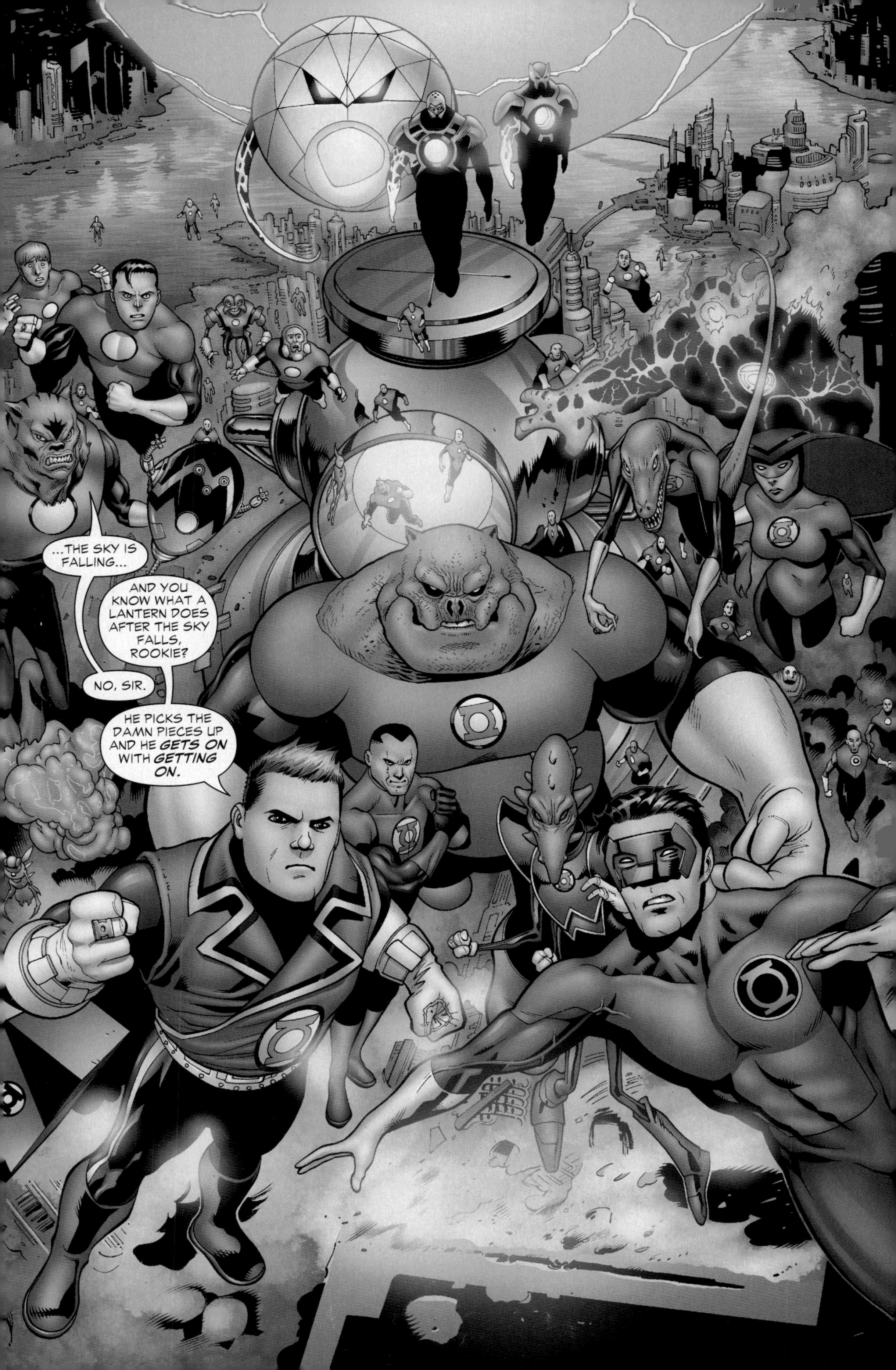
...THE SKY IS FALLING...
AND YOU KNOW WHAT A LANTERN DOES AFTER THE SKY FALLS, ROOKIE?
NO, SIR.
HE PICKS THE DAMN PIECES UP AND HE *GETS ON* WITH *GETTING ON*.

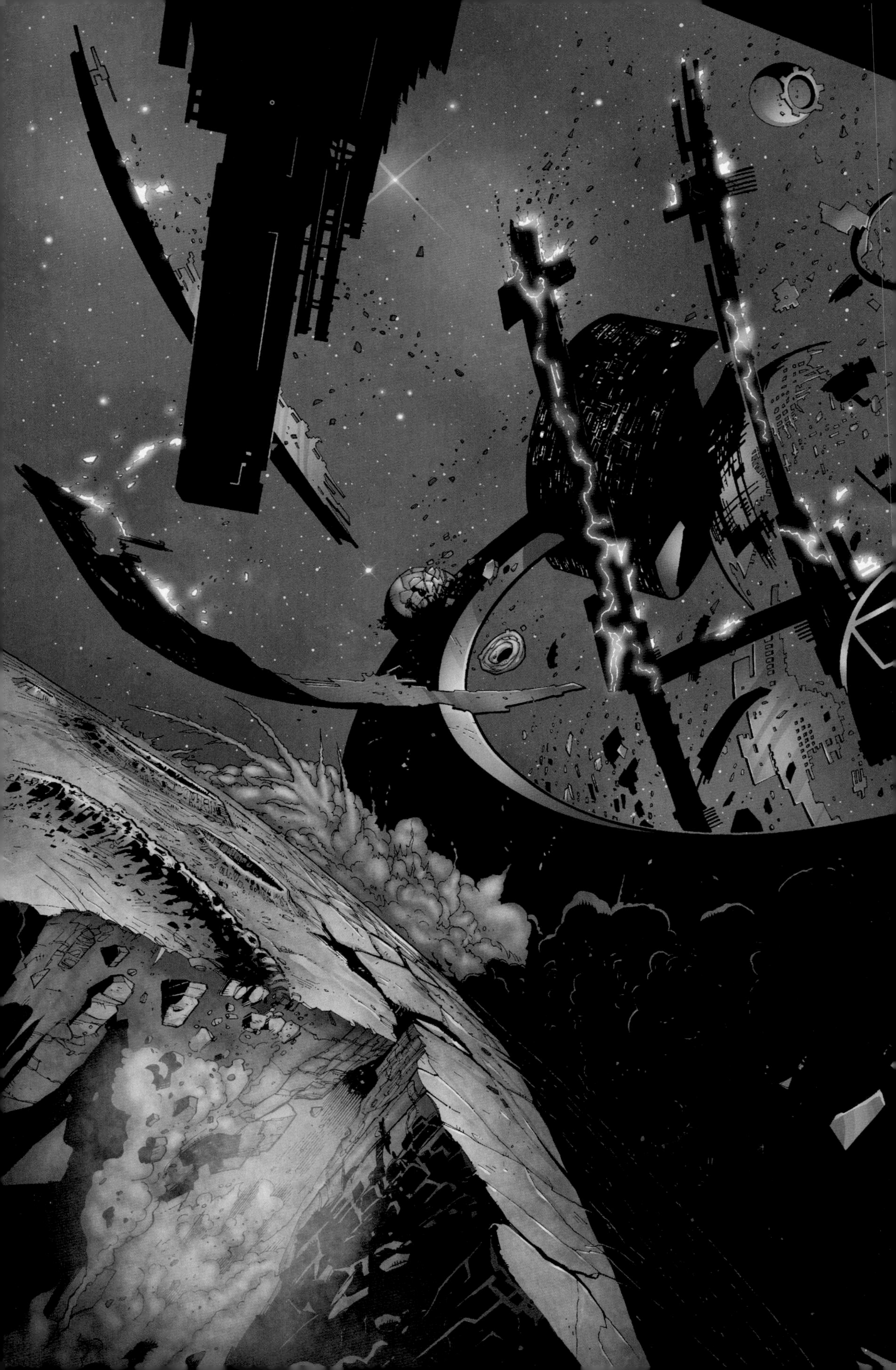

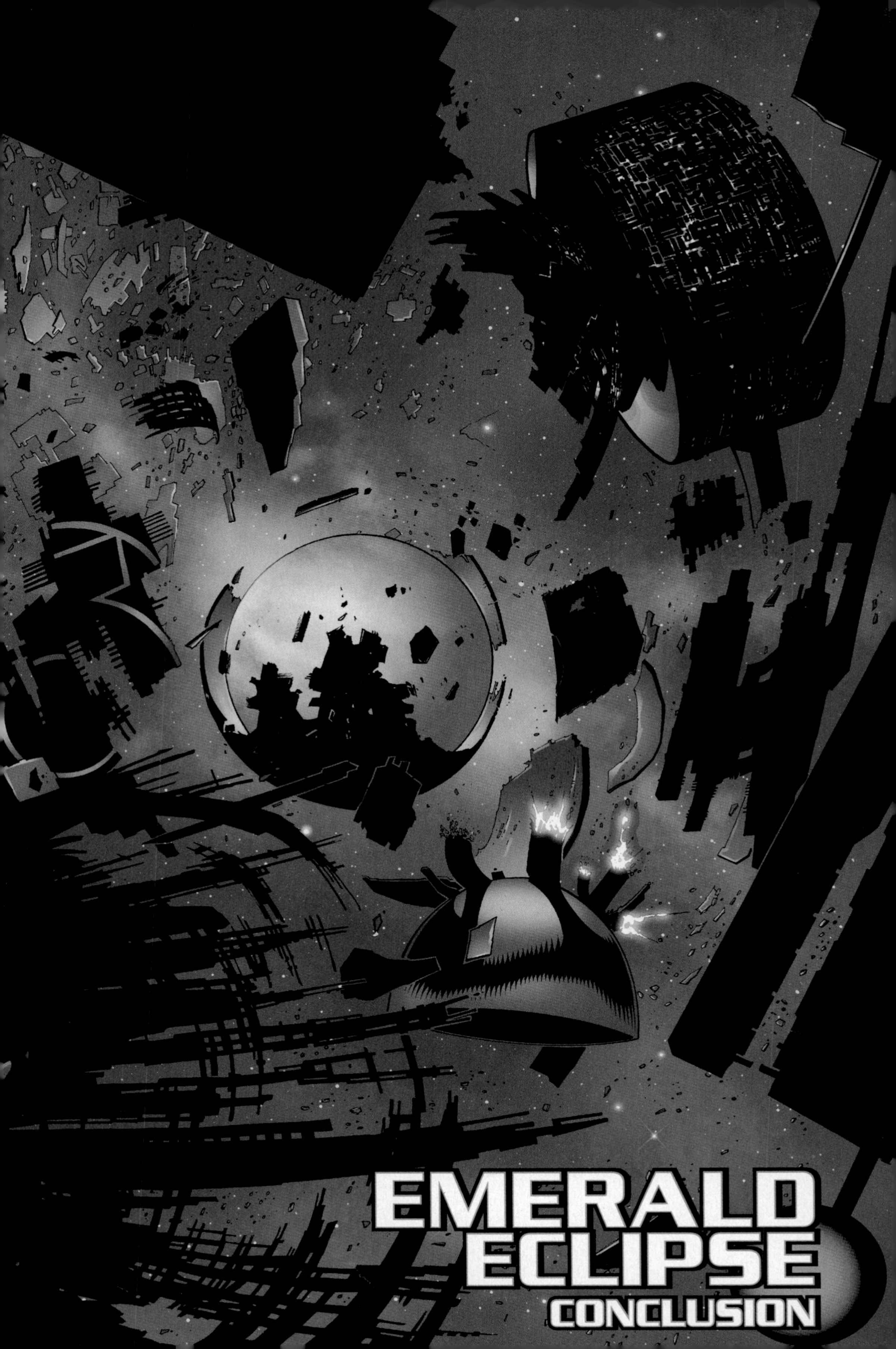
EMERALD
ECLIPSE
CONCLUSION

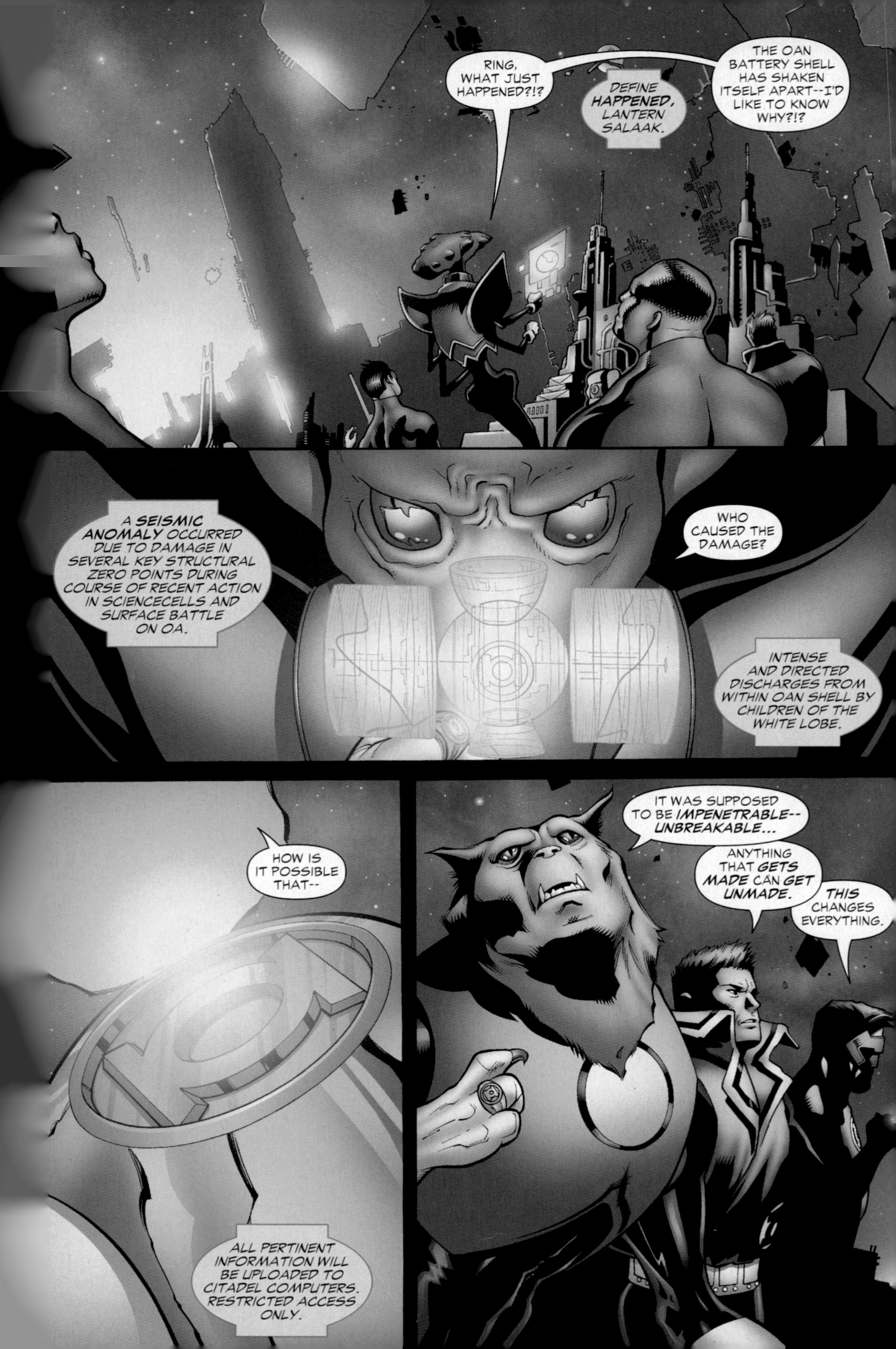
RING, WHAT JUST HAPPENED?!?
THE OAN BATTERY SHELL HAS SHAKEN ITSELF APART--I'D LIKE TO KNOW WHY?!?
DEFINE HAPPENED, LANTERN SALAAK.
A SEISMIC ANOMALY OCCURRED DUE TO DAMAGE IN SEVERAL KEY STRUCTURAL ZERO POINTS DURING COURSE OF RECENT ACTION IN SCIENCECELLS AND SURFACE BATTLE ON OA.
WHO CAUSED THE DAMAGE?
INTENSE AND DIRECTED DISCHARGES FROM WITHIN OAN SHELL BY CHILDREN OF THE WHITE LOBE.
HOW IS IT POSSIBLE THAT--
ALL PERTINENT INFORMATION WILL BE UPLOADED TO CITADEL COMPUTERS. RESTRICTED ACCESS ONLY.
IT WAS SUPPOSED TO BE IMPENETRABLE-- UNBREAKABLE...
ANYTHING THAT GETS MADE CAN GET UNMADE.
THIS CHANGES EVERYTHING.

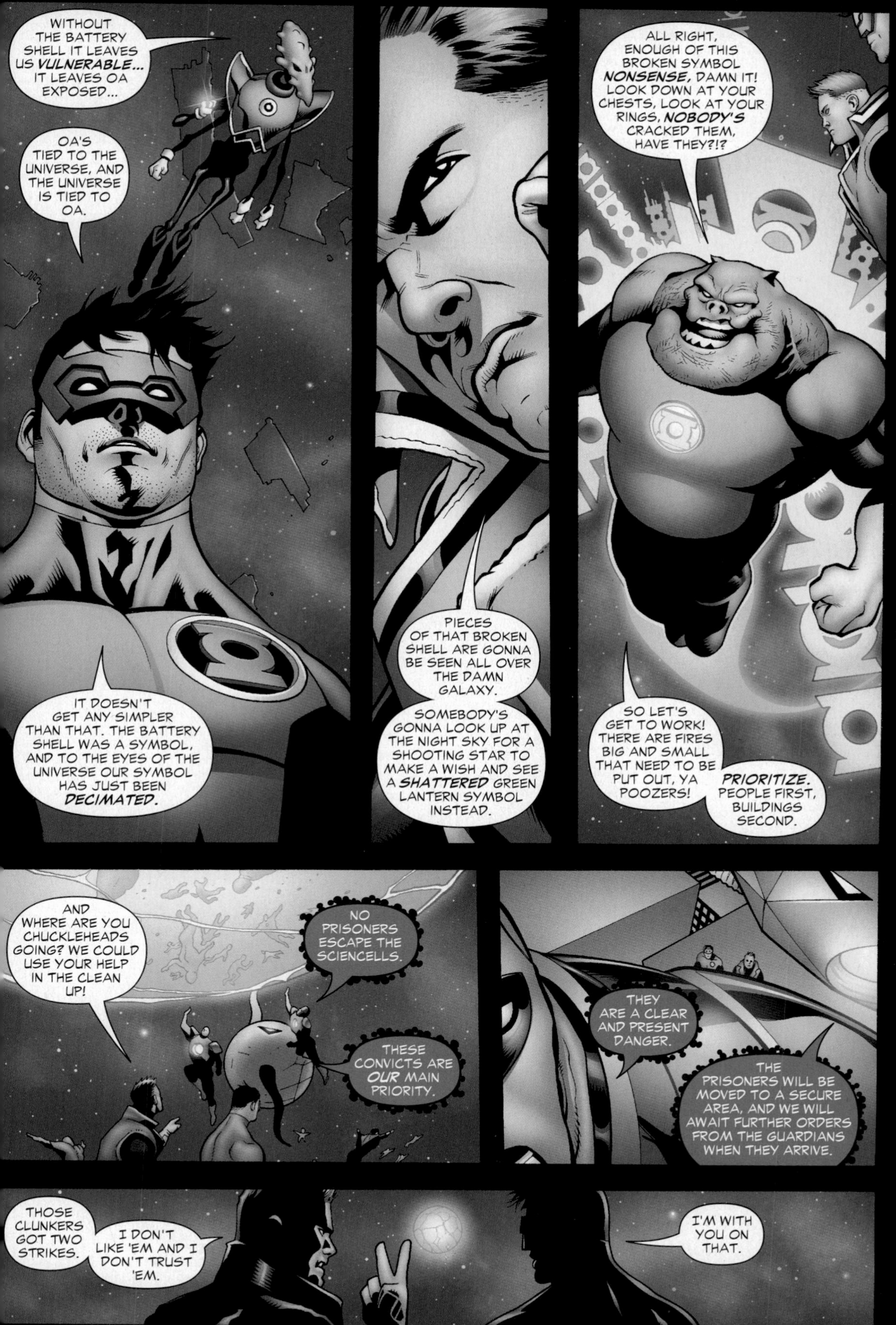
WITHOUT THE BATTERY SHELL IT LEAVES US VULNERABLE... IT LEAVES OA EXPOSED...
OA'S TIED TO THE UNIVERSE, AND THE UNIVERSE IS TIED TO OA.
IT DOESN'T GET ANY SIMPLER THAN THAT. THE BATTERY SHELL WAS A SYMBOL, AND TO THE EYES OF THE UNIVERSE OUR SYMBOL HAS JUST BEEN DECIMATED.
PIECES OF THAT BROKEN SHELL ARE GONNA BE SEEN ALL OVER THE DAMN GALAXY.
SOMEBODY'S GONNA LOOK UP AT THE NIGHT SKY FOR A SHOOTING STAR TO MAKE A WISH AND SEE A SHATTERED GREEN LANTERN SYMBOL INSTEAD.
ALL RIGHT, ENOUGH OF THIS BROKEN SYMBOL NONSENSE, DAMN IT! LOOK DOWN AT YOUR CHESTS, LOOK AT YOUR RINGS, NOBODY'S CRACKED THEM, HAVE THEY?!?
SO LET'S GET TO WORK! THERE ARE FIRES BIG AND SMALL THAT NEED TO BE PUT OUT, YA POOZERS!
PRIORITIZE. PEOPLE FIRST, BUILDINGS SECOND.
AND WHERE ARE YOU CHUCKLEHEADS GOING? WE COULD USE YOUR HELP IN THE CLEAN UP!
NO PRISONERS ESCAPE THE SCIENCELLS.
THESE CONVICTS ARE OUR MAIN PRIORITY.
THEY ARE A CLEAR AND PRESENT DANGER.
THE PRISONERS WILL BE MOVED TO A SECURE AREA, AND WE WILL AWAIT FURTHER ORDERS FROM THE GUARDIANS WHEN THEY ARRIVE.
THOSE CLUNKERS GOT TWO STRIKES.
I DON'T LIKE 'EM AND I DON'T TRUST 'EM.
I'M WITH YOU ON THAT.

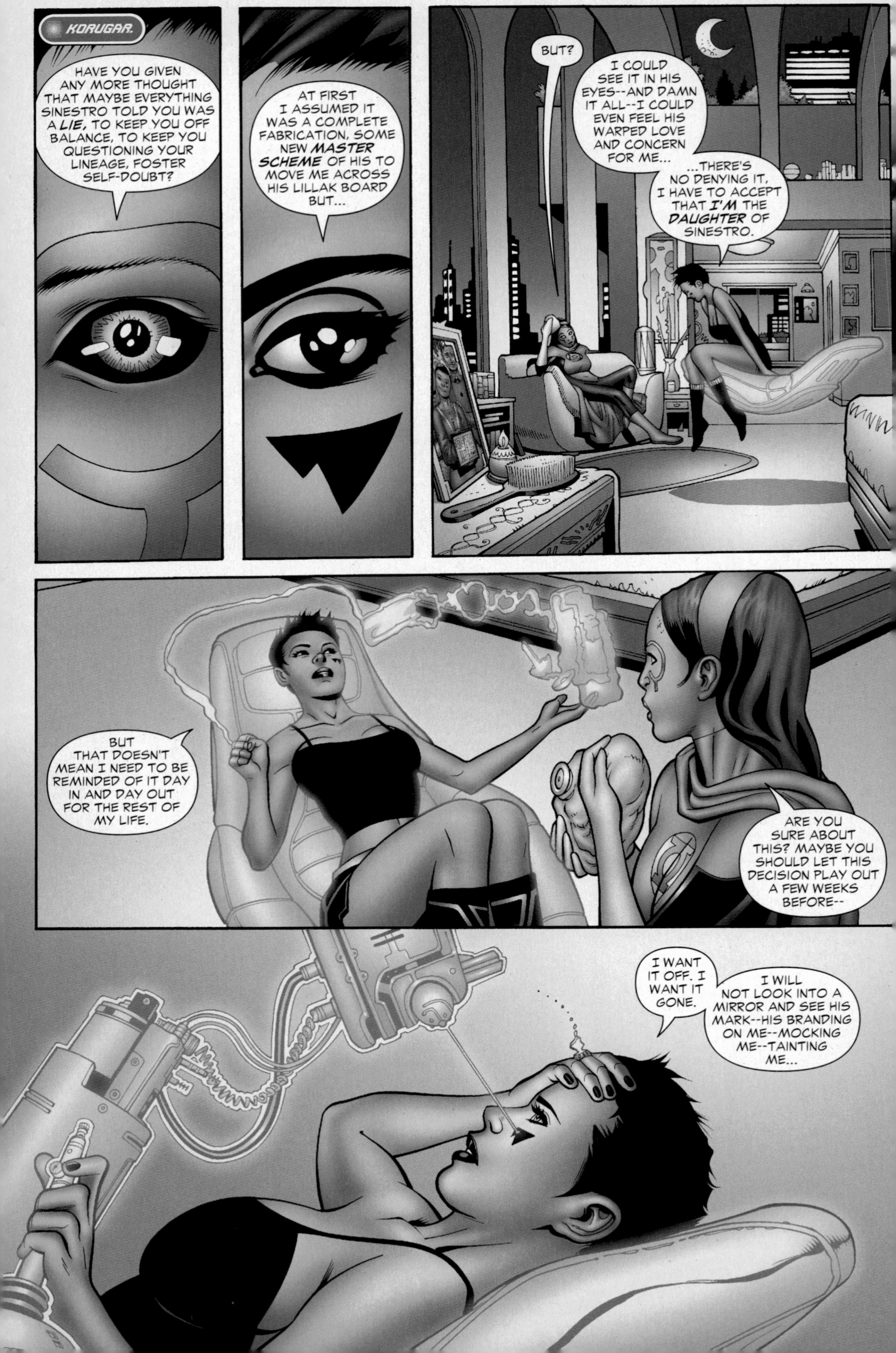
KORUGAR.
HAVE YOU GIVEN ANY MORE THOUGHT THAT MAYBE EVERYTHING SINESTRO TOLD YOU WAS A LIE, TO KEEP YOU OFF BALANCE, TO KEEP YOU QUESTIONING YOUR LINEAGE, FOSTER SELF-DOUBT?
AT FIRST I ASSUMED IT WAS A COMPLETE FABRICATION, SOME NEW MASTER SCHEME OF HIS TO MOVE ME ACROSS HIS LILLAK BOARD BUT...
BUT?
I COULD SEE IT IN HIS EYES--AND DAMN IT ALL--I COULD EVEN FEEL HIS WARPED LOVE AND CONCERN FOR ME...
...THERE'S NO DENYING IT, I HAVE TO ACCEPT THAT I'M THE DAUGHTER OF SINESTRO.
BUT THAT DOESN'T MEAN I NEED TO BE REMINDED OF IT DAY IN AND DAY OUT FOR THE REST OF MY LIFE.
ARE YOU SURE ABOUT THIS? MAYBE YOU SHOULD LET THIS DECISION PLAY OUT A FEW WEEKS BEFORE--
I WANT IT OFF. I WANT IT GONE.
I WILL NOT LOOK INTO A MIRROR AND SEE HIS MARK--HIS BRANDING ON ME--MOCKING ME--TAINTING ME...

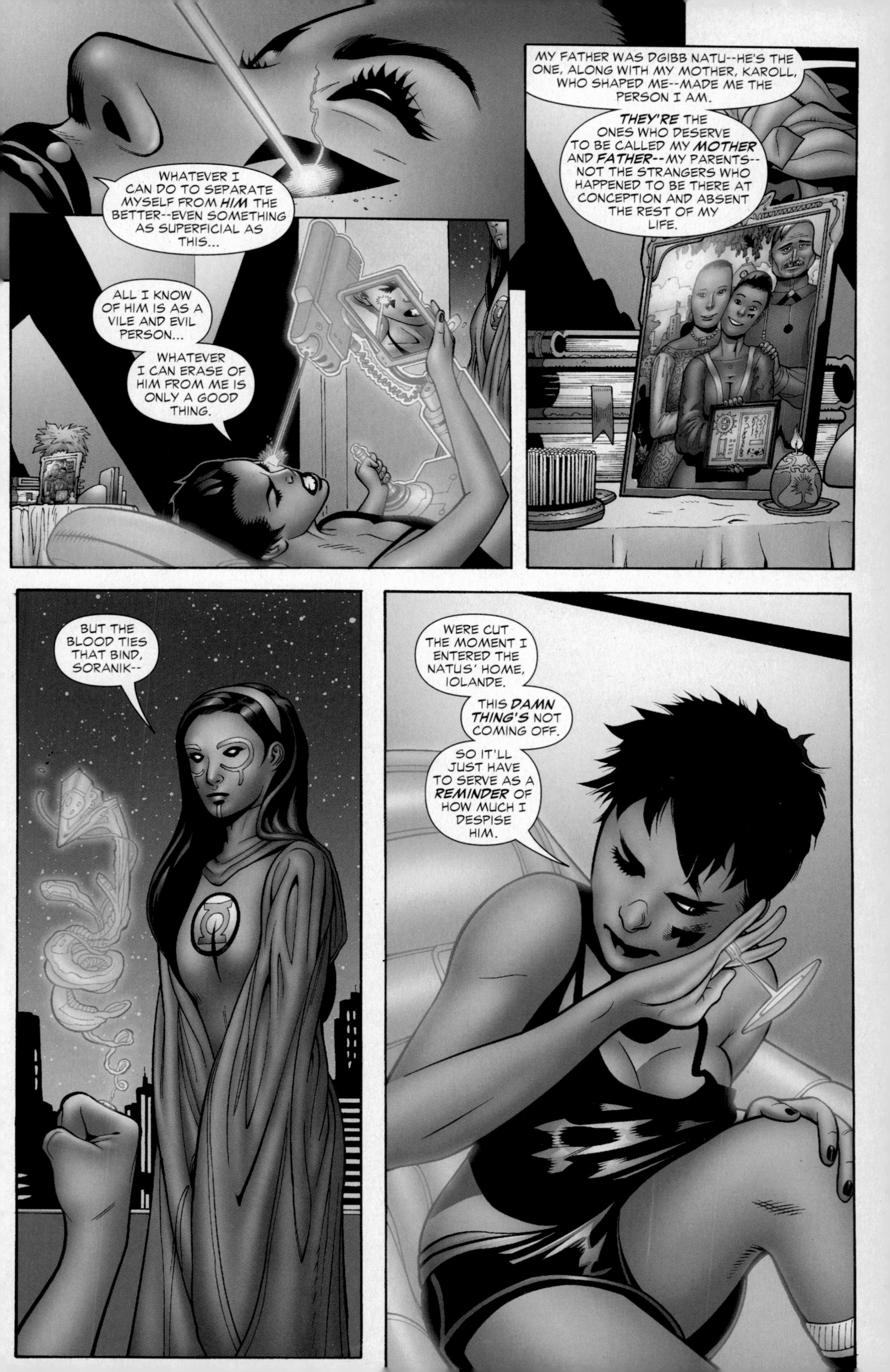
WHATEVER I CAN DO TO SEPARATE MYSELF FROM *HIM* THE BETTER--EVEN SOMETHING AS SUPERFICIAL AS THIS...
ALL I KNOW OF HIM IS AS A VILE AND EVIL PERSON...
WHATEVER I CAN ERASE OF HIM FROM ME IS ONLY A GOOD THING.
MY FATHER WAS DGIBB NATU--HE'S THE ONE, ALONG WITH MY MOTHER, KAROLL, WHO SHAPED ME--MADE ME THE PERSON I AM.
THEY'RE THE ONES WHO DESERVE TO BE CALLED MY *MOTHER* AND *FATHER*--MY PARENTS--NOT THE STRANGERS WHO HAPPENED TO BE THERE AT CONCEPTION AND ABSENT THE REST OF MY LIFE.
BUT THE BLOOD TIES THAT BIND, SORANIK--
WERE CUT THE MOMENT I ENTERED THE NATUS' HOME, IOLANDE.
THIS *DAMN THING'S* NOT COMING OFF.
SO IT'LL JUST HAVE TO SERVE AS A *REMINDER* OF HOW MUCH I DESPISE HIM.

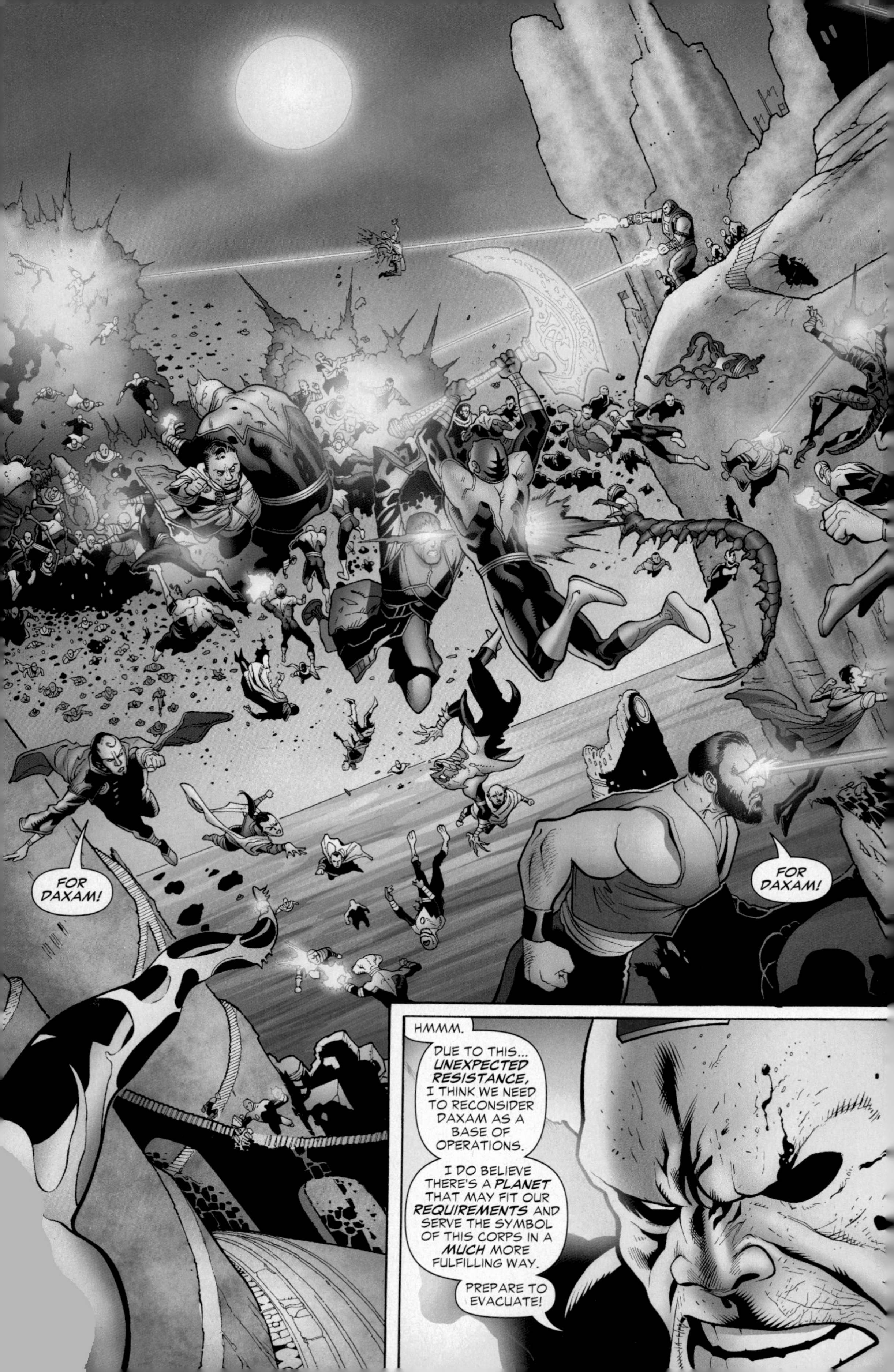
FOR DAXAM!
FOR DAXAM!
HMMM.
DUE TO THIS... UNEXPECTED RESISTANCE, I THINK WE NEED TO RECONSIDER DAXAM AS A BASE OF OPERATIONS.
I DO BELIEVE THERE'S A PLANET THAT MAY FIT OUR REQUIREMENTS AND SERVE THE SYMBOL OF THIS CORPS IN A MUCH MORE FULFILLING WAY.
PREPARE TO EVACUATE!

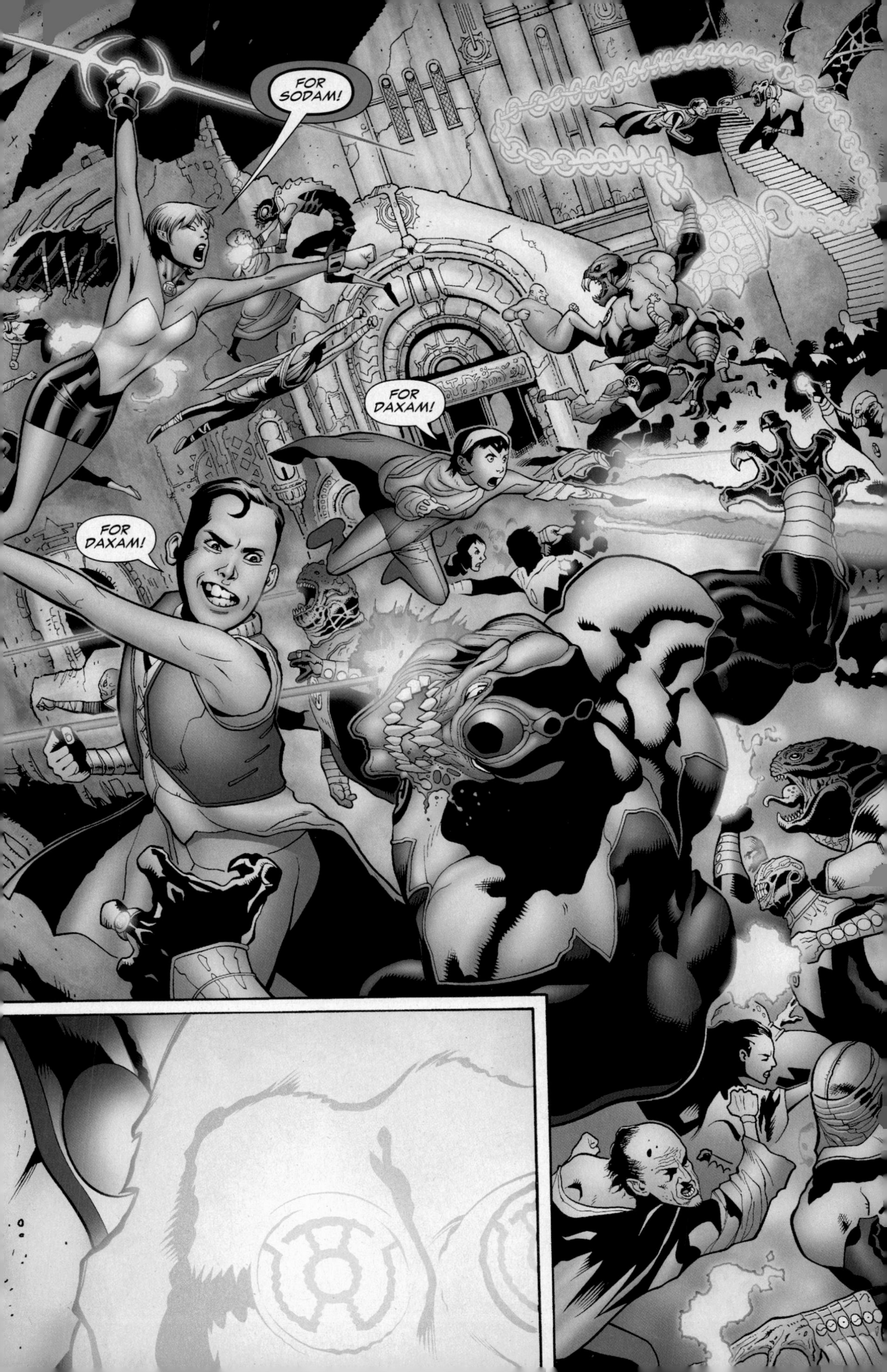
FOR SODAM!
FOR DAXAM!
FOR DAXAM!

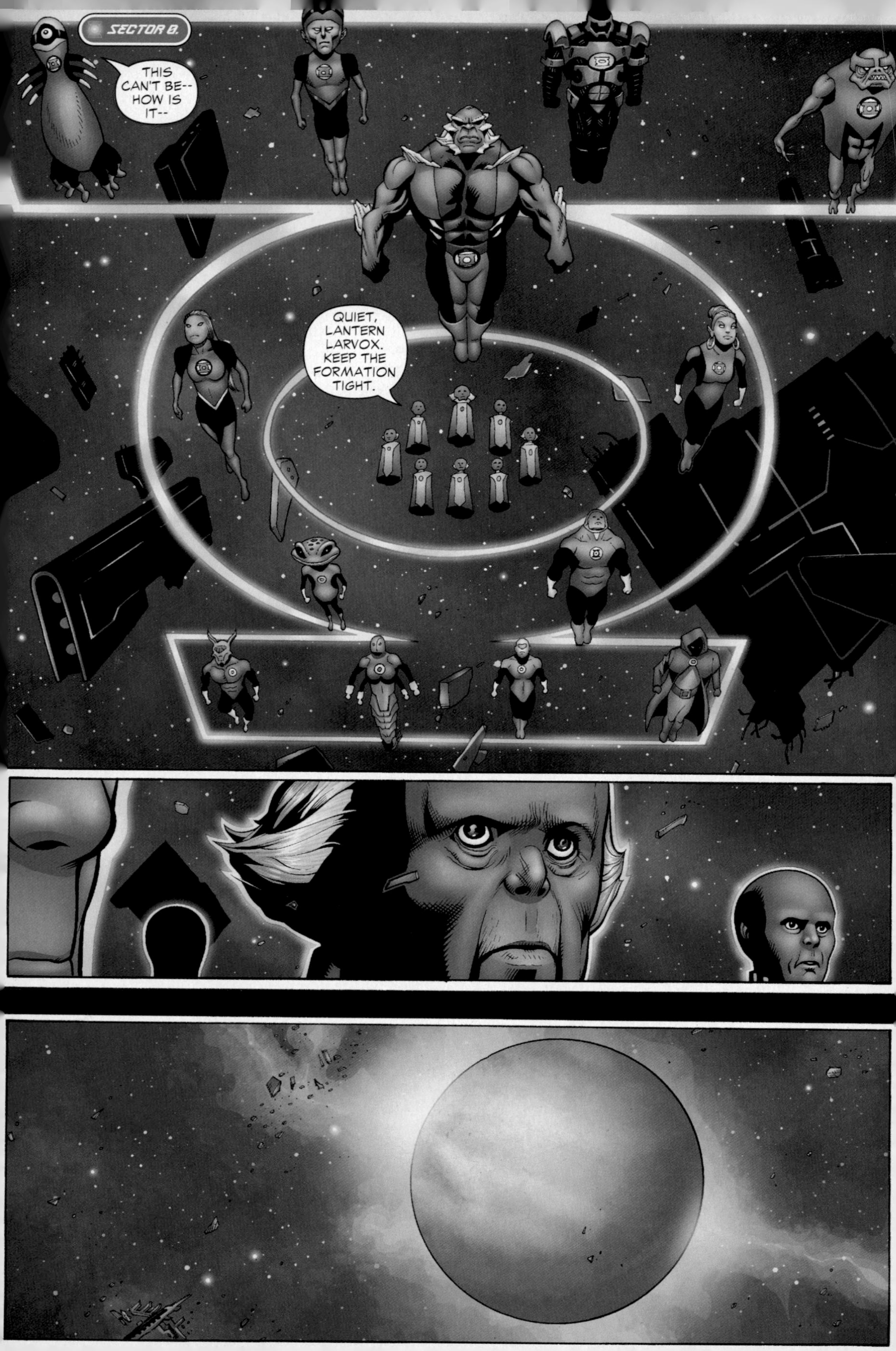
SECTOR 0.
THIS CAN'T BE-- HOW IS IT--
QUIET, LANTERN LARVOX. KEEP THE FORMATION TIGHT.

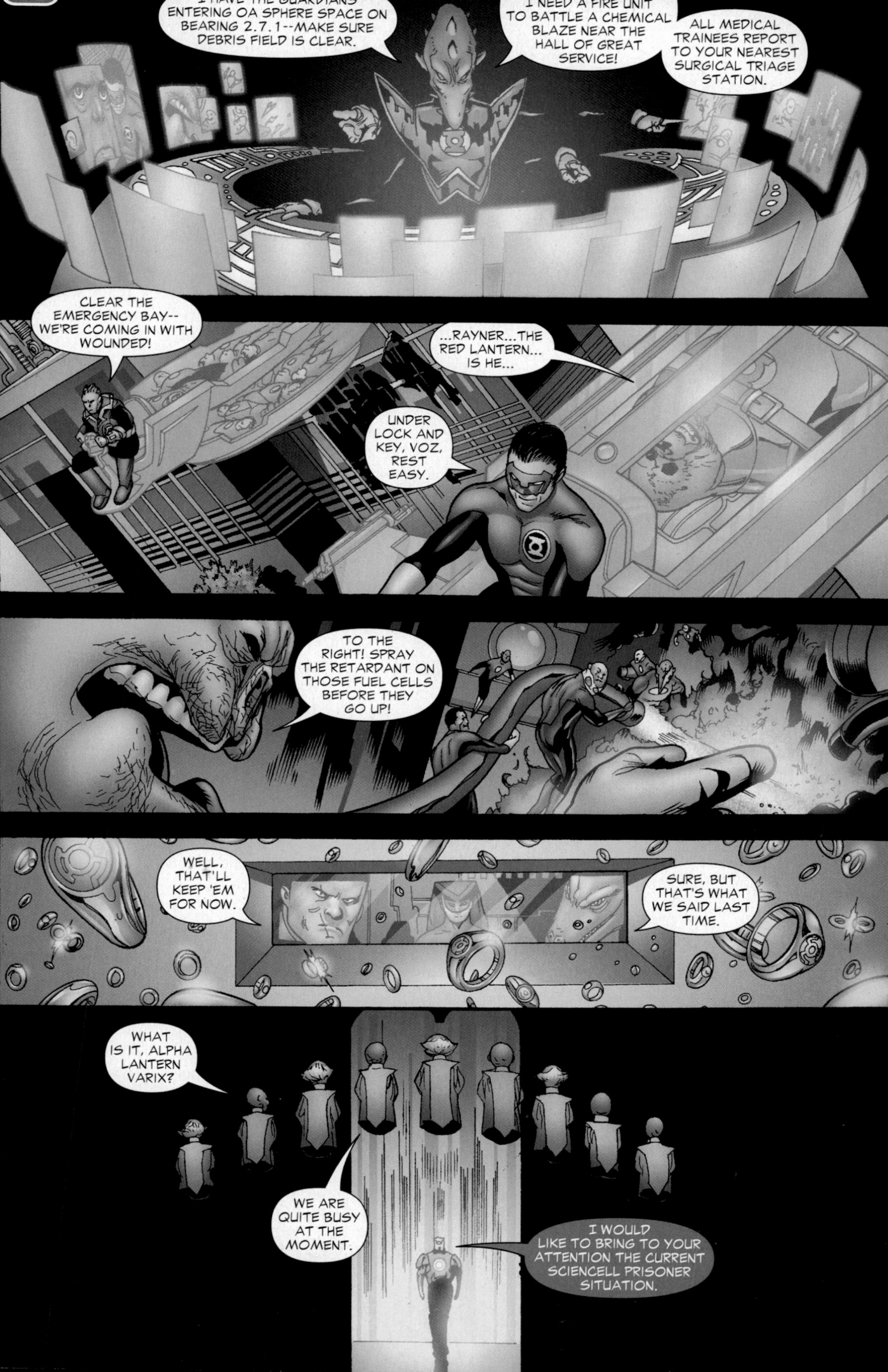

I HAVE THE GUARDIANS ENTERING OA SPHERE SPACE ON BEARING 2.7.1--MAKE SURE DEBRIS FIELD IS CLEAR.
I NEED A FIRE UNIT TO BATTLE A CHEMICAL BLAZE NEAR THE HALL OF GREAT SERVICE!
ALL MEDICAL TRAINEES REPORT TO YOUR NEAREST SURGICAL TRIAGE STATION.
CLEAR THE EMERGENCY BAY--WE'RE COMING IN WITH WOUNDED!
...RAYNER...THE RED LANTERN... IS HE...
UNDER LOCK AND KEY, VOZ, REST EASY.
TO THE RIGHT! SPRAY THE RETARDANT ON THOSE FUEL CELLS BEFORE THEY GO UP!
WELL, THAT'LL KEEP 'EM FOR NOW.
SURE, BUT THAT'S WHAT WE SAID LAST TIME.
WHAT IS IT, ALPHA LANTERN VARIX?
WE ARE QUITE BUSY AT THE MOMENT.
I WOULD LIKE TO BRING TO YOUR ATTENTION THE CURRENT SCIENCELL PRISONER SITUATION.

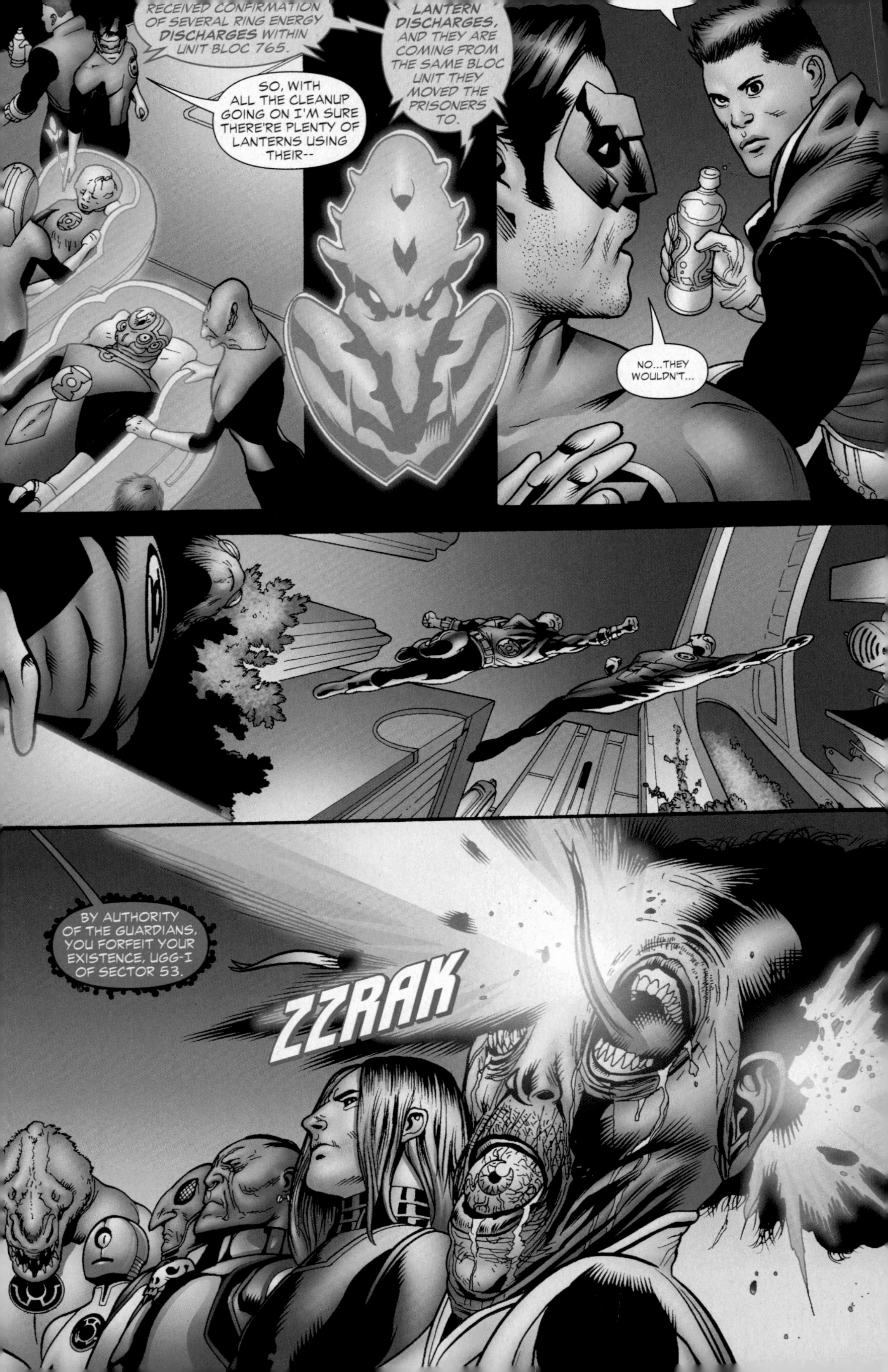
RECEIVED CONFIRMATION OF SEVERAL RING ENERGY DISCHARGES WITHIN UNIT BLOC 765.
SO, WITH ALL THE CLEANUP GOING ON I'M SURE THERE'RE PLENTY OF LANTERNS USING THEIR--
LANTERN DISCHARGES, AND THEY ARE COMING FROM THE SAME BLOC UNIT THEY MOVED THE PRISONERS TO.
NO...THEY WOULDN'T...
BY AUTHORITY OF THE GUARDIANS, YOU FORFEIT YOUR EXISTENCE, UGG-I OF SECTOR 53.
ZZRAK

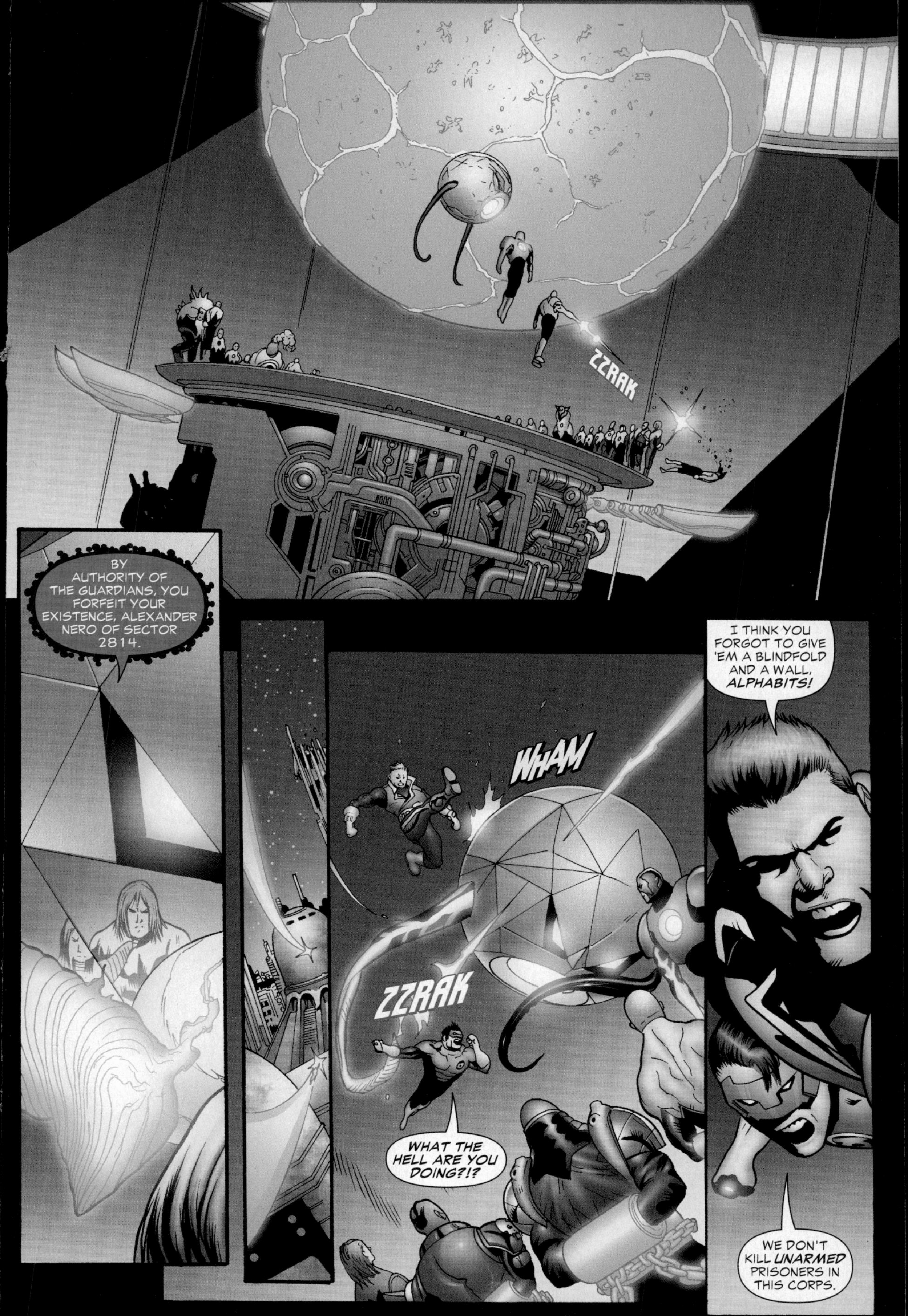
ZZRAK
BY AUTHORITY OF THE GUARDIANS, YOU FORFEIT YOUR EXISTENCE, ALEXANDER NERO OF SECTOR 2814.
WHAM
ZZRAK
WHAT THE HELL ARE YOU DOING?!?
I THINK YOU FORGOT TO GIVE 'EM A BLINDFOLD AND A WALL, ALPHABITS!
WE DON'T KILL UNARMED PRISONERS IN THIS CORPS.

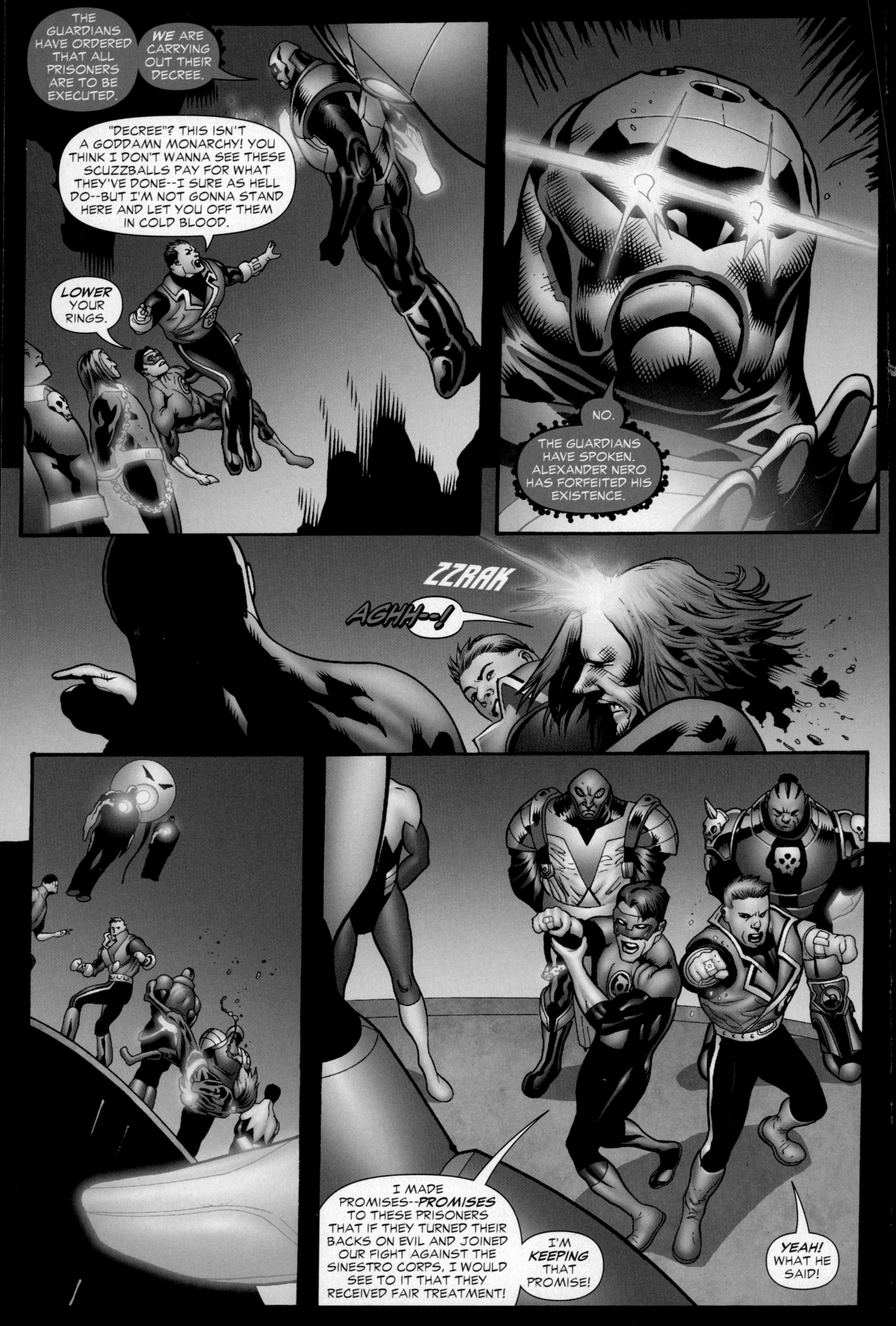
THE GUARDIANS HAVE ORDERED THAT ALL PRISONERS ARE TO BE EXECUTED.
WE ARE CARRYING OUT THEIR DECREE.
"DECREE"? THIS ISN'T A GODDAMN MONARCHY! YOU THINK I DON'T WANNA SEE THESE SCUZZBALLS PAY FOR WHAT THEY'VE DONE--I SURE AS HELL DO--BUT I'M NOT GONNA STAND HERE AND LET YOU OFF THEM IN COLD BLOOD.
LOWER YOUR RINGS.
NO.
THE GUARDIANS HAVE SPOKEN. ALEXANDER NERO HAS FORFEITED HIS EXISTENCE.
ZZRAK
AGHH--!
I MADE PROMISES--PROMISES TO THESE PRISONERS THAT IF THEY TURNED THEIR BACKS ON EVIL AND JOINED OUR FIGHT AGAINST THE SINESTRO CORPS, I WOULD SEE TO IT THAT THEY RECEIVED FAIR TREATMENT!
I'M KEEPING THAT PROMISE!
YEAH! WHAT HE SAID!

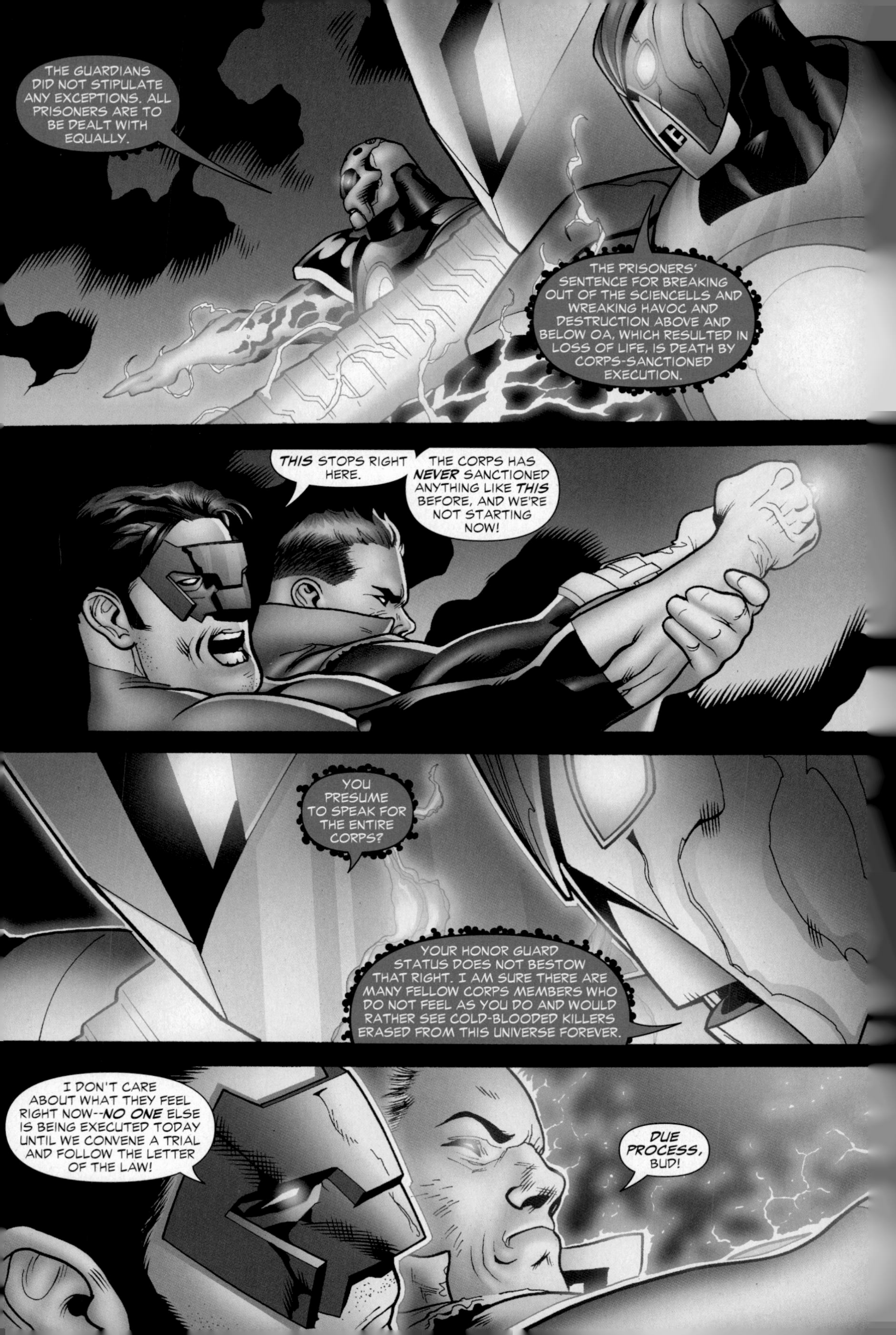
THE GUARDIANS DID NOT STIPULATE ANY EXCEPTIONS. ALL PRISONERS ARE TO BE DEALT WITH EQUALLY.
THE PRISONERS' SENTENCE FOR BREAKING OUT OF THE SCIENCELLS AND WREAKING HAVOC AND DESTRUCTION ABOVE AND BELOW OA, WHICH RESULTED IN LOSS OF LIFE, IS DEATH BY CORPS-SANCTIONED EXECUTION.
THIS STOPS RIGHT HERE.
THE CORPS HAS NEVER SANCTIONED ANYTHING LIKE THIS BEFORE, AND WE'RE NOT STARTING NOW!
YOU PRESUME TO SPEAK FOR THE ENTIRE CORPS?
YOUR HONOR GUARD STATUS DOES NOT BESTOW THAT RIGHT. I AM SURE THERE ARE MANY FELLOW CORPS MEMBERS WHO DO NOT FEEL AS YOU DO AND WOULD RATHER SEE COLD-BLOODED KILLERS ERASED FROM THIS UNIVERSE FOREVER.
I DON'T CARE ABOUT WHAT THEY FEEL RIGHT NOW--NO ONE ELSE IS BEING EXECUTED TODAY UNTIL WE CONVENE A TRIAL AND FOLLOW THE LETTER OF THE LAW!
DUE PROCESS, BUD!

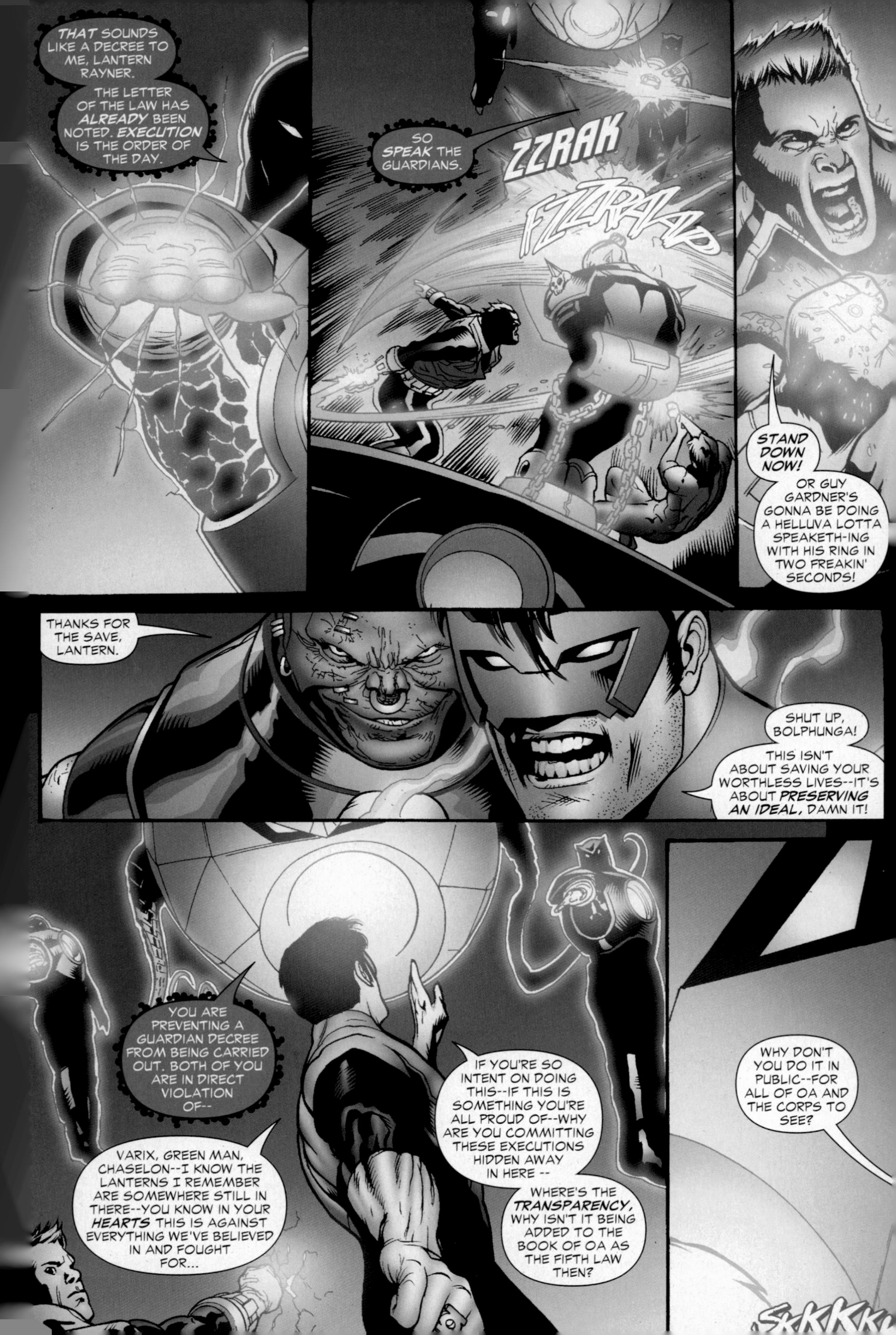
THAT SOUNDS LIKE A DECREE TO ME, LANTERN RAYNER.
THE LETTER OF THE LAW HAS ALREADY BEEN NOTED. EXECUTION IS THE ORDER OF THE DAY.
SO SPEAK THE GUARDIANS.
ZZRAK
FZZZRRAAAP
STAND DOWN NOW!
OR GUY GARDNER'S GONNA BE DOING A HELLUVA LOTTA SPEAKETH-ING WITH HIS RING IN TWO FREAKIN' SECONDS!
THANKS FOR THE SAVE, LANTERN.
SHUT UP, BOLPHUNGA!
THIS ISN'T ABOUT SAVING YOUR WORTHLESS LIVES--IT'S ABOUT PRESERVING AN IDEAL, DAMN IT!
YOU ARE PREVENTING A GUARDIAN DECREE FROM BEING CARRIED OUT. BOTH OF YOU ARE IN DIRECT VIOLATION OF--
VARIX, GREEN MAN, CHASELON--I KNOW THE LANTERNS I REMEMBER ARE SOMEWHERE STILL IN THERE--YOU KNOW IN YOUR HEARTS THIS IS AGAINST EVERYTHING WE'VE BELIEVED IN AND FOUGHT FOR...
IF YOU'RE SO INTENT ON DOING THIS--IF THIS IS SOMETHING YOU'RE ALL PROUD OF--WHY ARE YOU COMMITTING THESE EXECUTIONS HIDDEN AWAY IN HERE --
WHERE'S THE TRANSPARENCY, WHY ISN'T IT BEING ADDED TO THE BOOK OF OA AS THE FIFTH LAW THEN?
WHY DON'T YOU DO IT IN PUBLIC--FOR ALL OF OA AND THE CORPS TO SEE?

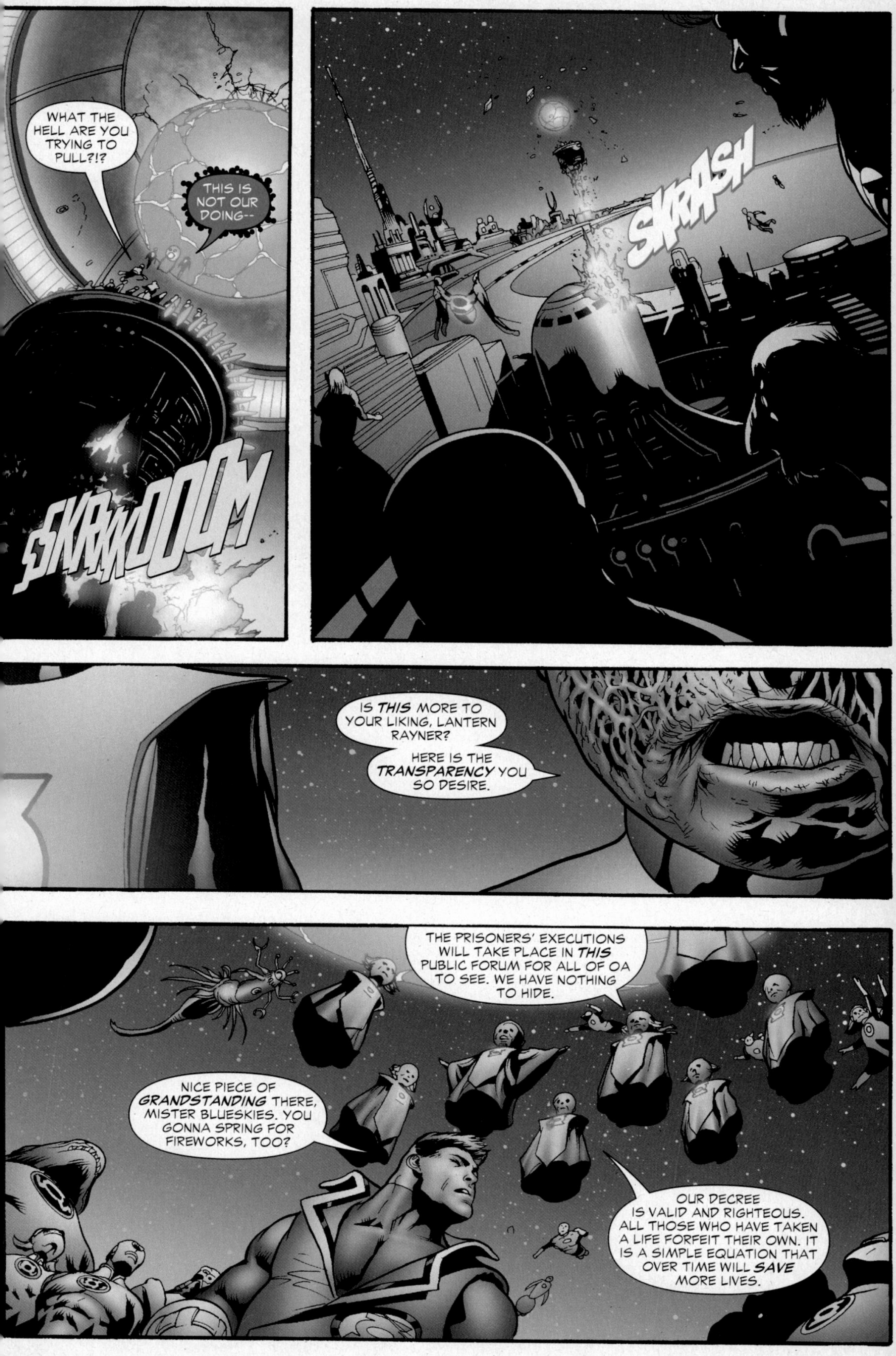
WHAT THE HELL ARE YOU TRYING TO PULL?!?
THIS IS NOT OUR DOING--
SKRAKOOOM
SKRASH
IS THIS MORE TO YOUR LIKING, LANTERN RAYNER?
HERE IS THE TRANSPARENCY YOU SO DESIRE.
THE PRISONERS' EXECUTIONS WILL TAKE PLACE IN THIS PUBLIC FORUM FOR ALL OF OA TO SEE. WE HAVE NOTHING TO HIDE.
NICE PIECE OF GRANDSTANDING THERE, MISTER BLUESKIES. YOU GONNA SPRING FOR FIREWORKS, TOO?
OUR DECREE IS VALID AND RIGHTEOUS. ALL THOSE WHO HAVE TAKEN A LIFE FORFEIT THEIR OWN. IT IS A SIMPLE EQUATION THAT OVER TIME WILL SAVE MORE LIVES.

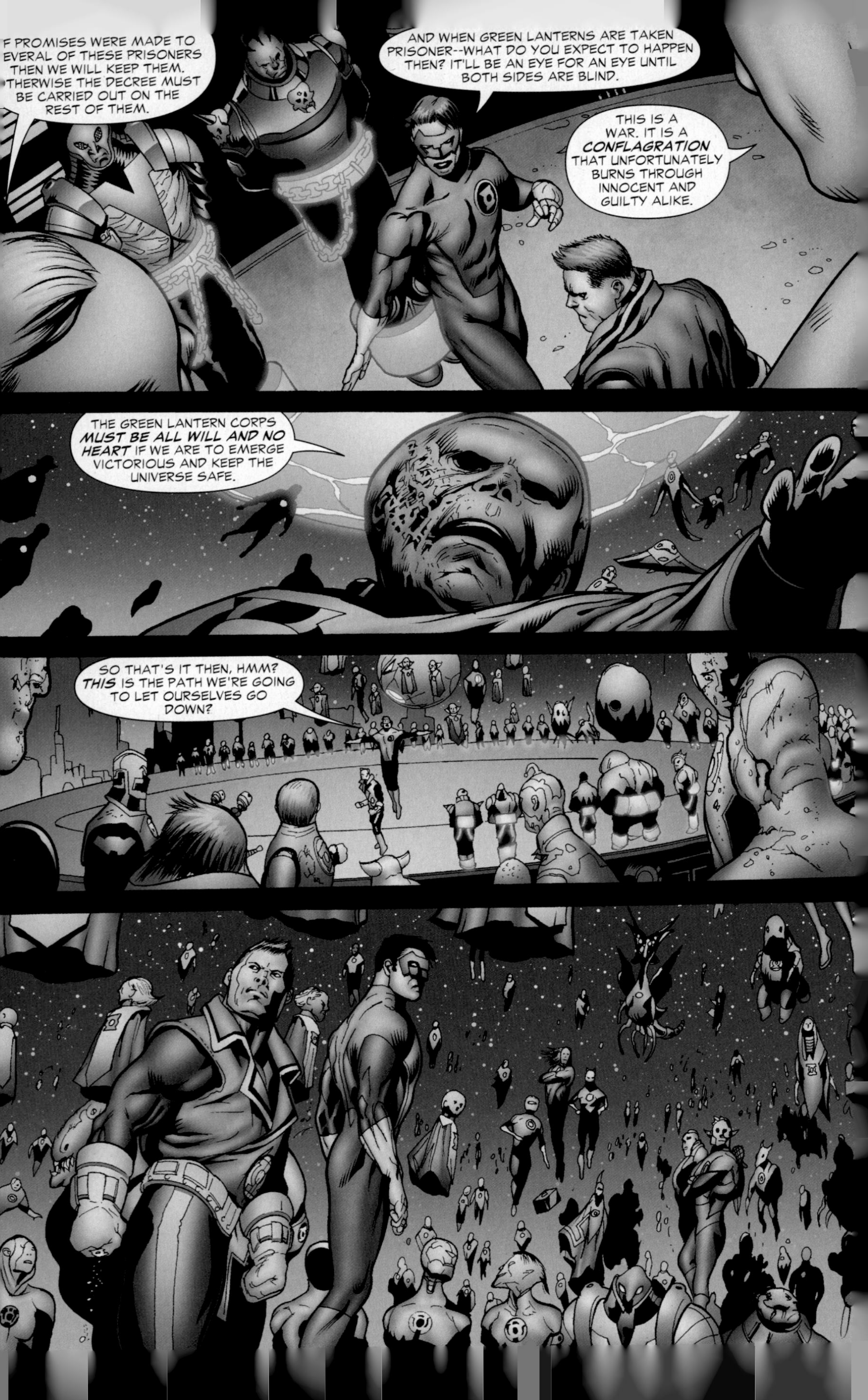
F PROMISES WERE MADE TO EVERAL OF THESE PRISONERS THEN WE WILL KEEP THEM. THERWISE THE DECREE MUST BE CARRIED OUT ON THE REST OF THEM.
AND WHEN GREEN LANTERNS ARE TAKEN PRISONER--WHAT DO YOU EXPECT TO HAPPEN THEN? IT'LL BE AN EYE FOR AN EYE UNTIL BOTH SIDES ARE BLIND.
THIS IS A WAR. IT IS A CONFLAGRATION THAT UNFORTUNATELY BURNS THROUGH INNOCENT AND GUILTY ALIKE.
THE GREEN LANTERN CORPS MUST BE ALL WILL AND NO HEART IF WE ARE TO EMERGE VICTORIOUS AND KEEP THE UNIVERSE SAFE.
SO THAT'S IT THEN, HMM? THIS IS THE PATH WE'RE GOING TO LET OURSELVES GO DOWN?

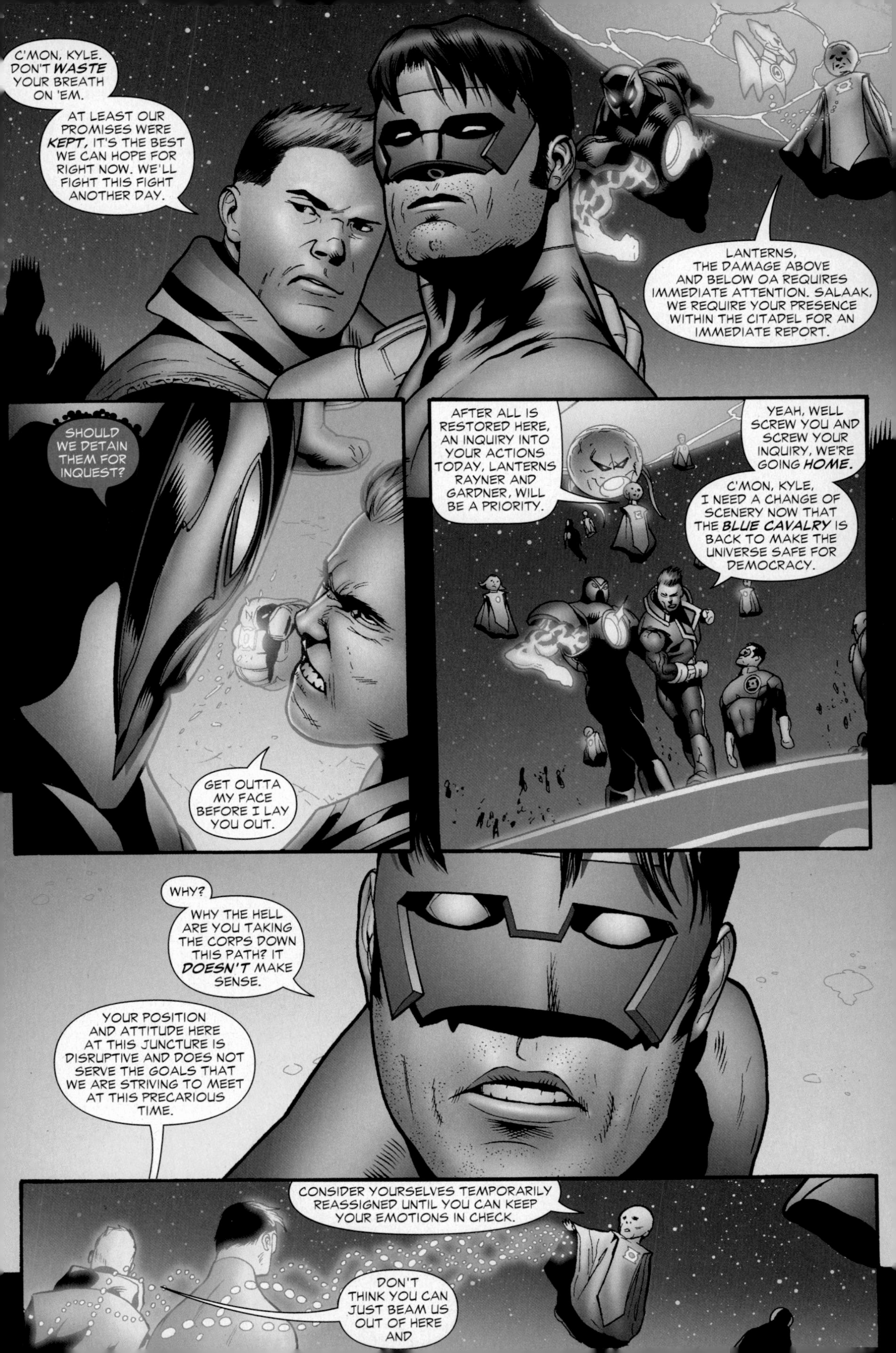
C'MON, KYLE. DON'T WASTE YOUR BREATH ON 'EM.
AT LEAST OUR PROMISES WERE KEPT, IT'S THE BEST WE CAN HOPE FOR RIGHT NOW. WE'LL FIGHT THIS FIGHT ANOTHER DAY.
LANTERNS, THE DAMAGE ABOVE AND BELOW OA REQUIRES IMMEDIATE ATTENTION. SALAAK, WE REQUIRE YOUR PRESENCE WITHIN THE CITADEL FOR AN IMMEDIATE REPORT.
SHOULD WE DETAIN THEM FOR INQUEST?
GET OUTTA MY FACE BEFORE I LAY YOU OUT.
AFTER ALL IS RESTORED HERE, AN INQUIRY INTO YOUR ACTIONS TODAY, LANTERNS RAYNER AND GARDNER, WILL BE A PRIORITY.
YEAH, WELL SCREW YOU AND SCREW YOUR INQUIRY, WE'RE GOING HOME.
C'MON, KYLE, I NEED A CHANGE OF SCENERY NOW THAT THE BLUE CAVALRY IS BACK TO MAKE THE UNIVERSE SAFE FOR DEMOCRACY.
WHY?
WHY THE HELL ARE YOU TAKING THE CORPS DOWN THIS PATH? IT DOESN'T MAKE SENSE.
YOUR POSITION AND ATTITUDE HERE AT THIS JUNCTURE IS DISRUPTIVE AND DOES NOT SERVE THE GOALS THAT WE ARE STRIVING TO MEET AT THIS PRECARIOUS TIME.
CONSIDER YOURSELVES TEMPORARILY REASSIGNED UNTIL YOU CAN KEEP YOUR EMOTIONS IN CHECK.
DON'T THINK YOU CAN JUST BEAM US OUT OF HERE AND

PROCEED.

AND THE PRISONERS THAT LANTERN RAYNER AND--

ARE TO BE SPARED AS PROMISED.

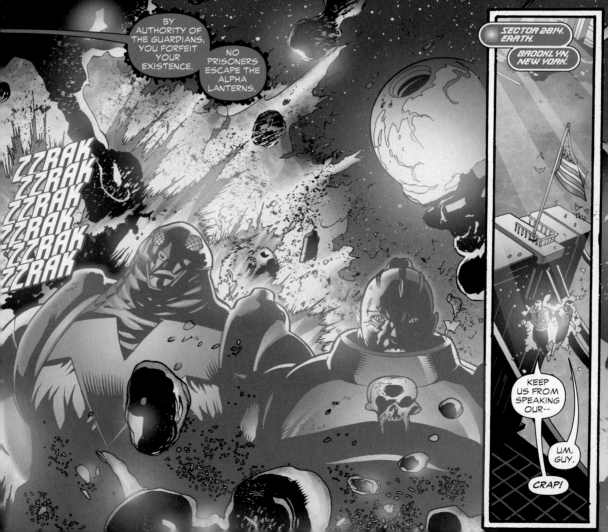

BY AUTHORITY OF THE GUARDIANS, YOU FORFEIT YOUR EXISTENCE. NO PRISONERS ESCAPE THE ALPHA LANTERNS.

ZZRAK
ZZRAK
ZZRAK
ZZRAK
ZZRAK
ZZRAK

SECTOR 2814. EARTH. BROOKLYN, NEW YORK.

KEEP US FROM SPEAKING OUR--

UM, GUY.

CRAP!

CAN WE HELP, ARISIA?

WE PROMISE WE'LL BE CAREFUL.

SURE, SINCE YOU BOTH SEEM TO BE *INVULNERABLE* NOW, I GUESS WHY NOT.

WE FOUND THIS ONE STILL BREATHING, BUT BARELY, SENATOR.

THROW HIM ON.

...UNNNN... NO...

AND THESE, SENATOR?

AAAGH!

THROW THOSE BODIES ON TOO.

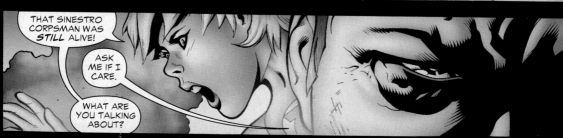

THAT SINESTRO CORPSMAN WAS *STILL* ALIVE!

ASK ME IF I CARE.

WHAT ARE YOU TALKING ABOUT?

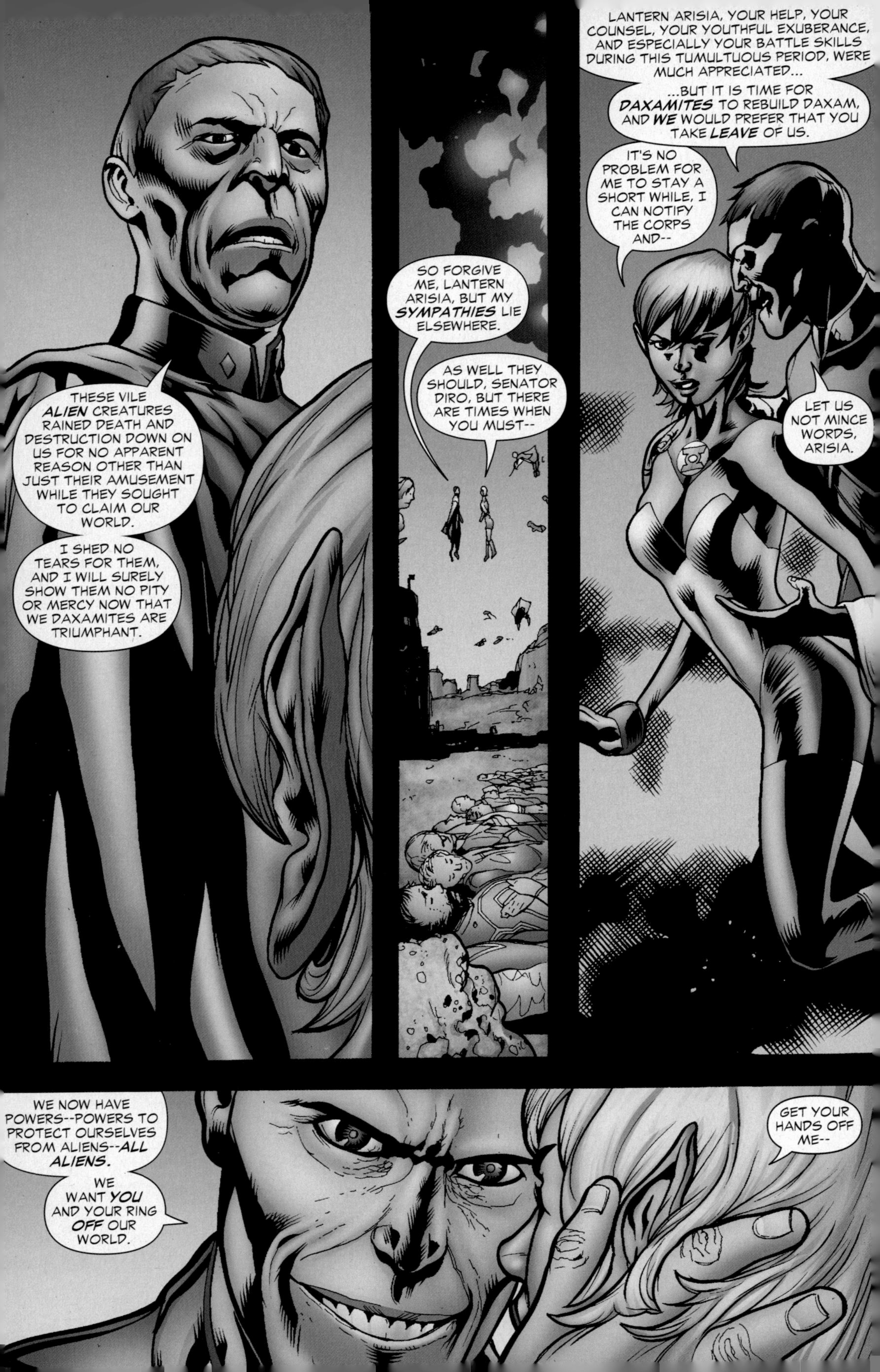
THESE VILE ALIEN CREATURES RAINED DEATH AND DESTRUCTION DOWN ON US FOR NO APPARENT REASON OTHER THAN JUST THEIR AMUSEMENT WHILE THEY SOUGHT TO CLAIM OUR WORLD.
I SHED NO TEARS FOR THEM, AND I WILL SURELY SHOW THEM NO PITY OR MERCY NOW THAT WE DAXAMITES ARE TRIUMPHANT.
SO FORGIVE ME, LANTERN ARISIA, BUT MY SYMPATHIES LIE ELSEWHERE.
AS WELL THEY SHOULD, SENATOR DIRO, BUT THERE ARE TIMES WHEN YOU MUST--
LANTERN ARISIA, YOUR HELP, YOUR COUNSEL, YOUR YOUTHFUL EXUBERANCE, AND ESPECIALLY YOUR BATTLE SKILLS DURING THIS TUMULTUOUS PERIOD, WERE MUCH APPRECIATED...
...BUT IT IS TIME FOR DAXAMITES TO REBUILD DAXAM, AND WE WOULD PREFER THAT YOU TAKE LEAVE OF US.
IT'S NO PROBLEM FOR ME TO STAY A SHORT WHILE, I CAN NOTIFY THE CORPS AND--
LET US NOT MINCE WORDS, ARISIA.
WE NOW HAVE POWERS--POWERS TO PROTECT OURSELVES FROM ALIENS--ALL ALIENS.
WE WANT YOU AND YOUR RING OFF OUR WORLD.
GET YOUR HANDS OFF ME--

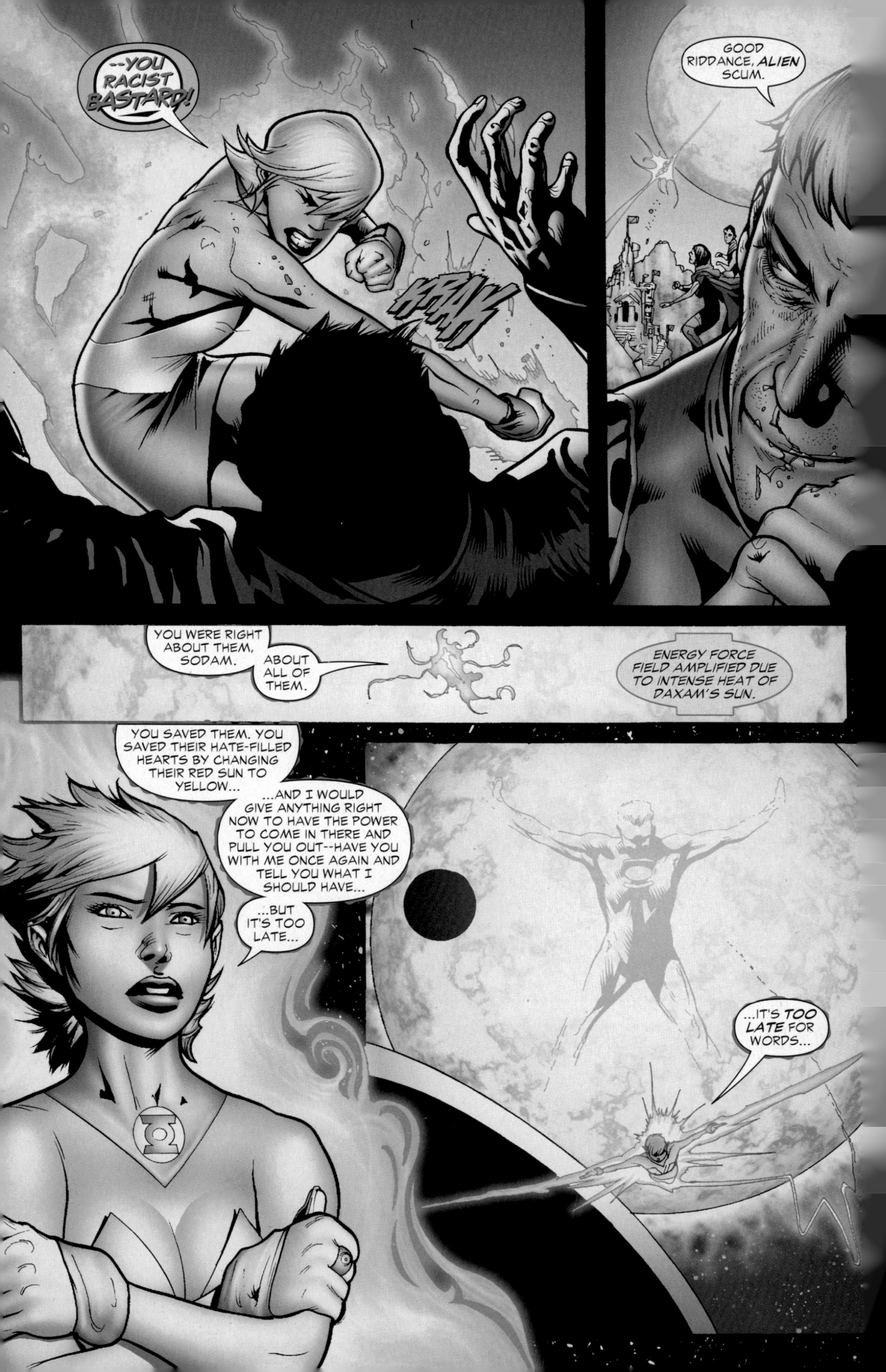
--YOU RACIST BASTARD!
KRAK
GOOD RIDDANCE, ALIEN SCUM.
YOU WERE RIGHT ABOUT THEM, SODAM.
ABOUT ALL OF THEM.
ENERGY FORCE FIELD AMPLIFIED DUE TO INTENSE HEAT OF DAXAM'S SUN.
YOU SAVED THEM. YOU SAVED THEIR HATE-FILLED HEARTS BY CHANGING THEIR RED SUN TO YELLOW...
...AND I WOULD GIVE ANYTHING RIGHT NOW TO HAVE THE POWER TO COME IN THERE AND PULL YOU OUT--HAVE YOU WITH ME ONCE AGAIN AND TELL YOU WHAT I SHOULD HAVE...
...BUT IT'S TOO LATE...
...IT'S TOO LATE FOR WORDS...

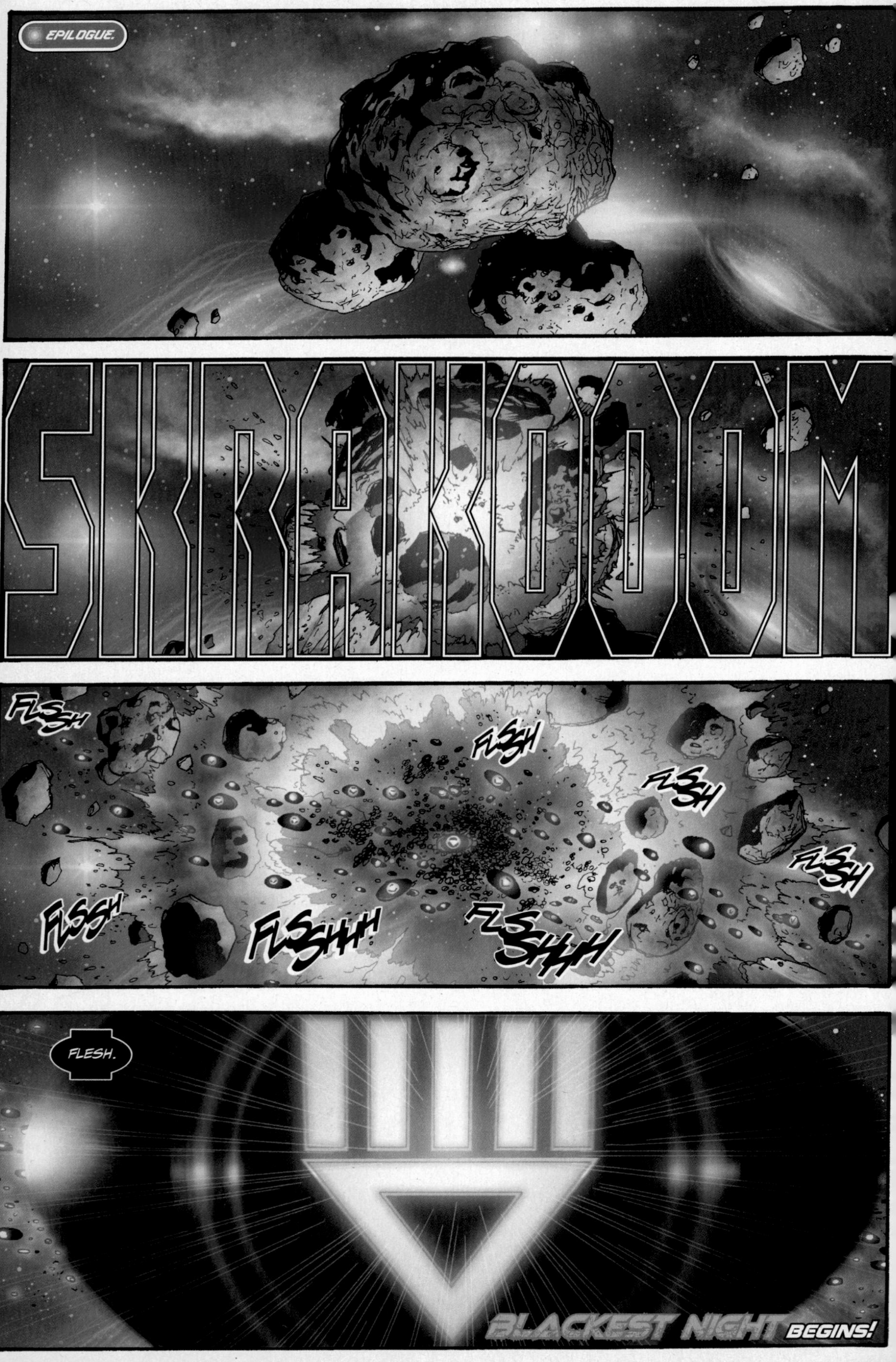
EPILOGUE.
SKRAKOOOM
FLSSH
FLSSH
FLSSH
FLSSH
FLSSH
FLSSHH!
FLSSHHH
FLESH.
BLACKEST NIGHT BEGINS!

GREEN LANTERN CORPS

EMERALD ECLIPSE

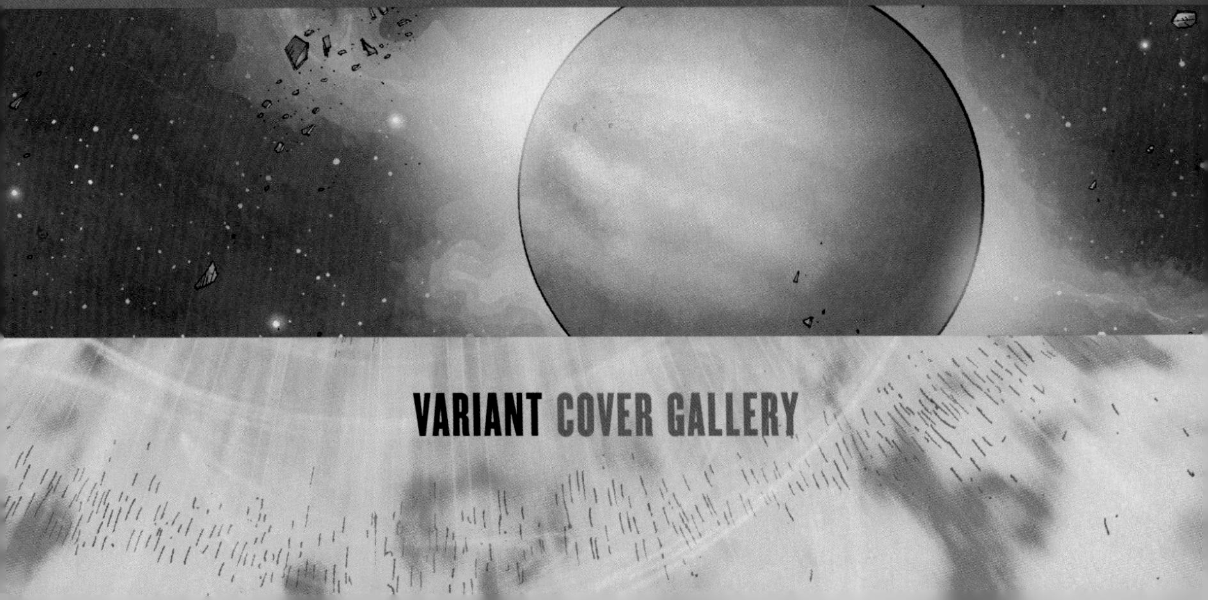

VARIANT COVER GALLERY

GREEN LANTERN CORPS #33 2nd printing by Patrick Gleason,
Rebecca Buchman & Randy Mayor

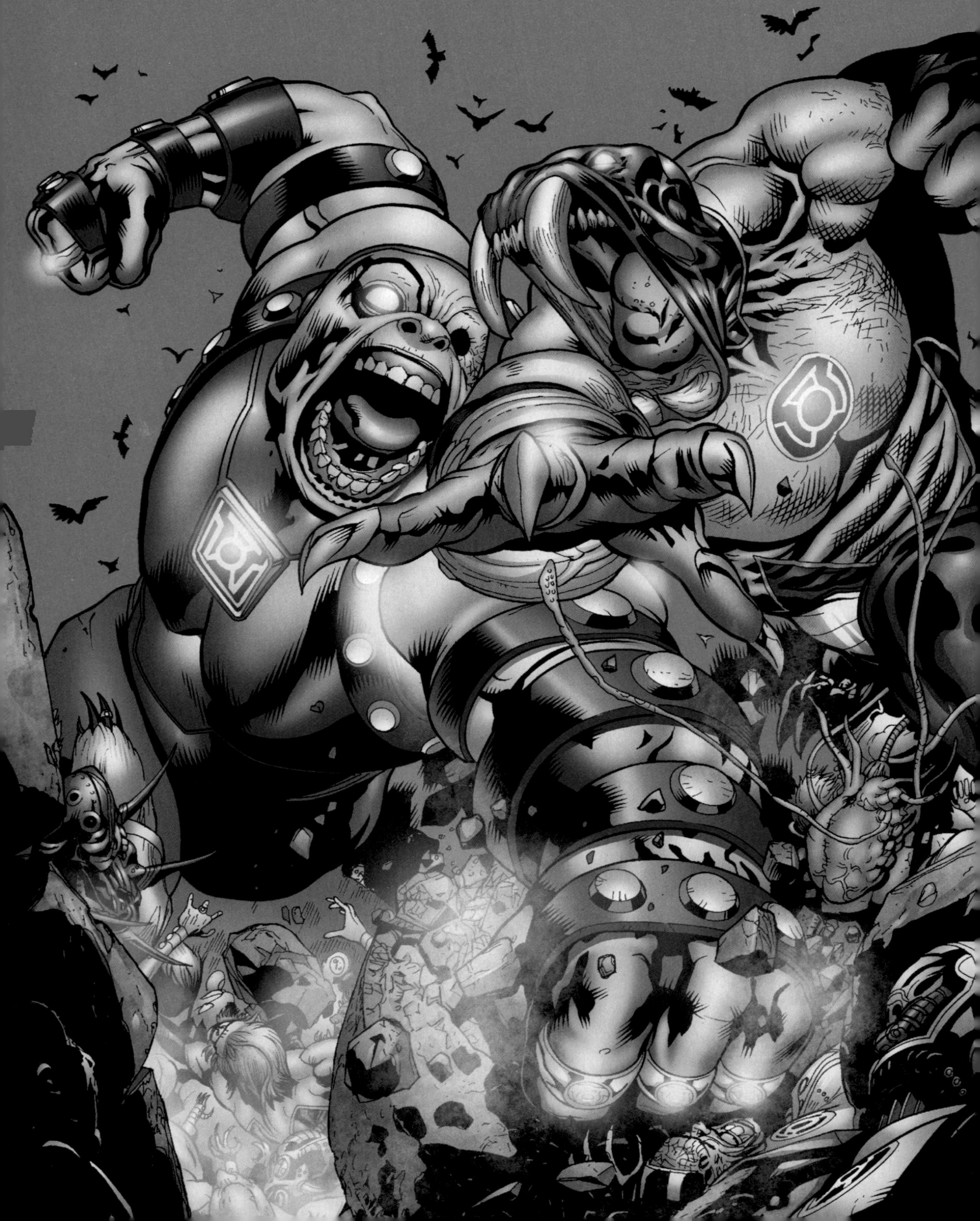

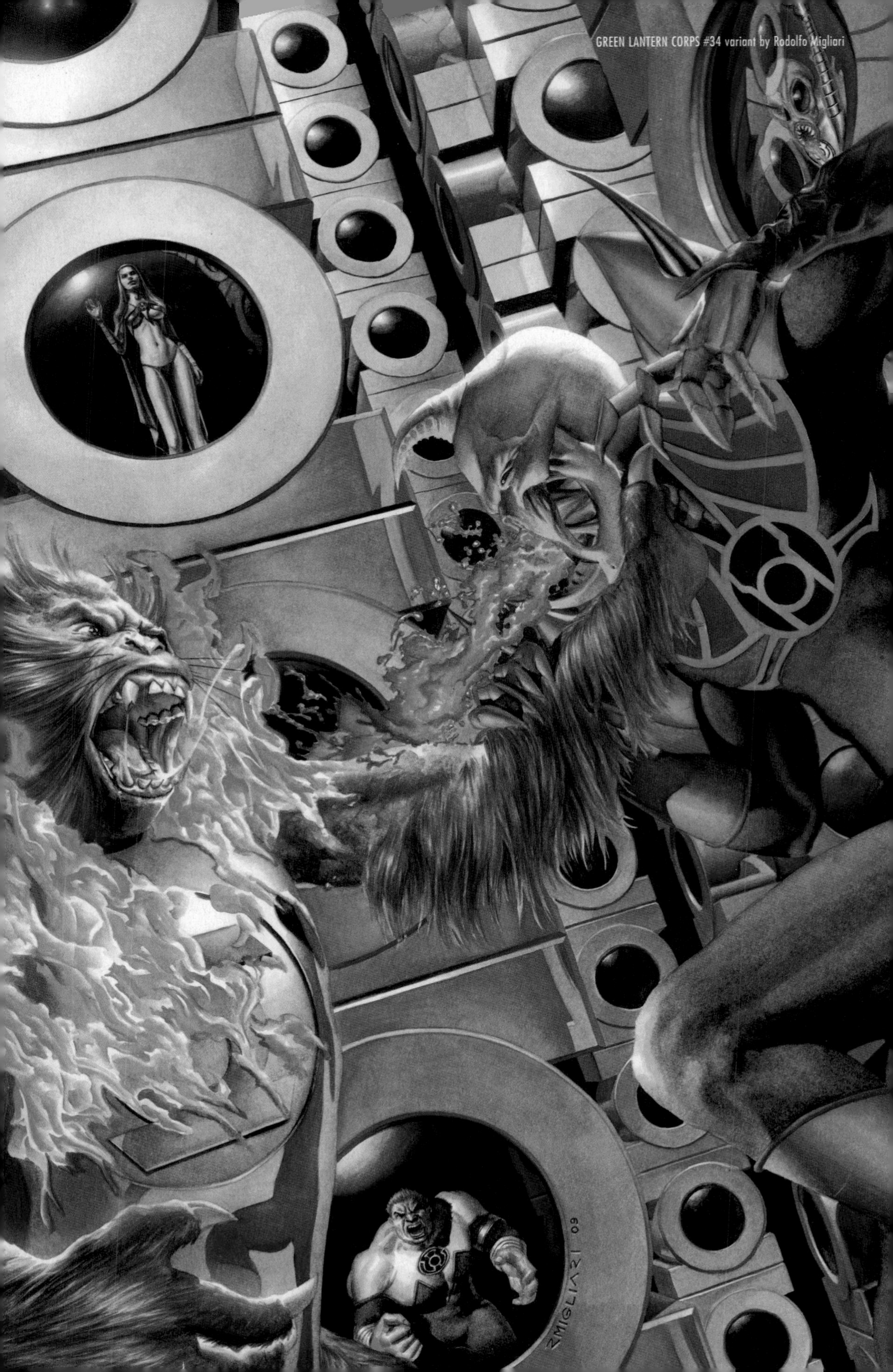

GREEN LANTERN CORPS #34 variant by Rodolfo Migliari

GREEN LANTERN CORPS #35 variant by Rodolfo Migliari

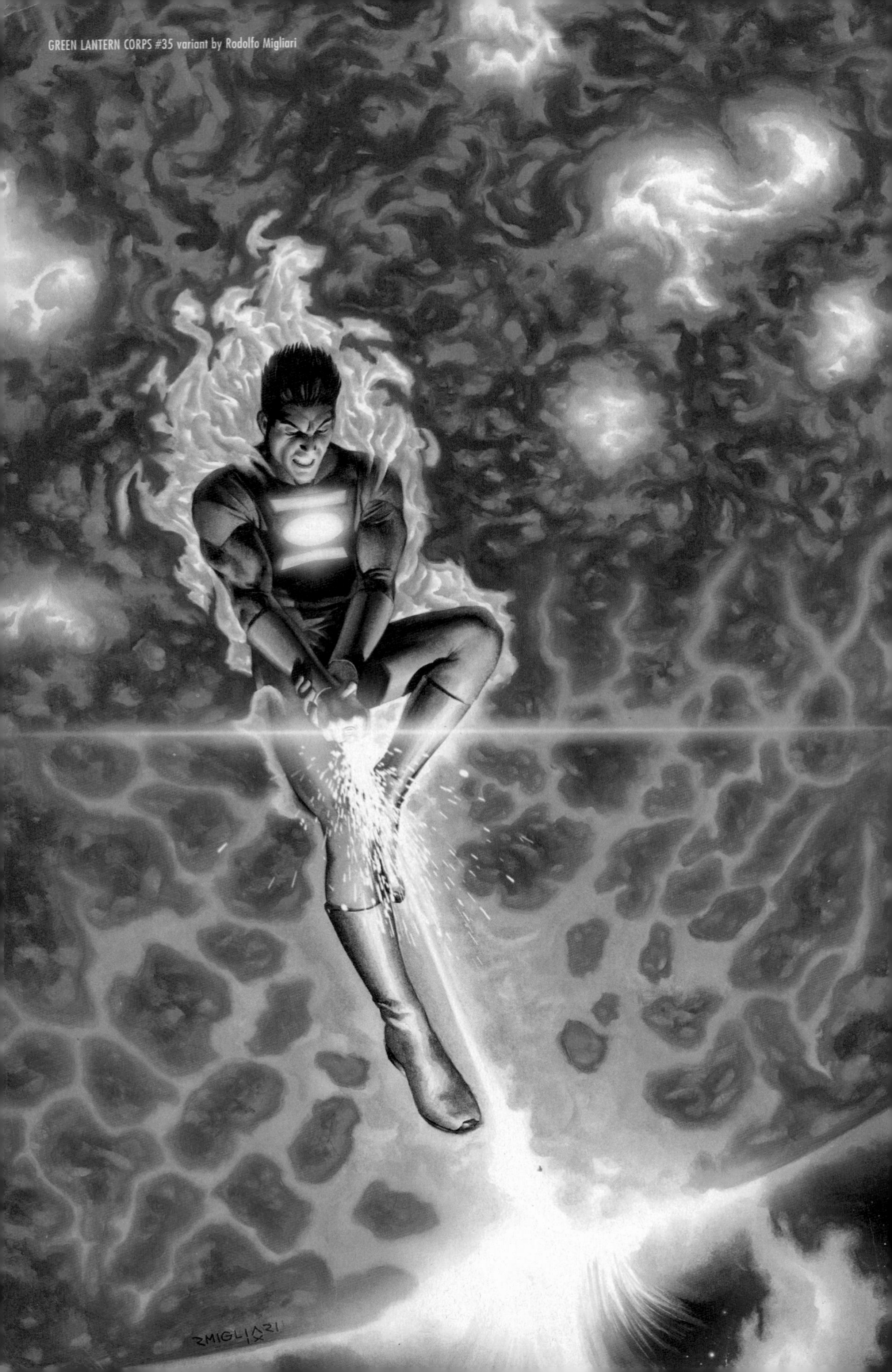

GREEN LANTERN CORPS #36 variant by Rodolfo Migliari

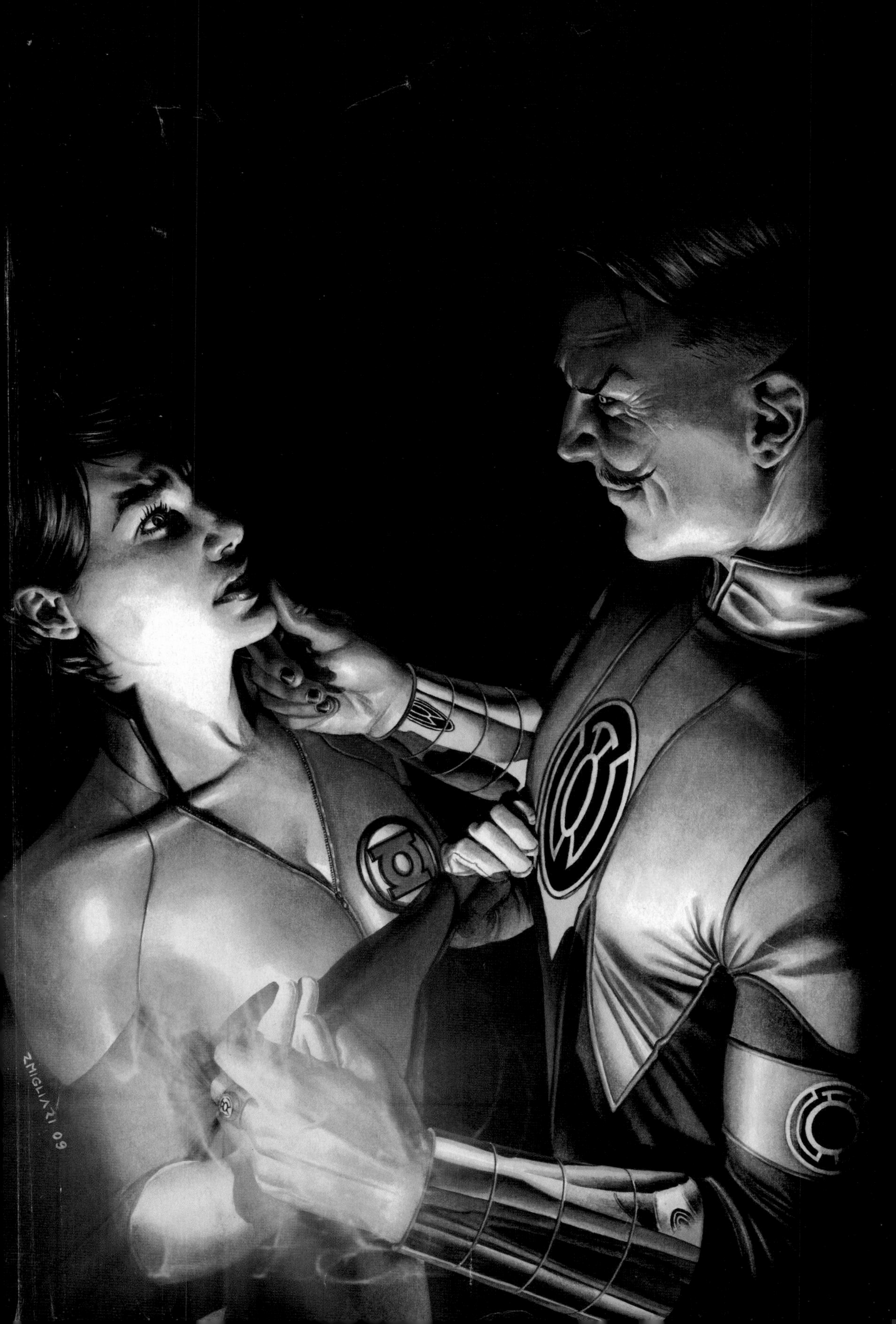

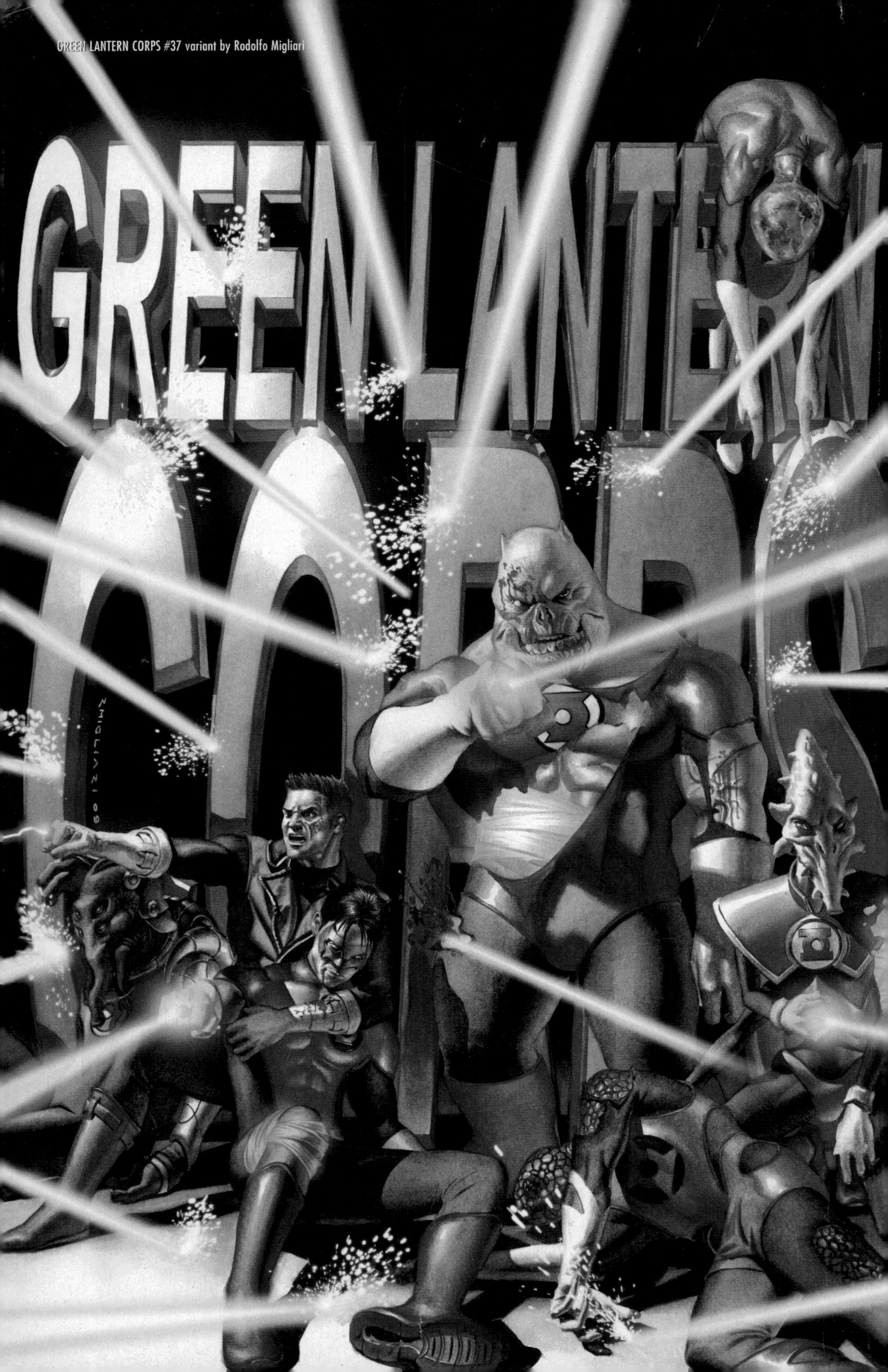
GREEN LANTERN CORPS #37 variant by Rodolfo Migliari

GREEN LANTERN CORPS #38 variant by Glenn Fabry

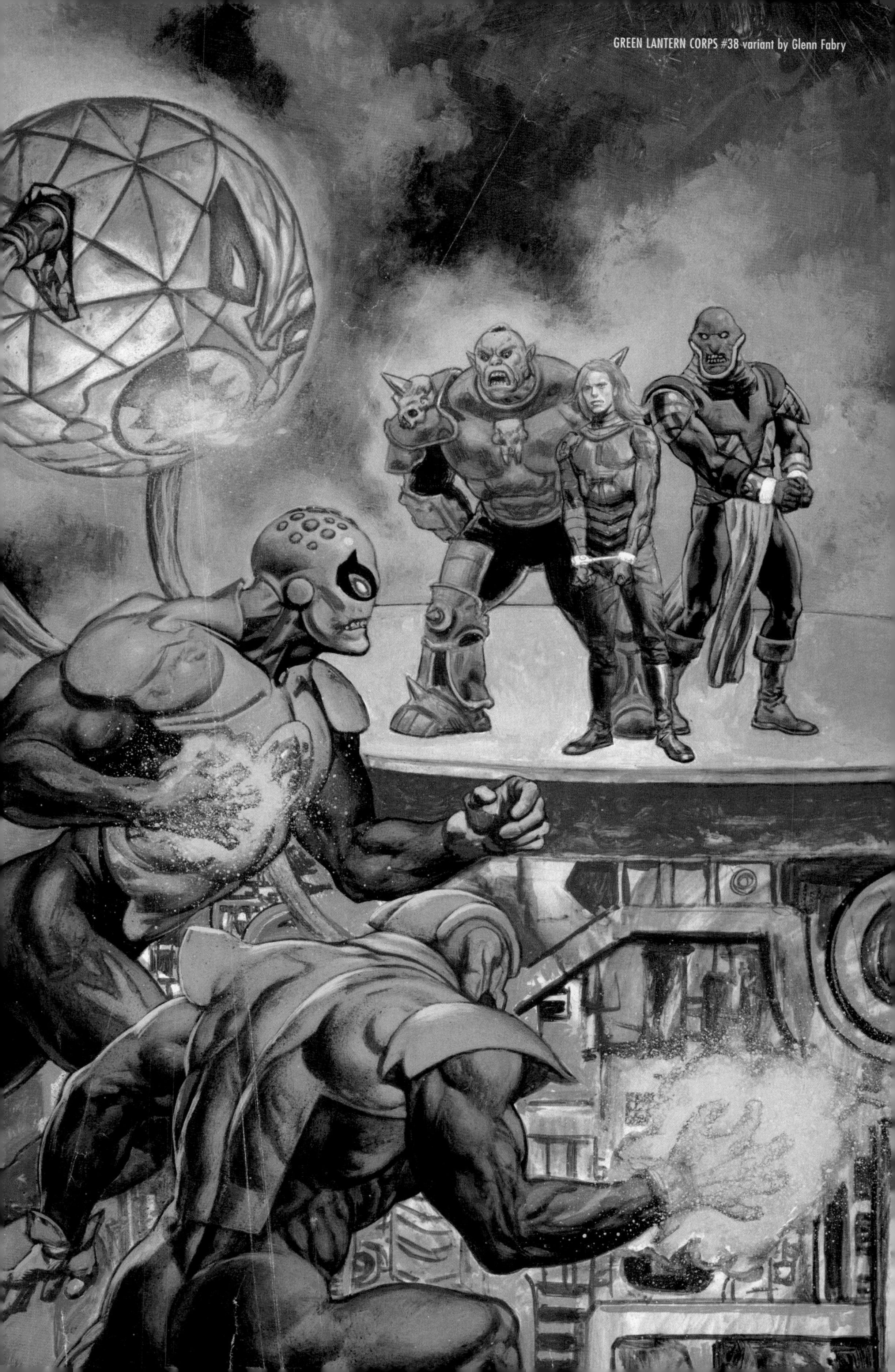